TeSelle

Macroeconomic Theory

Foundations of Modern Economics Series

Otto Eckstein, *Editor*

Richard Caves	American Industry: Structure, Conduct, Performance, 6th Ed.
Robert Dorfman	Prices and Markets, 3rd Ed.
James S. Duesenberry	Money and Credit: Impact and Control, 3rd Ed.
Matthew Edel	Economies and the Environment
Kenan and Lubitz	International Economics, 3rd Ed.
Charles L. Schultze	National Income Analysis, 3rd Ed.

Macroeconomic Theory

George T. McCandless Jr.
University of Chicago

Prentice Hall, Englewood Cliffs, New Jersey 07632

Library of Congress Cataloging-in-Publication Data

McCandless, George T.
Macroeconomic theory/George T. McCandless Jr.
p. cm.
Includes index.
ISBN 0–13–543323–1
1. Macroeconomics. I. Title.
HB172.5.M367 1991
339—dc20 90-7729
CIP

Editorial/production supervision: Joanne Palmer
Interior/cover design: Linda J. Den Heyer Rosa
Prepress buyer: Trudy Pisciotti
Manufacturing buyer: Robert Anderson
Cover Art: Megan McLean

Printed in the United States of America

10 9 8 7 6 5 4 3 2 1

ISBN 0-13-543323-1

Prentice-Hall International (UK) Limited, *London*
Prentice-Hall of Australia PTY. Limited, *Sydney*
Prentice-Hall Canada Inc., *Toronto*
Prentice-Hall Hispanoamericana, S.A., *Mexico*
Prentice-Hall of India Private Limited, *New Delhi*
Prentice-Hall of Japan, Inc., *Tokyo*
Simon & Schuster Asia Pte. Ltd., *Singapore*
Editora Prentice-Hall do Brasil, Ltda., *Rio de Janeiro*

To My Parents

Contents

Preface

This text is intended as an introduction to modern macroeconomic theory. It is not intended to be a giant, all-encompassing macroeconomic text, but rather to present both a fairly concise, coherent development of macroeconomic thought as a historical process and a serious discussion of the current issues in macroeconomics.

The book grew out of my own uneasiness with existing texts. It seemed that too many of these texts presented the classical model as an intellectually empty construct and the Keynesian model as if it were brought down from the mountain by Keynes. They failed to present the development of economic thought as a process in which the Keynesian model has an important, but not final, place. This approach began as I attempted to incorporate the models in Tom Sargent's *Macroeconomic Theory* into my macroeconomics classes. The dynamic analysis grew out of efforts to present the issues of expectations formation and the Phillips curve failure of the 1970s to my students.

The book is innovative in several ways. It presents a static model that captures much of the intellectual aspects of classical economics, a static Keynesian model, and dynamic Keynesian models with naive, adaptive, and rational expectations, all developed with essentially the same intellectual framework. The failure of each model to match or predict the data at some point in time is explored, and the next model is seen as a development to solve this failure in prediction. Dynamic models are almost never presented in undergraduate texts, but issues such as inflation (which is a rate of change) demand them. Their development here is consistent with the earlier, static, models and is fairly simple. Some very modern economic models are used but they are presented in a way compatible with undergraduate technical skills. The computer package follows the text very closely and allows the student to perform additional experiments quite easily. It is particularly useful in working out the dynamic models.

Chapters 2 and 3 develop some basic microeconomic tools. Chapter 4 begins the study of macroeconomics with a discussion of the problems of aggregation, national income accounts, and price indices. Chapter 5, following fairly closely on the material in the early part of Thomas Sargent's *Macroeconomic Theory*, develops the aggregate demand side of all of the models to follow. In this chapter is a discussion of the consumption function and the theories of permanent income and the life cycle hypothesis. Investment is discussed briefly but fairly deeply. Chapter 6 presents some exercises in the use of the aggregated demand curve for analyzing government policies.

Chapter 7 begins the historical development with a classical model (where classical signifies that all markets clear). In this chapter the basic version of the four-quadrant diagram that underlies all the models that follow is first constructed. Although this diagram initially appears to be quite complicated, it is constructed from a set of quite simple ideas and is a very compact and elegant way of combining these ideas. A section on supply side economics (of the Reagan variety) is included in this chapter. Chapter 8 begins with the failure of the classical models to provide policy suggestions during the Great Depression and develops a Keynesian model that permits unemployment and provides the standard Keynesian solutions to this unemployment.

Chapters 9 through 12 present dynamic versions of the Keynesian model in which the agents are given ever more information for predicting relevant variables. The standard Phillips curve is shown to be consistent with a dynamic Keynesian model in which individuals have naive expectations (where "naive" means the least amount of information). A shifting Phillips curve is generated with adaptive expectations a là Cagan and the Phillips curve disappears as a policy tool under rational expectations. Two general models (one Keynesian and the other a general equilibrium model) that give rise to business cycles are explored in Chapter 12.

Chapters 13 through 15 deal with issues of money and monetary policy. Chapter 13 contains some definitions of money and a short history of money and banking in the United States from colonial times to the present. This history is included because most students believe that what is has always been, and an illustration of the rich United States monetary history helps break this belief. Chapter 14 discusses the Federal Reserve System, monetary policy, bonds and interest rates, and the money-creating aspect of the banking system. This chapter ends with a reprise of the earlier models but with the effects of monetary policy on interest rates and investment included. Chapter 15 discusses policy options in a world with perfect foresight through an overlapping generations model of money. This is included for several reasons. First, a model is developed that generates a social security system. Then, the model generates a private demand for money; lastly, it is possible to explore what policy options are available to a government even when the citizens have perfect foresight with respect to government policy.

Chapter 16 uses game theory to explore the kinds of policies that are available to a government in a world with rational expectations. These explorations balance the policy ineffectiveness that was predicted by the extreme rational expectations model in Chapter 11. This is done by considering strategic policy options for the government in a simple game-theory environment. Chapter 17 deals with the effects of the issues presented in public choice theory on government policies.

Chapter 18 deals with international economics. It is a standard pure-trade theory model, in which issues of gains from trade, causes of trade, and some commercial policy can be developed. The basic issues of international (open economy) macroeconomics have been integrated with the earlier chapters, including some issues of balance of payments and exchange rates. The material developed allows some simple extensions of the models into a world with other countries.

I am grateful for the comments of the members of the classes at the University of Minnesota, Dartmouth College, and the University of Chicago where this text was developed. Additional helpful comments were given by Evangelos Falaris, Dennis Hall, Mustafa Koluman, Nicholas Noble, Charles Whiteman, Sharon Erenburg, and Ernst Stromsdorfer. Patricia Pitzele read and critiqued the entire manuscript, Barbara Belisle provided invaluable administrative support, and Susan Everly helped me prepare the index. At Prentice Hall, my editors, William Webber and Whitney Blake, my production editor, Joanne Palmer, and the rest of the staff were extremely supportive and friendly.

Macroeconomic Theory

1

Introduction

In which we are introduced to the heroine of our story, discover a little of her history, meet some of the men most important in her life, and become aware of some of her current trials.

We get the word economics from the Greek words $o\iota\kappa o\zeta$ (house) and $\nu o\mu\zeta$ (rule), or the rules of management of the household. "Household" was a very general term and could mean either the household of a single family or the household of a state or city-state. The early Greeks (Plato, Aristotle, and Epicurus, for example) wrote about economics. Aristotle, who was the most influential of these writers in Western thought, attempted to determine the **just price** for goods. His work in this area dominated economic thought in the Middle Ages and is still of interest to the more philosophically inclined economists of today.

From the mid-seventeenth century until fairly recently, economics was devoted almost entirely to the study of commercial arrangements; the interchange and production of goods. More recently, economics has developed into what Nobel Prize winner George Stigler calls the "Imperial Science" and has encroached on the realms of political science with an economic analysis of the behavior of politicians, returned to the household with an analysis of the formation and dissolution of families, and added education with an analysis of the formation of human capital or knowledge.

Economics has traditionally[1] been divided into two subcategories, microeconomics and macroeconomics. Microeconomics studies the behavior of individual **agents,** households or firms, as they attempt to maximize some kind of objective function[2]—their welfare or profit—in the face of such constraints as their incomes, time, likes and dislikes, prices, and taxes. It can be used rather successfully to explain or predict the changes in an individual's behavior in response to changes in these constraints. For example, economists can fairly accurately predict how individuals will change their purchasing patterns in response to some price changes. Microeconomic methods have been used to analyze such areas of human concern as the structure of industry, the introduction or removal of specific types of taxes, the optimal use of nonrenewable and renewable resources, schooling, occupation choice, marriage, toothbrushing, and (my personal favorite) household allocation of time and church attendance.

Macroeconomics is the study of economies in the large ("macro" is from the Greek word *makros*, which means "long") or, more accurately in its modern use, in the aggregate. It is the attempt to analyze the interrelated behavior of all the agents in an economy. Usually the macroeconomist tries to describe the behavior of each type of agent and the types of institutions through which these different types of agents interact. This is normally done with a mathematical model which, once constructed, is solved in order to determine how the macroeconomy will behave.

[1] This is a very recent tradition. According to the Oxford English Dictionary (supplement), the first use in print of the word "macroeconomic" was in 1948, when David Hawkins used it in the title of an article published in the November edition of the journal *Econometrica*. Interestingly enough, the word was not used in the text of the article, only in the title.

[2] Some psychologists claim that individuals who appear to act irrationally (the insane) can be viewed as having rational **processing** behavior, but have somehow collected information on life that is wildy at variance with sane norms.

Difficulties arise in macroeconomics for at least two reasons. In order to make the models tractable, massive simplifications occur. The nature of these simplifications determines the nature of the shortcomings in a particular model's ability to describe the real world. Second, data is insufficient to allow us reliably to distinguish innocuous assumptions from those that generate serious errors. Many—possibly infinitely many—models cannot be rejected by the data. The inability of macroeconomists to conduct careful experiments is a major obstacle in the search to generate an accurate model of the economy. It is a continual frustration to many economists that because of their inability to perform experiments they are unable to use the scientific method.

One of the major controversies in macroeconomics is the role of government, or more precisely of a central or federal government. There are two polar positions in this debate, with a bunch of folks falling in between. One position, currently called "liberal" even though this usage is at variance with the term's older definition, claims that the government must provide many services and a controlling or guiding role in the economy. Those who take this position believe that the government can and should make policy changes that change, in some beneficial way, current aggregate economic variables. The variables most often considered are aggregate output (called Gross National Product, GNP), inflation, and unemployment. The view taken is that the government itself has an understanding of the kind of trade-offs (represented by a mathematical function, called a trade-off function, that describes the preferences of the government) that it is willing to make between various values of these variables. It then wants to follow policies that will yield an optimal value to its trade-off function. (This is what a government will do, even though one may be unlikely to find many government officials who are able to describe either their own or their government's trade-off function.) Note that this position contains two possibly separate views: That a wide range of social services *should* be provided by government and that the government *can* control the aggregate economy.

The other position, currently called "conservative," usually claims that government *cannot* control the current aggregate economy and *should not* provide social services since the provision of those services by government only hinders the proper private operation of the economy. What a government *can* and *cannot* control are the crucial questions of macroeconomics. What it **should** and **should not** do are moral or political questions.

Modern economics is thought by many to have begun with Adam Smith[3] and his book *The Wealth of Nations*, published in 1776. In this book, Smith argued that the free interactions of individuals, each selfishly pursuing individual goals and attempting to become as well off as possible, generated the greatest welfare for

[3] Adam Smith, *An Inquiry into the Nature and Causes of the Wealth of Nations* (London: W. Strahen and T. Cadell, 1776). As with almost everyone else, Smith did not generate his ideas in a vacuum. Important influences on Smith include Hutcheson, Locke, and Smith's friend Hume. The general notion of the fine order of the natural universe that belonged to the system of Newton heavily influenced the 18th century.

society as a whole. Government, in this view, was small and had the role mainly of enforcing private contracts. The individuals who followed these ideals of a *free* interaction of individuals originally called themselves "liberals," and were against such policies as the government's granting of monopolies and other restrictions on free trade. This is the point of view of those currently called "conservative," while current "liberals" are those who favor government intervention. How this change in meaning came about is one of the mysteries of etymology.

Economic research in an environment with this contemporary conservative philosophical background is aimed mainly at understanding the *structure* of the economy and the nature of the interactions of its various agents. It has been long known that economies exhibit **business cycles,** alternating periods of boom and bust; periods of great business activity, high employment, and raising wages and profits, followed by periods of reduced business activity, increasing unemployment, and declining wages and profits. Macroeconomic research in the early part of this century attempted to explain these business cycles and to consider the effects of such economic institutions as banking laws, the nature of transfer schemes, and investment incentives on these fluctuations. This was the era we will consider in our **Classical Model.** (We are doing a little disservice to the historical economic usage of the term classical economics. Classical economics is often used to signify pre-marginalistic economic thought. This would include the works of Smith, Ricardo, and Marx. The economic theories of the early part of this century would be more accurately classified as neoclassical. For us, in this book, the terminological distinction is not important.)

The 1920s and 1930s saw the onset of the "Great Contraction," as Milton Friedman likes to call it, or the Great Depression, as almost everyone else calls it. During this time the old economic ideas seemed not to be working. The great unemployment and misery seemed far removed from the society described by Adam Smith and the many neoclassical economists who followed him. With something like one third of the labor force unable to find work, the classical model and its promise of full employment seemed of little relevance to the world in which people lived. More germane, a model that does not permit unemployment tells one nothing about how to get rid of it.

In 1936 in England, John M. Keynes published his book entitled *The General Theory of Employment, Interest, and Money.*[4] The economic model developed in that book—and since relatively few people actually read *The General Theory*, it's main ideas were spread by Keynes through his students at Cambridge University—described a world that *could* contain unemployment. Here was a model in which markets did not work perfectly. In his model, asymmetries existed in the labor market (a market that would determine full employment wages) and in the investment market (a market that would determine the interest rate so that savings and investment would equal each other). These asymmetries made it

[4] John Maynard Keynes, *The General Theory of Employment, Interest and Money* (New York: Harcourt Brace, 1935).

possible for the labor market not to clear—for unemployment to exist—and for the interest rate to fail to clear the investment market.[5]

The most important aspect of this model from a historical point of view, however, was that it provided a theoretical rationale for the economic intervention that the governments at that time so wanted to pursue. This does not mean that the **Keynesian Model** was being scientifically applied to regulate the economy; that was for much later. The mildly activist governments of the time finally had an economic theory that justified what they were doing and what they wanted to do. This, in part, was the reason for the phenomenal success of *The General Theory*. A second important result of this "Keynesian revolution" was a serious change in the direction of economic research. Instead of trying to understand how business cycles were generated in an economy, economists became concerned with trying to determine how to use short-term countercyclical policy to mitigate the effects of these cycles. The belief in this new approach, called **Keynesian Countercyclical Policy,** was reinforced by a statistical *correlation* noticed in the 1950s in both England and the United States by A. W. Phillips. Phillips noticed that periods of high unemployment tended to be correlated with periods of low inflation. Few doubt the ability of the government to generate inflation—this has a long and gory history—and if Phillips's discovery was interpreted as proving a *causal* relationship between inflation and employment, it could be viewed as strong statistical evidence in support of the Keynesian model and activist government policy.

By 1964, the Keynesian model had gained such acceptance that W. W. Heller, then chairman of the President's Council of Economic Advisors, persuaded President Johnson and the congress to pass a tax cut with the specific intent of pulling the economy out of the small recession it was then in. The idea was to use deficit spending during recessions and to tax more than the government spent during boom periods to help counter the business cycle. With varying degrees of faithfulness, especially with respect to the part about taxing more during good times, that policy has since been pursued in both the United States and many other countries. Through the 1960s these Keynesian types of policy were considered great successes, especially with the rising world standard of living and the long continued growth that was then being experienced in the United States and Europe. Robert Solow—who won the 1987 Nobel prize in economics, but not for this comment—declared that economists finally understood how the macroeconomy worked. Moreover, in the future it would simply be necessary to get better estimates of the parameters of these models to be better able to do the fine tuning that the economy would require.

A major crisis occurred in macroeconomics in the 1970s. As that decade's data, which showed a surprising combination of high inflation and high unem-

[5] A market clears when the price moves to the point where the quantity of a good or service that is demanded equals the quantity that is supplied. In terms of a labor market, the market clears when all of those who want work find it. The unemployed are those who do not want to work at the prevailing wage.

ployment came in and presented patterns unexpected for and unexplained by a Keynesian world, economists began seriously to question the predictions generated by that model, and some of the younger economists began to question the basis of the model itself. This set off a round of work aimed at discovering what was required to improve the Keynesian model in order to allow it to be better able to predict economic variables.

One of the major intellectual innovations in economics that grew out of this research was the inclusion of individuals' expectations into the macroeconomic models. It had been recognized early on that individuals' expectations were important in economics, but little had been done to incorporate those expectations into macroeconomic models. In *The General Theory*, Keynes had spoken of the effects and importance of expectations, but this style of development had virtually disappeared in the Keynesian theory that was developed by his most eminent followers. In response to the crisis of the 1970s, the Keynesian model was first augmented by the inclusion of the notion of adaptive expectations[6]. In adaptive expectations, an individual's expectations of inflation were formed by a learning process based on the inflation that he had observed over the last few years. This adaptive expectations model generated a shifting Phillips curve that could explain the data reasonably well. The adaptive expectations approach to changing the Keynesian model was well liked by the older economists because it preserved much of the theory that they already knew and required only minor adjustments in their lifetimes' beliefs.

A group of young economists suggested another way of viewing the macroeconomy. Noting a number of inconsistencies in the Keynesian model, they began concentrating on the microeconomic foundations of macroeconomics. This led to what is now called **Rational Expectations Theory.** At the core of this theory is the "Rational Expectations Critique" of economic policy making. This critique is as follows: Suppose one estimates an economic model, using statistical tools to find estimates of the variables and coefficients in a macroeconomic model, and does not explicitly include in that model the way that individuals' expectations of government behavior—to use one of the most important examples—influence their behavior. If one then uses this model to make predictions about what the economy will be like if the government changes its behavior, one will almost certainly get incorrect predictions. This is because the behavior of the individual agents will depend on what they think the government will do, and these expectations are incorporated in the values of the coefficients that are estimated. If the government changes its policies, individuals change their behavior, and the equations will then have different coefficients. The *old* set of coefficients is incorrect for forecasting the effects of a *new* policy. This way of viewing the economy, known as the New Classical economics, brought to the front, again, the whole question of the feasibility of helpful government action. If individuals guess correctly,

[6] The most important source for the idea of adaptive expectations comes from Phillip Cagan's study of the hyperinflations in Germany and other eastern European countries after World War I.

many of the government policies that would be beneficial in a world that behaved like a Keynesian model would not be beneficial—and would possibly even be harmful—in this brave new classical world. These economists do not say that all government policy is ineffectual, but they do demand a rethinking of the way government policy affects the economy and of the kinds of government policies that might be effective. The rational expectations theory has caught on, and in the past few years rational expectations has become such a common assumption in economic modelling that economists no longer bother to defend the assumption when they use it in a model.

Recent work in macroeconomics has dealt with the problem, mentioned above, of finding effective government policies in a world in which people have rational expectations. The search for solutions to this problem has led to models with perfect foresight (a known future, which is a kind of perfect rational expectations) and to economies in which strategic games are played by all of the agents and the actions of each agent depends on the actions of the other agents. In some of these strategic games, policies can be random and there can be private information that would help other agents in their predictions if it got out. The holders of this private information can manipulate that information (their reputations, for example) to some degree to get policies that can have aggregate effects. The process of collecting information and the problems that asymmetric information causes in economic processes have also been important areas of work. Rational expectations becomes much more interesting as a working hypothesis if it can be shown that a large number of learning models give results that converge to something that looks like a rational expectations model.

Before we go on to study these problems of macroeconomics, it is necessary to prepare a little background in microeconomics. The next several chapters present the small amount of microeconomics that we will be using in the construction of our macroeconomic models. This introduction to microeconomics is also intended to begin the (not too painful, I hope) process of converting you, my reader, from a human being into an economist.

2

Production

In which we examine the miracle of how the things we have are transformed into the things we want.

Economics has been called the study of society's attempt to satisfy individuals' unlimited wants with the limited resources that are available.[1] This definition is slightly absurd, since unlimited wants can, by definition, never be satisfied. However, the definition does suggest the nature of the economic problem. In this chapter, we are going to deal with the the economist's analysis of the conversion of the limited things that people have into the things that they want. This seemingly magical conversion is known as **production.**

FACTORS OF PRODUCTION

Generally, we don't have the things we want in the form we want them. What we have are **factors** and what we want are **goods.** (They don't call them "goods" for nothing.) Factors are the things that nature has given us or that have been left to us by history. The word "factor" comes from Latin and means a maker, a doer, or a generator. We can describe factors as being of three types: land, labor, and capital.[2] Remember that we don't really want any of these for themselves, but for what they can be turned into. (It may seem as if holding undeveloped land is a counterexample to the above statement, but this is not the case. The undeveloped wilderness is generating a set of esthetic services, which are a kind of good.) The division of factors into these three types is a bit of an artifact, but it is an artifact that helps us think about the world a little more carefully. Part of what we will need to define an **economy** is the quantity of each of the factors that it contains.

Land refers to all types of natural resources, whether renewable or nonrenewable. The eight feet of topsoil in Ohio is as much and as important a natural resource as is the oil under the ground in Texas or the silver in the mines of Potosí, the ancient Spanish silver mine high in the mountains of Bolivia. Renewable resources, like the Ohio topsoil, are called that because, with proper care, they can be used over and over again. Nonrenewable resources have some special charac-

[1] The Greek philosopher Epicurus did not see desires as unlimited but thought that individuals somehow got the erroneous idea that an unlimited number of goods was required to satisfy their wants. Epicurus taught that it was desirable to reduce one's desires to achieve contentment. Buddhists also have developed a value system by which maximum happiness is not achieved by maximizing the consumption of goods but by minimizing wants.

[2] We could define a very large number of factors. Land in a climate that is good for producing bananas could be considered one type of factor and a mountain hillside that is good for producing coffee could be another. This definition of factors could be extended until each good is produced by factors that are only used for that good. We would then have more factors than goods, which is not a very good way of simplifying the world.

teristic that cannot be recovered after use.[3] Usually this special characteristic is the historical accident of concentration. A particular ore deposit is exploited because that location contains a sufficient concentration of the ore to make the extraction worth the effort to someone. The exploitation of a resource is a testament to entropy, the tendency for the world to become more and more disordered. When we exploit a resource, we take it from a concentrated source and diffuse it around the world. It is not renewable, although it might be recyclable, because the concentration is lost.

Bauxite is mined from a specific concentration found in Jamaica, converted into aluminum by using the hydroelectric power in Iceland, and spread by users into a thin layer of beer cans all over the surface of the earth. The value of the resource, the bauxite in this example, is in the concentration, and that concentration is destroyed on extraction. The renewable water power that produced the hydroelectric power in Iceland is not destroyed in the process of converting the bauxite into aluminum, although the energy used is lost.

Land is given to us by nature even though different societies have their own ways of distributing the rights to use or ownership of the land. **Rents** are what we call the payments made for the use a specific piece of land to the agent who has the legal right of control over that land. Only rarely does the total quantity of land possessed by an economy change, although this does happen. Sometimes land, or any natural resource, becomes unaccessible, as did the soil in the town of Pompeii; sometimes it is made accessible, as when the Dutch took land from the sea, or farmers in Southeast Asia cut terraced rice paddies out of a mountainside; sometimes, through some negotiation process such as war, it is transferred from one economy to another, as in the German expansion during World War II, or as the seemingly greedy Libyan government attempts to take the phosphate deposits from Chad (which has few enough natural resources already).

Labor refers to human energy, more or less well controlled. We measure it in terms of person-years (or man-years under the old nomenclature), as the directed energy of one individual for one year. You should think of it as some basic unit of human energy that can be the base by which we measure labor. This basic unit is an almost completely untrained individual who is employed in the most menial of tasks. It may be quite difficult for members of a highly industrialized society to imagine such a unit of labor, for there is very little use for it in that society. A human being working carrying goods like a pack animal is about as close to a basic unit as possible, but even this type of work is usually combined with knowledge

[3] In almost all cases, we will not run out of our nonrenewable resources. This is true in spite of all the careless rhetoric to the contrary. We will use up the easily accessible concentration of nonrenewable minerals, for example, but there will continue to be other less easily extracted deposits available. As we use up easily available deposits, the price of these materials will rise and the more expensive sources will be exploited. These rising prices will change the use of these goods, and oil, for example, might become too expensive to burn. However, there will always be deposits of oil to be tapped.

about how to carry a load most efficiently. All labor that is at all useful comes combined with human capital.

Human capital is the knowledge or training that individuals have acquired in order to control their unit of labor more effectively. Wage differentials among individuals (**wages** being the payment that individuals receive when someone else has rented the use of their labor) are to a large part explained by the differentials in their training. One might argue, as surgeons often do, that a surgeon receives a higher wage than an auto mechanic, for example, because of the large quantity of human capital that the surgeon needs in order to control a scalpel correctly. This issue of wages gets fairly complicated—there is a whole area of economics devoted to the study of human capital and labor—but the basic idea of higher wages for more training seems to be a fairly well-observed phenomenon.

Individuals invest in human capital when they enter universities or special training programs, and they expect to get a return on this investment just as they would on any other type of investment. It seems reasonable that individuals should be able to borrow in order to finance their educations, since education will raise their earning power. The perpetual problems that the government has with the student loan program illustrates one major difference between human and other types of capital. If a person doesn't meet payments on a loan that was used to purchase a machine, the bank can take back the machine and sell it to someone else. It is very difficult to repossess human capital. It was possible to do so in the times of the ancient Romans, when debtors could be sold into slavery. It has been suggested that if college graduates who did not pay back their loans could be sold into slavery, (which in this case means that someone else could collect on the additional wages gained by their human capital) there probably would be no need for a government-run student loan program.

The quantity of labor in an economy depends on a number of historical accidents. The first of these is the set of accidents that causes the birth of the individuals in whom the labor is embodied. Another is the historical accident of the educational history of the members of the labor force. (A **labor force** is that part of the population that can work.) While this quantity of labor is unlikely to increase very rapidly, it can decline quite rapidly. (Although there have been examples of fairly rapid increases in the education level, except for the one-time jump in population that occurs when a society discovers sanitation and most of the children who were expected to die live instead, population growth is usually a fairly slow process.) World War I reduced the educated male population of England by a substantial percentage, as World War II did of Russia. The various plagues that have been recorded as destroying large parts of the population of Europe and the destruction wracked by the various European "childhood diseases" on the indigenous populations of the Americas, which thereby greatly aided the European conquest of those continents, serve as powerful reminders of the potential downward variability of the labor supply. In fact, the continuing decrease of the indigenous labor force was a great problem for the Spanish conquerors of the Americas and eventually led to the forced importation of Africans to replace that lost labor.

Capital, for the economist, refers to the machines used in the production process. Businessmen often use the term "capital" for the money that they invest or borrow in order to purchase their machines. We will use the word to refer to the machines themselves. The machines are goods that have been produced at some time in the past and are currently being used to aid in the production of other goods. (There are some philosophical issues, for the Marxists, as to whether there is anything special about goods that are being used in the production of other goods. While this is at the heart of the exploitation of labor question, we will ignore such issues here.) In a capitalist society, these goods earn rents for their owners from their use in the production process. Capital is a stock concept and is used to refer to the stock, or accumulated quantity, of machines in the economy. The accumulation, or flow, of additional capital is called **investment.** The capital that wears out during a particular production period is said to have depreciated and the quantity lost is called **depreciation.**

AGENTS

An economy possesses a number of different categories of **agents.** These categories are households, firms, government, and, as we will see later, financial intermediaries. An individual may be several different types of agent at the same time. We are using the artificial division of an individual into several types of agent in order to isolate the different kinds of decision problems that she must solve. An individual may have many roles: a member of a family, an investor, an employee, a manager of a firm, and a participant in governmental decisions. A farmer living in a small Vermont town who owns her own farm is an example of someone behaving as several different agents, for she is manager, owner of factors, main source of labor on the farm, and, on town meeting day, part of the government.

Households own all of the factors in the economy. They rent out these factors to firms and use that income to purchase the goods that they want to consume. The household is therefore both the supplier of factors and the demander of the final products. It is the preferences of the households for consumption of goods, even indirectly, that drive the economic machine. Some might argue that households do not own all of the factors, that some of the capital and land are owned by firms. (Doesn't IBM own its building and machines?) Firms, however, are owned by stockholders and stockholders are eventually households. There could be several layers in this, the stock of one firm being held by a second firm and the stock of this second firm held by a third and so on, but, eventually, the stock is held by an individual. There are no firms in the United States that own themselves. You might have read in the business section of your newspaper about a firm buying back its own stock. A buyback of a firm's stock merely reduces the number of shareholders and increases the percentage of the firm owned by the remaining shareholders. If the government owns something, it does so as a proxy for the citizens—the households—of the country.

The problem faced by individuals in the role of households supplying factors is to decide how much of the factors that they own they should rent to the firms. (How much labor to provide is probably the most important decision for the majority of households. This decision includes having to decide which and how many members of the household will enter the labor market to work outside the house and which and how many will work in the house.) As consumers they must decide how much of each of the commodities that they wish to have they will actually purchase, given the income generated by their factors. When they forgo the consumption of some goods and purchase capital, they are saving. (In this case they are investing as well. The distinction will be discussed later.) Households attempt to maximize their welfare or general well-being over time by their factor supply, investment, and consumption decisions.

Firms organize the production activities in the economy. They rent factors from households and combine them to produce goods. The objective of the firms is to maximize profits. Profits are the difference between the gross income earned by the firm from the sale of its products and the rentals it pays on the factors it uses. This does not mean that firms make profits. (Note that profits are what is left after the firm has paid the rentals on capital. This is different from the usual notion of profit that is used, for example, in determining a firm's federal income tax.) In fact, in a perfectly competitive economy there would be no profits, and all of a firm's earnings from the sale of its goods would go to pay wages and rentals. That firms attempt to earn profits even though they may not succeed should not be a strange idea. The object of a college's football team is to win games. Yet we have examples of football teams that have played more than forty games without winning one. Their objective is still to win games (in the case above, a more realistic objective may be to survive the next game, but they are *attempting* to win). The important idea is that the objective of the firm is to maximize profits.[4] This makes the behavior of the firm easy to describe.

Government collects and spends taxes. Taxes are forced contributions from the households. This ability to force contributions is an important characteristic of government. Why government expenditures exist can be rationalized through the idea of externalities. If there are services such as roads or defense that individuals can use without paying for them directly, it behooves a government to produce these services and extract payment from the citizens. This is because a market mechanism for generating payments for these services will usually result in a situation in which individuals will attempt to pay less for the service or good than it is really worth to them. A government can collect the "correct" amount from each user. If your neighbor pays something to help defend the country, for example,

[4] The problem is a little more complex than this. In a dynamic model the managers of a firm want to maximize the value of the firm (the value of the shares). To do this in a dynamic world, the managers need to think and plan for future as well as current profits. They want to maximize the entire stream of future profits. This entails discounting future profits so that, while their importance is recognized, they are not viewed as being as important as current profits.

you gain benefits from it—you are defended—whether or not you make any payments for this service. There are also such things as negative externalities. Pollution is an example of one of these. If a firm pollutes the air, it reduces its private costs but makes those who live near the factory and breathe the polluted air bear the costs of the bad air. In this case the government can make the firm pay the *real* costs of production. These costs would involve either compensating the neighbors for their losses caused by the bad air or cleaning up the air.[5] Governments do other things, mainly improving the condition of one subset of the citizens of the economy at the expense of other subsets. This is called the political process. For us, it is enough, for now, that they tax and spend.

THE PRODUCTION PROCESS

An economy operates as a circular process. Households provide factors to firms and receive rents for them. Firms produce goods and sell them to households for prices. The value of factors going to firms—the **income** of the households—equals the value of goods going to households—the **output** of the economy. Firms retain nothing; all rents, wages, and profits go to the households. Therefore, income equals output. If this were not the case, the economy would run down as either firms would not have enough earnings from their output to meet the rents on factors, or the households would not have enough income to purchase the output of the firms and the firms would be left with unsold product. This cyclical process of trade is an important concept. Figure 2.1 is a simple map of an economy that captures the above notions. (Note that the economic world is flat. This idea is carried through in that many of the equations that economists use to describe economic processes are linear.) If we measured the flow of the economy at either point A (income) or B (output), we would get the same result.

In one year, for example, the value of output that passes Line B is equal to the sum of the value of the goods produced and sold in the economy. The value of the production of chickens is equal to the price of chickens times the quantity of chickens delivered to households. Let p_c be the price of chickens and q_c be the number of chickens sold in the economy. Therefore, $p_c q_c$ is the price of chickens times the quantity of chickens and equals the value of chickens sold. Suppose that we index goods by numbers. An index already exists in the Universal Product Code (the bar codes on goods in supermarkets), so we can use that one if we wish. To express the total value of output we write

[5] There is a result in economics called the **Coase Theorem.** This theorem states that the reason there are externalities of this type is because property rights are not assigned completely. If one owned the right to breathe clean air, for example, one could sue a polluter and force a payment or a reduction in the pollution. In a world with low transaction costs, a full allocation of property rights would allow a private, free-market solution to these problems. Without this full allocation of property rights, a government can generate some second-best solutions.

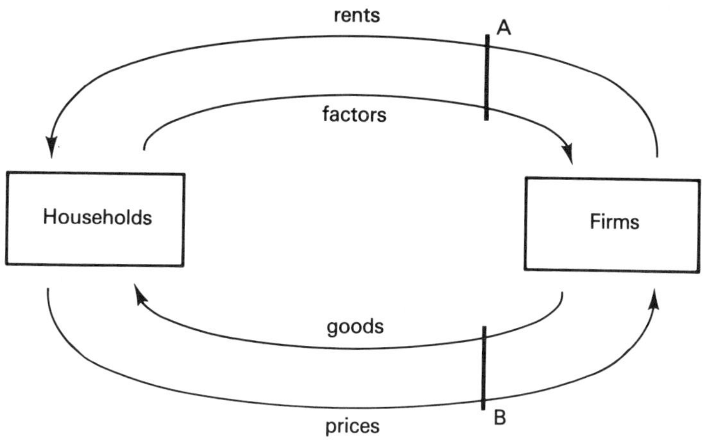

Figure 2.1

$$\text{total output} = \sum_{i=\text{all goods}} p_i q_i = p_1 q_1 + p_2 q_2 + \ldots + p_{\text{last}} q_{\text{last}}$$

The sign Σ means to sum up the $p_i q_i$s, letting $_i$ be, sequentially, the universal product code of all goods.

The value of income that passes Line A can be found in a similar manner. Let r_p be the wage (rental) of plumbers and let f_p be the quantity of plumbers' services used in the economy in one year. Then $r_p f_p$ is the total income of plumbers. Summing up all factors (plumbers' services can be thought of as one factor), we get the total income in the economy. We express this as

$$\text{total income} = \sum_{j=\text{all factors}} r_j f_j = r_1 f_1 + r_2 f_2 + \ldots + r_{\text{last}} f_{\text{last}}$$

where j is used to index all factors. Since income equals output, the revenues of households from renting their factors equals the sales of the firms.

We describe the results of the use of the factors to produce the goods by a **production function.** If the output of some good—compact disks, in this example—is Q_{CD}, and the quantities of the factors used in the production of compact disks are respectively L, Lb, and K, then we would write the production function in standard functional notation as[6]

$$Q_{CD} = f(L, Lb, K)$$

[6] Where L, Lb, and K represent the quantity of each of the factors that are used in the production of the good; L is the quantity of land, Lb is the quantity of labor, and K the quantity of capital.

For the nonmathematicians reading this, a production function can be viewed as a kind of computer program. One doesn't know quite how it works, but if one calls up the program for the production of compact disks, and gives the program the quantity of land (L), labor (Lb), and capital (K) that is being used in the production of compact disks, the program will give back the quantity of compact disks that will be produced. The computer program "knows" the most efficient technology available for converting any mix of land, labor, and capital into compact disks. If the technology changes, that will be reflected in the results of the program. We say that the technology is *embodied* in the production function.

In a simple world, one could imagine that there is really only one factor—the one traditionally chosen is labor—and that each additional unit of that factor always generates a fixed or constant increase in the output of the good. This type of production function has fixed coefficients and might look like this:

$$Q_{CD} = c \times Lb$$

where c is a number representing the number of compact disks that one unit of labor produces. Adding additional units of labor increases output proportionally. If there are only two goods in the economy—compact disks and beer, and the production function for beer also has fixed coefficients—$Q_B = b \times Lb_{\text{beer}}$, where Lb_{beer} is the quantity of labor being used in the beer industry—then we can easily draw a curve representing all of the production choices available to this economy. If there is full employment, then each worker not employed in the compact disk industry is making beer. If we reduce compact disk production by c units, the one unit of labor released from the compact disk industry goes to work in the beer industry and produces b units of beer. With these production functions, the trade-off of c units of compact disks for b units of beer occurs independently of the number of workers initially in each industry. Figure 2.2 shows the full set of

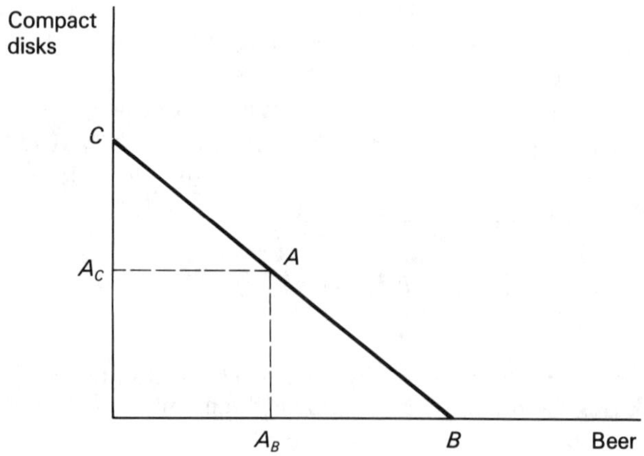

Figure 2.2

combinations of compact disks and beer that an economy with a total of 100 units of labor can produce.

If all of the labor is used for producing compact disks, then 100*c* units of compact disks (*c* units per unit of labor times 100 units of labor) and no beer can be produced. Point C represents this production combination. If only beer is made, then 100*b* units of beer can be produced. Point B represents this combination. Point A represents a point at which some of the labor is used for producing compact disks and some for producing beer. Since the coefficients are constant, the line representing the set of possible production points is a straight line. (We will discuss this set of possible production points again in Figure 2.4, illustrating the combinations of outputs that are possible in a more general world.)

In general, production does not take place using only one factor and production functions do not have a fixed coefficient between output and one factor. Normally, production functions display positive but diminishing marginal productivity for each of the several factors used. (**Diminishing marginal productivity** means that if the quantities of all but one of the factors were held constant, and the quantity of one of the factors were increased, output of the good would go up—the **positive marginal** product part—but the increase would be smaller for each additional unit of that factor—the diminishing marginal product part.) Table 2.1 shows an example involving the production of compact disks. If with a given amount of capital and land, one hundred workers could produce twenty-five thousand compact disks and 101 workers with the same amount of capital and land could produce 25,200 compact disks, the marginal product of the one hundred and first worker would be two hundred compact disks. This is the amount of additional compact disks produced by this additional worker. Since this industry displays diminishing marginal product, the one hundred and second worker, when the one hundred and two workers are working with the original quantities of land and capital, would increase production by some amount strictly less than two hundred compact disks. In the table, the marginal product of this worker is 150 compact disks, and the one hundred and third worker has a marginal product of one hundred compact disks. The information displayed in Table 2.1 comes from the

TABLE 2.1

# OF WORKERS	COMPACT DISKS	MARGINAL PRODUCT
100	25,000	
		> 200
101	25,200	
		> 150
102	25,350	
		> 100
103	25,450	

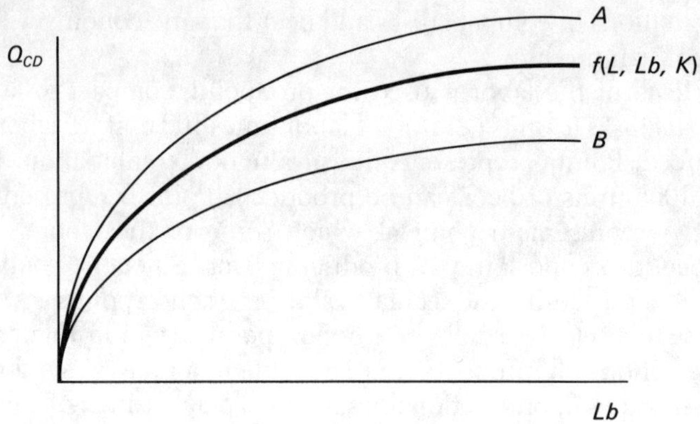

Figure 2.3

technology. Engineers determine the best methods for producing goods and that, expressed as the technology, determines the marginal product of workers or of any other factor.

The dark curve labeled $f(L,Lb,K)$ in Figure 2.3 shows the relationship between the amount of labor used in production and the output, assuming a fixed amount of land and capital. In the figure, we assume that we can continuously change the quantity of labor that we are using. If we think of labor as person-hours, then continously increasing or decreasing the amount of labor is reasonable. The slope of the production curve gets less steep as labor increases, because of the diminishing marginal productivity, but will not turn down, because we are assuming that labor always has a positive marginal product.

Increases in either land or capital will shift the whole curve except for the origin upward to a curve such as Curve A in Figure 2.3, and decreases will shift it downward to a curve similar to the one labeled B. Note that the curve would be similar but not necessarily identical in shape if either capital or land were on the horizontal axis and labor and, respectively, land or capital were held constant.

The production function contains information about the technology of the economy. We assume that the economy always uses the most efficient technology in the production of all of its goods. The most efficient technology is not necessarily the most sophisticated or the one that uses the most machines. The most efficient technology is the one that produces the most output given the combinations of factors being used. In an economy with little capital, such as what exists in parts of the Central African Republic, as a possible example, the most efficient technology for grinding flour may indeed be a stone mortar and pestle.

There is a story, possibly mythical, but instructive, about the choice of the most efficient technology where an economist is the hero. (Such stories are rare.) The Agency for International Development (AID), a United States government agency that helps less developed countries wanted to give a rice-milling plant to Indonesia. It gave the country one of the very large and very modern rice-milling plants that is used in the southern United States. It set the plant up in the middle of the rice-growing region. Unfortunately, Indonesia does not have the kind of transportation network that the United States has, and a rice farmer who wanted to use this milling plant would load his donkey with four or five sacks of rice and quite possibly spend several days traveling to the plant where the rice would be milled in a few seconds. The farmer would then take several days to return to his village. The whole process of milling the rice took two times several days plus a few seconds. After a few years, the farmers stopped coming to the plant, for the trip was dangerous and long, and it closed down. Several years later, some folks at AID were thinking of helping the rice growers of Malaysia by giving them a rice-milling plant. The transportation network in the rice-growing region of Malaysia is similar to that of Indonesia. Now here is where our hero comes in. He suggested that instead of repeating the Indonesia fiasco, AID should give each of the villages in the rice growing region a desk-sized, pedal-driven milling machine. This machine took fifteen minutes to mill one sack of rice, but because they were distributed to each village, there were almost no transportation costs. His suggestion illustrates that a simple, possibly even primative machine can be more efficient given a specific environment. These small milling machines represent the more efficient technology in a country where transportation costs are high.[7]

Improvements in technology come about through new ways of combining factors together. An improvement could be a new type of machine, but it may be something as simple as a new order in a production process. If someone discovers that the harvest can be increased by delaying planting until after the weeds begin to grow and the plowing of the fields can then turn the soil and kill the weeds, this discovery represents a technological improvement. The same factors are used, but they are just combined in a different way. A new machine has embodied in it a new way of combining the land, labor, and capital.

THE PRODUCTION POSSIBILITY FRONTIER

We can partially define an economy by the quantities of the factors, the agents and their methods of operating in the economy, and the production functions for the goods that are to be produced in this economy. This completes the picture of the physical, or production, structure of the economy. This information is sufficient to determine the full set of goods that *can be* produced in this economy. Limiting

[7] One should not come away from this discussion with the idea that big or modern is always bad. Some members of the "Small is Beautiful" crowd, in their drive for "appropriate technology," seem to take this point of view. Unfortunately, the low-tech approach to development does not have a large number of success stories to its credit. In fact, one of the famous failures in Mao's development of China was in his attempt to increase steel production with small backyard blast furnaces. The cost per unit was very high and the quality was very low. This project was fairly quickly abandoned.

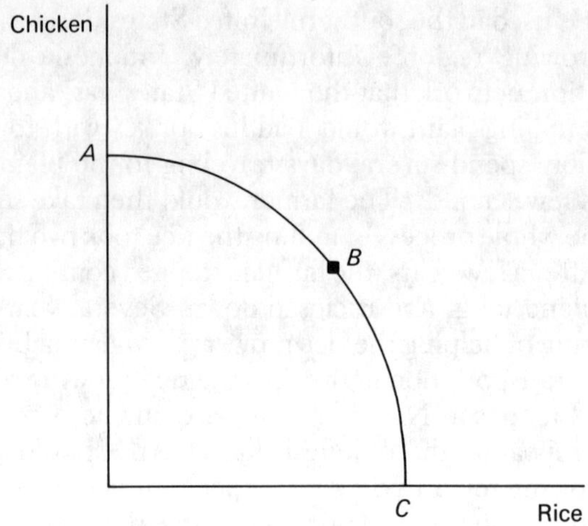

Figure 2.4

the discussion to an economy with only two goods (this page is two dimensional and it is much more difficult to draw curves in three, four, or more dimensions than it is in two), we can use this information to illustrate the set of possible combinations that the economy can achieve when it is being efficient. Figure 2.4 shows such a curve for an economy that can produce combinations of chicken and rice. Here, as distinct from Figure 2.2, the production functions for these goods display diminishing marginal productivity for each of the factors, and several factors are used in the production of each good. Since the curve illustrates the upper bound of the production possible in this economy, the curve is called, in one of the few rational namings of graphs in the social sciences, the **production possibility frontier** (PPF).

This production possibility frontier is concave to the origin, which means that it bows out in the middle. The diminishing marginal productivity causes it to have this shape as opposed to the straight line shape of Figure 2.2. Suppose that the economy was at Point A, producing only chickens. As the economy reduces its chicken production and moves into a combination of rice and chicken production, those factors given up in the chicken production are those that are least useful for producing chickens and most useful for producing rice. This means that initially, fairly large increases in rice production can be achieved with only fairly small declines in the production of chickens. As the production of rice increases, the factors left in the chicken industry are not as good at producing rice, and as chicken production drops, rice production does not increase as much as before. Hence the bowed-out shape of the PPF.

The production possibility frontier shows all possible production points. If

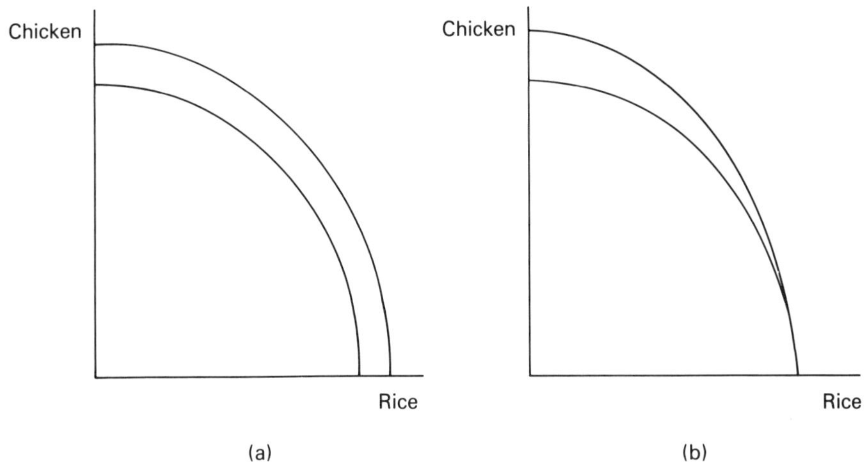

Figure 2.5

you were to observe an economy, you would, however, see only the point on the PPF where that economy chooses to produce. If it were an economy of carnivores, you might find them producing at Point A. If they were herbivores, you might find them at Point C. An economy of Jewish grandmothers making chicken soup might choose to produce at a point such as Point B.

The PPF will change as the quantity of the factors in the economy changes and will also change as the technology changes. An increase in the quantity of any one or more of the factors will cause a shift out, as in Figure 2.5a. Since the production functions display positive marginal productivity to each of the factors, an increase in any one of the factors means that more of each good can be produced when the economy is specialized in that commodity. For that reason the contact points on the axes move out. A similar argument can be used to show that there is a shift out at each point on the curve.

An improvement in the technology for producing chickens—a change in the way the land, labor, and capital are combined so that equal amounts of factors will generate more chickens—will cause the curve to shift out, as is shown in Figure 2.5b. Note that if the economy produces only rice, the technological improvement in the chicken industry will have no effect. However, whenever chickens are being produced, more of them are available with the original quantity of rice. An improvement in the technology for chickens does not necessarily mean that there will be more chickens. With certain types of preferences, it is possible that the economy will choose to produce more rice and the same or even fewer chickens. In this example, the technological improvement in the chicken industry freed factors that are now being used in the rice industry to increase rice production.

TRADE WITH OTHER ECONOMIES

If there are other economies around that have different quantities of factors, there might be possibilities for trade and each economy would not be constrained to choose its consumption point on or inside its PPF. We will continue with the chicken and rice example. Suppose that one economy, Country A, has relatively more of the factors that are good for producing chicken and the other economy, Country B, has more of the factors that are good for producing rice. Examples of possible PPFs are shown in Figure 2.6.

Country A could choose to produce at some point such as Point *a* and trade chicken, which it is good at producing, for rice and end up consuming at a point such as Point *c*. The line through Points *a* and *c* is the rate at which this country can trade chicken for rice with Country B. The slope of this line is the negative of the price of chickens in terms of rice. The line represents a price where *ae* units of chicken are traded for *ec* units of rice, and so *ae* is the distance from Point *a* to Point *e*. The slope is negative because the country must give up chickens to gain rice. Through trade, the quantity of rice is increased only by a reduction in the quantity of chickens. Country A has given up *ae* units of chickens in order to gain *ec* units of rice. Country B could produce at a point like Point *b* and choose to consume at Point *d*. The line through Points *b* and *d* is parallel to the line through Points *a* and *c* since they represent the same rates of exchange of chicken for rice. The distance from Points *b* to *d* is the same as from Points *a* to *c*. With only two economies in this example, the chicken that Country A gives up must go to Country B, and the rice that Country B gives up must go to Country A. So the distance from Points *b* to *f* represents a loss of rice that is equal to the increase in rice in Country A, repre-

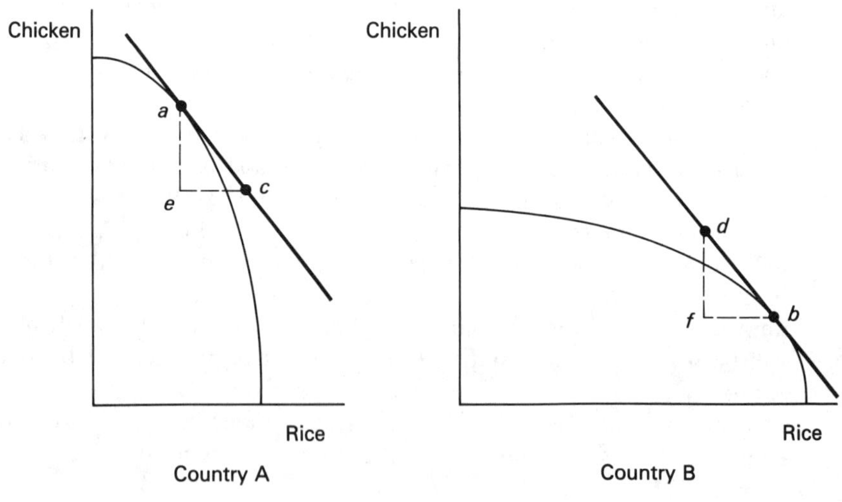

Figure 2.6

sented by the distance from *e* to *c*. The increase in chicken from Points *f* to *d* for Country B exactly equals the decrease of chicken from Points *a* to *e* in Country A.

Note that each country can consume a combination of chicken and rice that it cannot produce by itself. The consumption points, *c* and *d*, are above the PPFs. This increase in the potential consumption points presents the possibilities for both countries to be better off trading than by being by themselves. They produce what they are relatively good at producing and trade that for the good that they are not so good at producing. That trade can be advantageous is illustrated by the post-World War II export-led growth of Japan, Korea, and Taiwan and the stagnation of the nontrading countries of Albania, Burma, and, to some extent, Argentina. There is a distinction between better growth rates generated by trade and the improvement gained by opening up a country to trade that is illustrated above. The growth issue is not well understood.

This concept that countries can be better off by trading with other countries is true for individuals as well. Think of each of the PPFs in Figure 2.6 as the output possibilities for two single individuals, whom we will call Alan and Betty. Alan is good at growing chickens but not as good at growing rice as is Betty. If each specializes—in this example, neither specializes completely—then they both can consume more than they could if they produced for themselves. In the same way that nations gain from trade, so do individuals.

Certain less developed countries are often charged with not producing enough food to feed themselves. Those who make this complaint—for this observation is always in the form of a complaint—note that these countries are using their land for such cash crops as coffee and tea that they export and are not using the land to produce food to feed themselves. The little trade example above could have been made with tea on one axis and wheat on the other. The country that has the advantage in producing tea can make itself better off by specializing in the production of tea and exporting that tea for wheat to gain a combination of tea and wheat to consume that it cannot produce by itself. It is perfectly possible that by producing tea and importing wheat it can have more wheat to consume than it could produce if it used all of its land to grow wheat. Not being self-sufficient in food is not, in and of itself, an evil.

REPRISE

Production is the conversion of factors (things that we have) into goods (the things we want). Land, labor, and capital comprise the three categories of factors and one of the things we need to know in order to define an economy is the quantity of these factors that it possesses. The different economic decisions that an individual makes are thought of as being represented by the decisions of different agents. Agents include the household, which makes consumption decisions and owns all of the factors, the firm, which makes all decisions about organizing production, and the government.

A production function defines the technology by which factors get converted into goods. Production functions normally display positive but diminishing marginal productivity from each of the factors. Given the fixed factors of a given economy and the production functions for the goods available in that economy it is possible to construct a production possibility set, which shows all of the combinations of goods that the economy is able to produce. The upper boundary of that production possibility set is called the production possibility frontier (PPF). The PPF shows the maximum combinations of goods that can be produced, and, if the economy is efficient in its production, the actual production point will be on that PPF. Which point on the PPF is chosen depends on the preferences of the economy. The PPF shifts out with increases in the factors or with technological improvements, although these two shifts look slightly different. When trade with other economies is possible, then it is possible and likely that the economy can consume at a point above its PPF. It does this because it can get more of what it likes by specializing in one good (some set of goods, in the real world) that it is particularly good at producing and trading with other economies for goods it does not produce as well. Both economies gain by this trade.

EXERCISES

1. Suppose that there are 2 goods in an island economy—bananas and coconuts—and only one factor—labor. It takes 3 units of labor to collect 10 bananas and 4 units of labor to collect 10 coconuts. There are 24 units of labor on the island. Construct the production possibility curve between bananas and coconuts for this island economy.
2. Suppose that there are 2 goods in an island economy (fish and oats, as this island is off the coast of Scotland). There are two factors, labor and land, it takes 2 units of land and 4 units of labor to produce 5 fish, and it takes 6 units of land and 2 units of labor to produce 5 bushels of oats. There are 26 units of land and 16 units of labor on this island. Construct the PPF for this island economy.
3. Suppose that ginger beer is produced using land, T, and labor, L, to grow the ginger and convert it into beer. The production function for ginger beer is $Q_{GB} = 8 \times T^{1/2} \times L^{1/2}$. Graph the production curve for an economy with 36 units of land. An additional 13 units of land are then taken from the sea, as in Holland. Graph the new production curve.

3

Supply and Demand

In which we are introduced to Price. Poor Price is driven by forces much greater than herself to find her final equilibrium. She also faces powerful enemies who try to keep her from following her natural instincts.

INTRODUCTION

Once the goods are produced they must be distributed. Actually, the production and consumption decisions are intertwined, and both of them occur at the same moment. But let us suppose for a few moments that we have produced some goods, and we are interested in distributing them to the members of the economy. History has presented us with several examples of methods of distribution.

Sir John Hicks, in his *A Theory of Economic History*, suggests that early societies were a mix of command and custom societies.[1] The command society had a leader or group of leaders, and decisions came down from the top to the general population. A military-based society tended to be of this form, and societies that grew out of conquest continued for some time to follow this structure of the military organization that permitted the victory. The Roman colonial rule, the bureaucratic system of the Chinese, and the theocratic system of the Incan empire seem to be of this form. Allocation of resources were, to a greater or lesser degree, dictated by the central government. The Incan empire appears to be one of the most centrally controlled, with the local priest organizing the production and distribution of food products and in charge of sending the local contribution to the Inca. All of this was done without a written language or a method of accounting as we know it.

Custom societies that have survived to today tend to be small and fairly isolated. However, Hicks sees feudal Europe as a classic example of a custom society. In medieval Europe, the peasants had customary services to provide to the local lord and he had customary services to render to both his overlord and his peasants. Any ruler who expected to get more than was normal would encounter resistance and would be considered a tyrant. Simpler societies, usually aboriginal groups, had economies in which the whole tribe would participate and share the production based on a traditional allocation system. Part of the reason for this traditional system was to provide for the young and for those who had become too old to continue producing.

Neither of the above systems was based on the impersonal interchange of goods (although parts of the Roman and Chinese economies functioned this way). They depended on a repeated, habitual ritual of division of production. As societies grew, the number of products became larger, and the options more complex, these systems failed to continue allocating resources in a satisfactory way, although the Incan system, as best we can tell, successfully maintained a very large command economy. Sometimes, the leaders themselves were the main source of interest in the consumption of goods not traditionally provided by their economies and initiated exchanges with leaders of other economies that eventually led to international trade.

The impersonal interchange of one good for another preferred good is called

[1] John Hicks, *A Theory of Economic History* (Oxford: Oxford University Press, 1969).

commerce. The systematic interchange of such goods occurs in a **market,** whether this market is a physical place, such as a county fair or a store, or occurs over the telephone lines in connections between computers. The rate at which one good is exchanged for another is called the **price** of the good. The price of any good is the **opportunity cost** of forgoing any other good. Therefore, you should think of the price of a good not in terms of money that you need to pay for it, but rather in terms of the most favorable alternative to it. It is that next most favored alternative that you give up when you buy the good that you do in fact purchase. This is your forgone opportunity.

The workings of a market involve both the production and the consumption decisions of individuals. Economists believe that these decisions are based on different types of individual behavior. They therefore construct **supply curves** (functions) that contain information about production decisions and **demand curves** (functions) that contain information about consumption decisions. The combined information in these two curves, called a market, allows the analysis of price and output behavior.

A DEMAND CURVE

A demand function contains the variables that determine the single good consumption decisions of an individual and, when added up, of an economy. The quantity of a good that an individual will purchase is determined by 1, the price of the good; 2, the income level of the individual; 3, the tastes or preferences of the individual; and 4, the prices of other goods. We write such a demand function as

$$Q_D = D(p|Y, \text{tastes}, p_{\text{others}})$$

where p is the price of the good, Y is income, and p_{others} is a vector of prices of other goods. The vertical line separates the price of the good under study from the other variables that effect the demand decision. We define a demand curve as the curve that shows the purchases that a consumer will be willing and able to make at all prices, other things being equal. The items to the right of the vertical line in the demand function are those that are kept equal (constant) as we study the relation between the price of the good and the quantity of that good that is demanded. A demand curve of a general form is illustrated in Figure 3.1.

Note that the demand curve in Figure 3.1 slopes downward. This slope indicates that at lower prices people are willing to purchase more of a good than they are willing to purchase at higher prices. For almost any good—for example, apples—there are other goods that provide at least some of the same services that the apples provide. If the prices of the other goods are unchanged, then a high price for apples encourages people to look for other goods that provide much of the same set of services that apples provide and to purchase more of these goods. In

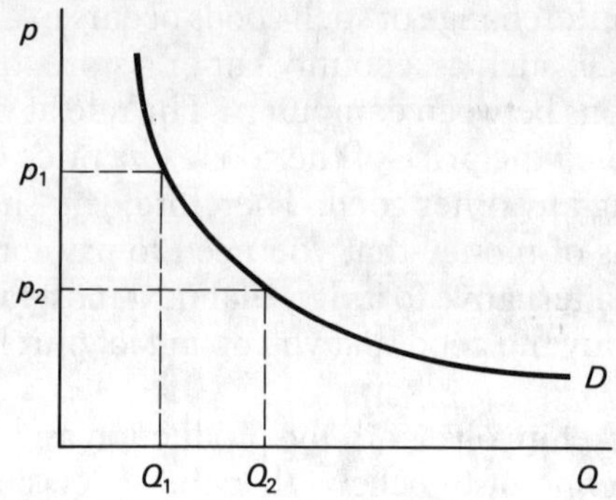

Figure 3.1

doing so they end up purchasing fewer apples. It is usually the case that there is no set of other goods that completely matches the set of services provided by apples—or almost any other good—and so, even at quite high prices, some apples will be purchased. The particular apple texture and taste—especially of Macintosh apples—is the special characteristic that differentiates apples from other goods and this means that even when the price of apples goes very high, some individuals will buy them. Trade-offs between goods give the demand curve for each good a downward slope.[2]

The fewer the characteristics of a good that can be matched by other goods, the more vertical the demand curve becomes. If there is nothing else to provide a particular mix of desired services, then the quantity purchased will change very slowly as the price changes. This gives an almost vertical demand curve. Goods such as insulin or other very specific medicines have a very steep demand curve for the person who suffers from the disease that they control. Other goods, such as grains like oats and rye, have a very flat demand curve, since there are many other goods that serve similar purposes. Addictive drugs are goods that initially have a fairly flat demand curve, but after repeated use the demand curve becomes vertical. British traders imported opium from India to China in the eighteenth and nineteenth centuries and sold it cheaply until the demand curve of opium addicts became vertical. They then raised the price and made enormous profits. Some criminal organizations in the United States have followed the British example by importing drugs and following a similar marketing strategy.

Movement along a demand curve occurs when the price of the good we are studying changes. This illustrates the quantity response to that price change. As prices change from p_1 to p_2 the movement along the demand curve signals that the quantity that individuals are willing to purchase has changed from Q_1 to Q_2. At lower prices individuals will want to purchase more of the good. If we look at the demand function

$$Q_D = D(p,|Y,\text{tastes},p_{\text{others}})$$

[2] The Appendix shows how a demand curve is derived using knowledge of an individual's preferences.

we can see that the demand curve relates the behavior of the variable before the vertical line, p, in the function to the value of the function (the value of Q_D). Changes in the variables that occur after the vertical cause *shifts* in the entire demand curve.

Following the usual "law of demand," the demand curve slopes downward. This is not an observation on nature similar to the "law of gravity," but is a statement about what we usually observe. There are good theoretical reasons for believing that the demand curve slopes downward almost all of the time. The basic notion is that each *additional* unit of a good will increase the happiness (that is, the well being or utility, the term most commonly used in economics) of an individual, but generally not as much as the units of the good that preceeded it. If the increased utility—happiness—is smaller, the price the individual will be willing to pay will also be less. As the price of a good increases, individuals will usually substitute away from that good towards other goods, which now give more happiness per unit of expenditure than the one whose price has risen.

Alfred Marshall, who can be held responsible for much of the development of the demand and supply analysis of markets, chose to put price on the vertical axis and quantity on the horizontal axis.[3] This is contrary to the usual form in mathematics, in which the **exogenous variable**—the variable that acts on the system being studied, but is not determined by it: the x in the equation $y = f(x)$—is on the horizontal axis and the **endogenous variable**—the variable determined by the system: the y in the equation $y = f(x)$—is on the vertical axis. In Marshall's system, price was viewed as being outside the control of the consumers and producers, who chose quantities in response to prices. In spite of mathematical convention, Marshall chose to put prices on the vertical axis, and economists have continued to do so since.

Marshall was very worried about the possible existence of a *Giffen Good*, which was a good for which the demand curve sloped upward—the higher the price, the more of the good a person would want to purchase. The example traditionally given of a Giffen good is potatoes in Ireland during the great potato famine. The story goes something like this: The basic Irish diet at this time was composed of potatoes and a few other things mainly mutton and a few vegetables. When the potato crop failed, the price of potatoes rose. The purchase of potatoes comprised such a large portion of the income of the Irish that the increased price of potatoes left them with too little income after purchasing the potatoes to buy other things. To maintain their diet, the story goes, they then had to buy more potatoes. One of the flaws in this story is that it doesn't explain where these additional potatoes came from (remember, it was the failure of the potato crop that began this cycle.) The data on Ireland during this time is insufficient to prove that this event ever took place, and many believe that it is more myth than fact.

While we have casually observed examples where higher prices have resulted in greater purchases of a product (one California wine producer followed the

[3] Alfred Marshall, *Principles of Economics*, 6th ed. (London: Macmillan, 1910).

advice of a marketing consultant and raised the price of his wine, thereby selling more bottles), the existence of Giffen goods has not been proved. There is, however, nothing in normal microeconomic utility maximizing theory that prohibits the existence of such a good. As will be shown below, a Giffen good can cause problems concerning the stability of the market equilibrium. This stability problem is what worried Alfred Marshall. Figure 3.2 illustrates the demand curve for a Giffen good.

In spite of the small possibility of a Giffen good, the vast majority of the evidence on the shape of demand curves is that these curves slope downward. There is some work that suggests that even if a demand curve had a portion that sloped upward, that could never be an equilibrium, and would never, therefore, be observed. In any case, all of our demand curves will slope downward.

Shifts in the demand curve come about by changes in the income, Y, of individuals, in their tastes, and in the price of other goods, p_{others}. The way to analyze the effects of changes in these variables is to fix the price of the good, change the variable of interest, and see what happens to the quantity that individuals want to purchase at the fixed price with the new value in place. If the price you fix is randomly chosen, the direction of movement you observe in the quantity demanded probably occurs at all prices. This is a shift in the demand curve.

Suppose that income rises. If a good is a **normal good,** at each price the consumer will wish to purchase more of the good than before. Individuals purchase increased transportation services in the form of more expensive cars as their incomes rise. If the good is an **inferior good,** the increase in income will make the individual wish to purchase less of the good than before at each price. Some goods can be both normal and inferior, but not at the same time for the same person. Consider hamburger. If a person is quite poor and has a diet that is composed mostly of beans and rice, a rise in her income will cause her to purchase more hamburger at each price as her income grows enough to include meat protein in her diet. In this case hamburger is a normal good. Consider someone in a middle-income bracket. As her income rises, she shifts away from the consumption of hamburger and purchases the more expensive and supposedly better cuts of beef.

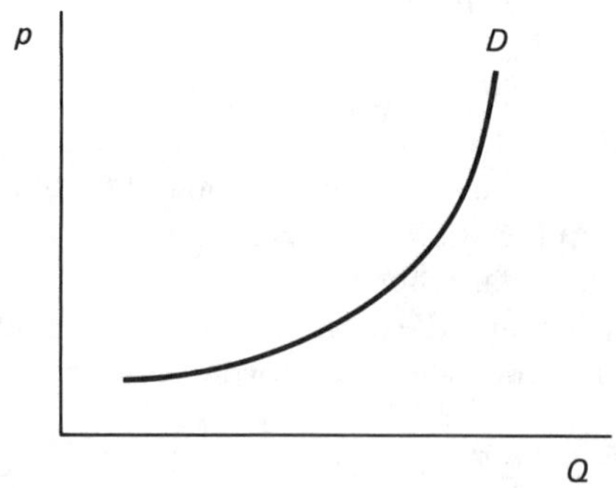

Figure 3.2

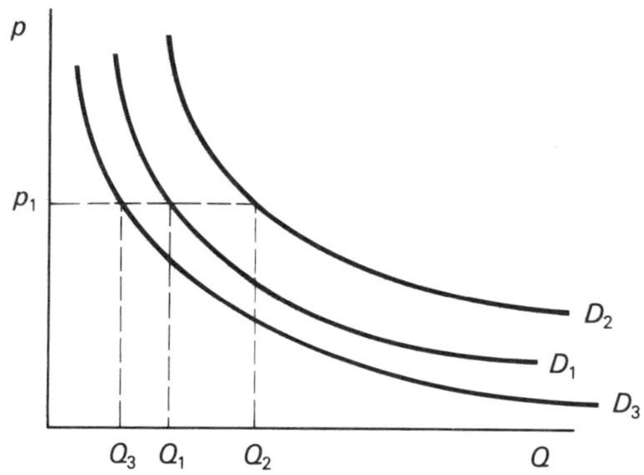

Figure 3.3

Her consumption of hamburger can decrease as a result of the rise in her income. In this case hamburger is an inferior good.

We use Figure 3.3 to illustrate these shifts in the demand curve in response to income changes. Arbitrarily choose some price, p_1, of hamburger. Given the initial taste, prices of other goods, and income, the quantity of hamburger that is demanded is Q_1, found at the price p_1 on the D_1 demand curve. If hamburger is a normal good, an increase in income will mean that more hamburger is desired at the price p_1. Suppose Q_2 pounds of hamburger is the amount desired at the price p_1 and with the new, higher income. The demand curve that represents quantity–price decisions at the new income level goes through the p_1–Q_2 point. D_2 is this new demand curve. There is a shift to the right of the demand curve because at every price more hamburger is demanded. (We know this because p_1 was arbitrarily chosen, and what happens at p_1 occurs at any other price.) If hamburger is an inferior good, an increase in income will shift the demand curve to the left, to D_3, for example. At some price, p_1, the quantity demanded declines from Q_1 to Q_3 as income increases and the individual chooses to consume less hamburger. At every price, the same behavior takes place, and the entire demand curve shifts from D_1 to D_3.

Changes in tastes can result, among other reasons, from peer pressure, advertising, and aging. Taste changes would cause shifts in the demand curve in the obvious manner. Advertising showing a large number of very healthy, attractive young people having a great time drinking some brand of cola will cause all those who want to become healthy, young and attractive, and to have a good time, to purchase more of this type of cola. (These are called "lifestyle" ads.)

Changes in the price of some other good usually will cause a shift in the demand curve, but the direction of the shift depends on the relation between the two goods. Goods can be either **complements** or **substitutes.** Substitutes are goods that serve the same or similar purposes. One might think of chicken and beef as alternatives or substitutes for meat protein in a meal, or wood or metal as alternative materials for the production of desks, or of cloth or leather as alternatives for book covers. When the price of a substitute rises, the demand curve for the good of interest shifts out as individuals shift away from the use of the now more expensive substitute. In Argentina, the demand curve for coffee shifts out when the price of Yerba Mate, a local herbal tea, rises. In many countries, when the price of chicken rises the demand curve for beef shifts out.

Complements are goods that are used together. Common examples are automobiles and tires, asparagus and hollandaise sauce, beer and pretzels, and, for the jaded, love and money. The concept behind complements is that the increased use of one of the goods results in an increased demand for the other. Therefore, a decline in the price of asparagus will normally lead to increases in the consumption of asparagus and this will lead to an increased demand for hollandaise sauce with which to cover the asparagus. Price declines in complements result in shifts out in the demand curve for the good of interest. Remember, a "shift out" is a change such as the one from demand curve D_1 to D_2 in Figure 3.3.

A SUPPLY CURVE

The supply function contains the information about the single-good production decisions that firms make. From our point of view, the most important of the variables that determines the level of production is the price of that good. Other important variables include the technology, the price of intermediate inputs—other goods used to produce this good—and the rentals on the factors used in production. We can write the supply function as

$$Q_S = S(p|\text{tech}, p_I, \text{rentals})$$

where tech is the technology and p_I is the vector of prices of intermediate inputs. These intermediate inputs are included because almost every industry uses the outputs of other industries in its production process. The automobile industry uses the output of the steel and plastics industries as inputs into the production of automobiles. The automobile industry uses factors such as labor, land, and machines to turn these intermediate inputs into cars. For the supply function given above, p_I is the vector or list, of prices of the intermediate goods, and the rentals are those paid to the factors used in the production process. As in the demand function, the vertical line separates variables that cause a movement along the supply curve (p) from the other variables that cause a shift in the supply curve. The supply curve is a graph that shows the quantity of the good that firms will be willing and able to produce at each price, other things being equal. With normal types of production functions as shown in Chapter 2, and with profit maximizing firms, the supply curve will always be upward-sloping. Figure 3.4 shows one such supply curve.

Supply curves need not be a straight line. This one was drawn straight simply for convenience. A supply curve could curve as does the Giffen good demand curve in Figure 3.2, or it could curve in the other direction. It will, however, always

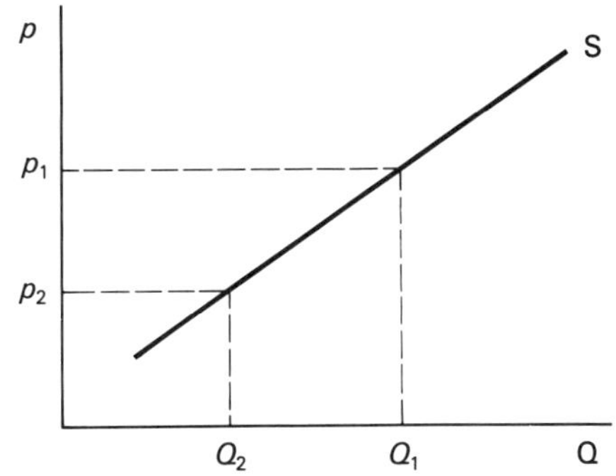

Figure 3.4

slope upwards, as in Figure 3.4. Changes in the quantity supplied as a result of changes in prices are illustrated on Figure 3.4 by the prices p_1 and p_2 and their respective quantities, Q_1 and Q_2. The supply curve shows that a decrease in the price from p_1 to p_2 will cause the quantity of the good produced by the firm to decline from Q_1 to Q_2.

If a firm wants to increase production it must hire additional factors of production and use additional intermediate inputs. Because the production function has diminishing marginal returns, each new worker produces less than the previous one had. (In the short run, at least, capital is thought of as fixed, and that guarantees diminishing marginal returns. The short run is sometimes defined as a time period too short to change the capital stock.) If wages are the same for all workers, a higher price for the good is needed to get the marginal product of the worker equal to his wage.

Improvements in technology will cause a shift outward in the supply curve. Increases in the prices of intermediate inputs or in the rentals paid to factors will cause a shift in the supply curve. Changes of these variables in the opposite direction will cause shifts in the supply curve in the opposite direction. Figure 3.5 illustrates a shift in a supply curve for potato chips from S_1 to S_2 caused by an increase in the price of vegetable oil, which is an intermediate input in the production of potato chips.

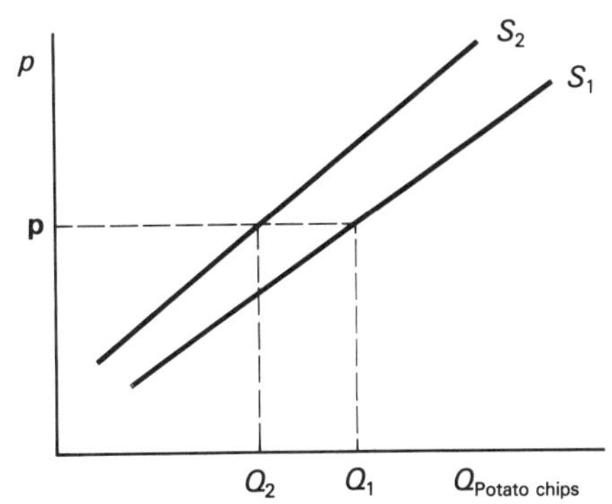

Figure 3.5

At each price for potato chips (**p**, for example), the firms will produce fewer chips after the rise in the price of oil then they had before. At the price **p**, the quantity drops off from Q_1 to Q_2. The shift in the supply curve need not be symmetric. It could shift more or less at higher prices than at low prices. Remember again that the curve need not be a straight line.

THE MARKET AND MARKET DYNAMICS

The quantity of the good actually sold and the price for which it is sold can be found by combining the supply and demand curves into a single graph that illustrates the market, as in Figure 3.6. On this graph, as on a pirate's map, the X marks the spot of interest. The point of intersection of the supply and demand curves is at the price where the quantity that firms are willing to produce is equal to the quantity that the consumers are willing to purchase. This is what we call an equilibrium. At an equilibrium, all who want to purchase at this price are satisfied, and there is none of the good left unsold. Here, p_e is the equilibrium price and Q_e is the equilibrium quantity. At this point the market is said to "clear."

We need some reason to believe that the intersection of the supply and demand curves at the equilibrium point—the (p_e, Q_e) point—will be the price and quantity observed in an actual market situation. If for some reason we are in an initial equilibrium, the point where the market clears, and a shift in either the demand or the supply curve causes the equilibrium to be at a different price and quantity, what is it that determines that price and quantity will move to this new intersection point? We need some rules or at least assumptions, about the dynamics of the market. These assumptions about dynamics are in addition to the assumptions that were needed to generate the demand and supply curves themselves. Paul Samuelson called the assumptions that are added to the supply and demand analysis the "correspondence principle."[4] We will name them after the

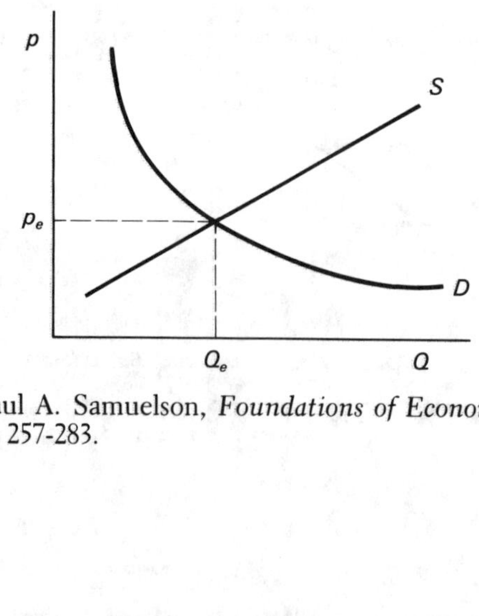

Figure 3.6

[4] Paul A. Samuelson, *Foundations of Economic Analysis* (New York: Atheneum, 1972), pp. 257-283.

man who wrote about them last century and call them the "Marshallian dynamics."

Alfred Marshall assumed that the price of a good would move when there was an inequality in the quantity of the good demanded and the quantity supplied at the current price. If, at some price, the quantity demanded (Q_d) is greater than the quantity supplied (Q_s), the price of the good will rise. One reason for this assumption is that those individuals who demand the good but cannot get it will offer a higher price to those who have it in order to assure that they too will get some of it. This competition among consumers will drive up the price when $Q_d > Q_s$. In a symmetric manner, if the quantity supplied is greater than the quantity demanded, the price will fall. The competition among the producers of the good, who don't wish to be left with some unsold, will drive down the price when $Q_s > Q_d$. In Figure 3.7, when the price is p_1 the Marshallian dynamics of the system will drive the price downward to the equilibrium price. When the price is p_2, the Marshallian dynamics will drive the price up to the equilibrium price. As the graph is drawn, at any price below the equilibrium, the dynamics will drive the price down towards the equilibrium price. At any price above the equilibrium, the dynamics will drive the price down towards the equilibrium. In both cases, the movement will not stop until the equilibrium is reached. The arrows show in which direction the Marshallian dynamics will drive the prices.

As mentioned above, one of the reasons that Marshall worried about a Giffen good was that it permitted the system to be unstable under his assumption about dynamics. If the demand curve is upward-sloping, as in Figure 3.8, it is possible but not necessary that his rules for dynamic adjustment would move a market away from the equilibrium rather than towards it. If the demand curve is upward-sloping, but not as steep as the supply curve, at prices above the equilibrium price, such as p_1 in Figure 3.8, Q_d is greater than Q_s. Under Marshall's rules of dynamics, this would cause the price to go *up*, away from the equilibrium, rather than down

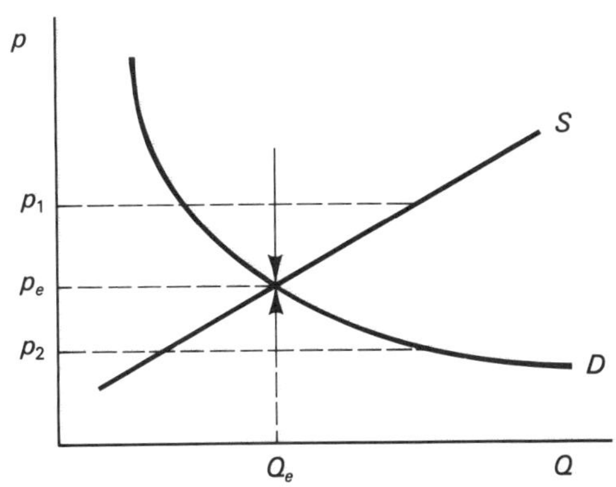

Figure 3.7

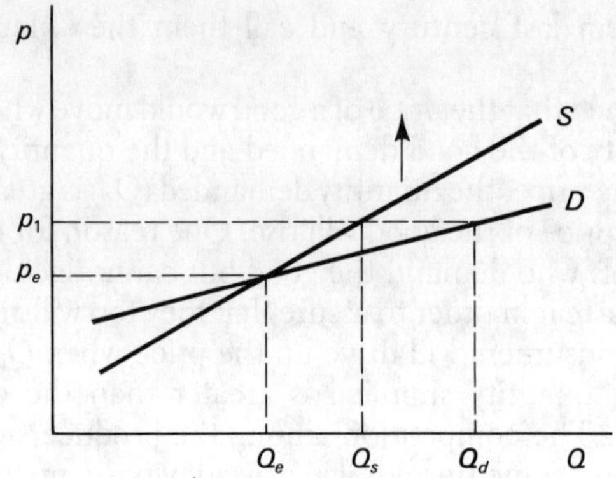

Figure 3.8

and back towards it. If a price is below the equilibrium, then Q_s is greater than Q_d and Marshall's rules of dynamics will cause the price to fall. This system is unstable because any movement away from the equilibrium will cause the price to explode away from the equilibrium. For the rest of this book we will outlaw Giffen goods, and we will have stable markets in all of our goods.

In the normal case, the Marshallian dynamic forces will always drive the price to the equilibrium unless there is some kind of legal restriction to the free movement of prices. Commonly imposed restrictions are **price ceilings** and **price floors.** A price ceiling does not let the price rise above a certain level, much as a ceiling in a room will not let a helium-filled balloon rise beyond it. A price floor does not let the price fall below some limit—the analogy with the floor of a room is valid. If there is excess supply at some price floor, the government which has imposed this price floor must intervene in order to purchase the excess supply, or the firms will compete and lower the price below the floor. A price ceiling that generates excess demand will continue in effect only when the government is strong enough to prevent citizens from bidding up the price of the good, usually in a "black market."

Figure 3.9 illustrates the analysis of a price floor using supply and demand curves. If p_1 is the price floor, the price is not allowed to fall below that price, the resulting quantity demanded in the market is Q_d, and the quantity supplied is Q_s. Since Q_s is larger than Q_d by a distance equal to the heavy line, the government must buy up that difference or the price will fall to the equilibrium. The dynamic forces of the market are stopped at the price floor by the actions of the government. The government cannot sell the goods that it has to purchase to maintain the price floor because, if it does, this additional quantity being supplied to the market by the government will drive the price down below the price floor. Price floors are fairly common in the markets for agricultural goods. They are sometimes called "price supports." Note that a price floor below the equilibrium will not have any effect because the dynamics are in the other direction, much as the floor of a room does not effect the height to which a balloon can rise. If the equilibrium price of wheat is already \$6 a bushel, the government achieves nothing by imposing a price floor

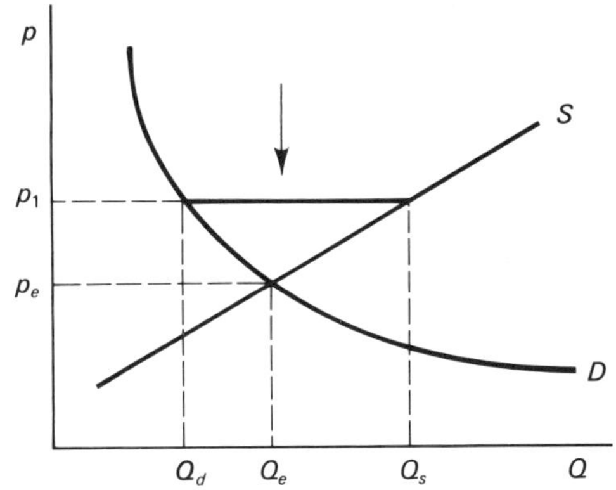

Figure 3.9

of \$4 a bushel, as it would do if it passes a law saying that it will purchase all the wheat that farmers want to sell to it at a price of \$4.

Figure 3.10 shows an example of an effective price ceiling. The government sets a price ceiling at price p_1. At that price the quantity that the consumers are demanding is Q_d and the quantity that the firms are supplying is Q_s. The difference is an example of a **shortage.** There are forces to remove this shortage. Firms may try to sell some of the good at a price above the ceiling. Nonprice mechanisms for the allocation of goods can also occur.

During wars, price ceilings are often accompanied by ration coupons. Goods then have two prices: one in money and a second in ration coupons. If the number of coupons which are issued is equal to the quantity produced, then the coupons serve as the allocating mechanism. Sometimes a market in ration coupons is allowed. If it is, the price of a ration coupon will be equal to the difference between price p_2 and p_1 in Figure 3.10. At the price p_2 all of the good that is produced is sold, and no one wants to purchase more. The price difference is "earned" by those who have the coupons to sell.

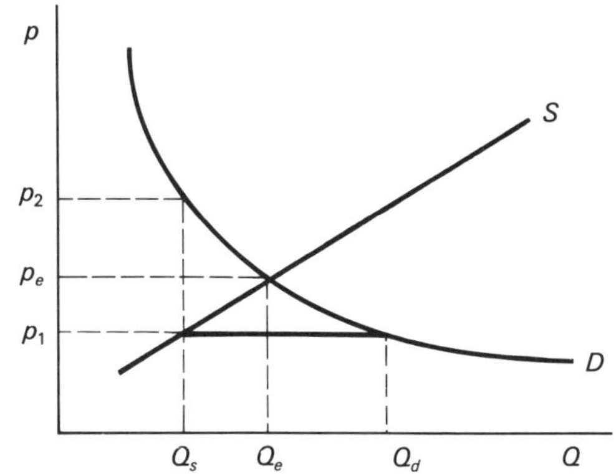

Figure 3.10

If the government can maintain that price for producers but doesn't use some kind of ration coupons, a black market may arise. In a black market, a good sells for more than its legal price. Again, the price in the black market will rise to p_2. In countries where prices are controlled, black markets are common. In Egypt in the 1970s, there were price controls on chicken and sales were rationed at the state run store, allowing one chicken per customer. Women from the poor section of Cairo would line up for their daily chicken, walk across town to the rich section of Cairo, and sell the chicken at the back fence to the cooks of the rich. These poor women would then take the profits gained by this transaction and buy the beans and rice for their families that they could not otherwise afford. This type of price control actually worked as a method of income transfer from the rich to the poor and provided a type of "employment" that may or may not be efficient given the local social structure.

In a country where the government is sufficiently strong and feared so that a black market doesn't arise, one often observes queues forming for controlled goods. Standing in line serves as the mechanism for allocating the goods in this type of system—the cost is of lost other opportunities for the use of time. One often sees bread queues forming in third world countries, and the "life in the queue" of the citizens of Moscow is well known and often depicted in recent Russian satirical literature. Because rent controls are just another type (albeit complicated) of price ceilings, housing shortages in major United States cities could be blamed on the rent controls. Because of political considerations, rent is usually controlled only after a person has an apartment, so the existence of rent controls often drives up the cost for the new renter. This is because this is often the only part of the market in which prices can adjust and because the owners are expecting to see even these newly rented apartments controlled (with some probability) in the future.

REPRISE

Demand and supply curves are the way economists divide up and analyze the private consumption and production decisions of the members of an economy. The demand curve shows how the desired quantity of a good changes in response to changes in the price of that good. Almost always, as the price of a good increases people decide to consume less of it. Shifts in the entire demand curve of a good come about from changes in tastes, prices of other goods and an individual's income.

The supply curve shows the desired level of production of a good as a function of the price of that good. This curve slopes upwards, so that as the price increases, firms wish to produce more. This curve shifts as a result of changes in technology, changes in the price of intermediate inputs, and the factors of production.

The intersection of the supply and demand curve give the market clearing price. This market clearing price can usually be obtained if there are no legal impediments to the movements of prices to that new equilibrium. Popular impediments are price ceilings and floors, which can usually be imposed only by some legal authority such as a government. (Note that we have ignored important considerations about the structure of markets. Such concepts as market power, product identity with a particular firm, and monopolies have not been dealt with at all. These topics are usually the province of microeconomic courses.)

This concludes the discussion of supply and demand curves. The major features of these curves will show up again and are quite important in this course. The macroeconomic models we develop will be based in part on some microeconomics. The market for labor, which has supply and demand curves as do most markets, will be of particular interest. This market will face restrictions of a price-floor type—unions and minimum wage laws—and the fact that these price floors keep the labor market from achieving a normal supply and demand equilibrium will be the basis for our Keynesian model. Our macroeconomic development will also look like supply and demand analysis as we use aggregate demand curves. Changes in the exogenous variables will generate shifts in the aggregate supply and aggregate demand curves in a form similar to the shifts in the normal, single market, supply and demand curves.

EXERCISES

1. Consider the market for coffee. If there is a freeze in Brazil, which damages a large portion of the Brazilian coffee trees, what happens to the equilibrium price and quantity of coffee?
2. Consider the market for wheat in the United States. A president of the United States imposes a ban on the shipment of U.S. wheat to a country that had previously been a major buyer of U.S. wheat. What happens to the price and quantity of wheat in the U.S. market? What happens to the world price of wheat? (Hint: There are many wheat producing countries.)
3. In Venezuela there has been a price ceiling on rice and beans, the major food of the poor. This ceiling is lower than the world price of each of the goods and is effective domestically. What must the government do to maintain this price ceiling and not have shortages? The International Monetary Fund tells the government of Venezuela that it can no longer maintain the ceiling on these goods and the government follows these directions. What happens to the price of each of these goods? Mangoes and bananas are also major food for the poor but do not have their prices controlled. What happens to the price of mangoes and bananas when the price ceilings on rice and beans are removed?

Appendix

The way that economists usually explain the demand curve is by beginning with a set of **preferences** for individuals. It is assumed that these preferences have the proper conditions so that they can be represented by a **utility function.** A utility function contains the description of an individual's preferences and represents these preferences by numbers. Suppose that an individual can choose between two sets of goods: To keep it simple, suppose that these are #1, a hardbound set of the complete works of James Joyce and a cheeseburger at the local fast food restaurant, and #2, a set of compact discs of all of Laurie Anderson's works and a dinner of sushi in the local Japanese restaurant. We know enough about this individual to know that #2 will be chosen. If we correctly represented this individual's preferences by a utility function (written as $U(x)$, where x is the set of goods we are interested in) the utility function would give a higher number for the choice of compact disks and sushi than for the choice of Joyce and a cheeseburger. Utility functions are ordinal. A higher number for one set of goods over another says that the first set is preferred, but the numbers do not tell us anything about how much more preferred it is. If two sets of goods, or two sets composed of different quantities of the same goods, produce the same number from an individual's utility function, then we say that the individual is *indifferent* between these two choices.

If we restrict the choices to bundles of quantities of two goods, we can represent the available choices and the individual's preferences on a graph. Let the two goods be wine and wool and the individual is concerned about how to keep warm. Different quantities of wine and wool will provide different amounts of comfort to this individual.

Figure 3.A.1 shows two possible bundles of wine and wool that we will assume the individual believes provides the same utility, or comfort. Bundle w_1 contains $wool_1$ units of wool and $wine_1$ units of wine. Bundle w_2 contains less wool, only $wool_2$ units of wool, but more wine, $wine_2$ units of wine. We show that these bundles provide the same utility by constructing an **indifference curve** that goes through both of them. An indifference curve shows all of the bundles that provide the same utility, and between which the individual is therefore indifferent. We also assume that more is better than less, although some people don't agree that that assumption is appropriate for all commodities. With this additional assumption, we can illustrate an entire indifference curve map, which shows the set of all the indifference curves for wine and wool, in Figure 3.A.2. As one moves in the direction of the arrow toward higher indifference curves, one is reaching higher levels of utility and is better off. Indifference curve u_4 in Figure 3.A.2 is the one that passes through points w_1 and w_2 in Figure 3.A.1.

On the wine–wool plane it is possible to represent a relative price between wine and wool. This relative price (p) is the quantity of wine one must give up to get

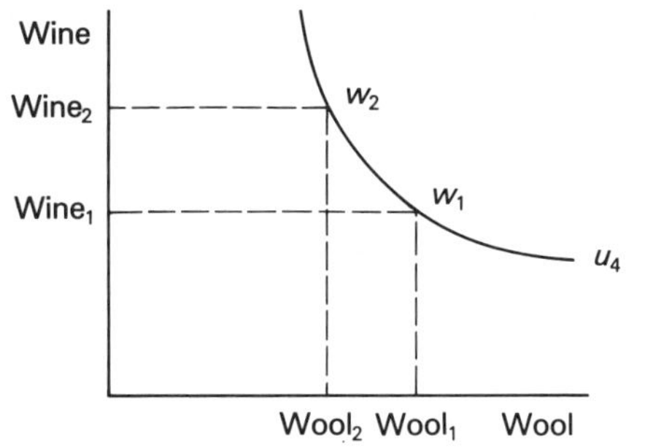

Figure 3.A.1

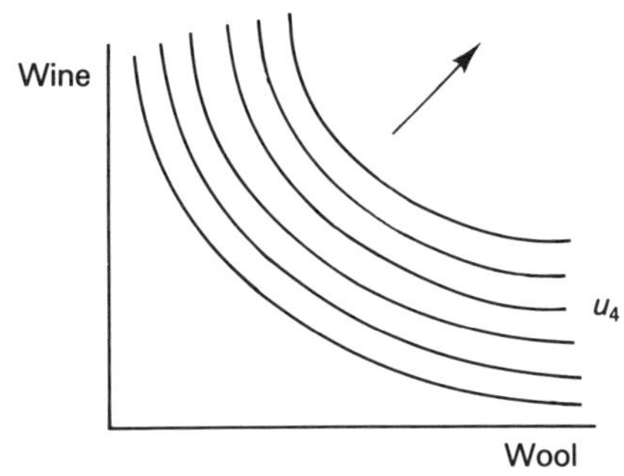

Figure 3.A.2

one unit of wool. A price measured in this manner is represented by the wine–wool plane by a line with a slope of $-p$. Price line p in Figure 3.A.3 shows one such price line. Price line p_2 represents a price line where wool is cheaper than at price p. Since wool is cheaper it will take fewer units of wine to get each unit of wool.

Figure 3.A.4 shows how to put the price line together with the indifference curves. (Some of the curves in Figure 3.A.2 were removed for clarity.) Let point x represent an initial quantity of wool owned by an individual. If the price is p_1, the individual can trade away some of that wool for wine along the line that starts at point x and goes up and to the left with the slope of $-p_1$. That line, called the **budget line,** represents all of the combinations of wine and wool that this individual can afford given that the price is p_1 and the individual begins with x units of wool. The economic problem the individual must solve is how to achieve the highest utility or well-being given the restriction of the budget line. The highest indifference curve the individual can reach is the one with utility level u_3. Point a is the desired consumption point given the restriction of price p_1 and the income in wool of x.

Note that a demand curve can be derived from this information about income and prices. Consider a demand curve for wine. Suppose that the individual

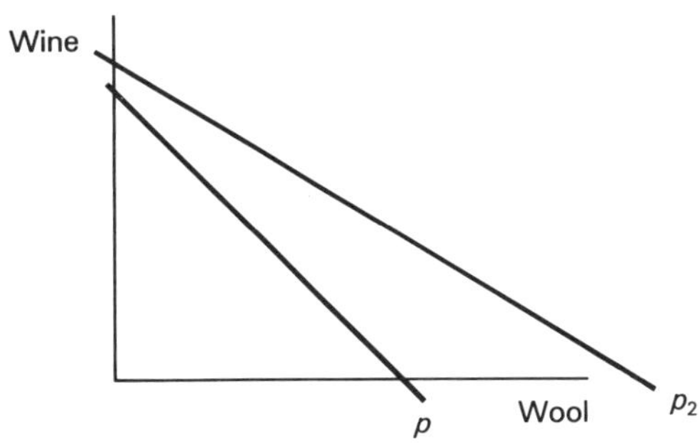

Figure 3.A.3

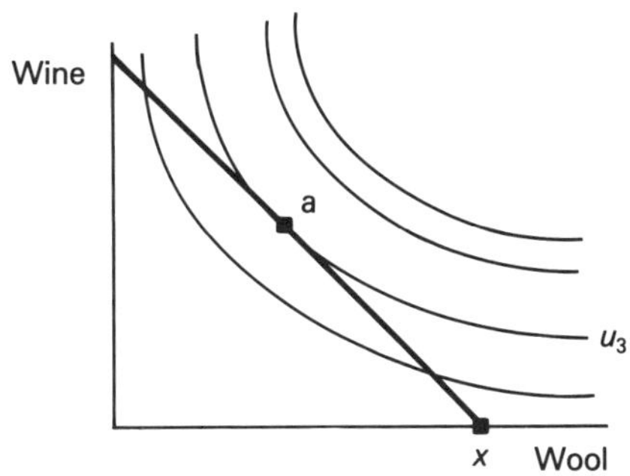

Figure 3.A.4

has x units of wool to start with (that is, the individual's income is x units of wool). Changing the slope of the line that comes out of point x will be changing the price of wine. The point where this line touches—is just tangent to—the highest possible indifference curve gives the preferred consumption point at that price and with that income. If one matches up the prices with the quantity of wine that the individual will choose to consume at those prices and graphs the resulting curve on a price–wine plane, one has a demand curve.

4

Aggregation

In which we discover the aggravation of aggregation, the magic single good of macroeconomics is introduced, the government's methods for measuring it are enumerated, and the intricacies of a price level are considered.

As we shift from the study of microeconomics to traditional macroeconomics, we must make several changes—not necessarily improvements—in our way of thinking.[1] We want to study an entire economy and the effects of government policies on this economy. To make this model simple enough to do this, we need to combine the many goods that we have been using into a single representative good. Once this combination is done there will no longer be any need for relative prices because there will be only one good, but we will need to continue the price idea in the notion of price levels. While we do not carefully explain the use or existence of money early on, the price level is the cost of an arbitrarily defined unit of the aggregate good in terms of this money.

Aggregation is tricky for another reason. Normally, an economist is interested in the level of welfare of individuals in a society. This use of the term **welfare** is not strictly related to the welfare system that provides support to the less advantaged in society. Rather it means the level of the well-being of each individual; some measure of the happiness or contentedness achieved by this individual in, normally, material terms. This welfare is measured by the level of **utility** that an individual achieves from his or her choices of goods to consume. We can construct utility functions for an individual that assign a number to every bundle of goods such that bundles with higher numbers are preferred. Utility is an **ordinal** concept, in that if we say that one bundle of goods provides an individual with more utility than another, we know that the first bundle makes the individual happier, but the notion of "how much" happier is not permitted. If one bundle of goods gives a utility that is in numeric terms, twice that of another bundle, we are not permitted to say that the first bundle makes the person twice as happy. We can only say that the first bundle is preferred.

The notion of utility permits us to compare the effects of different allocations of resources and different distribution systems on the welfare of an individual. If one system results in a higher utility number for an individual then it is preferred by that individual. When we look at groups of individuals and want to see if a system improves welfare for that group, we run into trouble. If one system, or government policy, for example, makes all individuals have a higher level of utility than another system does, it is superior. We are willing to say that if a policy allows one person to be better off and all others to be at the same level of utility, then it is a superior policy. This notion of optimality or superiority is called **Pareto optimality** after the Italian economist Vilfredo Pareto (1848–1923). An allocation of goods is called **Pareto superior** to another if at least one individual has a higher utility and no individual has a reduced utility. An allocation of goods that has no feasible allocation superior to it is called **Pareto optimal.** If we are at a Pareto optimal allocation, we can only make some person better off by making at least one other person worse off.

Almost all government policies involve the improvement of the utility level of some individuals and the reduction of the utility level of others when compared to

[1] See Chapter 1, footnote 1.

their situation before the policy. Those who gain belong to the political pressure group that is supporting the policy and those who lose are in the political pressure group that is against the policy. These members of the pressure groups will be active if the gains or losses are sufficient for them to divert resources from other activities to the political process. These issues are part of the microeconomics of government policy making. (We will discuss some of these items in Chapter 17.)

The macroeconomics of policy making ignores most of the above issues. With the aggregation of all goods into one good comes the aggregation of all individuals into the one "individual" of the economy. Questions concerning the distribution of the good are usually completely ignored and only the quantity and uses of this good are important. Increases in the one aggregate good in the economy provide for a *potential* Pareto superior distribution since there is more of the good to be distributed and therefore each individual could possibly get more. Whether that individual does or does not, in fact, get more, is not considered in this point in the presentation.

The one aggregate good is called output. We illustrated, in the circular flow diagram of Figure 2.1, that output, when measured as the sum over all goods of the quantity of production of each good times its current price, equals income. Output as measured by the Department of Commerce is called the **Gross National Product** (GNP—indicated in equations as Y) and is equal to the value of all legal goods that pass through markets in a given time period, usually a year. This definition means that illegal goods—all commodities and services that the government deems illegal and therefore "bad" such as illegal drug traffic, prostitution, and much gambling) are not included. Services and goods that do not enter markets also are not included. Therefore, neither the household services provided to the family by the adult member of that family who has traditionally been called "the housewife" nor subsistence farming appear in the GNP.[2] If the same individuals who now produce these goods were *paid* for their work, then these services and goods would appear in the GNP. Some recent efforts have been made to include these estimates of household production in the GNP but this is still preliminary.

GNP is usually divided into categories determined by the type of use. **Personal Consumption Expenditures** (henceforth called merely Consumption, indicated by C) are all those goods that are purchased by individuals for their personal use. We say that the individual as consumer is the final purchaser of these goods.

[2] In part, because subsistence farming is not included in the calculation, the GNP numbers for very poor countries tend to understate output. The per capita GNP (GNP per person) in India in the late 1970s was about US$250. The per capita GNP in the United States and the developed European countries was about US$10,000. It would be impossible to survive for a year on US$250 in the United States. Part of the explanation is that the subsistence production does not show up in the GNP of India, and is a fairly large part of agriculture output. This understates the GNP of India relative to the GNP of the more developed countries; exactly how much is unclear. In spite of this understatement of GNP in the poorer of the Asian and African countries, the people there are still, on average, very, very poor.

Consumption goods can be consumer nondurables (goods that are used immediately, such as food and clothing), consumer durables (goods, such as automobiles, dishwashers, and stoves, that produce a stream of services to the owner) and services.

Gross Private Domestic Investment (henceforth called Investment, I) contains all goods that have been purchased to help in the production of other goods. This category includes domestic and industrial construction (structures), durable equipment (stamping machines, tractors, and dump trucks), and the change in business inventories (goods that have not yet been sold). **Net Exports of Goods and Services** equals Exports minus Imports ($X - IM$). If this is positive, then the country is exporting more than it is importing and there is a net flow of goods out of the country. If it is negative, then the country is importing more than it is exporting and the end users in the country are consuming—when government expenditures and investment are viewed as a type of consumption—more than it is producing. We will generally assume that we are working with a **closed economy.** In this case both exports and imports are zero, and of course, net exports are zero.

The last on our list of end users of production in the economy is the government. **Government Purchases of Goods and Services** (henceforth called Government expenditures, G) are all of the product of the economy that goes to the government. This includes the government purchases of goods as well as the salaries of government employees. Government expenditures are somewhat independent of the government's collection of Taxes, T.

The **National Income Accounting Identity** is the name we use for an equation that states that the GNP (output) of an economy is equal to the sum of the different uses. This equation is

$$Y = C + I + G + (X - IM)$$

where the notation is given above. There are two sources for goods for an economy. It can produce them (given by Y) or it can import them (given by IM). $Y + IM$ is the total quantity of goods available. The four users of goods are consumers (indicated by C), investors (I), the government (G) and exporters (X). Since all goods in the economy are put to one of these uses, we can say that

$$Y + IM = C + I + G + X$$

The national income accounting identity is found by subtracting IM from both sides of the equation.

Sometimes we are interested in the net gains of an economy in any given year. In this case, investment is replaced in the national income accounting identity by net investment. Net investment is equal to total investment minus depreciation. Depreciation is the amount of the capital stock that wore out that year in the production of the output. Net investment is important if we are interested in knowing either how much our capital stock grew or the level of output available for distribution after the goods that wore out producing this output were replaced. The output, Y, that comes from the national income accounting identity when net investment replaces investment is called **Net National Product.**

Imagine that we wish to use the GNP to compare the output of an economy in two different years. Looking at data for the United States, we can observe that GNP in 1975 was 1,598.4 billion dollars, and that in 1985 the GNP was 3,998.1 billion dollars.[3] This would seem to indicate that on average each individual in the United States had 2.5 times as much to consume in 1985 as in 1975. For those of us who lived as sentient beings during those years, the general recollection is that while 1985 was a better year than 1975, it didn't feel as if we were that much better off. So what happened?

Remember that the GNP is the *value* of output. It is the sum of the quantity of goods times their prices and is therefore a nominal or money-denominated concept. If the majority of prices change in a systematic way, it is possible for the measured GNP to change enormously while the quantity of goods in an economy does not change at all. If all prices increased by a factor of 2.5 between 1975 and 1985, then the GNP, as measured, could have gone up by the indicated 2.5 and real, material output would not have changed at all. To find out what happened to the real output of the economy we need to know what did happen to prices between 1975 and 1985.

Table 4.1 is a very unscientific selection of goods and their prices in both 1975 and 1985. The prices come from the *New York Times* of September 19, 1975 and September 11, 1985. Note that most of the prices went up, but a few of them actually dropped. Many currently common items could not be on the list, since they either didn't exist in 1975 or were in a form sufficiently different from that of 1985 to make a comparison too difficult.

While the selection above is very mixed, it is sufficient to illustrate that a simple discussion about the direction of the movement of prices is impossible. Some prices rise, some fall. In order to find a direction for the movement of the

TABLE 4.1

ITEM	1975	1985
Bottom round roast (beef)	$1.39	$1.59
Tuna in a can	.49	.59
Wheat, hard #2 (bushel)	4.10	2.76
Silver (oz.)	4.61	6.03
Soybeans (bushel)	5.65	5.07
Tickets to "A Chorus Line"	15.00	45.00
Gallon of gasoline (wholesale)	.31	.82

[3] The GNP, consumer price index, producer price index, and the implicit price deflator for GNP are taken from the *1987 Economic Report of the President*, United States Government Printing Office, Washington, D.C.

price level, some method is needed to weigh the different goods and the movement in their prices in order to find some *index* of the movement of prices in general.

In order to construct a price index, the government constructs a representative basket of goods for the particular part of the economy that is of interest. If the government is interested in studying the effects of price changes on consumers, then the basket is designed to approximate the purchases of some representative consumer. The basket would contain the kinds of foods that this representative consumer—or family of two adults, two children, and, possibly, half a dog—purchases in a week, the expenditures on rent, clothing, automobile use, and entertainment. Whatever the choices for the basket, it contains specific quantities of specific products. Government employees can go to supermarkets, movie theaters, clothing stores, and so on, and find current prices for the items in the basket of goods. A **price index** (in this case a **consumer price index**) is constructed by dividing the current cost of the basket by the cost of the same basket in the base or reference period. The whole number is then multiplied by 100 to get an index rather than a decimal. Written as a formula, this is

$$\frac{\Sigma q_i \times p_{it}}{\Sigma q_i \times p_{ib}} \times 100$$

where the sums are over the goods in the basket, indexed by i, the quantity of each good is q_i, the price in time (t) is p_{it}, and the price in the base period is p_{ib}.

The consumer price index compares the cost of a basket of goods purchased by a representative consumer at retail prices at one time period with the cost of the same basket of goods at retail prices in the base time period. A **wholesale price index** uses the same basket as the consumer price index, but uses wholesale prices—the prices from the distributors to the retailers. A **producer price index** uses a basket of goods that approximates the purchases by firms in the economy and uses the prices that are paid to the firms. The **implicit price deflator for GNP** uses the retail prices for a basket of goods that is intended to represent the total purchases made by everyone—producer, consumer, and government—in the economy. Table 4.2 displays several price indices for the years 1975 to 1985. Notice that prices rose much faster in certain sectors of the economy (for example, the fuel sector) than in others.

In the implicit price deflator, the base year, as should be obvious from the table, is 1982. In the other three indices, the base year is 1967, so the value for 1967 is 100 in each of the indices. The capital goods and fuel price indices are producer price indices, in that they are the prices paid to firms for such capital goods as machines in one case and for fuel in the other.

Different countries have had different rates of changes in their price levels. (We call the rate of change in the price level the **rate of inflation.**) Just to give an illustration of this, Table 4.3 shows the consumer price indicies for 1975 and 1985 for a number of countries, with 1967 as the base year.

Canada had an inflation rate over these ten years very much like that of the United States. Japan and West Germany have had much lower rates, although

TABLE 4.2

YEAR	IMPLICIT PRICE DEFLATOR	CONSUMER PRICE INDEX	CAPITAL GOODS PRICE INDEX	FUEL PRICE INDEX
1975	59.3	161.2	162.5	271.5
1976	63.1	170.5	173.4	305.3
1977	67.3	181.5	184.6	372.1
1978	72.2	195.4	199.2	426.8
1979	78.6	217.4	216.5	507.6
1980	85.7	246.8	239.8	615.0
1981	94.0	272.4	264.3	751.2
1982	100.0	289.1	279.4	886.1
1983	103.9	298.4	287.2	931.5
1984	107.9	311.1	294.0	931.3
1985	111.5	322.2	300.5	909.6

Japan had a higher inflation rate than the United States between 1967 and 1975. France and Italy had higher inflation rates than the United States.

Now back to the original issue. If the nominal GNP in 1985 was 2.5 times the nominal GNP in 1975, what happened to the real GNP? The implicit price deflator for GNP rose from 59.3 in 1975 to 111.5 in 1985. Therefore, prices in 1985 were 1.88 times as great as in 1975. So real output in 1985 was 1.33 times that of 1975.[4] Since population in the United States was 1.108 times as great in 1985 as in 1975 (239.283 million in 1985 compared to 215.973 million in 1975), we can say that the per capita real GNP grew by only only twenty percent in that decade.

One must still be careful when using this type of calculation, especially when the years being compared are far apart. In the calculation of price indices we used a fixed basket of goods and compared the prices of this basket in two different time periods. The problem is with the *fixed* basket of goods. The actual basket of goods that people purchase, even on average, changes over the years. First, there is the introduction of new or improved goods that replace older goods. Currently automobiles are much used for private transportation. During the end of the last century, the main mode of private transportation was the horse or the horse and

TABLE 4.3

YEAR	CANADA	JAPAN	FRANCE	WEST GERMANY	ITALY
1975	160.1	205.8	178.9	144.2	186.8
1985	348.2	323.0	465.1	212.8	758.9

[4] This is calculated either by correcting the nominal GNP numbers by the price index and then dividing the 1985 GNP measured in 1982 dollars by the 1975 GNP, also measured in 1982 dollars, or by dividing the growth of nominal GNP (2.5) by the growth in prices (1.88). The end result is the same.

buggy. In a long term price index, which do we use? Even in shorter time periods, the basket of goods can change dramatically. In many colleges, students are now using personal computers where they once used typewriters, slide rules, pencils, and paper. If one wanted to calculate a price index for college students, how would one weigh each of these goods?

Baskets of goods change for reasons other than technological advances. Relative price changes can change the quantities of goods that individuals choose to consume. If in 1975 the price of potatoes was high and price of rice was low, the basket would have been likely to include a lot of rice and only a small amount of potatoes. If this basket is used to calculate the price index in 1985, and in 1985 the price of potatoes is low and rice is high, the effects of these price changes are underrepresented in the index. The actual 1985 basket of goods contains a lot of potatoes and little rice, but the index does not reflect this. If we use the actual basket in 1985 to calculate the index, then potatoes get too much weight and rice too little.

Unfortunately there is no good way around this problem. All price indices are incorrect inasmuch as they cannot correctly reflect the changing basket of goods, either in response to price changes or in response to technological changes. An economist or statistician who is constructing a price index may try to use his or her judgement to correct for the changing baskets, but to do this is more art than science.

SOME SAMPLE DATA

Figure 4.1 illustrates the per capita real GNP, real consumption, real investment, and real government expenditures for eight countries. Brazil, Ecuador, India, Kenya, and Saudi Arabia are developing countries (also called less developed countries.) Saudi Arabia and Ecuador are oil exporters, although Ecuador exports much less than Saudi Arabia. The graphs for both of these countries show the effects of the 1973 and 1979 oil price increases. The United States, Japan, and France are developed countries, although in the early 1950s many would have called Japan a developing country. The Latin American debt crisis shows up on the graphs of Brazil and Ecuador in the dip in GDP during the early 1980s. The debt crisis has caused investment in Brazil, Ecuador, and Kenya to drop in the 80s. By and large, the paths of GDP for less developed countries have been more volatile than for developed countries.

There are several interesting things to note about these graphs. The most obvious is the wide variety of growth experience that the different countries have had. Japan has almost ten times the per capita output in 1986 than it had in 1952. The growth rates of India and Kenya seem much smaller, but some of this is because these two countries have had much higher population growth rates, and the data is per capita. Output for Saudi Arabia seems to have the strangest path

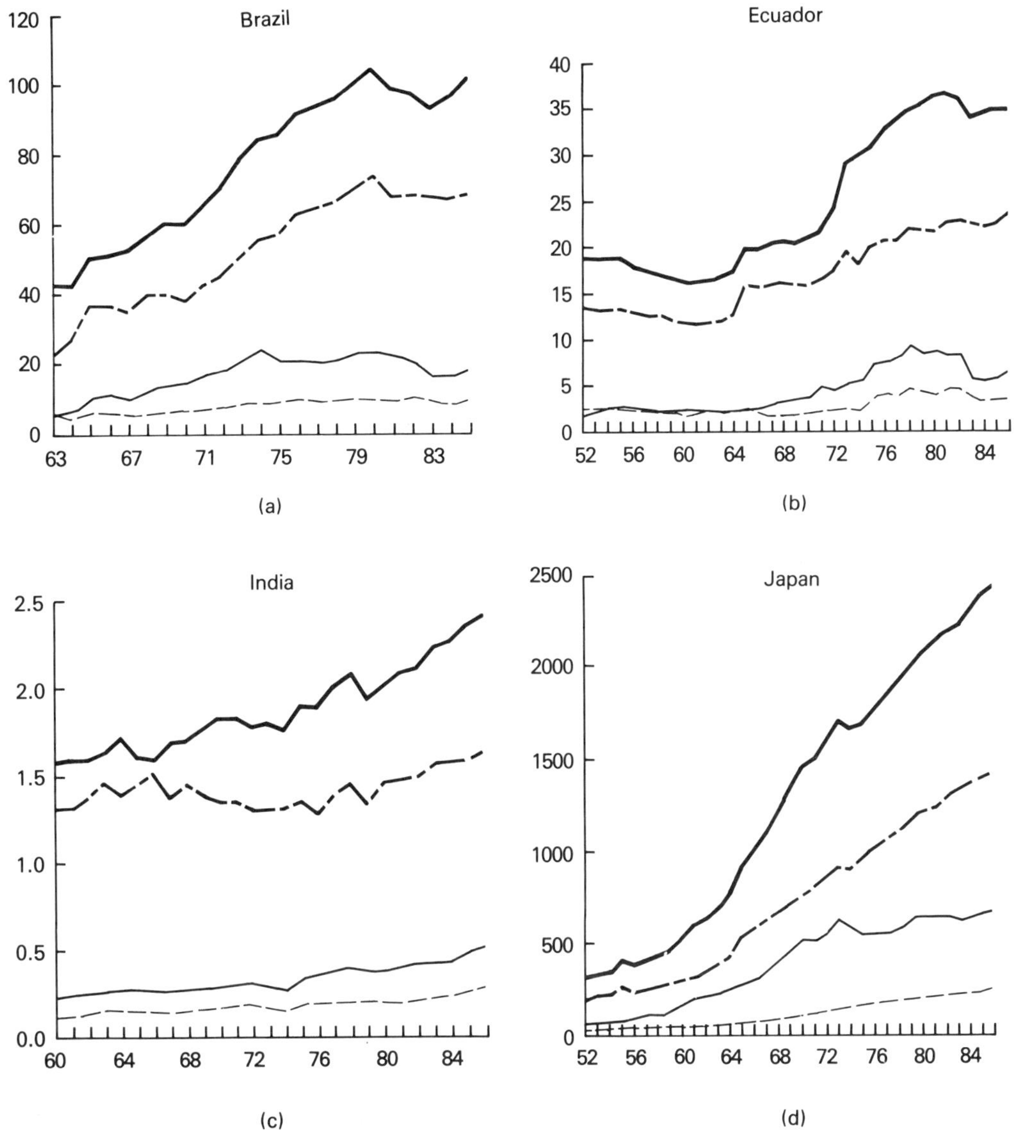

Figure 4.1

until one remembers that almost all of that production is in the form of oil and the output path closely follows the price path of oil. The consumption, investment, and government expenditure paths for Saudi Arabia are much smoother.

Look at the time path of consumption in each of the graphs. Note how smooth that path is. It has considerably smaller oscillations than the GDP except in India, where those two paths are very similar. Now look at investment. The

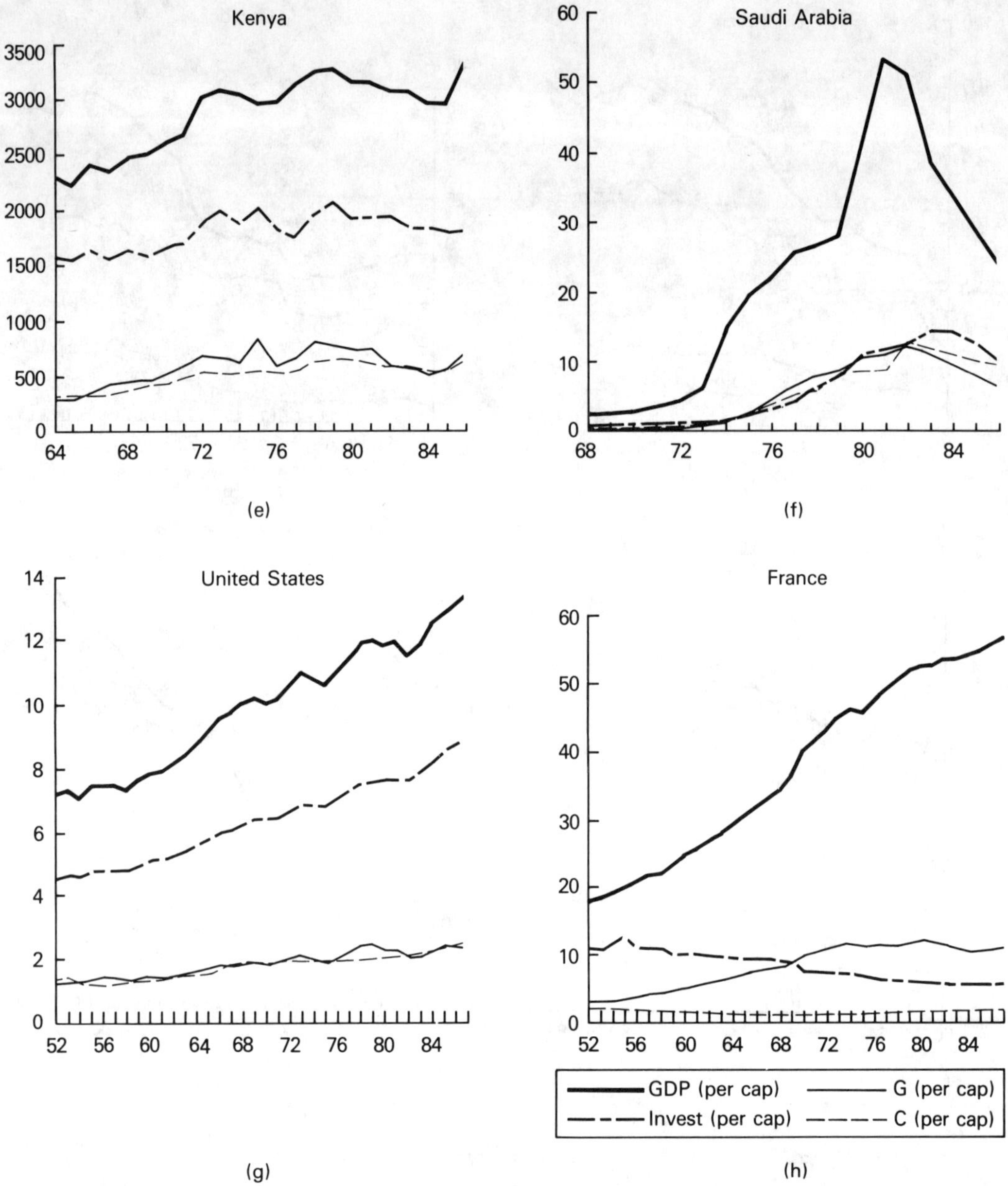

Figure 4.1 con't

cycles in the time paths of investment are much greater than those in consumption, and, as a percentage of its value, the oscillations are much greater than those in GDP. Again, India is the exception. In India the majority of investment decisions are made by the government and are likely to have a different relationship to the other economic variables than they do in a country where the majority of the investment decisions are privately made. The characteristics of the time path of consumption and investment are very interesting to business cycle economists. We will attempt to explain some of these characteristics in Chapter 12, when we discuss business cycles.

Figure 4.2 illustrates consumption, investment, and government expendi-

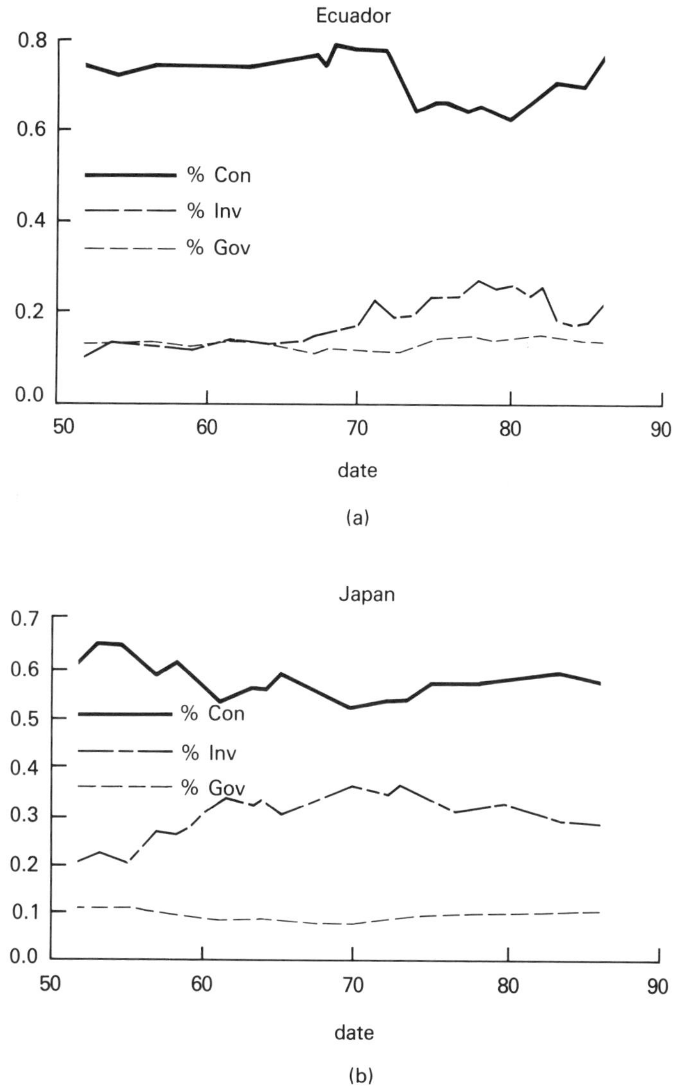

Figure 4.2

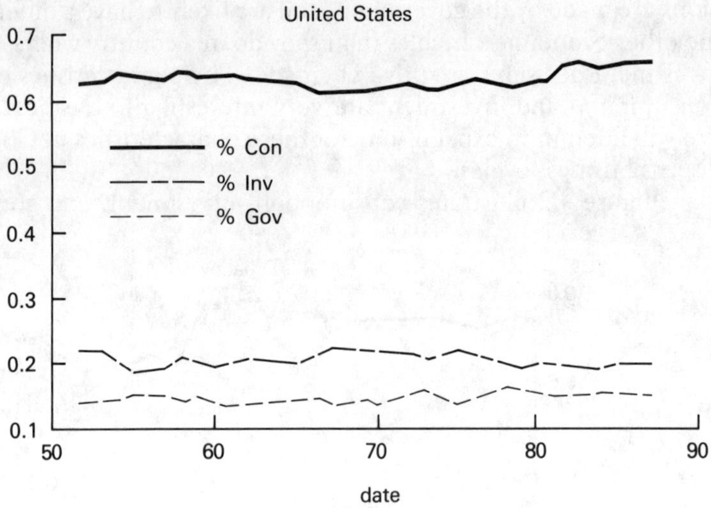

(c)

Figure 4.2 con't

tures as a percentage of GNP for Ecuador, Japan, and the United States. Here we can see some important differences among these three countries. Consumption in Japan represents the smallest percentage of GNP of this small sample, while it is the highest in Ecuador. This represents, to some degree, the poverty of Ecuador and its need to consume a large portion of its output. In the United States, consumption is a fairly constant percentage of GNP, but rises during the 1980s.

The most interesting of the illustrated variables is investment. The percentage of output that is devoted to investment in Japan is much higher than in the other two countries. Investment in Japan reaches almost forty percent of its GNP in the early 1970s, while in the United States investment is fairly constant at fifteen percent of output. (Note that investment in the United States is private investment and government expenditures include investment by the government. The data for Japan and Ecuador include government investment in the investment numbers.) Investment in Ecuador is about the same as in the United States as a percent of GNP until the early 1970s. Then investment as a percentage of GNP jumps. Notice that periods of high rates of growth of output correspond with periods of higher investment. Japan, the country with the highest percentage of GNP in investment, also has the highest long term rate of growth in output.

Figures 4.1 and 4.2 are intended to illustrate some of the relationships between our main economic variables. The first figure gives an idea of the growth rates of these variables since World War II, and the second better illustrates how different countries distribute their output among the different users. Use these figures as reference, especially when we consider business cycles. The fact that

Japan consumes such a small percentage of its output, and uses only ten percent of that output for government expenditures, means that the savings rate is very high. (Income that is not spent on consumption or contributed as taxes is saved.) This very high savings rate in Japan will come up again in Chapter 18 when we discuss foreign investment.

REPRISE

It is not unreasonable to suggest that macroeconomics began with the collection and calculation of data aggregates, and only later did economists attempt to produce macroeconomic theories to explain regularities in those data. The main aggregates we defined are gross national product, consumption, investment, and government expenditures. The rest of this text is concerned with explaining relationships among these variables and the time paths that each of these variables follows.

The main economic aggregates are found by summing up the values of all of the commodities that we define as falling into each of these catagories. Since prices are needed for determining these values and prices change over time, we use price indices to correct for general price movements. Relative price movements—changes in the price of one good relative to another—complicate the process of correcting for general price movements and we must accept that our data is a very rough approximation of reality.

EXERCISES

1. Consider an island economy with four goods: cotton cloth, hammocks, rice, and fish. In 1975 the prices of these goods in the local currency, shark's teeth, were 7, 16, 3, and 6, respectively. In that year the average family consumed 2 units of cotton cloth, 3 hammocks, 31 units of rice, and 23 units of fish. In 1985 the price of each of these goods rose to 24, 39, 5, and 17, respectively, and the average family consumed 3 units of cotton cloth, 2 hammocks, 42 units of rice, and 20 units of fish. How much shark's tooth inflation was there between those two dates?

5 Aggregate Demand

In which we find that the desires of the entire economy can be expressed in just one equation. We encounter a lifetime of earning and consuming as well as the forces that cause the members of an economy to invest. All this, and government, too, combine to form one simple curve.

INTRODUCTION

A macroeconomic model is a simplified version of an economy. It normally is presented as a system of equations which represent the modeller's assumptions about human behavior, or, in models that are not very good, about persistent correlations among different economic variables. Since the world is extremely complex, a model usually contains exogenous variables, variables whose values are given by something outside the system being analyzed; by the government, for example, or another economy, or god, . . . and is solved for a set of endogenous variables, the items determined *by* the system. The standard practice has been to use these systems of equations to do comparative static experiments.

In a **comparative static** experiment, the model is solved for an equilibrium (values of endogenous variables are found) for one set of values of the exogenous variables. The experimenter then changes the value of one or more of the exogenous variables that are of interest—usually variables that the government can (or thinks it can) control—and resolves the model to find the new values for the endogenous variables. The economist can then compare the two sets of solutions for the endogenous variables and use these results to predict how the economy will respond to the particular policy change. Note that in comparative statics one only looks at the initial and final solutions, which might be called equilibria, for use in policy making; one ignores the *path* that the economy takes as it moves from one of these equilibrium to the other. Dynamic economic analysis of these paths can be very difficult. For that reason and for some historical reasons connected with the nature of Keynesian economic analysis, it has not been frequently done until quite recently. (This is not strictly true since there was a school of business cycle theory that existed alongside early Keynesian analysis but lost the postdepression popularity race among policy makers. Modern dynamic macroeconomics might be thought of as a resurgence of that school.)

Various mathematical techniques are used to solve the models. In general, the more complicated the model, the more complex the mathematics needed to solve it. A serious problem in economic research is outrunning mathematical knowledge (not just the reasearcher's mathematical knowledge, though that happens frequently enough, but the entire body of mathematical knowledge). In order to avoid many of these mathematical complications, we will make a number of very strong assumptions that operate as simplifications to allow us to reduce our model to two equations, which we can then solve graphically. These two equations will separate consumption decisions and production decisions, as was done in the microeconomic model presented earlier.

Consumption decisions are summarized on an **aggregate demand curve.** This curve shows the response of desired **consumption** of output in an economy to changes in the price level. The behavioral aspects come from dividing demand into three components: 1, the demand for consumption goods; 2, the demand for investment goods; and 3, the demand for goods by the government. This division should remind you of the National Income Accounting Identity ($Y = C + I + G$) that we discussed in the last chapter, but with foreign trade ($X - IM$) removed.

Production decisions are summarized in the **aggregate supply curve.** This curve incorporates knowledge of the production technology and activities in the labor market and allows us to show how the production of output responds to changes in the price level. It is on the production side that we will be able to incorporate the expectations of unions, or of individual workers acting though their unions, and of firms into the model and generate time paths of some of our endogenous variables. The study of these paths is not really pure dynamic analysis, because we are following a number of comparative static equilibria that are linked by expectations functions. Still, the analysis should give a flavor of the nature of dynamic problems.

The intersection of the aggregate supply and aggregate demand curves yields the equilibrium price level and the equilibrium output level for an economy much as the intersection of the single market supply and demand curves gave the equilibrium for the market. We will be interested in how these equilibrium values, the endogenous variables of interest, change with changes in government policy variables, those exogenous variables that government can control.

AGGREGATE DEMAND

We use the National Income Accounting Identity for a closed economy, one without international trade, to describe the way we divide aggregate demand into its components. As you recall, the National Income Accounting Identity is the equation,

$$Y = C + I + G + X - IM$$

where C is the demand for consumption goods, I is the demand for investment goods, G is the demand by the government for the goods it uses (known as government expenditures), X is exports, and IM is imports. In a closed economy, which has no trade with any other economy, both the exports, X, and the imports, IM, will equal zero. We will henceforth leave exports and imports out of the national income accounting identity so it becomes $Y = C + I + G$. Each of the three sources of demand will be considered separately and then the functional forms that we get for them will be summed and solved as a function of output in terms of the price level and the exogenous variables.

Consumption demand and investment demand are derived from the behavior of households. (While in a good economic model this derivation is explicit, such a model would be too sophisticated for our purposes.) We will consider some of the optimizing behavior that could lead to an investment function and several of the theories that give us specific values for some of the parameters of our consump-

tion function. These theories are based on microeconomic theory, but this will be used only lightly in our initial development.

THE CONSUMPTION FUNCTION

We want to write a consumption function of the form

$$C = C(z_1, z_2, \ldots, z_n)$$

where $C(z_1, z_2, \ldots, z_n)$ is the function that describes the relationship between the yet undetermined variables $z_1, z_2, \ldots$, and z_n, and the consumption that results from different values for these variables.[1] Although as written here the function is very general, we will construct a very specific linear (afine) consumption function. First, we need to determine the variables, the z_is, that effect an individual's consumption. The most obvious one is the individual's income. The greater one's income, the more one can consume. This seems a simple proposition. Contrary to the circular flow diagram of Chapter 2, consumers don't have control over the total income in an economy. (Total income equals total output, since all results of production—rents and profits—are paid back to households. Firms keep nothing.) Any of you who have received paychecks know that you don't have control over your total income. There is a number, imaginary although it does not begin with *i*, on the stub of the check. It is usually called something like "gross wages." The dollar amount on the check attached to this stub has only the slightest resemblance to this gross wage number. The government extracts a forced contribution of a share of the total income in the form of **taxes.**

Initially, we will assume **lump sum taxes** so we can leave production decisions free of tax-induced distortions or inefficiencies. The amount of lump sum tax that an individual pays is not related to any of the economic variables that are under that individual's control. The government determines the amount of tax a person pays by what *might* (and, to the individual, often does) seem to be a random process. (This tax system operates as does the entire society in Jorge Luis Borges's short story "The Lottery of Babylon.")[2] In particular, the amount of tax does *not* change systematically with changes in income.[3] A lump sum tax is an economist's

[1] Whenever we write the functional form $X = X(a, b, c)$, for example, we are stating that we believe that some variable X has its values determined by the variables inside the parenthesis. If the reader is unfamiliar with functional notation, think of $X(a, b, c)$ as a computer program called X that asks for the values of *a*, *b*, and *c*, in this example, and returns the value of X.

[2] Jorge Luis Borges, *Ficciones* (New York: Grove Press, 1962).

[3] This assumption will be changed later when we will consider the effects of changing income tax rates on the supply and demand for labor. This income tax is not a lump sum tax as it will affect production decisions.

artifact, as none have ever been sighted in the wild. The portion of total income (Y) the consumers have control over is their **disposable income,** or income minus taxes ($Y - T$).

We can now write a preliminary linear consumption function as

$$C = a + \beta \times (Y - T)$$

where a is the intercept (or the amount of consumption when disposable income is equal to zero), and β is the slope of the line giving consumption as a function of disposable income. The $\times$ denotes "times." This consumption function can be written even more explicitly in terms of the economic ideas it incorporates. The portion of each *additional* dollar of disposable income that is spent on consumption is called the **marginal propensity to consume** (mpc). This mpc is the slope of the line obtained when consumption is plotted against disposable income. With consumption on the vertical axis, this is equal to the parameter β of the above linear consumption function.

Using total yearly quantities of consumption and disposable income from 1960 to 1985 in the graph in Figure 5.1, we can see that the estimated mpc—the slope of the straight line that is drawn in the graph and whose equation is given above as the line that best fits the data points—is .9136, or approximately .9. The value of the parameter a of the linear equation is close to zero—it equals -9 in an equation where many of the data points are in the several thousand range. Each additional dollar of income results in about a 91.36¢ increase in consumption. Each point, as shown by the boxes in Figure 5.1, shows the aggregate consumption

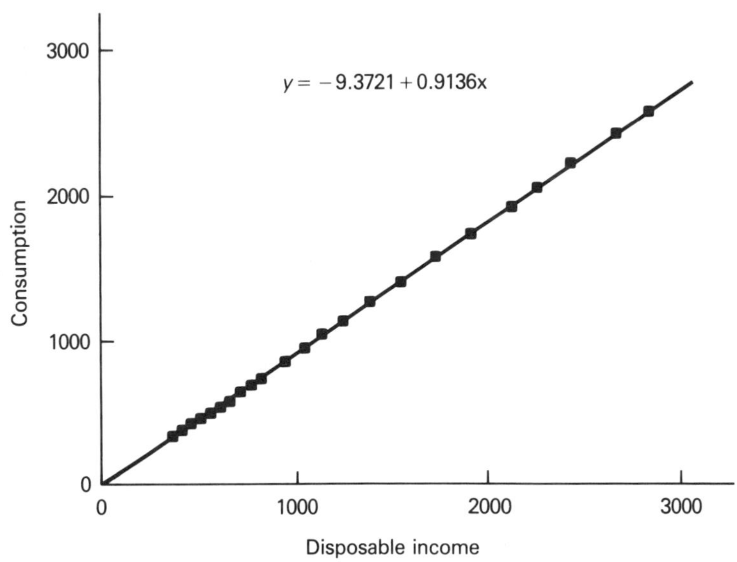

Figure 5.1

and disposable income for a different year. This technique, which uses the total yearly, monthly, or weekly values as data points when estimating the mpc, as we did with the graph above, is called **time series estimation.** This is because the separate data points represent different moments in time, and the whole collection represents a series of time-period-based data points.

Very different estimates of mpc have been obtained by looking at **cross sections** of the economy in any given year. In cross-sectional estimation, the data points come from different families in the economy in the same year. It was noticed that poor people (students, as a possible example) spent more than their current incomes while people who were quite well off spent considerably less than the 90% suggested by the time series estimates. (Families with disposable incomes in the $100,000 range spent somewhere around 50% in 1982.) Apparently, as people moved to higher income brackets they saved a greater portion of their disposable incomes. The same method of finding a linear consumption function can be used with the cross-sectional data. Estimates for the mpc using cross-sectional data range from .50 to .70, with different studies getting different numbers, and the value of *a* significantly greater than zero in all cases. This means that a graph of the consumption–disposable income relationship, similar to that shown in the graph in Figure 5.1, based on cross-sectional data, will have a much flatter curve and an intercept well above the origin. Figure 5.2 shows two such estimated cross-sectional consumption function lines and a corresponding per capita time series consumption function line with a slope of .9. The line CS_2 represents a second cross-sectional estimation at a time when the general income and consumption level in the economy was higher.

The fact that we get a different estimate of the mpc when we use time series data as compared to when we use cross-sectional data has bothered many economists. A theoretical microeconomic justification is needed to explain these different estimates. Two major ideas have been proposed—the permanent income hypothesis and the lifecycle hypothesis. Note that we are attempting to find a

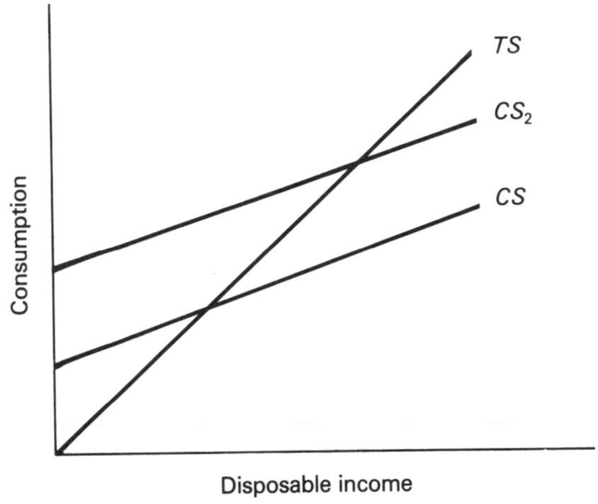

Figure 5.2

theory of individual behavior that will result in a line with a slope of .9 when we look at the aggregate data and a slope of .5 to .7 when we look at the individual data points.

Milton Friedman has suggested a **permanent income hypothesis.**[4] The different estimates can be explained, according to this hypothesis, if individuals view their income as being comprised of two components. These two components are permanent income and temporary income. Permanent income is the income that individuals expect to get. Temporary income is surprise income. Because an individual does not know what his income will be when he makes his consumption plans, he makes those plans based on what he *thinks* his income will be. Individuals need to do this because many of their purchases must be planned, and decisions about which automobile to purchase and what type of living accommodations to have, to name just two of the more important, involve long-term plans. Because these decisions occur before the actual consumption and before the income is earned, an individual needs to base these types of expenditures on his expected or, as Friedman called it, permanent income. Friedman hypothesized that an individual plans to consume ninety percent of his permanent income.

As the year unfolds, individuals find that their income is not what they expected. Because of either good or bad fortune (luck?), their income is either larger or smaller than expected. This difference between actual and expected income is called surprise or temporary income. Friedman assumed that individuals consume almost none of their temporary income. This is illustrated by the fact that people who win lotteries (single prize lotteries, not the ones that make a payment for each of twenty years) tend to save almost all of those winnings. Temporary incomes are unexpected, and for the economy as a whole are expected to be zero. If people's expectations are based on fact or are, on average, accurate, then all the temporary incomes in the economy will sum to zero. If we look at time series data, we see that the average income level in the economy is the economy's average permanent income, since the temporary incomes cancel out. That would mean that the mpc from time series data should be .9, as it actually is. When we look at cross-sectional data, we see that temporary income is included. Incomes are equal to permanent *and* temporary income, while consumption decisions are based only on permanent income. People with positive temporary incomes—those who are rich and have an income to the right of the average income level for the economy—will consume a relatively smaller portion of their incomes, less than .9, while people with negative temporary incomes—the poor—will likely consume more than their incomes. (They might, for example, borrow.) So the "best" line running through these cross-sectional points will be below the time series lines for incomes that are greater than average and above the time series line for incomes that are less than average. Since the average is where the cross-sectional line crosses the time series line, there is a "rotation" in the cross-sectional line when

[4] Milton Friedman, A *Theory of the Consumption Function* (New York: National Bureau of Economic Research, 1956).

compared to the time series line. Estimating the mpc (slope) of a line representing the cross-sectional data will yield a much smaller value than .9, something like the .5 to .7 we get with cross-sectional data.

The **Life Cycle Hypothesis** suggests a different way to explain the difference in the estimated mpcs. During each person's life there are periods when he consumes more than he earns and there are periods when he consumes less than he earns. During the early part of one's life, one has consumption needs, but those needs are provided by someone else—usually one's parents. This period, during which one consumes more than one earns, continues through college and into the early part of working life. As one approaches middle age, the level of income usually increases, but consumption expenditures have steadied at a level well below income. People in this age group know that retirement is coming up and usually are saving to help cover consumption during that period. When you graph income and consumption over one's lifetime as a function of age, you get a graph like Figure 5.3.

On average, individuals consume only ninety percent of their income. In part, this may be because they don't know when they will die and they do not want to have their income run out before their lives do. (Kenneth Arrow once said that the major uncertainty for people in planning their lifetime's consumption is not knowing when they will die.)[5] So if the distribution of old and young stays fairly constant, then, on average, the economy will consume ninety percent of its disposable income and the slope of a time series graph will be .9. The cross-sectional data will give a line of flatter slope. Individuals with a relatively high income, who are in the middle age period of their lives, consume a relatively small proportion of their incomes. Those with relatively low incomes consume more than their incomes. We get the same kind of rotation as we observed in the permanent income explanation. Graphing consumption as a linear function of disposable income will yield a line with relatively small slope, .5 to .7.

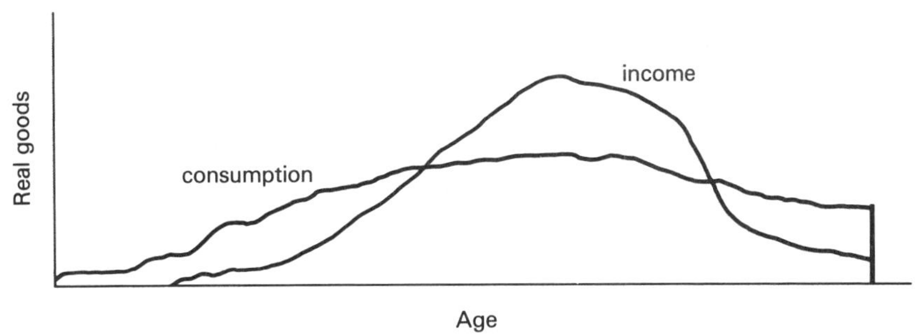

Figure 5.3

[5] Nobel prize winner Kenneth Arrow provided the foundation for the modern theory of risk in *Essays in the Theory of Risk-Bearing* (Amsterdam: North Holland Publishing Company, 1970).

It is possible to combine the life cycle and permanent income hypotheses into one fairly unified concept. Permanent income can be viewed as the discounted value of expected future income. (Don't panic, I'll explain these terms.) Imagine that individuals have a good idea of what their future income streams will be. (An example of an income stream is shown in Figure 5.3.) How do they view this future expected income and take it into account in their current consumption decisions?

Given the choice between one dollar today and one dollar a year from now, most people would choose the dollar today. This is not just because there might be inflation, an increase in the dollar price of most goods, but because spending that dollar now can provide immediate benefits, while the dollar next year gives delayed benefits. To find out what one dollar a year from now is worth today for some consumer, one can offer that consumer choices between the guaranteed dollar a year from now and some amount of money today. Suppose the choice is between ninety-five cents today and one dollar in one year, and the consumer chooses the ninety-five cents. This choice says that the ninety-five cents now is worth more to the consumer than the one dollar in a year. Suppose that we keep subtracting one cent from our offer of money today until we find the amount that just equals the promise of one dollar in a year. Suppose that this occurs at eighty-five cents. At this offer, the consumer is equally pleased with having eighty-five cents today or one dollar in a year. The two options are equal. We can use this information about the consumer and say that this individual discounts income one year in the future by .85. Therefore, .85 is this individual's *discount rate,* and an offer of one hundred dollars a year from now would be viewed as being discounted to be worth only eighty-five dollars today.

Suppose that today is January 1, 2000. Someone with a discount rate of .85 is promised one hundred dollars on January 1, 2002, two years from now. What current value does this person place on this expected one hundred dollars? In other words, for what amount of money today would he exchange this promise of one hundred dollars two years in the future?

On January 1, 2001, the promise will come due in exactly one year. We know that this individual discounts a one year promise by .85, so on January 1, 2001, the promise will be worth eighty-five dollars. (One hundred dollars in one year is worth eighty-five dollars today.) But January 1, 2001, is one year from today. For our individual, every dollar promised on this date is worth only .85 dollars today. The promise of one hundred dollars on January 1, 2002 is worth eighty-five dollars on January 1, 2001 and is worth $.85 \times \$85$, which equals \$72.25, on January 1, 2000. So \$72.25 is the worth, to this individual, of a promise of \$100 two years in the future.

Notice that the value of this two-year-ahead promise is \$100 dollars times .85 times .85 or

$$.85^2 \times \$100 = \$72.25$$

For a promise of \$100 to come three years in the future, the \$72.25 is discounted once again to give

$$.85 \times 72.25 = .85^2 \times \$100 = .83^3 \times 100 = \$61.4125$$

We can use the discount rate of each individual to find out how he or she evaluates the expected lifetime stream of income. Suppose that someone living in the year 2000 will earn one hundred thosuand dollars for the next five years and then will retire and earn nothing. She knows this and wants to evaluate the present value of her income stream. The present value of an income stream is the amount of money that a person would be willing to take today instead of waiting for the promised future income stream. How much is this expected five years of one hundred thousand dollars worth today?

We can find the present value of the income stream by discounting each of the expected payments by the correct discount rate. The income expected this year is not discounted and is worth one hundred thousand dollars . The income expected in 2001 is coming one year in the future and, given a discount rate of .85, is worth \$85,000 today. The combined worth of two years of income at one hundred thousand dollars is \$185,000 today. Table 5.1 shows the dates, the incomes and the discounted value of these incomes for the remaining five years of work. The sum of the discounted values is the present value of this stream of income.

The nominal value of the income stream is five hundred thousand dollars, but discounting the future income payments by .85 for each of the years one must wait for the payment gives us a present value for this stream of "only" \$370,863. Notice that most state lotteries announce their prizes in terms of the nominal value of the stream of payments. If the prize were five years of payments of one hundred thousand dollars the state would call it a half-million-dollar prize, but the winner, if he discounts the future by .85, should behave as if the gain were only \$370,863. The present value of a two-million-dollar lottery prize spread out in

TABLE 5.1

DATE	INCOME (DOLLARS)	DISCOUNT FACTOR	DISCOUNTED VALUE (DOLLARS)
2000	100,000	$.85^0 = 1$	100,000
2001	100,000	$.85^1 = .85$	85,000
2002	100,000	$.85^2 = .7225$	72,250
2003	100,000	$.85^3 = .614125$	61,413
2004	100,000	$.85^4 = .52200$	52,200
		Present value of stream =	\$370,863

twenty yearly payments of one hundred thousand dollars each is \$640,826, with the last year adding only \$4,560 to the present value calculation. The one hundred thousand dollars that comes twenty years in the future is discounted by $.85^{19}$, which equals .0456. Now suppose that individuals use the present value of future income as a proxy for permanent income. We can write the permanent income version of the consumption function for the individual who earns one hundred thousand dollars for five years and then retires as

$$C_{2000} = \alpha + \beta \times (\text{present value of income}) = \alpha + \beta \times (370{,}863)$$

Consumption in the year 2000 is a linear function of the present value of the expected future income. We want to determine α and β. From the evidence we discussed above, a change in income of one dollar that is viewed as permanent will result in a change in consumption of ninety cents. For the person in our example, a permanent increase in income of one thousand dollars means an additional one thousand dollars in each of the five years left of work will result in an increase of nine hundred dollars in consumption in the year 2000. Using a chart like Table 5.1, we can calculate the increase in the present value of income from the five years of an additional one thousand dollars. That increase in present value is \$3,708.63. We now want to find the value of β for the above consumption function that will cause C_{2000} to increase by nine hundred when permanent income goes up by 3708.63. This β ~~if and~~ is found by dividing nine hundred by 3708.63 to get $\beta = 900 / 3708.63$ or .2427.

If this individual receives a temporary increase in income for only the year 2000 which will not continue into future years, then the increase in present value of income is only one thousand dollars, not the \$3,708.63 that we found from the permanent income increase. If the above equation correctly describes behavior, then consumption in the year 2000 will increase by .2427 × 1000, which equals \$242.7. Using the present value of income in place of Friedman's permanent income gives us a model that gives the same kind of response to permanent and temporary income that Friedman suggested, but also gives a better description of what determines "permanent" income.

This form of consumption theory has been used recently to explain why consumption does not vary as much over time as does income. If short term wiggles in income are viewed as temporary, then they have a much smaller effect on consumption, and consumption has smaller wiggles than does income. We will return to this idea in Chapter 12, where we discuss business cycles.

Because we are aggregating data in our macroeconomic analysis, we are interested in how consumption changes as the income of the whole economy changes. In this situation, one could believe that the relative positions of individuals in the economy (or at least the relative distribution of rich and poor people in that economy, even though individuals may shift into or out of these groups) remain fairly stable as all incomes change (perhaps by some general increase in income in the economy). It would seem that the mpc estimate from time series data is more in keeping with our needs. Whenever we need a value for the mpc, we will use a number that approximates the time series value: .9. Therefore, we can rewrite our consumption function as

$$C = \text{mpc} \times (Y - T)$$

remembering that the mpc is equal to .9. Since the *a* was approximately equal to zero, we will drop it.

The second component of the consumption function that we will consider is wealth (Wel). High levels of wealth allow individuals to smooth over sharp changes in their income. Putting wealth into the simple consumption function we have here might help us capture some of the ideas in the combined life cycle–permanent income model. Wealth might represent some portion of expected future incomes. We would expect high levels of wealth to be consistent with high levels of consumption. The marginal change in consumption resulting from a change in wealth is called the **marginal propensity to consume out of wealth.** We would expect this to be quite small relative to the standard mpc, with a value considerably smaller than .1. We will use the symbol μ (called mu) to represent the marginal propensity to consume out of wealth. The consumption function can be expanded to

$$C = \text{mpc} \times (Y - T) + \mu \times \text{Wel} \tag{5.1}$$

An economist named A. C. Pigou was one of the first to consider the effects of wealth on consumption and therefore the effects that arise in consumption from changes in wealth are known as the **Pigou Effect.**[6]

Two questions concerning wealth remain: what comprises it, and how is it denominated? We will limit wealth to household holdings of money and bonds. The government issues the money and individuals hold it, often in a bank. There are two sources of bonds: the government and firms. The government issued bonds to help cover the deficit and this helped pay for some past government expenditures. Firms issue bonds in order to get funds that the firm can use to invest. The sum of these is referred to as **nominal wealth,** since both money and bonds are measured in dollar terms. Yet it is not the dollar value of wealth that is important to people. Rather, it is what that wealth can buy that has an effect on consumption decisions. If both the nominal value of their wealth and the price level doubled, the real value of their wealth would be left unchanged. If this happened, individuals would not change their consumption behavior. In the real economy, much wealth is held in real assets—in land or as machinery, for example. Some of this is held in the form of stocks, such as the shares of firms that are traded in the New York Stock Exchange. In spite of the stock market drop of October, 1987, we will

[6] A. C. Pigou, "The Classical Stationary State," *Economic Journal* LIII (1943): 343–351.

assume that this real property aspect of wealth does not change much and therefore doesn't much affect consumption decisions. Summarizing the above considerations, we get

$$\text{Wel} = (M + B_g + B_p)/p$$

where p is the price level, M is the money stock, B_g is the stock of government bonds, and B_p is the stock of bonds privately issued by firms. We can rewrite the consumption function (equation 5.1) as

$$C = \text{mpc} \times (Y - T) + \mu \times (M + B_g + B_p)/p$$

Notice that prices, p, enter into the consumption function, which is in terms of real goods and not of dollars, for example, only through the Pigou Effect. In this model, changes in the price level results in changes in consumption only so far as they change real wealth. These effects of prices on wealth will be the main way we get prices to be important in the Aggregate Demand function.

Robert Barro has revived an interesting argument made by David Ricardo about government bonds.[7] This argument, called **Ricardian Equivalence,** claims that it does not matter, in terms of lifetime utility, if the government taxes now for current government expenditure or if it borrows the funds now and pays back the loans by taxing in the future. Especially in a closed economy, it is possible to think of government bonds as measuring what we have borrowed from ourselves and promise to bay back to ourselves in the future. If we think of government bonds this way, should they be included in nominal wealth? Barro and Ricardo say no. If I wrote a note to myself promising to pay me one hundred dollars in a year—with interest, of course—am I one hundred dollars wealthier? Surely not. The argument for Ricardian equivalence extends this idea to the whole economy. If the government issues bonds, the only effect is to change the date at which the taxes will be paid. Issuing government bonds shifts taxes into the future.

The validity of Ricardian equivalence hinges on several factors. One major factor is the same aggregation problem that we first observed in Chapter 4. Only if taxes are collected in the future in the same proportions, with each person paying the same taxes, plus interest, he or she would have paid today, is there no individual effect. Individuals need to know that this shift will have no effect on their lifetime income stream in order for them to act as if it has no effect. This "superationality", as it is called, is required for the equivalence to hold. There is the additional problem of passing on the cost of paying off the bonds from one generation to another. Individuals who die before the taxes are collected gain from

[7] Robert J. Barro, "Are Government Bonds Net Wealth?" *Journal of Political Economy* 82 (November–December 1974): 1095–1118.

David Ricardo, "Funding System," in *The Works and Correspondence of David Ricardo*, ed. P. Straffa (Cambridge: Cambridge University Press, 1957).

this procedure, while the new generation who never benefited from the government expenditures will have to be taxed to pay for it.

It is possible that the government bonds will never be paid off. The government might simply roll them over, issuing new bonds every time that the old ones come due. The British government has issued bonds called Consols that are never to be paid off—buyers get an infinite number of interest payments, at two percent of the face value per year, but never the initial payment back. The government could also pay off the bonds by issuing new money. The welfare or utility effects of exchanging the bonds for money are difficult to analyze without an explicit model of money. This is because increasing the amount of money in the economy by issuing new money to buy back the bonds can act like a tax. (See Chapter 15 for details on how this can be so.) Depending upon whom this tax is imposed, the Ricardian equivalence does or does not hold.

THE INVESTMENT FUNCTION

Next is investment. Investment is the flow of current goods that is put aside to aid in the continuing production of goods. Investment includes new machines that firms use to produce goods, factories, and office buildings, and other construction done by firms, and the inventories that firms keep on hand to meet orders and smooth out production. The total accumulation of the past net investments is called capital. Following a standard practice in introductory expositions, for the majority of this development we will simply fix investment at some level and not worry about how it got to be at this level. Therefore, investment is constant, or exogenous, or

$$I = \mathbf{I}$$

Before we go on, however, it is important to consider what an investment function should, or could, look like. It is often assumed in the construction of Keynesian-type macroeconomic models that the interest rate (roughly, the percentage of the amount borrowed that must be paid to the lender each period for the use of the amount borrowed) has an important effect on firms' investment decisions. With this in mind, the investment function is usually written as

$$I = \mathbf{I}(r)$$

where r is some relevant interest rate, and it is assumed that the investment decreases as the interest rate rises.

Keynesians explain this kind of relationship between investment and the interest rate by equating the marginal productivity of investment with the interest rate, as a condition that holds in equilibrium. At any time each firm has a number of projects in which it might invest. It is likely that some of these projects have potential for generating a higher rate of return than others. If we order these projects, with the ones that offer the highest rate of return first and the rest in order of their rates of return, we can generate a graph for the firm's investment opportunities.

Figure 5.4 illustrates the possible investment opportunities for a small firm with five possible projects. The height of each segment is the rate of return that project will yield and the width is the cost of that project. Project 3 will give a rate of return of fifteen percent and it will cost $15,000 ($55,000 − $40,000) to put it into production. If the prevailing market interest rate is sixteen percent, then only projects 1 and 2 will earn a return higher than the interest rate the firm will have to pay to get the money, or would give up by not lending its money to someone else. If we imagine that all the firms in the economy have curves like this one we can sum them all up to find out the total investment the economy will want to make at each interest rate. Summing up all of these firms smooths out the curve and we get an interest rate–investment relationship such as the one in Figure 5.5. Notice that the curve is drawn so that it is almost vertical on the right. Keynes was much occupied with the notion that as interest rates fell there would be a floor after which further declines in the rate would *not* yield additional investment. This is known as the **liquidity trap.**

Modern investment theory thinks of investment as the result of businesspeople changing the stock of capital that their firm needs as they attempt to maximize a discounted stream of expected future profit flows. (This is the same kind of discounting we used in the discussion of the effects of changes in permanent or temporary income on the consumption function.) The value of a firm, and therefore of all the shares of stock of that firm held by the public (from a model

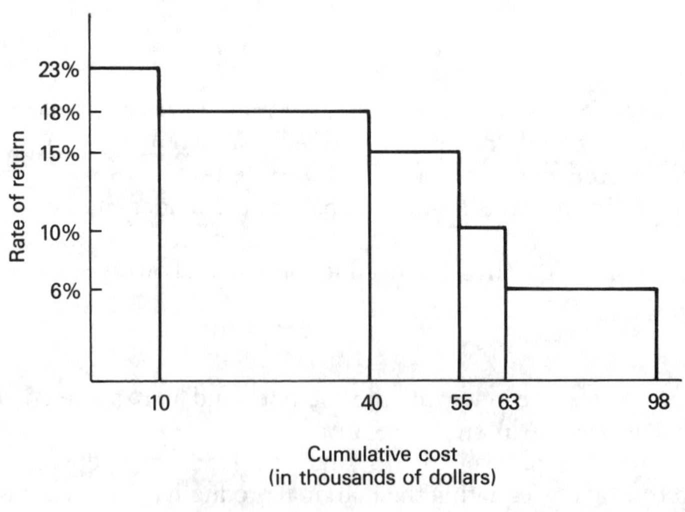

Figure 5.4

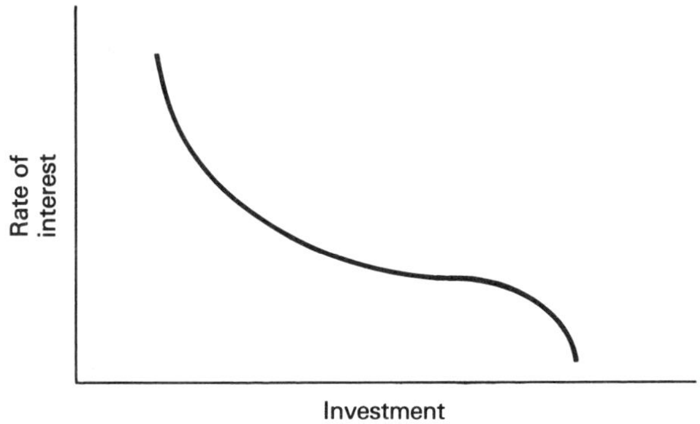

Figure 5.5

called the **Capital Asset Pricing Model**), is equal to this discounted expected flow of profits. We assume that stockholders want the managers of their firms to maximize the value of their shares. As before, revenues that are not going to occur until some future date need to be discounted because individuals find one unit of consumption worth more now than at some time in the future. Recall our discussion of discounting, in which we used an example in which consumers believed that one unit of income next year was worth only .85 units of income today. (Note that .85 is an example. Different individuals may give greater or lesser weight to delaying income. Young children, for example, want everything now and might have a discount rate of .1. Someone who is very patient might have a discount rate very near one, .98 for example.)

Managers of firms need to plan today to generate future profits. They make plans for the future size of their labor force and the amount of capital they will want to have in place at different future dates. Some projects take a long time to build—an automobile plant or hydroelectric power-generating plant may take ten or more years to plan and get into production. These projects require investment for many years before profits are generated. It is possible to speed up the construction of capital equipment and plants—it might be possible to build an automobile plant in five years—but it usually costs much more to make large quick investments than to make the same investment somewhat more slowly. A premium must often be paid in order to get quick delivery of machinery from its manufacturer, training costs are higher if it is to proceed quickly, and construction of a building costs more the faster it is to go. (Overtime payments to labor are just one reason for this last complication.) Divesting—that is, selling off some capital—quickly is more expensive than doing so slowly would be. It takes time to find a buyer of capital equipment, but reducing the price of the equipment will speed up that process. (A broker might buy the equipment, if the price were low enough, and then look for a buyer.)

Keeping in mind the cost of changing the capital stock, for any given long-term investment plan we can calculate a firm's expected profits for each future year. Let t stand for today—this year—and then $t + 5$ will stand for five years into the future. Using year $t + 5$ as an example, the expected profits for that year equal the expected revenues in the year $t + 5$, minus the wage bill—wages times the number of workers—in year $t + 5$, minus the cost of investment—price of capital goods times the amount purchased—in the year $t + 5$, minus the cost of putting the capital equipment in place. This is

$$\begin{aligned} \text{Expected profits}(t+5) = {} & \text{Revenues}(t+5) \\ & - \text{wages}(t+5) \times \text{number of workers}(t+5) \\ & - \text{price of capital equipment}(t+5) \times \\ & \quad \text{investment}(t+5) \\ & - \text{cost of putting in investment}(t+5) \end{aligned}$$

The current value of all the stock or shares of a company is the discounted expected value of future profits, according to the Capital Asset Pricing Model. Given an investment plan for a firm, the optimal number of workers needed each year is estimated, and the expected profits for each future date can be calculated. We then discount future profits by the discount factor to find the value of the firm. If the discount rate is .85, the value of a firm is

$$\begin{aligned} \text{Value of a firm at time } t = {} & \text{expected profits at time } t \\ & + .85 \times \text{expected profits at time } t+1 \\ & + .85^2 \times \text{expected profits at time } t+2 \\ & + .85^3 \times \text{expected profits at time } t+3 \\ & + \ldots \end{aligned}$$

The optimal investment plan is found by choosing the plan that maximizes the discounted stream of expected future profits and therefore maximizes the current value of the stock in the stock market. Aside from a lot of complicated nomenclature, this microeconomic-based theory of investment illustrates that entire paths of investment decisions depend on the **expectations of the future path** of prices and wages. However, to solve this theory of investment we also need a good theory on how those expectations are formed.

This development was intended to illustrate what is required for a good micro-based macroeconomic theory. As you can see, it is quite complicated. We will keep this theory in the back of our minds as we discuss investment and our models, but in the formal development we will be limited to either a constant (exogenous) investment function or one that is a simple function of the interest rate.

GOVERNMENT EXPENDITURES

The government chooses to consume a certain amount of goods. (These government expenditures are designated by G.) It purchases material for defense, hires soldiers and tax collectors, builds roads, maintains national parks, and performs many additional functions. Since different government actions and expenditures benefit different individuals, there is considerable disagreement about what are appropriate government expenditures. Transfers, such as welfare and social security payments, do not count as government expenditures in our definition (although they do in government account books) because no goods are purchased and used. Income is transferred from one individual to another and is washed out in our aggregate models. The government pays for these goods by collecting taxes, T (lump sum, just like in the consumption function); by borrowing from the Federal Reserve System, which prints new money and gives it to the government, ΔM; or by borrowing directly from private citizens, ΔB_g.[8] If government expenditures exceed taxes, the government borrows from the Federal Reserve System (see Chapter 14) or from individuals and this shows up in the economy directly as an increase in the flow of money into the economy, ΔM, or as as increase in the flow of government bonds to the public, ΔB_g. In this model, a positive ΔM will show up in the money stock in the next period as an increase in M, and a positive ΔB_g will show up next period as an increase in B_g. If taxes exceed government expenditures some of the government debt to the federal reserve system is retired, and money leaves the economic system. Writing this out as a simple equation, the government faces the **Government Budget Constraint** of

$$G = T + \Delta M/p + \Delta B_g/p \tag{5.2}$$

where T is taxes, G is government expenditures, ΔB_g is the change in government bonds, ΔM is the change in the money supply, and p is the price level. Thus, $\Delta M/p$ is the real value of the change in the money supply, and $\Delta B_g/p$ is the real value of the change in government bonds. Note that G and T are chosen by Congress exogenously and need bear little relation to each other. Equation 5.2 should hold so sales or purchases of government bonds and money make up the difference between G and T. This government budget constraint shows what happens in the model as a result of **fiscal policies.** Fiscal policies are changes in taxes or government expenditures and can result in changes in the money stock or the quantity of government bonds.

Note the difference between M and ΔM; M is the stock of money, while ΔM is the flow of money into the economy in a given period as a result of a failure of taxes to cover government expenditures. If ΔM is negative, then taxes exceed expenses. The flow of bonds into the economy generated by the same government activites that generated ΔM is represented by ΔB_g. Both ΔM and ΔB_g are flow variables

[8] The Federal Reserve System is the central bank of the United States and issues all the money in the United States economy. Note that United States currency is called Federal Reserve Notes. The Federal Reserve System doesn't really give the government new bills in exchange for the bonds that the government—the treasury—gives to it. Rather all of this is done with bookkeeping entries. Bonds are allocated to the Federal Reserve System in the accounting books of the Treasury and the FRS allocates deposits in bank accounts for the Treasury. No paper money moves in these transactions.

which are changed by changes in fiscal policy, while M and B_g are stock variables that are changed by the past history of the flow variables or by monetary policy. Monetary policy will be covered in Chapter 14.

THE AGGREGATE DEMAND CURVE

There are four equations that represent all of our assumptions about the behavior on the demand side of our model. They are listed below.

(1) $Y = C + I + G$	Accounting Identity
(2) $C = \text{mpc} \times (Y - T) + \mu \times (M + B_g + B_p)/p$	Consumption
(3) $I = \mathbf{I}$	Investment
(4) $G = T + \Delta M/p + \Delta B_g/p$	Government Budget

Replacing C and I in the national income accounting identity, (1), with what they equal in equations (2) and (3) gives

$$Y = \text{mpc} \times (Y - T) + \mu \times (M + B_g + B_p)/p + \mathbf{I} + G$$

Because we are looking for a relationship between the price level and income, we want to bring all of the parts of the equations with income in them over to the left hand side of the equal sign. We then get the equation

$$Y - \text{mpc} \times Y = \mu \times (M + B_g + B_p)/p + \mathbf{I} + G - \text{mpc} \times T$$

Solving for Y by dividing both sides by 1 − mpc) gives us the aggregate demand curve

$$Y = [1/(1 - \text{mpc})] \times [\mu \times (M + B_g + B_p)/p + \mathbf{I} + G - \text{mpc} \times T]$$

Holding the exogenous variables (M, B_g, B_p, $\mathbf{I}$, T, G) and the parameters (mpc, μ) fixed, we can graph Y as a function of p, the price level. This is an equation of the form

$$Y = X/p + Z$$

From the above equation, X is equal to

$$X = [1/(1 - \text{mpc})] \times [\mu \times (M + B_g + B_p)]$$

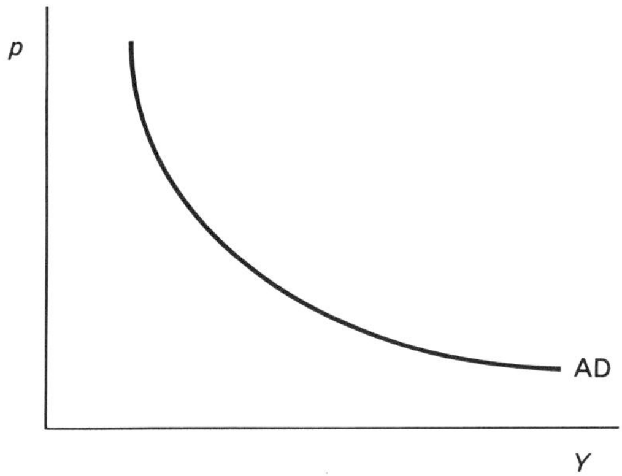

Figure 5.6

and the constant, Z, is equal to

$$Z = [1/(1 - \text{mpc})] \times [\mathbf{I} + G - \text{mpc} \times T]$$

This kind of equation is graphed as a rectangular hyperbola. Figure 5.6 shows just such a graph.

This is the graph of the Aggregate Demand curve that we will be using for much of this book. Note that the reason that the AD curve is a function of prices is because of the Pigou Effect. The curve slopes downwards because changes in prices change the way individuals value their nominal wealth and that changes consumption behavior. While this curve *looks* like a regular demand curve, in that it is downward sloping, the reasons for this shape are fundamentally different.

REPRISE

The aggregate demand curve is generated from the National Income Accounting Identity, the consumption function, the investment function, and the governments budget constraint. The National Income Accounting Identity sums up all of the sources of demand in the economy. The consumption function expresses the reactions of the consumers to changes in their disposable income and their wealth. The estimated coefficient of the consumption function with respect to disposable income is different depending on whether time series or cross-sectional data is used. Explanations for this difference, and an increased understanding of consumer behavior, come from the Permanent Income Hypothesis and the Life Cycle Hypothesis of consumption. (For some economists, these two hypotheses are combined into one. The expectations about income over one life cycle are part of the Permanent Income Hypothesis.)

The investment function that is used in the full model is very simple: investment is exogenous. It does, however, have a fine pedigree. Behind the simple investment function that we are using is the slightly more complicated and more Keynesian function in which investment is based on the interest rate. This is sometimes called the **Marginal Product of Capital** theory of investment. We also consider a more microeconomic model of investment decision where managers maximize the current value of the firm. This leads to an investment function that is based on expectations about the economy's future microeconomic variables; in particular, the demand for the firm's goods and the expected wages and cost of capital.

The Government's Budget Constraint highlights the connection between taxes, government expenditures, the flow of new government bonds, and the flow of new money. This equation expresses some of the trade-offs that a government policy maker faces.

This full demand side of the model can be resolved into one equation in two unknowns. The aggregate demand curve has both output and price level as unknowns, and the actual price level and output cannot be determined until the aggregate supply side is added. The next chapter discusses how changes in the exogenous variables, which are mainly but not exclusively generated by government policy, result in shifts in the AD curve.

EXERCISES

1. Construct a consumption function where the taxes are no longer lump sum, but are a fixed percentage of income. Use this consumption function to construct an aggregate demand function for an economy with an income tax that is a fixed percentage of income. Do not substitute the government budget constraint in for G.
2. Consider the conbined life cycle–permanent income model of consumption. The discount factor is .95, and a one unit permanent change in disposable income results in a .9 change in consumption. How much will consumption change as a result of a one time only $100 increase in disposable income, which will take place in the current period and disappear next period?
3. In the Consumption function, as we developed it, an exchange by the government of government bonds for money—an exactly equal exchange—has no effect on the amount of consumption. Why? If Ricardian equivalence is true, should this exchange still have no effect on the amount of consumption? Explain.

6

Shifts in the Aggregate Demand Curve

In which the simple curve from the last chapter gets more complicated, as we see how both government and other sources of surprises cause it to jump around.

INTRODUCTION

As constructed in the preceding chapter, the aggregate demand curve in Figure 6.1 shows the relationship between the aggregate demand for output and the price level when M, B_g, B_p, T, G, ΔM, ΔB_g, and **I** are held constant. Just as a change in one of the exogenous variables to the right of the vertical line in the normal demand function causes a shift in the single good demand curve, a change in one of these exogenous variables in the Aggregate Demand function causes a *shift* in the Aggregate Demand curve. This is very different from a change in the price level with the exogenous variables in the above list held constant, which is analyzed by a movement along the AD curve. The nature of these shifts, and the set of shifts that is permitted, is of considerable interest, for this is the first step in analyzing the results of government policies.

Events that generate changes in the exogenous variables controlled by the government—T, G, M, B_g, ΔM, and ΔB_g—are fairly easy to imagine. New governments, new individuals in positions of authority in an old government, or new responses to the current economic situation because some old policy has been deemed not to be functioning correctly, are all some of the large set of possible sources for these types of exogenous changes. If government policy is determined by a large group of individuals, such as a combination of two houses of congress and a chief executive, it may be viewed by some of the agents of the society as exogenous.

However, a government's economic policy is rarely completely exogenous. One can build models for the behavior of politicians in terms of their own desires—their own utility functions—and the desires or utility functions of their constituents, and these kinds of models might be able to predict fairly well the government policy response in the face of different economic situations. In this case, the past and current path of the economy might provide useful information as to the kind of policy that the current government, with its set of constituents,

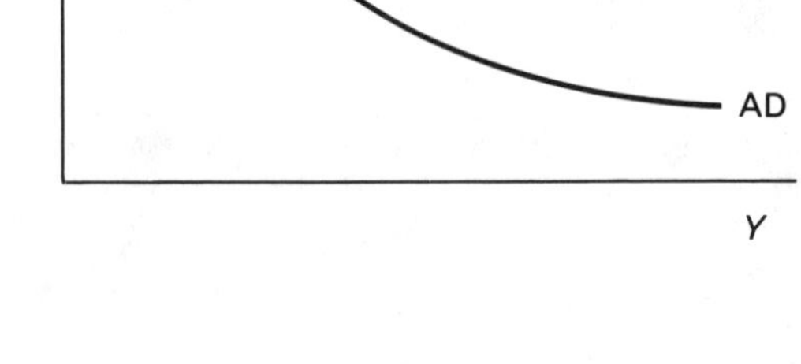

Figure 6.1

will follow. Nonetheless, we will find it much simpler in the beginning to think of the government as having a number of possible exogenous policies to choose from; therefore, our job as economists is to determine the results of each of these policies. The politicians then choose from that set the policy that they prefer. Once the set of results that correspond to the potential policy set is determined, then it may be that the choice that the politicians will make can be determined from economic theory.[1]

It is a bit more difficult to imagine what could be the source of an exogenous change in the other, nongovernment-controlled variables: Investment, **I**, and private bonds, B_p. One thing we could do is to suppose that people just decided that they should invest more or less—perhaps they were attacked by some wave of optimism or pessimism. In any case, it is quite likely that the value of **I** increased for some reason not determined inside our system. Some of these possible reasons were discussed in Chapter 5 in the section on investment, and we will heuristically appeal to these reasons when we wish to consider changes in investment or when we want to consider policies that we have reason to believe will change investment as a secondary effect. We will not change private bonds.

AN EXAMPLE OF A CHANGE IN INVESTMENT

In this first example, we will avoid the problem of the exogeneity of government policy by choosing to consider one of the variables that, at least at this point, we do not consider to be under the control of the government. This variable is investment. Suppose that some wave of pessimism attacks firms causing them to all suddenly believe that the future will be worse than the present, and thus they decide to reduce their investments. We want to see what this will do to the AD curve.

The simplest way to observe what happens to the aggregate demand curve from changes such as the ones mentioned above is to first fix the price level at some arbitrarily chosen value. Then, change the exogenous variable and calculate the resultant change in aggregate demand at the fixed price level. Suppose aggregate demand increases at that price level. Since the price level was chosen *arbitrarily* the implication is that the change in the exogenous variable resulted in an increase in aggregate demand at any and all price levels. This change at all price levels is represented by a rightward *shift* in the aggregate demand curve.

[1] This is really quite a complicated issue. If it is possible for the economist to model the set of politician's choices and their results, then it should be possible for households to do the same thing. This model then predicts the policy actions of the government and the resulting changes in household behavior. This change in household behavior might end up changing the result of the policy. The models of the politicians' behavior need to be updated with this response of the households and a cycle of reactions from politicians to households, each reacting to the other, can go on forever—or be solved by the mathematical tools of game theory.

Back to the example of an exogenous change in investment. Suppose I declines to some value less than its initial value of **I**, say to $\mathbf{I}_1$. Assume that all the other exogenous variables remain fixed. We must compare the aggregate demand for output, Y_1, at some arbitrarily chosen price, p_1, before the change to the aggregate demand for output at that same price level after the change. We will call the new aggregate demand for output Y_2. First calculate—by writing out the AD function—the initial aggregate demand for output at the price level you chose. Call it p_1. That AD function is written as

$$Y_1 = [1/(1 - \text{mpc})] \times [\mu \times ((M + B_g + B_p)/p_1) + \mathbf{I} + G - \text{mpc} \times T]$$

Write out the AD function with the new value for the changed exogenous variable but at the original price level, p_1. In this case, that gives a new aggregate demand for output of Y_2, where

$$Y_2 = [1/(1 - \text{mpc})] \times [\mu \times ((M + B_g + B_p)/p_1) + \mathbf{I}_1 + G - \text{mpc} \times T]$$

Point A on Figure 6.2 shows the initial aggregate demand Y_1 on the aggregate demand curve AD_1 at price level p_1.

To find the change in aggregate demand, we subtract Y_1 from Y_2. Doing so yields

$$Y_2 - Y_1 = [1/1 - \text{mpc})] \times [\mathbf{I}_1 - \mathbf{I}]$$

Only the effects of investment are left in this equation because all the other exogenous variables have not changed, and subtracting an unchanged variable from itself cancels it out. Since **I** is greater than $\mathbf{I}_1$, this means that the change in aggregate demand is negative, or a leftward shift in the AD curve. Since $1/(1 - \text{mpc})$ is approximately equal to 10 $[1/(1 - .9) = 1/.1 = 10]$, the change in aggregate demand is approximately ten times that of investment. Point B on Figure

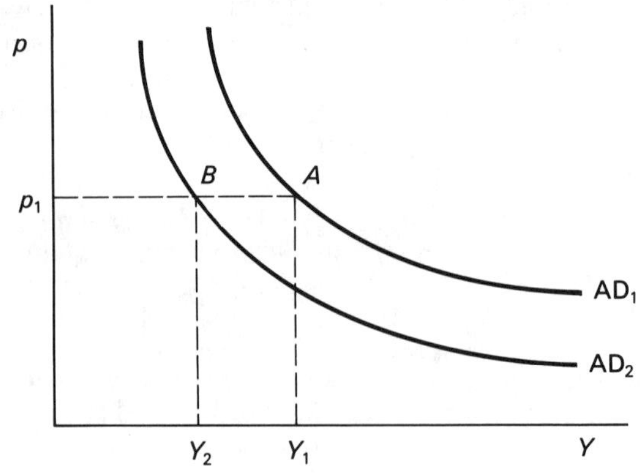

Figure 6.2

6.2 represents the change found above—the new value of aggregate demand is Y_2 at the price p_1. The horizontal distance from point A to point B is $1/(1 - \text{mpc}) \times [\mathbf{I}_1 - \mathbf{I}]$ as calculated above. Since p_1 was chosen randomly, the entire AD_1 curve shifts left to AD_2.

EXAMPLES OF GOVERNMENT POLICIES

Six of the other exogenous variables are often thought to be under the control of the government. These are M, B_g, T, G, ΔM, and ΔB_g. Before we discuss the results of changes in these policy variables, a brief discussion of the difference between M and ΔM is necessary. (The differences between B_g and ΔB_g are of the same type as those between M and ΔM, however, in that case the relationship holds for government bonds instead of money.)

M is the stock of money held by households. It is rather like the mound of poker chips piled up in front of a player. ΔM (which can be either positive or negative, as we will see below) is the flow of money into and out of the economy as the result of government's fiscal policy. It is caused either by the government using issues of new money each period to finance the then-current federal deficit, or by the government retiring old money when there is a budget surplus. (This has happened.) The real value of ΔM—that is, $\Delta M/p$—changes in response to changes in the other variables in the government's budget constraint. Since it is a flow variable, one can think of ΔM as being the changes that take place in the player's pot as the game progresses. These are the winnings and losings from each hand that flow into and out of the stock of chips.

Changes in M caused by ΔM are *not* the only way that M can change. There are several ways that the government can change the stock of money without changing the flow as measured by ΔM. The government could print money and distribute it in some random method to the citizens of the country. Milton Friedman once made the famous suggestion that the money can be thought of as being dropped from helicopters. While this is very unrealistic, there are some important reasons for making the distinction between the instantaneous changes in the stock that result from some kind of government policy—the kind of changes that result from **monetary policy** and fall under the control of the Federal Reserve Board—and the changes in the flow of money into the economy that are controlled by the budget process—a fiscal deficit or surplus—and will, over time, cause changes in the stock. In our poker chip example, the helicopter money is as if someone dropped an extra pile of chips in front of some of the players. ΔB_g reflects the use of new government bonds to finance the fiscal deficit or surplus. Changes in B_g, the instantaneous changes, result from monetary policies that change the mix of money and government bonds in the economy.

What would be the result of some instantaneous change in the money stock, M, by the gifts to all of the citizens—that is really, by monetary policy—for example? M would increase from some M_1 to some M_2. Holding p constant at some p_1, as we did above when we considered investment and looking at the equation for aggregate demand,

$$Y_1 = [1/(1 - \text{mpc})] \times [\mu \times (M_1 + B_p + B_g)/p_1 + \mathbf{I} + G - \text{mpc} \times T]$$

we can see that the increase of Y would be

$$Y_2 - Y_1 = [1/(1 - \text{mpc})] \times \mu \times (M_2 - M_1)/p_1$$

where $M_2 - M_1$ is the increase in the money stock. This increase in Y at a fixed price level, p_1, would result in a rightward shift in the aggregate demand curve. At each price, p, aggregate demand has increased by $[1/(1 - \text{mpc})] \times \mu \times (M_2 - M_1)/p$. In Figure 6.2, this would be represented by a shift from AD_2 to AD_1. (Note: In Figure 6.2, Y_1 and Y_2 are the reverse of those in the example directly above.)

Exogenous changes in ΔM, ΔB_g, G, or T are not that simple. They are related to each other by the government budget constraint,

$$G = T + \Delta M/p + \Delta B_g/p$$

$\Delta M/p$ is the real value of the government expenditures that are funded by the issue of new money, and $\Delta B_g/p$ is the real value of government expenditures funded by new bond issue. The sum of $\Delta M/p$ and $\Delta B_g/p$ is the amount of government expenditures that are *not* paid for by taxes. (This can be positive or negative. It is negative when the government taxes more than it spends.)

An exogenous increase in T with both ΔM and $\Delta B_g/p$ constant can occur only if G increases the same amount as does T. Otherwise, the government budget constraint will not hold. Policies where the change in T equals the change in G are called **Balanced Budget Policies.** They are so called because if the government budget had been balanced before the policy—that is, if T equaled G—then the budget would still be balanced after the policy. Other government policies are possible. The government can reduce T, keep G and ΔB_g constant, and therefore increase $\Delta M/p$ by increasing ΔM. It may change G, keep T and ΔB_g constant, and pay for the change in expenditures with a change in the money flow, ΔM. A complicated policy, whereby all four change somehow, yet so that the government budget constraint still holds, is also possible (and more than likely). An example of this type of policy is one where the government promises to reduce taxes and increase military spending while reducing no other government expenditures, and pays for the difference with an increase in both ΔM and ΔB_g—that is, with an issue of both new money and new bonds.

We will examine only one of the above policies here. (It is strongly recommended that the reader attempt to determine the direction of the shift of the aggregate demand curve that would result from the other policies mentioned.) Let us look at the last of the policies mentioned above: let T decrease, G increase, and then, in the complete version, $\Delta M/p$ and $\Delta B_g/p$ must increase to make up the difference.

First, fix p at p_1. (Remember to first fix the price level every time you analyze a policy that changes the aggregate demand side of the model.) T decreases from T_1 to T_2, and G increases from G_1 to G_2. Using the government budget constraint, we can see that the sum of the change in money flows, $\Delta M_2 - \Delta M_1$, and the change in the flow of new government bonds into the economy, $\Delta B_{g2} - \Delta B_{g1}$, must be

$$(\Delta M_2 - \Delta M_1 + \Delta B_{g2} - \Delta B_{g1})/p_1 = G_2 - G_1 - (T_2 - T_1)$$

which is positive and greater than the absolute value of the change in taxes, $T_1 - T_2$. If we really wanted to keep track of the paths of M and B_g through time, we would use each period's ΔM and ΔB_g to update these paths. We will ignore this complication in most of what we do. Only the changes in T and G show up directly in the Aggregate Demand curve.

The initial AD function is

$$Y_1 = [1/(1 - \text{mpc})] \times [\mu \times (M + B_p + B_g)/p_1 + \mathbf{I} + G_1 - \text{mpc} \times T_1]$$

After the changes in government expenditures and taxes, it is

$$Y_2 = [1/(1 - \text{mpc})] \times [\mu \times (M + B_p + B_g)/p_1 + \mathbf{I} + G_2 - \text{mpc} \times T_2]$$

The change in aggregate demand at price p_1 is equal to

$$Y_2 - Y_1 = [1/(1 - \text{mpc})] \times [G_2 - G_1 - \text{mpc} \times (T_2 - T_1)]$$

where $G_2 - G_1$ is positive and $T_2 - T_1$ is negative (because taxes decrease). Since we are subtracting mpc $\times$ $(T_2 - T_1)$, we are subtracting .9 times the negative change in taxes. The second part of the above equation in square brackets equals the increase in government expenditures plus .9 times the absolute value of the change in taxes. In this example, if G increased \$200 million and taxes dropped \$300 million, then the part of the above equation in square brackets, assuming mpc = .9, equals \$200 million plus .9 × \$300 million or \$470 million. To find the shift in the AD curve, that change is multiplied by 10, since 1/(1 − .9) equals 10. The shift out in the AD curve at price p_1 is \$4.7 billion. The net result of this particular policy is a shift in the AD curve that is a tenfold response to the increase in government expenditures added to a positive-valued ninefold response to the decline in taxes.

EXERCISES

1. Suppose that the government, adopting a balanced budget policy, cuts taxes and government expenditures by the same amount. What is the resultant shift in the AD curve? How large is this shift compared to a cut of the same size in taxes alone? How large is this shift compared to a cut in government expenditures alone? Are the directions of these shifts the same?
2. Use the AD curve you constructed in Exercise 1, Chapter 5, where taxes were collected as a percentage of income. A cut in the percentage of the income tax will result in what kind of shift in the AD curve?
3. Milton Friedman has described monetary policies, using the analogy "helicopter money." This is new money that is dumped onto the economy by helicopters and causes an increase in M (and of the exogenous variables *only* M is changed). What does this policy do to the AD curve? How is it different from an exchange of government bonds for money (called open market operations)?
4. Consider a model in which investment is a function of income: $I = i \times Y$, where i is a constant (say $i = .05$). Construct the AD curve for this economy. Do the balanced budget policies of Exercise 1 generate larger or smaller shifts in the AD curve of this exercise than in Exercise 1?

7

"Classical" Aggregate Supply Curve

In which we construct our first complete model. But first, we create an aggregate supply curve by much curve flipping. The production side of this classical economy is one in which all markets clear, so no one is ever unemployed without wanting to be.

INTRODUCTION

What we will call the "classical" economic model—the one that held sway before the 1930s—assumed that all markets worked perfectly.[1] Wages and prices adjusted to clear all markets. (A market clears when the price adjusts so that the quantity produced exactly equals the quantity people want to buy. This is the same as an unrestricted, single good market equilibrium.) This meant that wages—that is, a real wage, the wage in terms of the good produced—adjusted until all the people who wanted work at that wage found work and at the same time employers were employing exactly the number of workers they wanted to employ. There might have been people who were not working, but they were doing so voluntarily; the unemployed were those who chose not to enter the labor market at the prevailing wage. Those people preferred leisure to the income they would receive at the prevailing wage. At the equilibrium wage, no one who wanted work was without a job.

We will construct an aggregate supply curve to complete the model begun with the aggregate demand curve that we constructed in the preceding chapters. This aggregate supply curve will show the quantity of output of the one aggregate good in the economy that the productive sector of that economy is willing to produce at each price level. This curve is loosely similar in concept to a standard supply curve, which shows the quantity of some particular good that firms are willing and able to produce at each price. In this chapter, the aggregate supply curve that we develop is "classical"; it assumes that markets work perfectly. In future chapters, we will construct other aggregate supply curves under other sets of assumptions about labor market behavior.

THE PRODUCTION FUNCTION

The one good in the economy is produced using all of the stock of capital and that portion of the labor stock that firms wish to hire at the wage that is determined by an equilibrium in the labor market. No other factors of production exist. Capital is the accumulated past net investments in the economy and is generally considered to be unchanged and unchangeable *during* any period.(Today's investment, **I**, isn't involved in production until the next period, so no amount of investment today can change the existing capital stock. As far as we are concerned, the capital stock is fixed *in* each period.) The capital stock can—and often will—change from one period to the next. The assumption that the capital stock is fixed during any

[1] Economists at that time did not use a model in the form we are building. Our model does, however, incorporate all their basic assumptions in a very organized method, and gives the main results that arose from the "classical" models.

given period is made to simplify the analysis. In a model with discrete time periods, such as we will be using, some of the characteristics of the continuous-time "real world" seem to get lost. But investment does take time to come on line—to become productive—and our one-period lag in investment becoming a part of the capital stock captures something of this delay.

Labor is also used in production. Since the quantity of capital is fixed, or predetermined, and the amount of labor that can be used in production in any period is allowed to change, we can graph a relationship between the amount of labor being employed and the output, or production, in the economy. With fixed capital, output is a function only of the quantity of labor.

The information concerning the technology available to the economy is expressed in a production function of the form,

$$Y = f(L, K) \tag{7.1}$$

where Y is the quantity of output produced, L is the labor, and K is the capital being used in production. Thus, $f(L, K)$ is the function—black box or computer program—that tells us the level of output generated by any given combination of capital and labor. If we fix capital at K, our production function, which we show below as a **production curve,** tells us how output changes as the amount of labor being employed changes. Figure 7.1 shows this relationship.

With a labor force of L_1 and capital stock of K, Figure 7.1 shows that Y_1 units of output would be produced. The shape of the production function, with fixed capital, shows that the technology exhibits positive but diminishing marginal returns from labor. The "positive" part of the phrase means that each additional worker produces some positive additional amount of output. With this condition, the production curve may increase forever or may approach an asymptote, but will not turn downward. A downward-sloping production curve means that additional workers actually reduce the amount of output. At the very least, one can ask the additional workers to stay out of the way and their contribution to production will be zero. The "diminishing" part of the marginal return assumption means that the

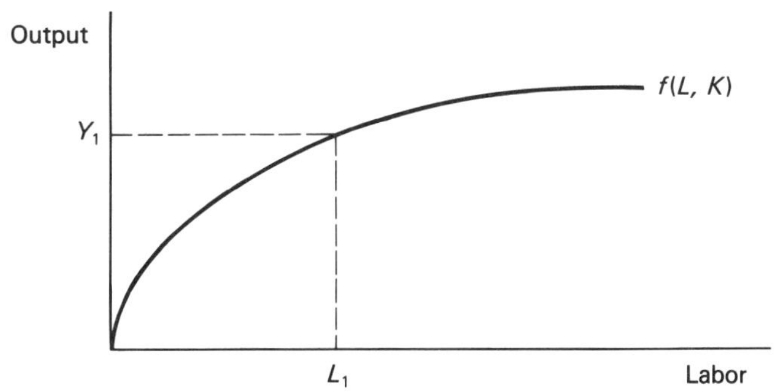

Figure 7.1

increase in total production by a new worker will be something less than the increase in total production generated by the last worker hired just before that new worker. If the 256th worker generated an additional fifty-six units of output, the 257th worker will generate some positive amount of additional output less than fifty-six units. The additional output generated by the 258th worker will be something less than the additional output generated by the 257th, and so on. Since these new workers add less to total production than did the ones before, each additional worker is less valuable to the firm, and to the economy, than the one hired before him or her. This characteristic of the production function is important in determining the behavior of firms in the labor market. In fact, this production function characteristic generates the demand curve for labor.

THE LABOR MARKET

In a competitive economy, workers are paid a real wage equal to their marginal product—the amount that output increases because of their labor.[2] Therefore, we can write a relationship between real wages and a function of labor and capital that is related to the production function. (This function is really the partial derivative of the production function with respect to labor.) This function can be written as

$$w/p = f_L(L, K)$$

where w is the nominal wage—the wage in terms of money—and p is the price level. The equation is written $f_L(L, K)$, called "f sub L," to remind us that it is related to the production function $f(L, K)$.[3] The function $f_L(L, K)$ tells us the slope of the production function at each value of L and K. An examination of Figure 7.2 will show that the slope of the production curve gets flatter and flatter as the quantity of labor increases.

The lines labeled A, B, and C illustrate the slope of the production curve, $f(L, K)$, at points L_1, L_2, and L_3, respectively. Notice that as the quantity of labor increases the slope of the lines gets flatter. At each point on the production curve, the slope is the contribution to output of the last, infinitesimally small increase in labor. A firm will be willing to pay workers a real wage no greater than their marginal product, this increase in output from the last, infinitesimally small

[2] The real wage is the wage in terms of the one good produced. In a more general setting, it represents the quantity of real goods that the workers can purchase with their wages. It is equal to the nominal wage divided by the price level.

[3] The function $f_L(L, K)$ gives the partial derivative with respect to labor of the production function, $f(L, K)$, for all sets of L and K. When K is fixed at some constant value, the partial derivative with respect to labor is nothing more than a function that gives the slope of the production curve, Figure 7.1, at each quantity of labor. Since the production curve approaches an asymptote, the wage function, $f_L(L, K)$, approaches zero as the amount of labor increases.

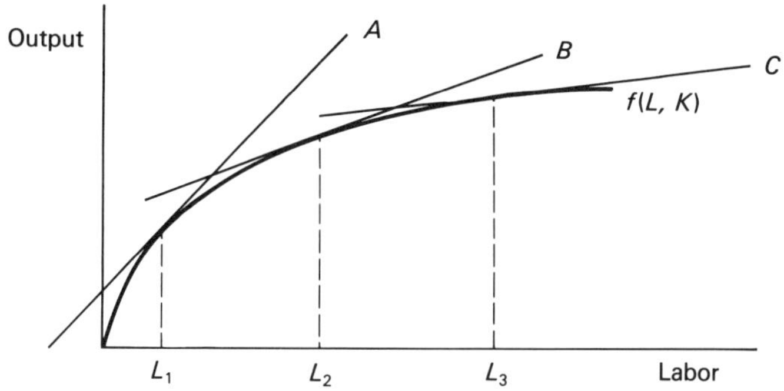

Figure 7.2

increase in output, and will be willing to hire workers up to the point where their marginal product is equal to their wage. To pay a wage that is greater than the marginal product means that the worker is not generating sufficient output to cover that wage and the firm loses profits on that worker. A profit-maximizing firm would not hire a worker at such a wage. If the marginal product of the last worker is less than the wage, there are some unexploited profit opportunities still available to the firm.

Figure 7.3 shows a graph of the value of the slope at different quantities of labor. (For now, ignore the label on the vertical axis.) The vertical distances on the graph at points L_1, L_2, and L_3 equal the slope from Figure 7.2. The equation 7.2 is the inverse of a **demand curve for labor** since it can be interpreted as giving the quantity of labor that firms will be willing to hire at each real wage. (The demand curve for labor shows the real wage firms will be willing to pay at each quantity of labor. Taking the inverse of a two-variable equation creates a new equation, in which the role of the endogenous and exogenous variables are switched.) When K is fixed at some **K**, the equation 7.2 is a relationship between real wages and the quantity of labor that firms will want to hire, or demand. At low real wages—the real wage equals money, or nominal, wage divided by the price level and represents the wage in terms of the one good in our economy—firms will want to hire many

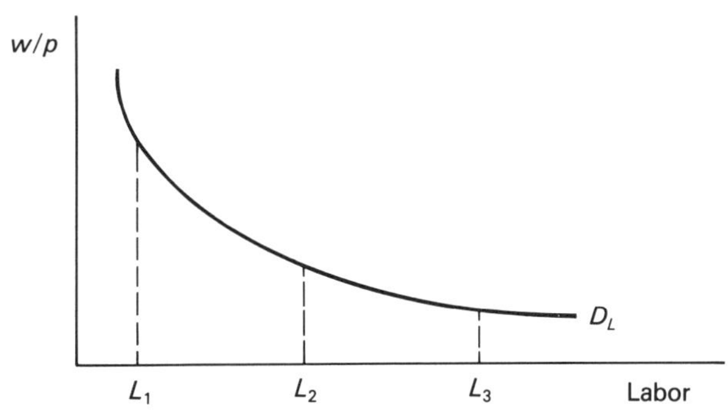

Figure 7.3

workers, because a large number of workers can be hired before the marginal product drops below the low real wage. At high real wages few workers will be wanted because the firm can only hire a few workers before their marginal product drops below their real wage. If workers can be hired continuously—for 27.3 hours a week, for example—then workers will be hired until the marginal product of the last second worked by the last worker hired is exactly equal to the real wage. Figure 7.3 shows a demand curve (D_L) for labor that incorporates all of these considerations.

There is also a **supply curve for labor.**[4] Households are willing to offer greater amounts of labor into the market as the real wage increases. One way this can be explained is by considering the value of the leisure given up to work to earn income. If individuals view leisure as a good (as opposed to a "bad"?), then households view different wages as the different prices that they must pay for their leisure, since the price of leisure is the forgone wages; individuals choose to consume a mixed bundle of goods and leisure. It is believed that, up to some point, a higher per hour real wage will cause households to offer more labor or labor hours to the labor market. A labor supply curve (S_L) is shown in Figure 7.4.

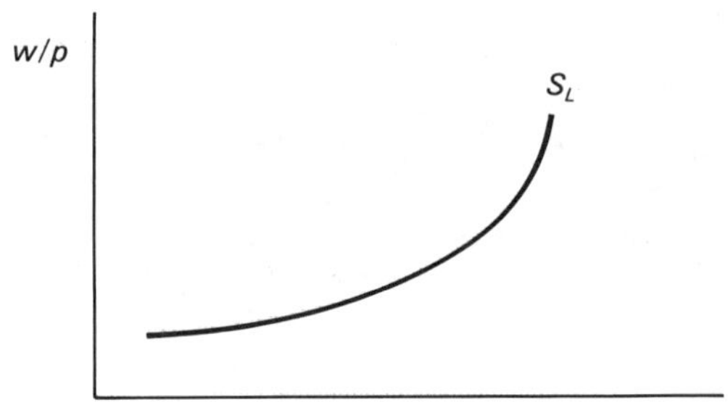

Figure 7.4

Note that we have abstracted a bit here. Such institutional items as unions, labor contracts, and the forty (or thirty-seven and a half) hour week are ignored. It is possible in our model that a household offers 26.5 hours of labor a week at some real wage rate. It must be admitted that the institutional structure of the formal portion of the labor market in most countries means that this sort of behavior is seldom seen. There is also a possibility that the supply curve for labor has a strange shape. At high real wages, individuals may choose to consume *more* leisure in response to increases in their wages. In some of the less developed countries, for example, a worker may enter the labor market from the subsistence agricultural sector in order to earn a specific amount of money in order to make a specific purchase. (In some third world subsistence economies, families send their sons into the cities for short periods of time to earn money to purchase specific goods, like radios, and/or to pay the head tax that many of these countries impose.) In this

[4] The appendix to this chapter shows how a supply curve for labor can be constructed given individual preferences between income and leisure. This approach uses the indifference curve analysis developed in the appendix to Chapter 3.

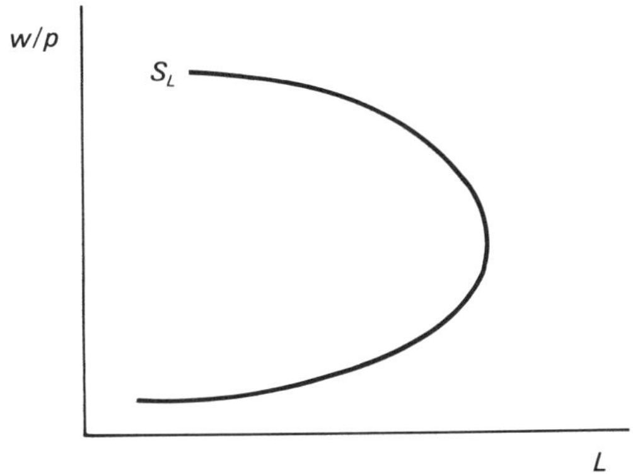

Figure 7.5

case the supply curve for labor could be backward bending. Figure 7.5 shows such a supply curve. In the top half of this labor supply curve, increased wages result in less rather than more labor being supplied to the labor market. At higher wages, workers from the subsistence sector need to work less to earn the money necessary to purchase the particular good that they temporarily migrated to the city to obtain. It has also been suggested that this kind of supply curve for labor occurs for individuals in such high-paying occupations as medicine, especially as they get older. We will ignore this possibility and assume that our supply curve for labor is as in Figure 7.4.

We now put the labor demand curve from Figure 7.3 and the labor supply curve from Figure 7.4 on the same graph in Figure 7.6a (note that the axes have been rotated so that the real wage is on the horizontal axis and the quantity of labor is on the vertical axis[5]) and at the intersection of these two curves we find an equilibrium (labor market clearing) real wage, **w/p,** and an equilibrium amount of labor **L.**[6]

[5] If you have trouble visualizing any of these changes in the positions of the graphs, the best way to see what is happening is to draw the graph in its normal position and then rotate the page in the suggested manner and hold it against a window (if the page was flipped) to see how the curves go. It is better to do this during the daylight hours.

[6] One of the reasons that the backward-bending supply curve for labor was dropped is that it complicates the labor market. It is possible to get two equilibrium wage rates or none at all. The following figures illustrate this point.

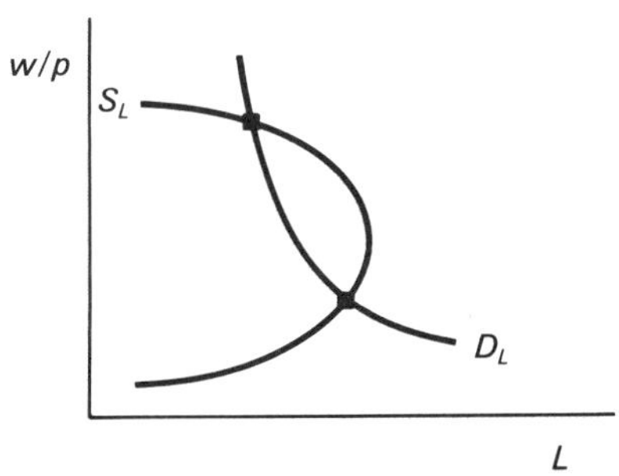

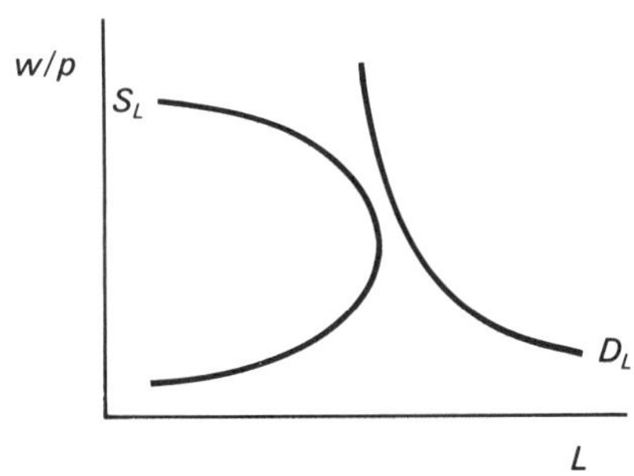

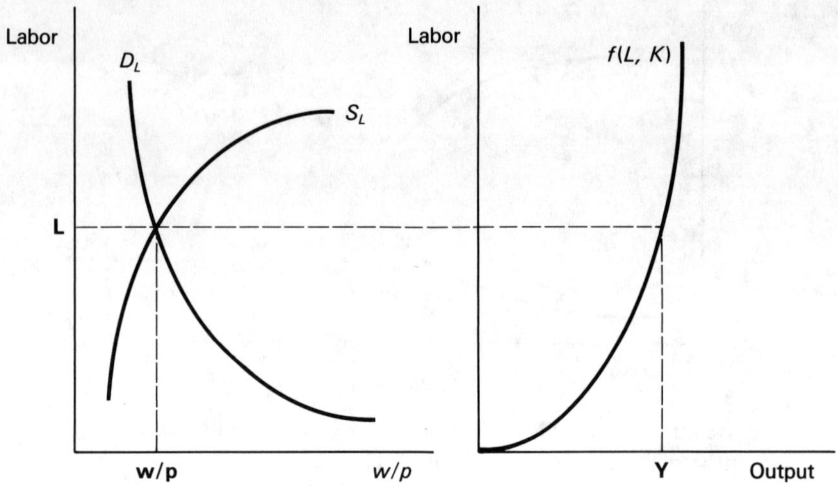

(a) (b)

Figure 7.6

In this case, **L** can also be referred to as the full employment level, since all of those who wish to work at the prevailing wage are employed. Figure 7.6b shows the graph of the production curve. It is Figure 7.1 with its axes flipped. Since **L** is the amount of labor being supplied and used, we can use the production curve graph to tell us how much output is being produced. Measuring across to the production curve at **L** and then down, we find that output is **Y.** Note that this is the level of output that is consistent with the equilibrium in the labor market. In later models,

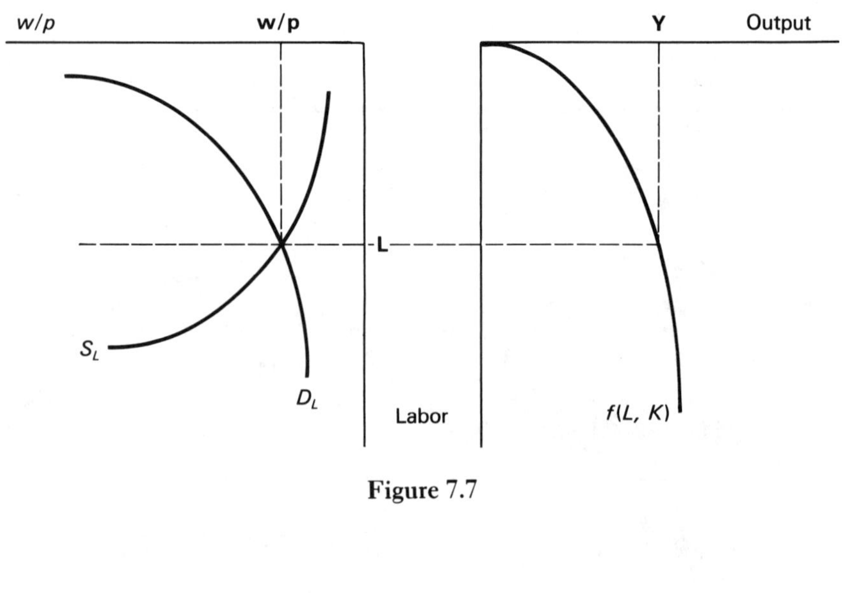

Figure 7.7

the output that is generated at the equilibrium in the labor market will be called the **full employment output.**

Figure 7.7 shows the graphs in Figures 7.6a and b flipped to the orientation that we will use in the AS curve. First the labor market curve was switched, so that the labor axis backed up against the labor axis of Figure 7.6b. These axes are measuring the same things in the same units. Then both of the graphs were flipped top to bottom. We now have output on a horizontal axis, and are preparing for the AS curve. Notice that real wages increase as we head left on the w/p–L plane, that labor increases as we move downward, and that output increases to the right on the L–Y plane.

THE PRICE—REAL WAGE CURVE

We are almost to our aggregate supply curve—that is, the curve that shows the quantity of output that is produced in the economy at each price level. First, think of real wages as a function of the price level. In the classical model, we are always in equilibrium in the labor market. The real wage is determined by the supply and demand curves for labor, which is a function of real wages. As the price level, *p*, changes, the equilibrium real wage, **w/p,** remains unchanged. This is because only real wages affect consumer and producer decisions in the labor market. That means that when there are changes in the price level, the nominal wage, *w*, must change in a way exactly proportional to the change in the price level in order to keep real wages at their equilibrium value. Under these conditions, we would get a relationship between real wages and the price level as shown in Figure 7.8. This

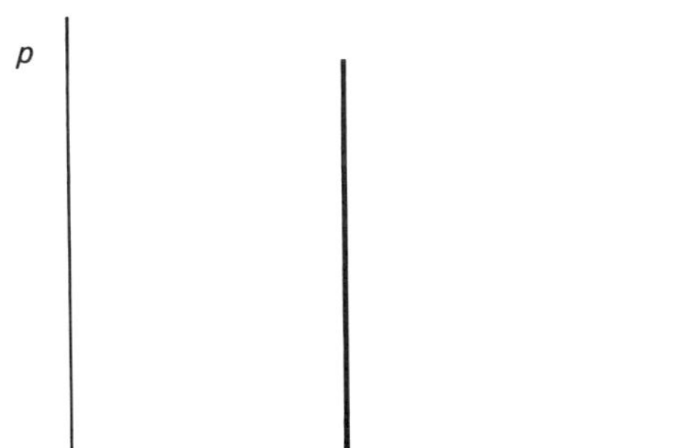

Figure 7.8

curve (in this case, a straight line) shows that, because of the rapid adjustment in the nominal wage, real wages are unaffected by price changes. The vertical line is directly above the equilibrium real wage, **w/p,** that we found in Figure 7.6a, and that is on the horizontial axis in Figure 7.7.

If we flip the price–real wage plane so that the price axis is on the right, we

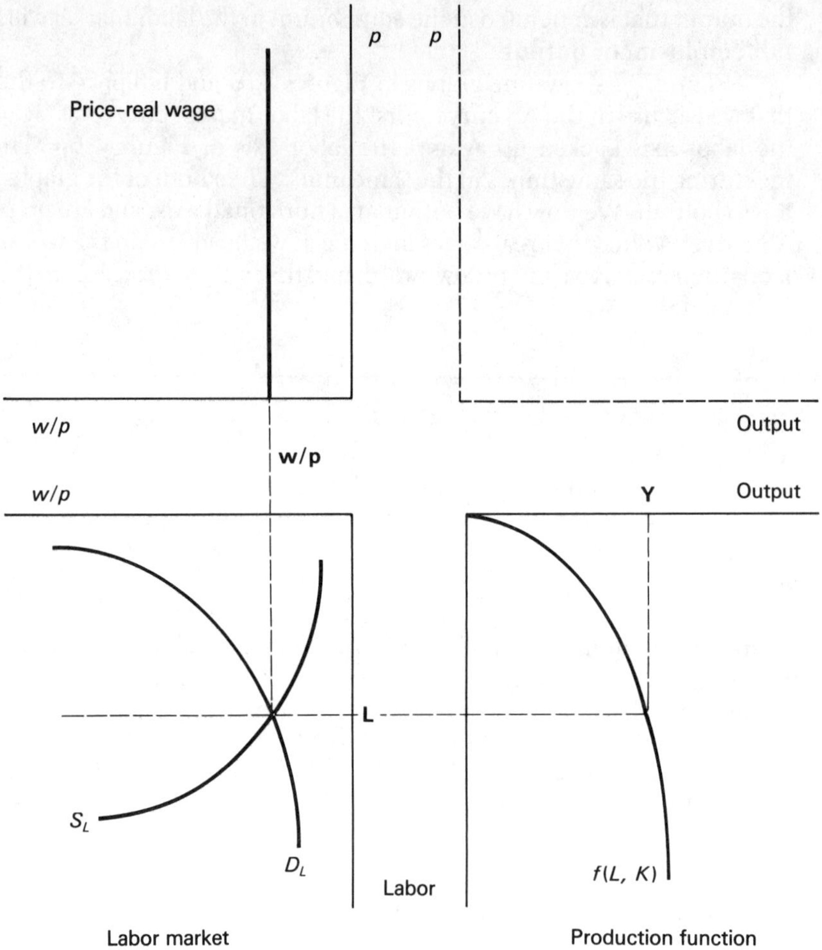

Figure 7.9

have the real wage being measured in the same way that it was in Figure 7.7. The price axis heads upward above the labor axis. This is shown in Figure 7.9. We would then also have a price–output plane being formed to the right of the price–real wage plane. In Figure 7.9, the price–output axis is drawn in with dotted lines. On this part of the graph we construct the aggregate supply curve.

THE AGGREGATE SUPPLY CURVE. FINALLY!

Figure 7.10 puts together all of the above topics. This is not difficult to do, but be careful, here, to keep track of the way that the axes are labeled.

The southwestern section, called the labor market quadrant, shows the

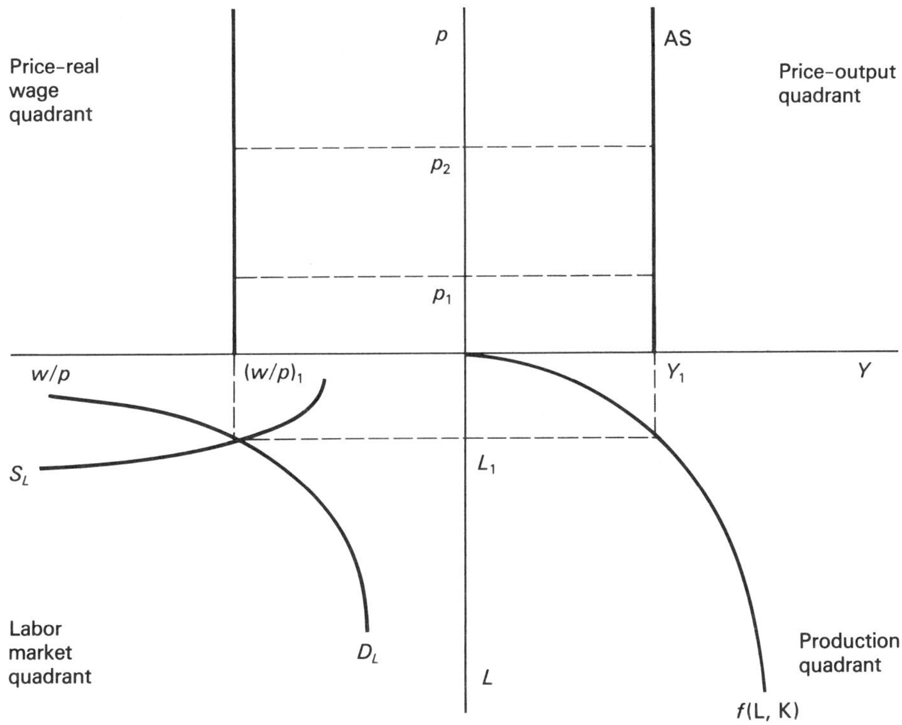

Figure 7.10

supply and demand curves for labor (This is Figure 7.6, flipped both horizontally and vertically.) The southeastern section, called the production quadrant, shows the production curve graph (Figure 7.6b, flipped vertically). The two of these, as in Figure 7.6, determine the real wage, $\mathbf{w/p_1}$, the employment level, $\mathbf{L_1}$, and the output, $\mathbf{Y_1}$. The bottom part of this graph looks just like Figure 7.7. The northwestern section, the price–real wage quadrant, is Figure 7.8 flipped horizontally, and shows how real wages change with the price level. We can now use these three sets of graphs to construct the AS curve on the northeastern section, the price–output quadrant. Figure 7.10 is a version of Figure 7.9, with the duplicate axes combined together as one. We automatically have a price–output quadrant generated by the unification of the pairs of axes.

To generate the aggregate supply curve, we want to find out how much output will be produced at each price. We choose some price level (for example, p_1) and find that at that price level, the real wages are the equilibrium real wage $(w/p)_1$. At this real wage the labor supplied and demanded in the labor market is L_1. When used with the capital stock, K, that quantity of labor generates output Y_1. So we have one point on the Aggregate Supply curve, point P_1–Y_1. At any other price level (for example, p_2) the real wage, the quantity of labor is supplied and demanded in the labor market, and the output is the same as at price p_1. So point p_2–Y_1 is another point on the aggregate supply curve. Output does not change in this classical aggregate supply curve when there are changes in the price level. This is continued for many more prices and the summarized results are shown in the price–output quadrant. The vertical line, labeled AS, is our "classical" aggregate supply curve.

EQUILIBRIUM IN THE CLASSICAL MODEL

Combining the aggregate demand curve from Chapter 5 and the "classical" aggregate supply curve that we have just derived, we find the equilibrium output and price level for our classical model. Figure 7.11 shows such an equilibrium, where the entire structure that generated the AS curve as in Figure 7.10 has been left out. At the intersection of the AD and AS curves we find that the equilibrium level of output is **Y** and the equilibrium price level is **p**.

Note that in this model the quantity of output is determined entirely by production considerations. (Because the AS curve is vertical it does not matter in terms of the equilibrium output where the AD curve crosses the AS curve.) It is the equilibrium price level that is determined, however, by the interaction of the AD and AS curves. The higher the AD curve, the higher the equilibrium price level. Shifts in the aggregate demand curve caused, for example, by certain government policy changes have no immediate effects on total output but will change the price level and may change other variables of interest: for example, consumption. A very important result of the classical model is that no demand-side policy can change current output. Demand-side policies that have effects on investment decisions can change the capital stock in the future and these changes will have important effects on the growth *path* the economy follows but not on the current output level. An example of one such demand side policy, and how it does not change current output, might be useful.

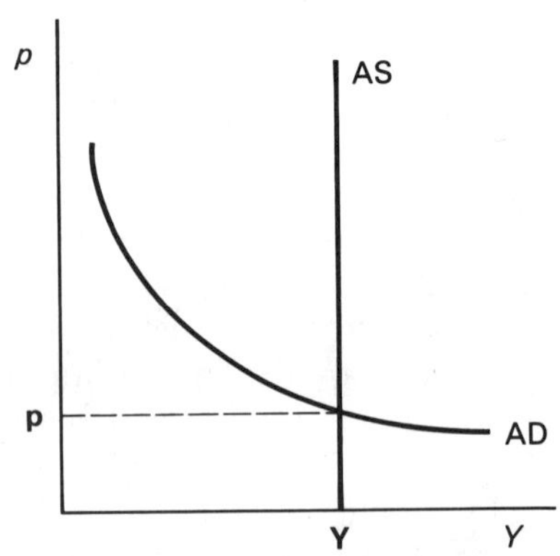

Figure 7.11

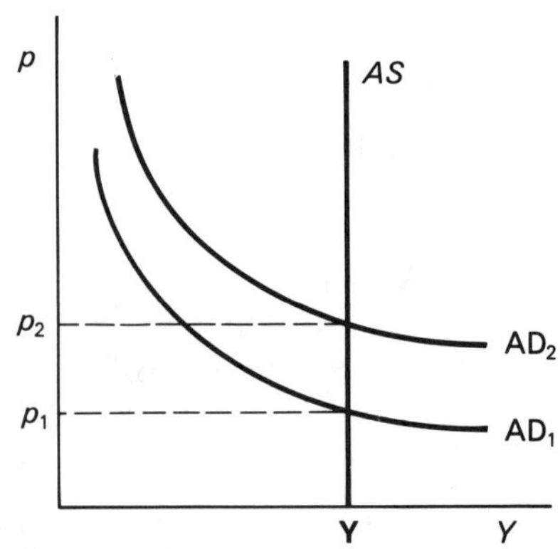

Figure 7.12

A POLICY EXAMPLE

Suppose the government increases taxes, T, and government expenditures, G, the same amount. From the government budget constraint,

$$G = T + \Delta M/p + \Delta B_g/p$$

we can see that the increases in G and T balance each other out, and no change in $\Delta M/p + \Delta B_g/p$ will result from this policy. Of the variables in the aggregate demand function,

$$Y = [1/(1 - \text{mpc})] \times [\mu \times ((M + B_g + B_p)/\text{p}] + I + G - \text{mpc} \times T]$$

only T and G will change, and these will increase by the same amount. Comparing the initial demand for output at some price, p_1, to the demand for output at that price after the change, we have

$$Y_2 - Y_1 = [1/(1 - \text{mpc})] \times [G_2 - G_1 - \text{mpc} \times (T_2 - T_1)]$$

Since because of the balanced budget assumption in the example, $G_2 - G_1$ equals $T_2 - T_1$, we can write the above equation as

$$\begin{aligned} Y_2 - Y_1 &= [1/(1 - \text{mpc})] \times [G_2 - G_1 - \text{mpc} \times (G_2 - G_1)] \\ &= [1/(1 - \text{mpc})] \times (G_2 - G_1) \times [1 - \text{mpc}] = G_2 - G_1 \end{aligned}$$

This means, at any fixed price level, that the demand for output, Y, increases; therefore, the AD curve shifts right, or out, by exactly the change in government expenditures. This is shown in Figure 7.12. The new aggregate demand curve is labeled AD_2. The resultant equilibrium price is p_2—output is unchanged at **Y**.

At this new equilibrium price level p_2, we find that the government either prints more new dollars, ΔM, or new bonds, ΔB_g, to cover the same real deficit, or buys more to cover the same real surplus. A slight manipulation of the government's budget constraint gives

$$G - T = \Delta M/p + \Delta B_g/p$$

Since G and T declined by the same amount, $\Delta M/p + \Delta B_g/p$ remains the same—that is, real value is unchanged. However, the equilibrium price, now p_2, is higher, so a larger ΔM and/or ΔB_g is needed to get the same real value as before.

Note that consumption declines. Remembering that the consumption function was

$$C = \text{mpc} \times (Y - T) + \mu \times [(M + B_g + B_p)/p)$$

we can see that consumption falls for two reasons. First, the increase in taxes decreases disposable income $[(Y - T)$ shrinks when Y is fixed]. Second, with the stock of money and bonds, M, B_g, and B_p, constant during the period, the increase in the price level reduces real wealth. The same change in consumption can be demonstrated by looking at the National Income Accounting Identity. Since $Y = C + I + G$, and since Y and I are unchanged, then if G increases, C must go down by the same amount, to allow the National Income Accounting Identity to continue to hold. It is useful to remember both of these methods for finding consumption movements. Sometimes it is possible to find out what would happen to consumption by using one of these methods (say, with the National Income Accounting Identity) when it is difficult or ambiguous using the other (say, the consumption function).

To summarize, an equal increase in taxes and government expenditures left total output unchanged, shifted output from individual consumption to the government, and raised prices.

SUPPLY SIDE ECONOMICS—THE CLASSICAL VERSION

The Reagan administration made its mark on economics, for either good or bad, with the introduction of a theory known as **supply side economics.** This theory concentrates on the long-term effects of government policies on the productive, or "supply," half of the aggregate demand and supply model. As we saw above, short run government fiscal policies—changes in taxes and government expenditures—do not change the aggregate level of output in the period in which they take place. If they do not have effects on investment, the capital stock, or the labor market, then they may not ever have effects on aggregate output. The Reagan supply side theory concentrates on the effects of government income tax policy on investment.

Assume that a cut in government taxes—one that, for simplicity's sake and contrary to events, is matched by an equal reduction in government expenditures—that generates an equal-sized increase in investment. (It is not at all obvious why investment must increase that much, but this is *their* theory.) Therefore, G and T are both reduced; from the government budget constraint, there is no change in either $\Delta M/p$ or $\Delta B_g/p$, and I increases by the decline in T. The aggregate demand curve is

$$Y = [1/(1 - \text{mpc})] \times \{\mu \times [(M + B_g + B_p)/p] + I + G - \text{mpc} \times T\}$$

Let the subscripts $_1$ and $_2$ respectively refer to before and after the change. Then

$$Y_2 - Y_1 = [1/(1 - \text{mpc})] \times [I_2 - I_1] + G_2 - G_1$$

Since $I_2 - I_1$ equals $G_2 - G_1$ in absolute value, but with opposite signs, the net result, if we use an mpc equal to .9 is a shift out in the AD curve equal to 9 times the increase in investment. That is the same kind of shift that is illustrated in Figure 7.12, but in this case the shift is much larger. Output does not change, but prices rise. Because this was our assumption, investment has gone up, and from the consumption function

$$C = \text{mpc}(Y - T) + \mu \times [(M + B)/p]$$

we see that disposable income increases, but real wealth declines. The use of the consumption function gives us an ambiguous result about the direction of the change in consumption. However, the National Income Accounting Identity says

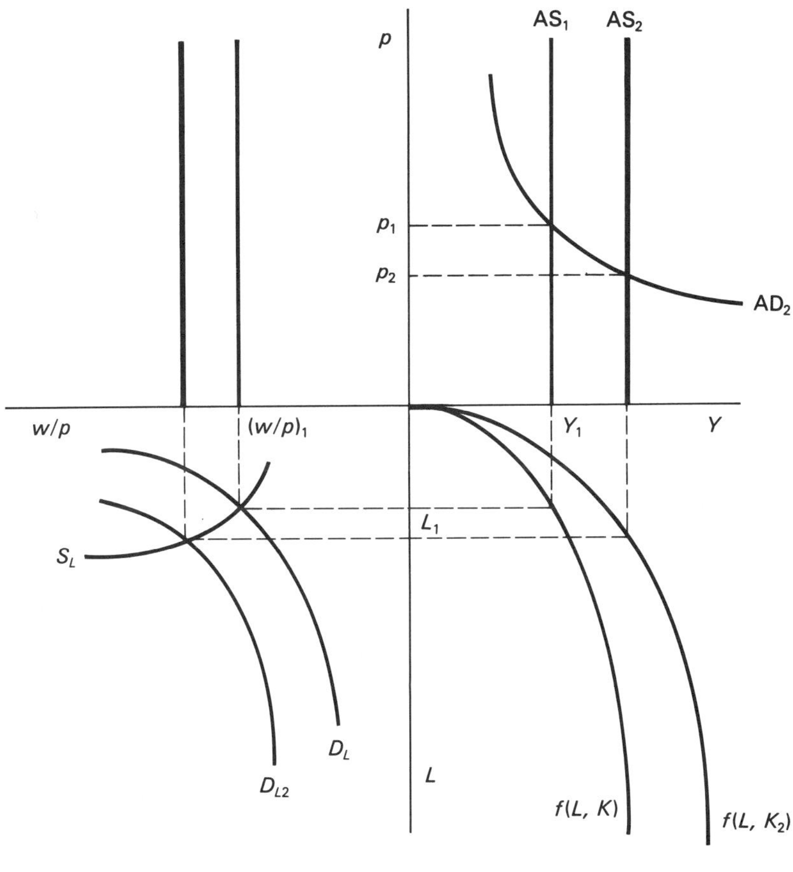

Figure 7.13

that consumption is unchanged. With $Y = C + I + G$, when Y does not change and I increases by the same amount that G declines, the changes in I and G cancel each other out, and C remains constant.

The important part of this supply side economics theory comes next. The increase in investment in the first period results in an increase in the capital stock in the second period, so K increases to K_2. As a result of this increase in K, both the production curve and the demand curve for labor will shift out. The demand curve for labor shifts out because with the additional capital the marginal product of labor increases, and because this is equal to the real wage that firms will offer, at each level of labor the offered wage will be higher. Figure 7.13 shows the result of these changes, which cause the shift out in the AS curve from AS_1 to AS_2.

We get a new equilibrium in the labor market at a higher real wage. This is illustrated by the intersection of the S_L and the D_{L2} curves under the new, thicker price–real wage line. More workers are employed, and with the new, higher production curve, we get a new, higher level of output. The AS_2 curve shows this new output level. If the government does not change its policies from period one to period two, the new equilibrium will give a higher output at a lower price level, p_2, than the equilibrium in period one. Consumption also goes up between these two periods as government expenditures and taxes remain unchanged. If investment does not change, then all of the increase in output goes to increased consumption.

This version of supply side economics promises us increased consumption without great inflation. In our example, we even get declines in the price level. If this would work as promised, it would be a wonderful thing indeed.

A (SLIGHTLY) OPEN ECONOMY

Many countries, especially the poorer ones (which are called, depending on the level of optimism of the speaker, developing countries; less developed countries, or LDCs; or underdeveloped countries) are very much influenced by changes in their exports and imports. These influences come from the several different ways in which foreign trade can change an economy. One way these changes can come about is from unbalanced trade, when the value of exports is greater than that of imports, or vice versa.[7] Differences in the values of imports and exports can occur only when something else is moving between the countries to balance out the values of trade. This something else is usually some kind of asset, such as an

[7] We really need a world with at least two goods, one foreign and one domestic, in order to get trade. In our one good model, the kind of trade mentioned above is silly, since you would export the one good and import the same amount of it. If we did have two goods, we could allow the relative price of the domestic and foreign goods to change, as in a supply and demand analysis, to give us an equilibrium in which the value of the exports and the value of the imports, as measured in the one macro good, would be equal.

investment in physical assets (in which an import is exchanged for ownership of some of the capital stock of the country) or the purchase of bonds or money. Sometimes, in what is called a **gold standard** or **fixed exchange rate** regime, the difference in the flow of goods is made up by a flow of gold, which in this situation is not considered a good, but an asset like bonds or money.[8] Imported goods can also be borrowed from other economies, and this foreign debt can be paid back at some other time by making exports greater than imports. We will discuss a number of these situations later, but first we want to look at a very simple example that concentrates on the possible aggregate supply effects of changes in exports and imports.

If we are to consider a slightly open economy version of our model, one thing we would have to do is return imports and exports to the National Income Accounting Identity and have that

$$Y = C + I + G + X - IM$$

where X equals exports and IM equals imports.

Suppose that we start with what might be the most neoclassical of the assumptions that we could make about imports and exports. Assume that only goods can move internationally—there is no international borrowing or lending, nor any other movement of other assets between countries—and that trade is always balanced. In that case exports will always equal imports and the net result on the AD curve of considering a model with any open economy will be zero. The exports and imports cancel each other out in the National Income Accounting Identity equation (X minus IM equals zero) and the AD side of the economy is determined solely by domestic considerations. (It would look exactly the same as the one from Chapter 5.)

An assumption that is often made when talking about LDCs is that their domestic output is determined to a large extent by the amount of imports that they can afford. Because most of these countries are either fairly small, or poor enough so that their industrial material markets are small, they import intermediate goods. An intermediate good is one that has gone through some processing but is not in a form in which it can be used by consumers. The industries in the LDC specialize in the final conversion of these intermediate goods into final or consumer goods.

[8] Exchange rates are the price of one currency in terms of another. In a fixed exchange rate regime, the government of the economy chooses a price at which it promises to exchange its money for the money of other economies. If the price is such that the other economies want to buy more of this economy's money than its private citizens want to provide, then the government provides the difference. If the citizens of this country want to buy more of the other monies than the other economies want to provide at this price, the government of the economy will sell gold to the other economies to purchase the money that its citizens want. The important thing here is that the price is fixed by the government and this government makes up the difference in the value of the imports and exports by either buying or selling gold.

Sheet steel that may be made into pipes, automobile parts, or a computer are assembled in the LDC. This means that, in our model, the production function is a function of imports as well as labor and capital, and we write it as

$$Y = f(L, K, \mathrm{IM})$$

instead of

$$Y = f(L, K)$$

as we did in equation 7.1. The production curve in Figure 7.1 will shift out or in as the imports increase or decrease in much the same way that it would shift if there were changes in the capital stock. Since we are dealing with a model where imports equal exports, the quantity of imports is limited by the quantity of exports. This is a binding constraint in the long run but may not hold for any one period. The country may borrow imports if it has an obviously short-term decline in its exports.

Consider the case of Venezuela. Venezuela is a member of the Organization of Petroleum Exporting Countries, OPEC, and about ninety percent of its exports are in some form of oil. In the 1980s, Venezuela increased its exports of aluminium and iron, but oil still dominated. Changes in the price of oil have a very important effect on Venezuela's non-oil output. In 1986 the price of oil, in United States dollars, fell from over twenty to about ten dollars a barrel. Restrictions from OPEC agreements—whose flouting caused Saudi Arabia to generate the price decrease in the first place—prevented Venezuela from increasing its oil exports enough to maintain the earlier level of imports. Figure 7.14 shows the analysis of these changes IM dropped from IM to IM_2, and that caused both the shift of the production curve that is shown in the movement from the thin to the thick production curve in the graph, and the change of the demand curve for labor from D_{L1} to D_{L2}. The equilibrium real wage dropped, as shown by the shift from the thin to the thick price–real wage line in the northwest quadrant. Combining all of these changes gives us a shift in the aggregate supply curve from AS_1 to AS_2.

The equilibrium in the price–output involves an increase in prices and a fall in output. If the government does nothing with respect to the AD curve through fiscal or monetary policies, then the fall in the price of oil shows up, as it did in Venezuela, as inflation accompanied by declining real wages and output. This is an example of a case where an external shock—the oil-price fall—has an effect on both prices and the output of an economy. Unfortunately, there was not much that the Venezuelan government could do in this situation unless it could borrow some imports in order to reduce the shift back in the production curves and the demand curve for labor. This is likely to be a wise policy if the reduction in the oil price was temporary, for after the oil prices return to "normal," the loan could be paid off by spreading the effects of the shock over several periods. Since it could not borrow all that it wanted to, the oil-price drop generated inflation and output

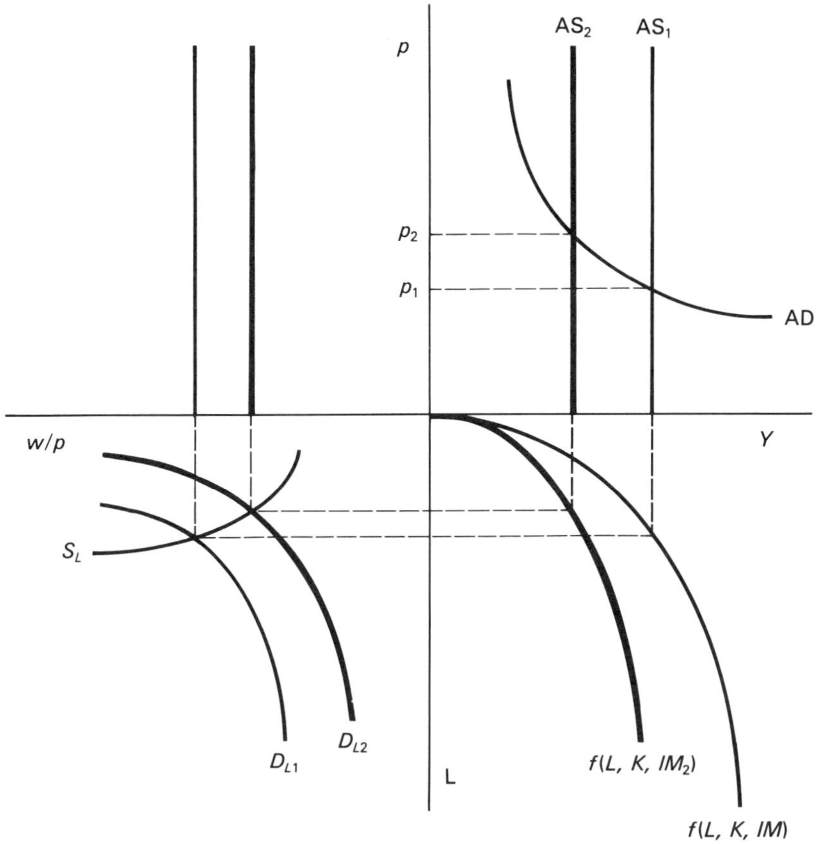

Figure 7.14

reductions. The import reduction was handled by allowing the exchange rates to raise. (However, this was done in a confused and very complicated way, as the exchange rate for most goods rose from 7.5 Bolivares per dollar to 14.5 B/\$, while some special goods continued at 7.5B/\$ and some others went free and rose to about 20 B/\$.) Since most of the imports were now more costly in terms of domestic money, only those firms that felt they could cover the cost increases and still sell their goods imported intermediate goods.[9]

The same story can be told about other oil-producing countries, such as Nigeria and Mexico; and about many other countries with other commodities, such as Colombia and coffee, for example.

[9] The actual method of price changes and import licence allocation in Venezuela was byzantine in its complexity. The description given above captures the main features of the events in Venezuela in 1986 but should not be construed as being completely accurate in detail.

REPRISE

The classical aggregate supply curve is generated by a labor market in which there is no involuntary unemployment. The equilibrium in the labor market determines the number of workers being hired and this quantity of workers is used with the current capital stock to generate output. This output can be read directly off the production curve. This level of output is independent of the prevailing price level, because the nominal wage adjusts to keep the real wage at the equilibrium real wage. The classical aggregate supply curve is vertical.

The classical aggregate supply side of the model can be written as a system of equations. These equations are

(1) $Y = f(L,K)$	Production function
(2) $w/p = f_L(L_D,K)$	Demand curve for labor
(3) $L_s = S_L(w/p)$	Supply curve for labor
(4) $L_s = L_D$	Labor market equilibrium

These equations, along with the equations at the end of Chapter 5, define the Classical model in mathematical terms. When K is given, the above four variables are a closed system. They can be solved for the variables Y, L_D, L_S (and since from equation (4) they equal each other, they also equal L), and w/p. In fact, equations (2) and (4) can be solved for L and w/p, the labor market, and the result of these
equation (4) they equal each other, they also equal L), and w/p. In fact, equations
in the text. The aggregate demand half of the model—the equations in Chapter 5—is not needed to find the output, but is needed in order to find the price level.

Changes in exogenous variables in the aggregate demand function—government fiscal policy variables—will not change output in the period in which they first change. They might change the price level and consumption. If investment changes, that will change the capital stock during the next period, and that will show up as a shifting of the AS curve. Changes in output in the classical model occur over the long run. Short-run changes—those taking place in one period—do not occur.

It is recommended that the reader attempt to analyze some other policies in the classical model. A tax cut not matched by a government expenditure cut is one example; some exogenous change in the labor supply is another.

EXERCISES

1. Suppose that an earthquake destroys much of the capital stock of California. (The people escape unharmed.) What does this do to the aggregate supply curve in a model of the Californian economy? If this incident does not change

the AD curve, what happens to equilibrium price and quantity in California? (In this problem consider California as a closed economy.)

2. Use a classical aggregate supply curve to solve for the price level and output changes that result from the policies in Chapter 6, Exercises 1–4.
3. (An exercise for those who know some calculus.) Use the production function we used for exercises in Chapter 2: $Q_{GB} = 8 \times T^{.5} \times L^{.5}$. Suppose that there are 36 units of land. What is the demand function for labor? Suppose that the number of units of land increases to 49. What is the demand function for labor?

Appendix

Assume that the two goods are income, measured in real terms, and leisure, the time spent enjoying not doing any work. Individuals have preferences about the combinations of income and leisure that they want to consume. These preferences can be illustrated by the usual type of indifference curves. (See Appendix: Chapter 3.) However, there is an upper bound on the amount of leisure that can be consumed. That limit is the total amount of time that available. So, in one day, the maximum amount of leisure that can be consumed is twenty-four hours. Figure 7.A.1 shows a set of indifference curves for the decision between income and leisure, with the upper bound of twenty-four hours for leisure drawn in.

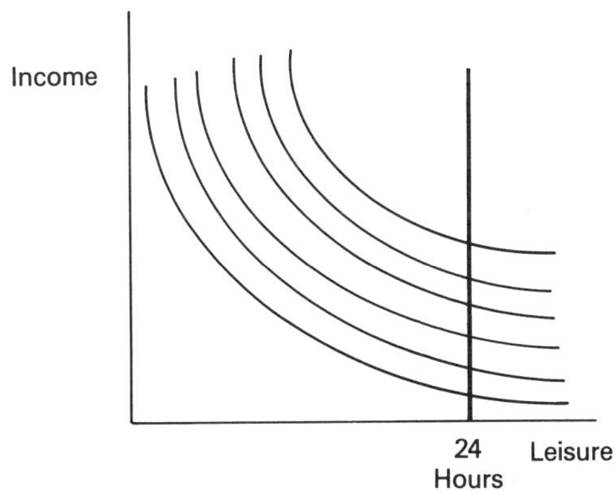

Figure 7.A.1

Work time is leisure given up. If an individual can earn a particular wage for the time spent working, a decision to consume leisure is a decision not to get the wage that could have been earned in place of the leisure. Likewise, a decision to work longer hours is a decision to forgo leisure. The wage an individual earns is the price that individual pays for leisure.

Each individual is endowed with an "income," measured in terms of leisure, of twenty-four hours. For each hour worked, the quantity of leisure consumed drops by one hour. Just as we drew a budget line out of the wool income level in Figure 3.A.4, we can draw a budget line out of the maximum amount of leisure with a price between leisure and income equal to the wage rate. (The slope is the negative of the wage rate.) Figure 7.A.2 shows five different wage rates drawn from

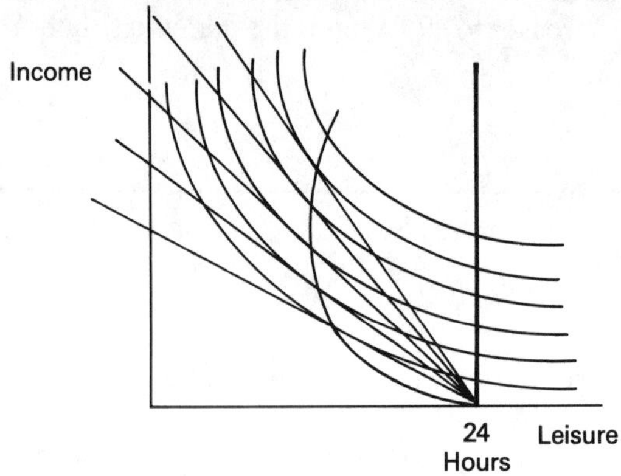

Figure 7.A.2

the twenty-four hour maximum leisure point. At the wage that the slope of each of these lines represents, the line is a budget line between income and leisure. The individual chooses the preferred point of consumption of leisure and income: The point where an indifference curve is tangent to the budget line. The thick curve connects up the chosen consumption points for the whole range of wages. Notice that as the wage increases from zero—the horizontal wage line—the amount of time that the individual is willing to work first increases and then, as the wage gets very high, decreases.

An individual who cannot get a good wage (because of lack of salable skills, for example) will not want to work very much and will choose to consume leisure. An individual with the same set of preferences between leisure and income, but who can earn a bigger wage, will choose to work more. The individual who cannot earn a good wage is not lazier than the higher-paid person—they have the same preferences over income and leisure—but is choosing to consume more leisure because it costs less than it does for the higher wage-earner. The individual who can only get a low wage would choose to work more if a higher wage were available. It is the low wage, not some inherent laziness, that generates the observed low level of work effort.

If the information on the curved line in Figure 7.A.2 were to be graphed on a real-wage labor plane, that graph would be the supply curve for labor shown in Figure 7.4, complete with the swung-back portion. A supply curve for labor can be generated directly from a set of preferences between income and leisure.

8

The Keynesian Model

In which we construct a Keynesian aggregate supply curve that allows for unemployment and tells us what to do about it. Keynesian economics saves us from a great depression, or so the model says.

INTRODUCTION

In the early 1920s a serious recession hit England. Unemployment, measured as those people covered by the unemployment insurance system who were looking for work and unable to find it, reached 22.4% for men and 25.9% for women in May of 1921.[1] While the unemployment rate had been in the neighborhood of two percent during 1919 and 1920, and has been estimated to have been only 2.4% in 1913, a serious coal miners strike from April to August of 1921 seemed to set off the recession. The unemployment rate in England stayed above ten percent except for only one year during the rest of the interwar period and in that year, 1927, the rate was 9.4%. Figure 8.1 shows the history of unemployment in England during that period.[2]

These continuing high levels of unemployment were not consistent with the concept of a fully employed economy that was a basic feature of the classical model. The model did not even permit economists to create examples of situations with unemployment and was therefore powerless to give answers about what to do when the real economy was experiencing unemployment. Although many other countries experienced higher levels of unemployment or slower growth in output

Figure 8.1

[1] From A. C. Pigou, *Aspects of the British Economic History 1981–1925*. (London: Macmillan, 1974) This is the Pigou of the Pigou Effect.

[2] Data for this figure is from Derek H. Aldcroft, *The Inter-War Economy: Britain, 1919–1939*. (New York: Columbia University Press, 1970.)

than did England during the Great Depression of 1929 to 1939 (the United States, Canada, France, and Belgium had a worse time of it than did England during this period), this early experience with high levels of unemployment, which began in 1921, made these issues of particular, and particularly early, interest to British economists.

In 1936, John Maynard Keynes, even then one of the most eminent of English economists, published a book entitled *The General Theory of Employment, Interest, and Money*. In it he argued that certain assumptions of the classical model were not valid, or were valid only in very special cases. In particular, he argued that labor markets did not work perfectly, as witnessed by the high unemployment that many countries were then experiencing. Both the changes that he made in the theory of the operation of the labor market and others about the operation of capital markets resulted in a rather startling change in policy results. The output level of the classical model was determined solely by the technical considerations of the production function and the equilibrium in the labor market. This output was therefore unaffected by changes in aggregate demand. Keynes's new model predicted that in times of economic contraction—a depression, for example—changes in the aggregate demand curve could result in real, immediate changes in output. His model allowed the equilibrium level of output to change in response to changes in the exogenous variables in the aggregate demand function.

In England and some other European countries, this activist policy prescription fell on the ears of willing listeners, for government officials felt certain that they could shift the aggregate demand curve. Although it took till the 1960s for the United States government to attempt to *systematically* use this activist policy, Keynesian theory justified the kinds of policies that politicians already wanted to use in their attempt to help the developed economies of the western world get out of the Great Depression. Much of the economic profession and all liberal (in the sense of interventionist) politicians welcomed this new theory, and from the late 30s until the 70s, the Keynesian model became *the* macroeconomic model.[3] (Things went so far that in the early 1970s the Republican President, Richard M. Nixon, could say "We are all Keynesians now."[4])

While *The General Theory* is generally credited for beginning this "Keynesian Revolution," the book itself is seldom read, and is, quite frankly, almost unreadable. Keynes, who produced several clear and beautifully written books before and after this one, seemed to have lost his writing skills for his masterwork. Keynesian theory, as it is known today, spread from the lectures that Keynes gave at Cambridge University in England through the writings of the students who attended those lectures. It was those students who, in the 1950s or so, converted

[3] As with all new ideas in economics, the younger economists were the first to embrace the Keynesian model. Many of the older economists, especially Republicans in the United States, never gave up their classical views. Since the older economists tend to die off first, the new ideas became the prevalent theories of the profession.

[4] Always one with great timing, Nixon said this just as the modern, rational expectations macroeconomic theory that rejects Keynesian theory began to gain support.

the theory into a set of mathematical formulation that is somewhat different than what one can make of Keynes' book, *The General Theory*.[5]

In the version of the Keynesian model we will construct, the aggregate demand curve will be identical to that of the classical model. The changes we will make in the classical model will all be in the aggregate supply curve; specifically, in the market for labor. In particular, workers are resistant to declines in the money wage (say as prices fall), but are not as resistant to declines in the real wage. A quotation from Keynes' *General Theory* might help emphasize this point.

> Now ordinary experience tells us, beyond doubt, that situation where labour stipulates (within limits) for a money-wage rather than a real wage, so far from being a mere possibility, is the normal case. Whilst workers will usually resist a reduction of money-wages, it is not their practice to withdraw their labour whenever there is a rise in the price of wage-goods. It is sometimes said that it would be illogical for labour to resist a reduction of money-wages but not to resist a reduction of real wages. But, whether logical or illogical, experience shows that this is how labour in fact behaves.[6]

Keynes made changes in the classical model in terms of his assumptions about the behavior of sectors of the economy other than the labor market. These other changes, such as changes in the investment–savings market, only reinforced the results that he got with his changes in the labor market.

THE KEYNESIAN AGGREGATE SUPPLY CURVE

For our Keynesian model we make a modification to the operation of the labor market. We will assume that in the previous period—last year, say—workers, or the unions that represent them, signed contracts with their employers for a fixed money wage for work done in the current period. Supply and demand curves for labor still exist, but the real wage need not always be the one where the labor market is in equilibrium.

At this fixed money, or nominal, wage, **w**, the relationship between the price level and the real wage is quite simple. An increase in the price level causes a decrease in the real wage and vice versa. This is because the real wage is equal to the fixed nominal wage, **w**, divided by the price level. A function of this type yields a curve that is a rectangular hyperbola. Figure 8.2 shows this **price–real wage relationship.**

Yet this is not the complete relationship. We will assume that if the price level

[5] This is, in a negative context, the argument of A. Leijonhufvud, in *On Keynesian Economics and the Economics of Keynes*. (New York: Oxford University Press, 1968.)

[6] John Maynard Keynes, *The General Theory of Employment, Interest, and Money* (New York: Harcourt Brace, 1935), pg. 9.

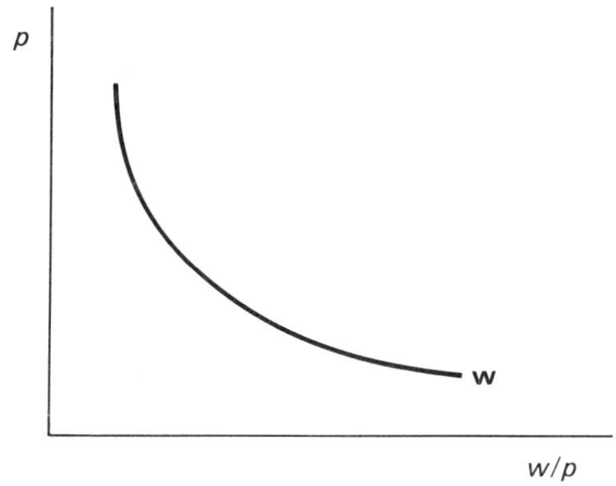

Figure 8.2

gets high enough the labor supply curve really does become effective. That is, the real wage rate becomes sufficiently low, causing enough workers to leave the marketplace that the supply of labor is less than the demand for labor by firms. Yet firms are receiving a high price for their goods and want to produce a lot. So at the point where the demand for labor is greater than the supply, the Marshallian dynamics *will* begin to work. Firms will bid up the nominal wage rate until the real wage rate rises to the equilibrium level. Real wage rates below the equilibrium real wage will not be observed because firms are free to raise the nominal wage if the market forces—the Marshallian dynamics—are pushing them in that direction. The contract between the unions and the firms can be broken in order to increase the nominal wages for the workers if the firms so desire. Any union official who refused an offer of increased nominal wages would quickly lose his or her job. Because of the asymmetry described in the quotation from Keynes, the firms are *not* able to *lower* the nominal wage when the real wage is too high and the demand for labor is less than the supply. The employed workers, or their union, resist the decline in their money, or nominal wage. This asymmetry generates a kink in the price–real wage curve. At high enough price levels, the Keynesian model will look like the classical model.

At low price levels, where **w**/p is above the equilibrium real wage, the money wage, **w,** that was contracted for the previous period holds sway. The contract between the union and the firms prevents non-union workers from bidding down the money wage, so the real wage increases. In Figure 8.3 we show the price–real wage line of Figure 8.2 above the labor market, with both flipped horizontally so they can be used in the form required to construct the AS curve. Once a wage rate, **w,** has been contracted, this graph allows us to observe the results of different price levels in the labor market. Thus, **p** is an example of a price level that produces a real wage (**w**/**p**) that is greater than the equilibrium real wage. Firms demand only L_D units of labor while L_S units of labor are being offered by households. $L_S - L_D$ is the amount of unemployment in the economy and $(L_S - L_D)/L_S$ is the unemployment rate. It is the existence of some institutional forces—the union's con-

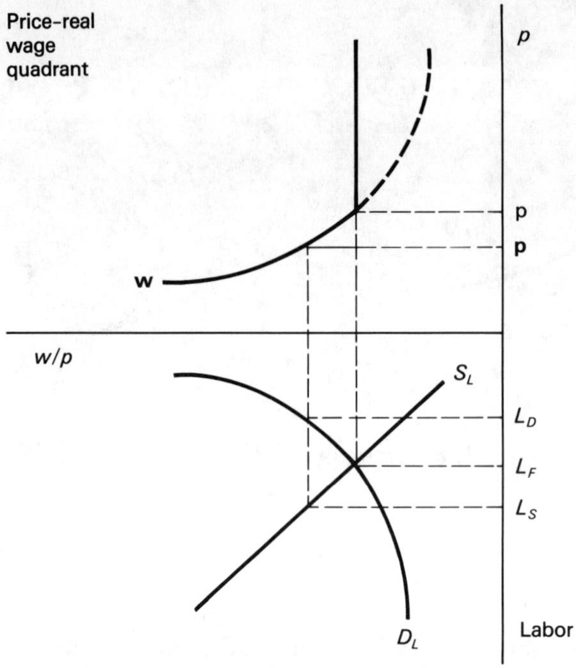

Figure 8.3

tract with the firm, in this example—that prevents the real wage from moving towards equilibrium.

The thick line in the price–real wage quadrant of Figure 8.3—the part without the dashes—represents the relationship we have just developed between the price level and the real wage in the economy. At prices above p, the money wage adjusts to make the real wage equal to the equilibrium real wage, and the labor market is in equilibrium at L_F, the full employment level. Consider some price above p. If the nominal wage, **w**, continued to prevail, the dashed line would give the real wage. Tracing down into the labor market at that real wage, one observes that the quantity of labor demanded is greater than the quantity being supplied by the households. The firms will offer higher nominal wages in order to drive the real wage up to the equilibrium real wage. For price levels above p, the Keynesian model is identical to the classical model. At prices below p, the contracted money wage **w** holds and a drop in the price level causes the real wage to increase, reducing employment and increasing unemployment.

We can incorporate this price–real wage curve into the aggregate supply side of the classical model to find the Keynesian aggregate supply curve. This is illustrated in Figure 8.4. We use a setup similar to Figure 7.7, where we constructed the classical aggregate supply curve, but replace the price–real wage quadrant with the upper half of Figure 8.3. The lower half of Figure 8.3 is already the labor market quadrant of the model we used to construct the classical aggregate supply curve. At a price level below the kink in the price–real wage curve such

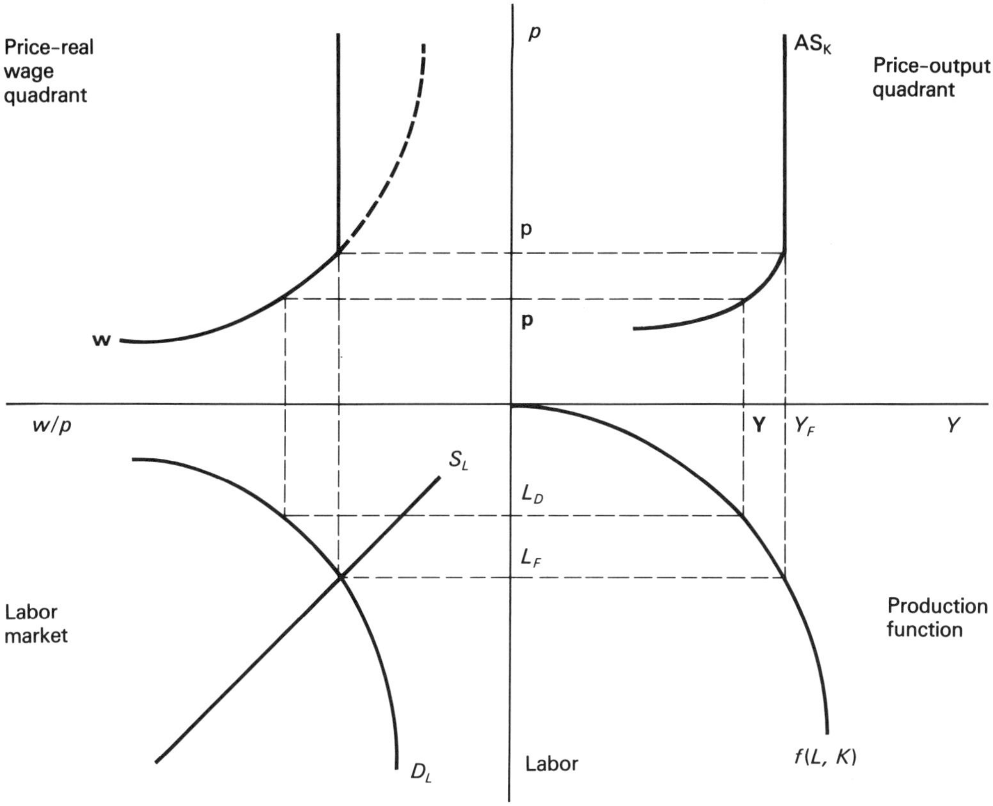

Figure 8.4

as **p**, we trace from the price **p** on the price axis to the price–real wage curve **w**, down to the real wage **w/p** (not written in on the graph), to the demand curve for labor. That gives the demand for labor, L_D. In this region of the graph, the demand curve for labor determines the number of workers actually employed. Tracing that quantity of labor over to the production curve, we find the output level, **Y**. The point (**p**, **Y**) on the p–Y plane is one point on the Keynesian aggregate supply curve. Other points on this curve, at other prices below the kink, can be found with the same process. One begins at the price level, finds the real wage, finds the labor demand, and then finds the output generated by this quantity of labor. The process begins at the price axis and ends at the output axis. Maintaining that order is very useful when attempting to draw a Keynesian aggregate supply curve.

At a price level greater than the one at which the contracted nominal wage, divided by that price level, is equal to the equilibrium real wage above the kink, the Keynesian aggregate supply curve is identical to the classical aggregate supply curve. This is shown in the vertical part of the Keynesian aggregate supply curve, which looks just like a classical aggregate supply curve. At price levels above the kink, the output is always the full employment output level, Y_F.

With a fixed money wage, as the price level drops the real wage increases. This causes firms to cut back on employment (the demand curve for labor here determines the amount of labor hired), and this reduced employment causes a reduction in output. The results of this interaction between prices, real wages, employment, and output is a swing left in the lower portion of the Keynesian aggregate supply curve (AS_K). It is worth emphasizing that the level of output in the economy when the real wage is equal to the equilibrium real wage is the full employment output for the economy (Y_F). When the price level is at or above p, then the real wage is the equilibrium real wage and all those who want to work can find it.

Many economists have described the Keynesian model as a short-run model, one that is useful for predicting or adjusting economic behavior over just a few years but is not so useful for longer periods. The basis for these comments is that the excess supply of labor and the high money wages that occur at low price levels face the possibly slow, but inexorable, workings of market forces. Eventually, it is argued, unemployed workers will bid down the money wage and the economy will move towards an equilibrium real wage. In the long run (a decade, perhaps) some believe, the Keynesian aggregate supply curve would degenerate into a classical AS curve. Keynes, however, was explicitly concerned with the short-run effects and the possibility of reducing short-run misery during a recession or a depression. For, as he is often quoted as saying, in the long run we are all dead.

KEYNESIAN EQUILIBRIUM

We solve our Keynesian model by combining the aggregate demand curve from Chapter 5 with the Keynesian aggregate supply curve. Figure 8.5 is an example. Note that all the interesting results of the Keynesian model occur when the AS and AD curves intersect on the bent portion of the AS curve, below the kink. On the vertical portion of the Keynesian AS curve the results are identical to those of the classical model and, since we have already seen that model, these results will be neither new nor interesting. Whenever you are solving a Keynesian model, be sure that your initial equilibrium is on that bent or curved portion.

The initial equilibrium is at an output level, **Y**, which is below the full employment level output Y_F, and at price level **p.** The real wage associated with this equilibrium is the real wage, **w/p.** The quantity of labor employed is L_D and the rate of unemployment is $(L_S - L_D)/L_S$, which, in this example, is a positive amount of unemployment.

Let us consider a government policy that is popular during periods when the output level is well below the full employment level of output. Suppose the government cuts taxes but makes no change in government expenditures. From

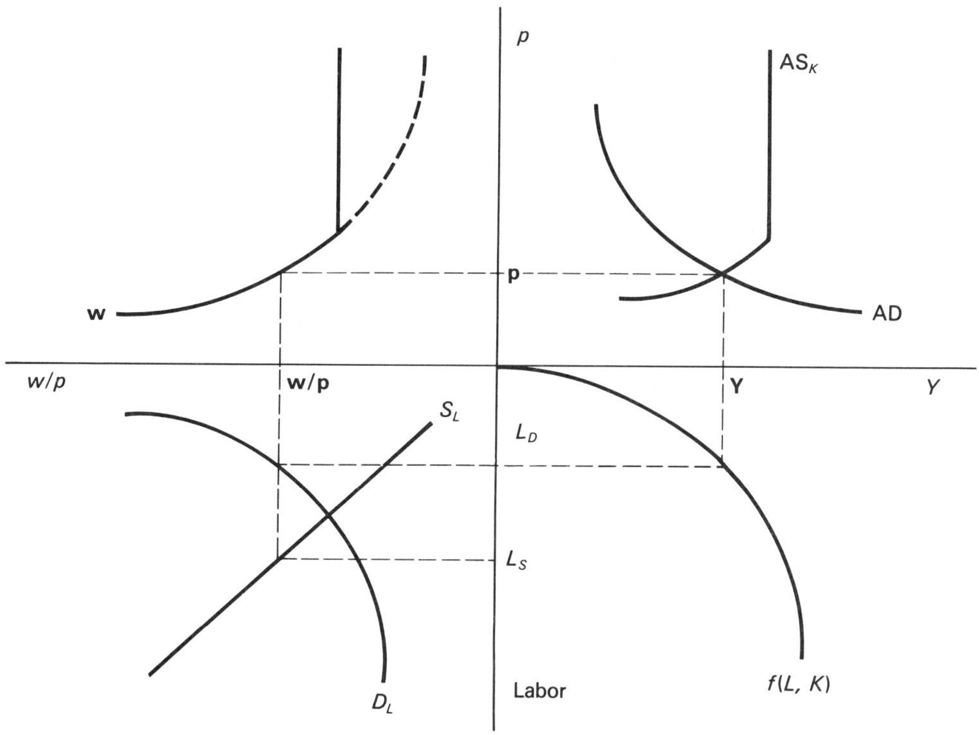

Figure 8.5

our earlier work with the aggregate demand curve, we know that this government policy causes a shift in the AD curve to the right. (You should be able to work this out using the material on the AD curve from Chapter 5.) As shown in Figure 8.6, the AD curve shifts out from AD_1 to AD_2. Prices rise from p_1 to p_2, which is smaller than the rise that would have occurred in the classical model. If a classical model were initially at output Y_1, this shift in the AD curve would raise prices to the point on AD_2 directly above Y_1. Because this AS curve is sloped, the rise in prices is smaller than that. Output increases from Y_1 to Y_2. Real wages drop from w/p_1 to w/p_2. Along with this drop in real wages, unemployment is reduced. Note the smaller distance between the labor supply curve and the labor demand curve at the real wage, w/p_2, than at w/p_1.

The shift in the AD curve increased prices which, with the money wage fixed, reduced real wages. This decline in real wages increased employment, and decreased unemployment by a greater proportion since, at the lower real wage, some people decided not to look for work; that increased production, or output. It would seem that in times of recession, a rational policy for an individual who believes the assumptions of the Keynesian model is to recommend a tax cut, or an increase in government expenditures. This would generate some inflation, but would lower unemployment and increase output.

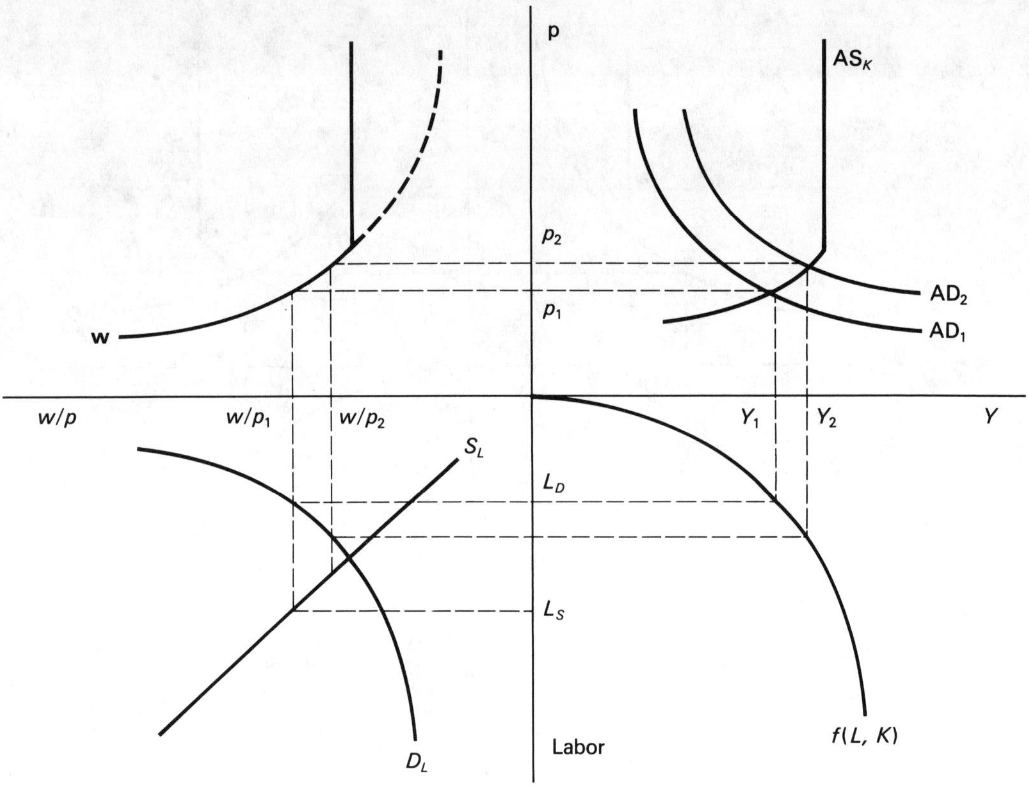

Figure 8.6

THE KEYNESIAN VERSION OF SUPPLY SIDE ECONOMICS

In Chapter 7, we worked through results of the Reagan administration's version of a supply side tax cut in the classical model. The assumption that we made, following the assumption of the Reagan administration, was that a cut in taxes, matched by an equal-size cut in government expenditures, would increase investment by the amount of the tax cut. The Reagan administration's assumption was that all of the tax cut would go into increased investment. There is considerable disagreement among economists as to how much of a tax cut ends up as increased investment.

The aggregate demand side of this model is identical to the one in Chapter 7. The AD curve shifts out to AD_2 (as it does in Figure 8.6, but not by the same amount). The immediate results are increased output, and therefore income; a higher price level; and a lower real wage. This is one place where the results are different from those of the classical model. In the Keynesian model, we get an immediate increase in output from this set of policies.

In the next period, the increased investment results in an increased capital stock for this economy. Assume that no demand-side policies change, so the aggregate demand curve, AD_2, is still the appropriate aggregate demand curve to use. We need to construct a new aggregate supply curve.

Assume, for simplicity's sake (even though it might not be true), that the nominal wage does not change. We will consider changes in the nominal wage in future chapters, but now we will concentrate on other aspects of the model, so the price–real wage curve, **w**, is the one we will continue to use. The increased investment causes an increase in the capital stock to K_2. This increased capital stock causes the production curve and the demand curve for labor to both shift outward. These shifts are shown in the labor market quadrant and production function quadrant of Figure 8.7.

The shift in the demand curve for labor changes the equilibrium in the labor market. The new equilibrium is where DL_2 and SL cross. This is also gives us the new equilibrium real wage and the new vertical portion of the price–real wage

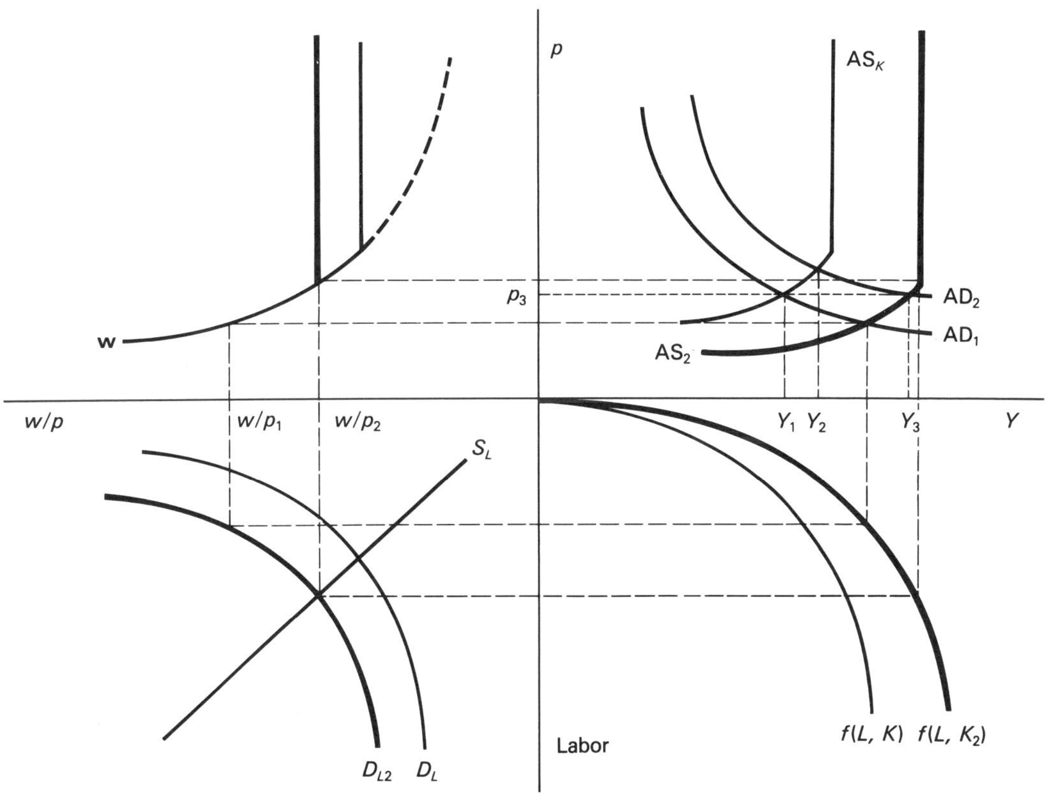

Figure 8.7

curve. The new vertical portion of the price–real wage line is drawn in the thick line in the price–real wage quadrant. Tracing over at the new equilibrium quantity of labor to the new production curve we find the new full employment level of output. That is drawn as the new, thicker, vertical portion of the AS curve. One other point on the new AS_2 curve is traced from prices to real wages to labor demanded to the quantity of output. This generates another point on the AS_2 curve. Connecting these points gives the swung-back portion of the new AS_2 curve. This new AS_2 curve intersects the AD_2 curve at price p_3 and output level Y_3, which are the new equilibrium levels of price and output. The new AS_2 curve was constructed in exactly the same method as the first, but it is necessary to keep careful track of which demand curve for labor and which production curve are the relevant ones. The new equilibrium price, p_3, is below p_2, but could be below, above, or equal to the initial price, p_1. The relative sizes of the shifts in the AS and the AD curves determine which of these is the relationship between p_3 and p_1 for a given policy.

The Keynesian model says that if the assumptions of the model are correct in charting how a decline in taxes and government expenditures shows up in increased investment, then there would be an increase in output with some inflation immediately, and a big increase in output with dropping prices a bit later. The warning about these policies is that neither we nor the Reagan administration have ever explained why all tax cuts should go to increased investment.

THE KEYNESIAN MULTIPLIER

A notion popular among politicians and economists of the Keynesian persuasion is a **multiplier.** This multiplier is a simple, constant number that is used to calculate the effects of some government fiscal policy on output. It has been used as a teaching tool by Keynesian economists in order to present their ideas to politicians in a simple form.

The multiplier is a number that represents the change in output, ΔY, that results from some change in government policy such as a change in government expenditures, ΔG. The multiplier (which is a pure number, without any units) is equal, in this case, to $\Delta Y/\Delta G$. While he was trying to get Congress to agree to a tax cut, W. W. Heller, President John F. Kennedy's Chairman of the Council of Economic Advisors, claimed that the multiplier was four.[7] When Herbert Stein, the Chairman of the Council of Economic Advisors under Richard Nixon, was

[7] In this case the multiplier is $-\Delta Y/\Delta T$. The minus sign is included because a cut in taxes generates a shift out in the aggregate demand curve and that, with a Keynesian aggregate supply curve, usually causes an increase in equilibrium output.

trying to get a cut in government expenditures, he claimed that the multiplier was one. While a tax increase and an expenditure cut of equal magnitude will result in slightly different shifts in the AD curve (the tax increase is a bit smaller), the difference is not enough to explain the estimates of one and four that these eminent economists found. The multiplier does not seem to be a constant, even for Keynesians.

These different estimates in the multiplier can be explained by looking at the AS and AD curves of our model. Note that a tax cut of one billion dollars, say, will always generate the same size shift in the AD curve, independent of the initial location of that curve. In Figure 8.8, the shift from AD_1 to AD_2 was generated by a tax cut of that size, as was the shift from AD_3 to AD_4. The horizontal shift at each price level on each of these curves is the same distance, so there is a specific sized shift in the AD curve generated by some specific ΔT.

What that ΔT will yield in terms of an output change depends on the initial location of the AD curve. This should be very clear from Figure 8.8. On the flatter part of the AS curve, the shift in the AD curve, from AD_1 to AD_2, generates a rather large increase in output. In this case, $-\Delta Y/\Delta T$ is very large. Where the AS curve is steeper, the same size shift in the AD curve, from AD_3 to AD_4, generates a much smaller increase in output. Here, $-\Delta Y/\Delta T$ is much smaller. In the limit, on the vertical part of the AS curve, the multiplier will be equal to zero, since a shift in the AD curve will only raise prices and not change output.

In a Keynesian model it makes sense to speak of multipliers. It does not seem to make much sense to speak of the value of the multiplier as if it were a constant. The above analysis shows that the value of the multiplier depends on the initial equilibrium of the economy. Note that both Heller and Stein could have been correct. Heller's estimate would be more likely if there were a lot of unemployment initially, and Stein's if there were almost full employment.

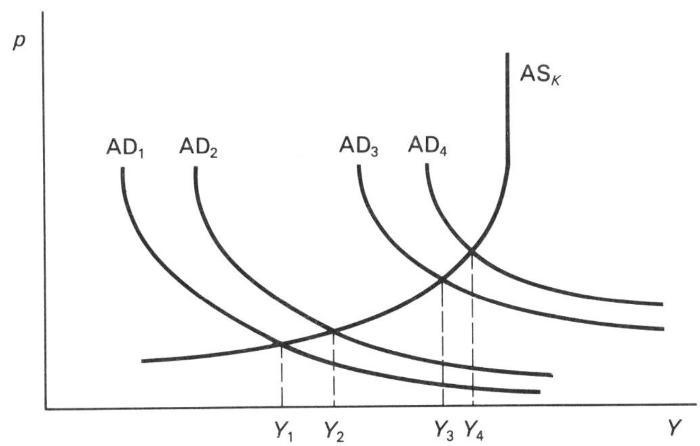

Figure 8.8

REPRISE

The Keynesian model diverges from the classical by assuming that labor markets do not always clear. Because of that, equation (4) at the end of Chapter 7 does not hold. We must write that equation as $L_S \neq L_D$. In our particular development of this model, unions and firms contract for a nominal wage; that nominal wage usually entails some unemployment among nonunion workers, and might entail some unemployment among the less senior members of the union as well. The government's aggregate demand-side policies can, in this static Keynesian model, reduce unemployment by generating inflation, which lowers the real wage.

Solving for either output or the price level in the Keynesian model requires both the AS and the AD curves. Remember that in the classical model output was determined by the AS side alone. The reason the Keynesian model needs both halves comes from the nominal wage contract and the fact that the labor market does not clear. The nominal wage is given to us, but it is the real wage that determines the number of workers hired, and the amount of output they produce. To get the real wage once we have the nominal wage, we need the prevailing price level. The price level is solved by both the AS and AD curves. Therefore, the price level and output must be solved for simultaneously in the Keynesian model.

It might be helpful to write out the equations that comprise the AS side of the Keynesian model. These are similar to the equations in the classical model that are given at the end of Chapter 7, but the differences are very important. The first two equations are the same as before.

(1) $Y = f(L, K)$ Production function

(2) $w/p = f_L(L_D, K)$ Demand curve for labor

To these equations we add the nominal wage agreement. So

(3) $\mathrm{w} = \mathbf{w}$ Nominal wage equation

where **w** is exogenous (in this static model). The labor market equilibrium equation does not hold, and it is very possible that

(4) $L_S \neq L_D$

However, this inequality is permitted only on one side. The supply for labor can be greater than the demand, but we are allowing the firms to bid up the nominal wage so that we will never observe that the supply for labor is less than the demand for labor. Because of this, equation (4) should be written as

(4) $L_S \geq L_D$

If we consider only the curved part of the Keynesian AS curve—the equal part occurs on the vertical part of the AS curve—equation (4) is a strict inequality. Equations (1) through (3) can be solved by substituting **w** for w in equation (2), taking the inverse of this new equation (2), having an equation where L_D is a function of p, and substituting for L_D in equation (1). This gives a single equation in which both p and Y are unknowns. The AD curve is an independent equation in both p and Y, and a system of both the AD and the Keynesian AS curve can solve for both p and Y.

The short-term policy implications of the Keynesian model are quite simple. If unemployment is too high, use some government policy that will shift out the AD curve, and unemployment will come down. Some annoying inflation will be generated when you do this. "Cooling down" an economy that has too much inflation, or is growing "too" fast, can be done by following a policy that shifts the AD curve back towards the price axis. This will reduce the inflation, or generate a deflation, but it will increase unemployment. These are the responses that are at the heart of the Keynesian countercyclical policies. At least one problem that arises is that these short-term policies may or may not make for good long-term policies. Further discussion of this last comment will wait for the chapter on Business Cycles, Chapter 12, when we consider countercyclical policies more carefully.

EXERCISES

1. Consider a model with a Keynesian aggregate supply curve. What happens to equilibrium output, price level, real wages, and consumption, if the government cuts taxes and keeps all other exogenous variables unchanged?
2. Consider Exercise 1. How are the results on the endogenous variables of the economy different if the tax cut is accompanied by an equal-size government expenditure cut?
3. Consider a Keynesian economy with an income tax. (See exercises, Chapter 5.) What does a tax cut do in this economy? How does this tax cut affect the demand and supply curves for labor?
4. In a Keynesian economy, consider an investment function where $I = i \times Y$ where $i = .05$. In period one, the government cuts lump sum taxes by 10%. Find the equilibrium in period one and period two. No additional policy changes occur in period two.
5. Assume that California is best described as a Keynesian economy. Suppose that an earthquake destroys much of the capital stock of California. (The people escape unharmed.) What does this do to the aggregate supply curve in a model of the Californian economy? If this incident does not change the AD curve, what happens to equilibrium price and quantity in California? (In this problem consider California as a closed economy.)

9

The Phillips Curve

In which Mr. Phillips finds a curve, and all the Keynesians adore him. The correlation he found between inflation and unemployment was viewed as a confirmation of the Keynesian model. To show this, expectations are added and our Keynesian model slowly goes dynamic.

INTRODUCTION

In 1958, an English economist named A. W. Phillips published a paper in which he observed, in the historical data for England, a relationship between wages and unemployment that seemed to hold.[1] He noted a negative correlation between the percent change in wages, sometimes called "wage inflation," and the unemployment level. He observed that during periods when wages increased only a little or actually declined, unemployment was high. During periods when increases in wages were large, unemployment was relatively low. Figure 9.1 shows a graph of

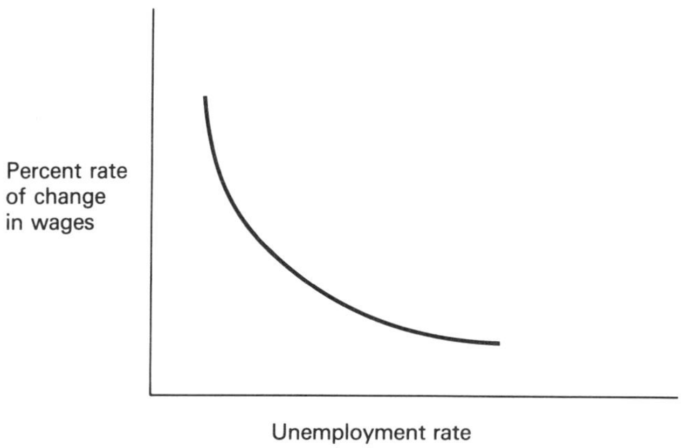

Figure 9.1

such a relationship. This correlation had been commented on long before by some American business cycle theorists, but it had not attracted much general attention. After the publication of Phillips' paper, this correlation between wage inflation and unemployment came initially to be known as **Phillips Curve.**

The inverse relationship that was observed between wage inflation and unemployment also seemed to hold when one compared the (price) inflation rate to the unemployment rate. Note that this says that there is a correlation between the **rate of change** of prices and the portion of the labor force that is unable to find work. Figure 9.2 shows data points for these variables for the United States from 1954 to 1969. A line is drawn on this graph that is, in a casual sense, "close" to most of the points, and this line approximates the curve in Figure 9.1 rather well. Modern discussions of the Phillips Curve usually refer to relations between the (price) inflation rate and the unemployment rate rather than to Phillips's original case, that of the relationship between the rate of change of nominal wages and the unemployment rate.

[1] A. W. Phillips, "The Relation between Unemployment and the Rate of Change of Money Wage Rates in the United Kingdom 1861–1959," *Economica* 25 (November 1958): 283–299.

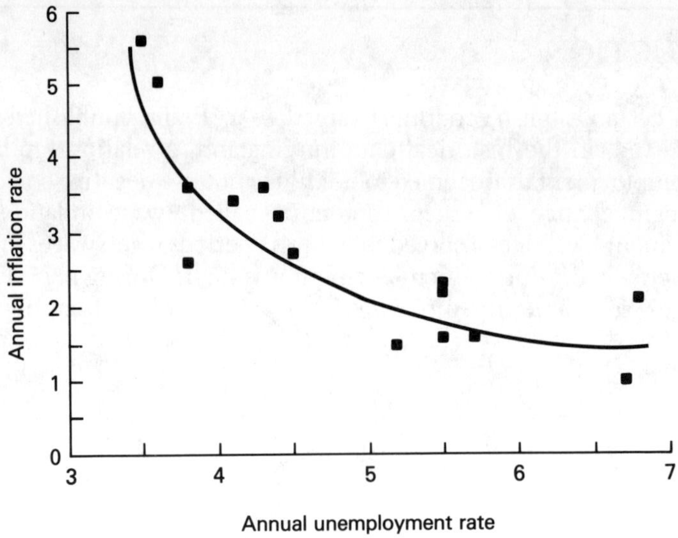

Figure 9.2

The 1958 paper by Phillips caused a great deal of commotion among economists. Why this should be so is not obvious. The correlation that Phillips found was already known, so his discovery wasn't really pathbreaking. His statistical techniques were better than those that had been used previously, but that wasn't enough to warrant the response that his paper received. His primary good fortune, as is often the case with people whose names are remembered, was that his timing was right.

The 1950s observed a widening popularity of the Keynesian economic model, which coincided with a continuing growth in size and economic involvement of national governments. Phillips's curve was viewed as giving some empirical support to the Keynesian model. As we shall show presently, a Keynesian economist would not be surprised that such an inflation–unemployment relationship existed. Further, many economists who favored an activist government macroeconomic policy—and most Keynesians could be safely included in this group—interpreted the Phillips curve as demonstrating a *causal* relationship (which is much stronger than a mere correlation) between inflation and unemployment. Simply put—as it still often is—they claimed that high inflation could cause low unemployment. Governments knew that they could create high inflation, since they have been doing this from time immemorial, so they reasoned that they could use this power to inflate to reduce unemployment whenever it got uncomfortably high, or whenever the political situation dictated—for example, six months before an election.

However, interpreting an observed correlation as a causal relationship is a very tricky and dangerous intellectual leap and can often lead to problems. For a period in the 1960s it was noted that there existed a correlation between the GNP and the number of hits achieved by the Phillies, Philadelphia's baseball team. This correlation poses all kinds of interesting questions. Does a causal relationship exist? Which way does the relationship go for this data? Do hits by Phillies change the GNP, or is it the other way around? Can we get a Phillies curve? If indeed Phillies' hits drive the GNP, think of the government's policy possibilities: It might be socially optimal for the government to pass a law that reduces the strike zone for the Phillies, or one that forces the opposing pitchers to throw underhand. With these suggestions we seem to be bordering on the absurd. This example is one where very few people—and then only Phillies' fans—would interpret the observed correlation as causality in either direction. There is little in the way of a reasonable model of how the world works to back up such a causal claim.

Real difficulties in determining causality arise in cases where there are several, conflicting, *reasonable* models of the world that allow correlations like the one observed in the Phillips curve. Some of the models may imply causality going one way, some the other. A third set of models might attribute the correlation to an independent third variable, which drives both of the observed variables. In such a world as this neither of the two observed variables "causes" the other. In all of these cases, the observed data are unable to help us decide which of our possible models is the correct interpretation of the world. Individuals are free (free, that is, from data restrictions) to choose whichever of the models suits their policy tastes.

A second issue that arises with the Phillips curve is that in order to study this phenomenon we need to introduce dynamics into our models. Since the Phillips curve relates the *rate of change* of prices and the unemployment level, we need to add some kind of dynamics to our previously static models in order to generate a model that can deal with these rates of change. We need a structure in the model that will relate the behavior or decisions of one period to those of the next.

To generate these dynamic models, we will simplify a seemingly continuous world into discrete time segments and those time periods in our model will be connected in three ways. First, we will consider exogenous variables to remain unchanged across time unless the results of changes in one of them is the particular experiment we are conducting. Second, the capital stock, **K**, will be changed by nonzero net investment. Total investment minus depreciation is net investment, and this is the amount by which the capital stock changes. We will usually start with net investment equal to zero in order to simplify the changes in the capital stock. Third, and most important, periods are connected to one another because certain kinds of contracts are signed in one period but only come into operation in the next period. In particular, labor contracts between unions and firms are signed on one date and last for some specified period of time (usually one or two years). We are defining a period as the time for which labor contracts hold. In order to keep things simple, imagine that the unions and firms sign contracts on the last day of each period and those contracts will be in effect for the entire next period.

Since unions and firms do not *know* how the variables in the economy that are important to them will change in the period during which the contract is in effect, which is, of course, in the future, they have to *predict* the future values of those variables based on the information that is available to them at the time of signing. The method they use for making these predictions and the way that information is used to make the predictions are specified in their **expectations function.** This expectations function is written as

$$E_t X_{t+n} = f_n(\mathbf{Z})$$

and says that the expectation at time, t, of the value of X at the time $t + n$ is a function, $f_n(\bullet)$, of the information, **Z,** that is being used. The notation, n, is used to represent the fact that we can make predictions n periods into the future. The function, $f_n(\bullet)$, will be slightly different for different n. In other words, the function that is used for predicting ahead three periods is slightly different from the one that we use for predicting ahead two periods. We will consider the effects on our Keynesian model of three different types of expectations functions: "naive," "adaptive," and "rational." As we move from naive to adaptive to rational expectation functions, we will permit unions and firms to use more information to form their expectations. This will be expressed by letting the vector, Z, contain increasing amounts of information.

We will deal with the inflation–unemployment causal relationship later. In order to demonstrate why the Phillips curve was viewed as providing empirical support for the Keynesian model, we need to show that a correlation between inflation and the unemployment rate is consistent with **naive expectations,** the simplest version of the Keynesian model. We will also consider the kind of policies that the government can use to take advantage of the fact that unions have this kind of expectation formation. As mentioned above, unions and firms decide on a money (nominal) wage for each period in the last moments of the previous period, and the nominal wage that is agreed upon is not changed, unless full employment is reached, during the entire current period. The government, however, can make changes in its policy variables *during* a period. This gives the government a special position in the economy that allows it to effectively pursue activist policies. It will be able to know what nominal wage the unions and firms have signed for, and, unless full employment is reached, it knows that wage will not change. The aggregate supply curve will be fixed in a Keynesian shape and, in this case, will not change during a period. The government will be able, in the short run, to exploit this fixed aggregate supply curve.

THE PHILLIPS CURVE AND THE KEYNESIAN MODEL

Let us assume that we are in a period of relative economic calm, a period when the government balances its budget and does not try to manipulate the economy too much. Inflation has been relatively low—1 to 2 percent—and is expected to remain so. (1959 to 1965 was such a time—the points in the 1 to 2 percent inflation range in Figure 9.2 are from that period.) Under such conditions, unions and firms might expect price levels to remain as they are, constant over time, and aim their money wage contracts accordingly. We will call this type of expectations "naive" because, while forming them, individuals know very little about the world. The only information that they have is the current price level. This naive expectations function can be expressed as

$$E_t(p_{t+1}) = p_t \tag{9.1}$$

This equation says that the price expected at time t, E_t, for the time $t + 1$ price, p_{t+1}, is the price that occurred at time t, p_t. Unions and firms bargain and sign a contract for a money wage, w_t, but this is not normally a money wage that results in the full employment (labor market equilibrium) real wage.

The money wage for which unions—or nonunion workers with skills that make them particularly valuable to the firm—and firms contract is one that will result in a higher-than-equilibrium real wage at the current price level. (When individuals have naive expectations, the current price level is also the price level that is expected for next period.) This is because unions can exert some monopoly power and bargain for a wage that will ensure its members a higher-than-equilibrium real wage. If it can't why would anyone join a union?[2] This, however, will create some unemployment. The result of this bargaining on the labor market is similar to what would happen if a government mandated a minimum money wage that would be large enough so that the real wage would be greater than the equilibrium real wage at the expected price level.

The contract negotiations between firms and unions are not allowed to drive the real wage upward without bound. If they were to do so, more and more union members would be put out of work. The threat of this happening is enough to keep some of the marginal members of the union, those most likely to lose their jobs, from voting for union leaders who would follow such a policy. Second, the major threat that the union has at its command in its campaign for raised wages is a strike. It is costly to the members of the union to have to use that threat; they must go without wages for a while. So union members are faced with a trade-off between higher wages as a result of a prolonged strike, or somewhat lower wages from a strike concluded earlier, or even the mere threat of a strike. Third, firms are likely to resist allowing the real wage to rise too high. They can instead go out of business, close down plants, wait out the strike, attempt strikebreaking activities, or move their plants to another town, state, or country.

Figure 9.3 shows a situation in which firms and unions arrive at a higher-than-equilibrium real wage. There, **w** is the contracted money wage when price

[2] Unions serve other purposes as well. If there is a local monopsony on the side of the firm—the firm is the only employer in town, for example—then the monopoly power of the unions works counter to the monopsony power of the firm and can result in equilibrium wages. If there were not a union, the monopsony power of the firm would allow the firm to pay less-than-equilibrium wages. (Not too much less, though, because workers would then have sufficient incentive to move to another location to work for a different firm.)

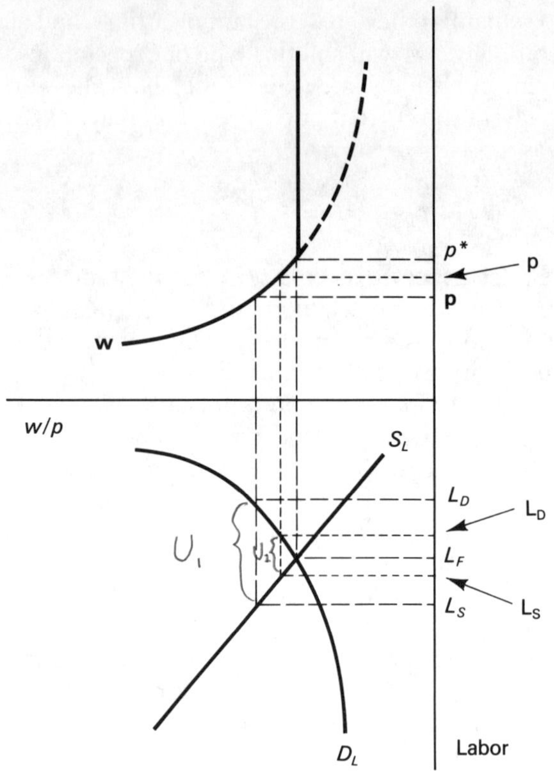

Figure 9.3

level $\mathbf{p}$ is the current and expected price level, so $\mathbf{w/p}$ is the expected, desired, and contracted real wage (although the contract specifies the nominal wage, $\mathbf{w}$). Unemployment rate U_1, which equals $L_S - L_D/L_S$, is the unemployment rate that is consistent with firms and unions receiving their desired real wage, and p^* is the price level that would result in full employment.

If the price level $\mathbf{p}$ actually occurs next period, that represents a situation with no inflation ($\pi_1 = 0$), and the unemployment rate, U_1, equal to $(L_S - L_D)/L_S$. If there is inflation—say the price level rises to p—then the unemployment rate will be U_2, which equals $(L_S - L_D)/L_S$. The inflation rate in this case is $\pi_2 = (\mathrm{p} - p)/p$. We divide the change in prices $(\mathrm{p} - p)$ by p because that is the initial price, which was set last period, we are looking for the inflation rate, and that is the *rate* of change of prices. If prices rise to or above p^*, the economy is at full employment. So at an inflation rate of $\pi_3 = (p^* - p)/p$ or greater, unemployment is zero. Plotting the inflation rates and unemployment rates given above yields the Phillips curve shown in Figure 9.4. This shows that, at least in one way, the Keynesians of the late 1950s were right: The Phillips curve is consistent with the Keynesian model and can be derived from it when one makes the appropriate assumptions about expectations (i.e., naive expectations).

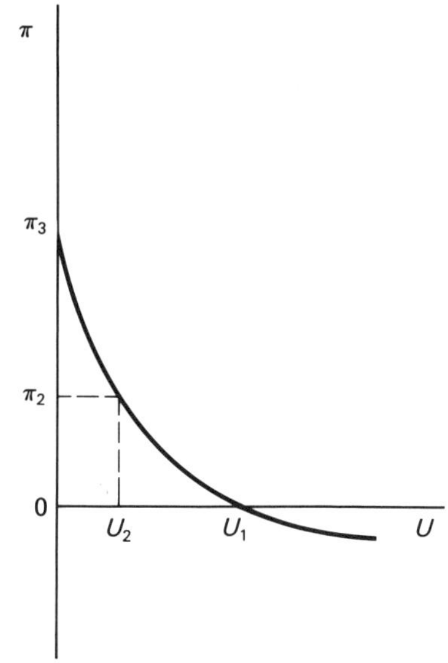

Figure 9.4

GOVERNMENT POLICY UNDER NAIVE EXPECTATIONS

In a world with naive expectations the Phillips curve can be exploited, and the government can change its policy to *cause* inflation and reduce unemployment. As a starting point, imagine a world in which the government has been following the same policy for a long enough time so that the effects of all possible shocks have died out—in some models this could be a very long time—and the equilibrium from one period to the next is the same price–output point. With the unions getting what they want (or, at the least, what they bargained for), the aggregate demand, AD_1, and the aggregate supply, AS, curves must intersect at price **p** in Figure 9.3. This would fulfill the union's expectations and result in unemployment of $L_S - L_D$ (again, in Figure 9.3). This **stationary state equilibrium** of the AS and AD_1 curves is drawn in Figure 9.5. It is called a stationary state equilibrium because it will be repeated from period to period. (Note that we need investment, I, to be exactly equal to depreciation in order to have a stationary state. This prevents changes in the capital stock that would cause shifts in the production curve and in the demand curve for labor. Shifts in these curves would not be consistent with a *stationary* state equilibrium.) With the AD_1 curve as it is drawn in Figure 9.5, the price level that occurs is the price level that the unions expect, and which is the same as the one that occurred during the preceding period. Unions will contract for the same real wage and, with no expected change in prices, that action will result in the same nominal wage. There are no changes in employment, in

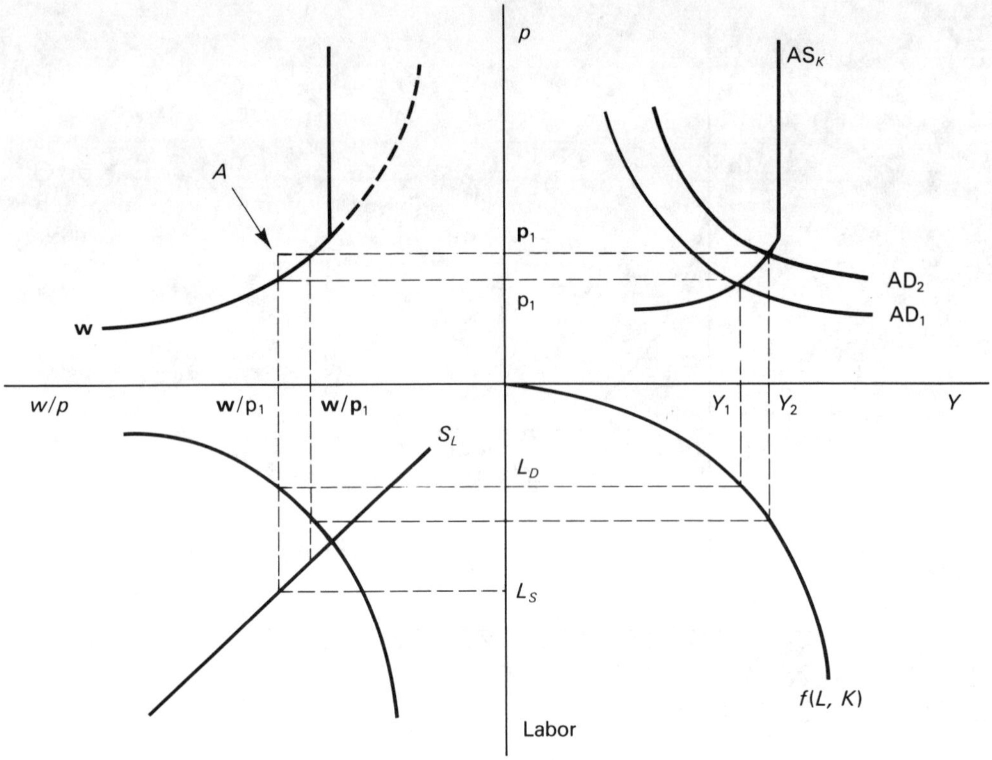

Figure 9.5

equilibrium output, in prices, or in real wages. Time may pass, but the economy, in a stationary state, will look exactly the same from one period to the next. Note that although the labor market is not in equilibrium (supply and demand of labor are not the same quantities at the real wage **w/p**), we can say that the model is in equilibrium. This is so because all the laws (in particular in this case the rule of expectation formation) of the model are fulfilled.

Suppose that after the world has been in a stationary state for some time, there is some kind of a shock to the economy in a period that we call "period one". This could occur as a change in the AD curve, generated by an exogenous change in investment or by a government policy change. Assume that the AD_1 curve shifts out to some new, higher AD_2. This would cause the equilibrium price level to increase from p_1 to $\mathbf{p}_1$, and output to increase from the stationary state value of Y_1 to Y_2. The unions and firms stay on the same money wage line **w,** so the real wage declines from $\mathbf{w}/p_1$ to $\mathbf{w}/\mathbf{p}_1$. The lower real wage causes more workers to be hired, and output to increase to Y_2. The lower real wage also means that households will be supplying less labor to the labor force. Unemployment has been decreased during period one because more people are being employed and fewer are in the labor force.

The price that the unions and firms see at the end of period one is $\mathbf{p}_1$. With naive expectations, $\mathbf{p}_1$ is also the price they will expect to see in period two. Writing out their expectations function, we have that $E_1p_2 = \mathbf{p}_1$, which we read as saying that the expectation during period one of the price for period two equals $\mathbf{p}_1$. Given these expectations, unions and firms will bargain for a nominal wage, $\mathbf{w}_2$, such that the real wage $\mathbf{w}_2/\mathbf{p}_1$ will be the same as the real wage they had expected to have in period one, $\mathbf{w}/p_1$. The nominal wage curve that represents the new nominal wage, $\mathbf{w}_2$, will pass through the point labeled A in Figure 9.5. Point A is strictly above the old wage line $\mathbf{w}$ at the intersection of price p_1 and the old preferred real wage w/p_1. With this new nominal wage curve, if price level $\mathbf{p}_1$ is the level that actually occurs, the real wage and the employment level will be what the unions and firms want. The output level will be Y_1. The new nominal wage curve will generate a new AS curve. The new price–real wage curve is drawn in as $\mathbf{w}_2$ in Figure 9.6.

The new, curved portion of the aggregate supply curve must go through point $\mathbf{p}_1 - Y_1$ on the p–Y plane. The new nominal wage rate, $\mathbf{w}_2$, was chosen so that when the price level is $\mathbf{p}_1$, the real wage will be the same as the real wage w/p_1. The real wage, w/p_1, was the one that resulted in the output Y_1. Since the new nominal wage $\mathbf{w}_2$ will give the real wage w/p_1 at price $\mathbf{p}_1$, it will also generate the output Y_1. So $\mathbf{p}_1 - Y_1$ is a point on the new AS_2 curve. The price level that will yield full employment also goes up because the new nominal wage line, $\mathbf{w}_2$, intersects the vertical line above the full employment point—that is, the equilibrium point in the labor market—at a higher price level than in period one. These two points can be used to approximate the AS_2 curve that will occur in the second period. Where that curve and the AD_2 cross the graph shows the price and output level that will occur if the government does not change its policies from period one to period two. (If the government did change its policies this would require a new AD curve, and the new equilibrium would be the intersection of the AS_2 curve and this new AD_3 curve.) The price and output levels that result from the intersection of the AD_2 and AS_2 curves are denoted p_3 and Y_3 respectively. Note that this position is one with some inflation and with an output level, Y_3, that is higher than the firms' and unions' preferred level, Y_1, but lower than Y_2. This is shown in Figure 9.6.

We can summarize events in the example we just discussed. The same pattern of events holds for other examples, but some other variables may change in periods other than the first one. For example, a policy might involve changing one variable in period one and then changing it back to its old value in period three. Which variables change depends on the time path of government policies. We begin in a stationary state.

Stationary State. At price p_1, w/p_1 is the desired real wage, $(L_S - L_D)/L_S$ is the rate of unemployment, and Y_1 is the output. Since unions and firms are in agreement on the real wage, if no exogenous variables change this equilibrium can continue indefinitely.

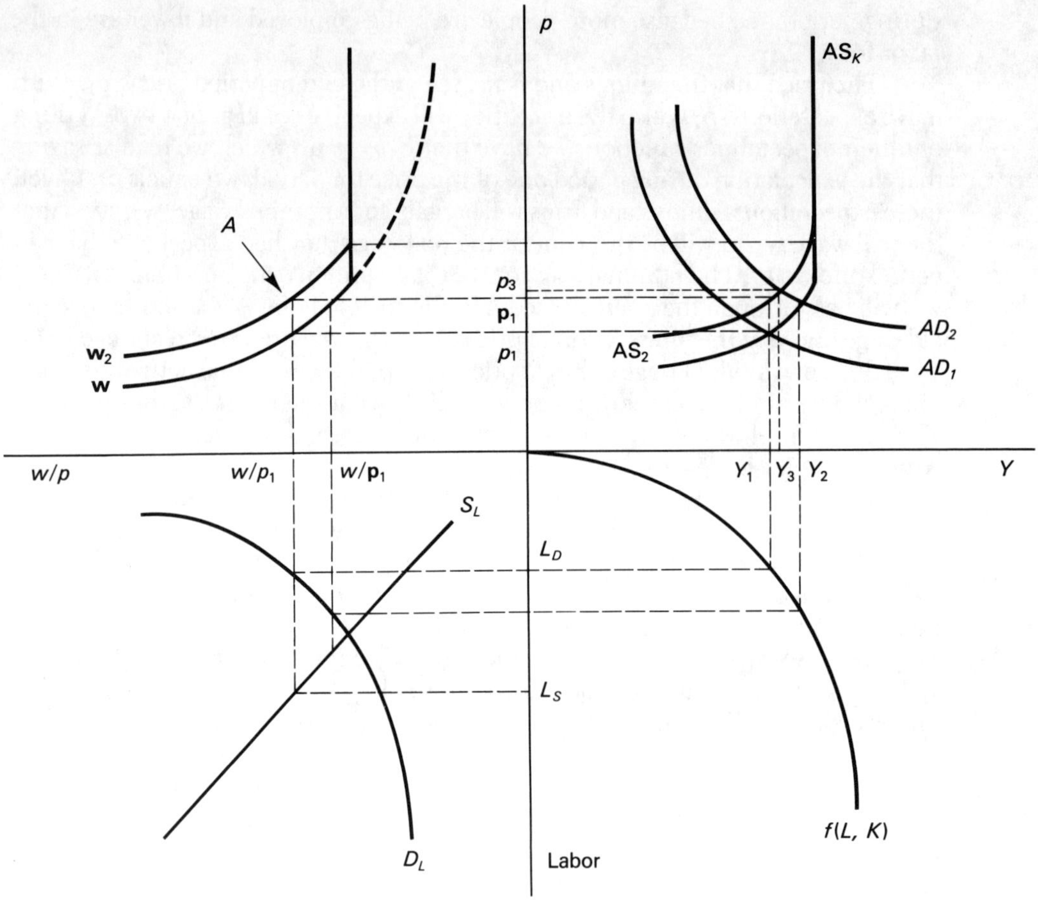

Figure 9.6

Period One. The government's policy shifts out the AD curve to AD_2. Prices rise to $\mathbf{p}_1$, real wages decline to $w/\mathbf{p}_1$, and more labor is employed. Output increases to Y_2. With naive expectations, everyone expects the price in period two to be $\mathbf{p}_1$. At the end of period one, unions and firms contract for a new wage, w_2, such that $w_2/\mathbf{p}_1$ equals w/p_1. This new nominal wage does not go into effect until period two begins.

Period Two. If we assume that there are no changes in government policy, the AD curve continues to be AD_2. At the beginning of period two, the new nominal wage, w_2, goes into effect. There is a new nominal wage curve representing this wage, and this generates a new AS curve, AS_2. This new equilibrium is at p_3 and Y_3, p_3 is the period two price level, and, with naive expectations, it will be expected to continue into period three. At the end of period two, the unions and firms contract for a new nominal wage, w_3, such that w_3/p_3 equals w/p_1. This new nominal wage does not take effect until period three.

Period Three. Period three follows the same pattern as period two, but with a higher nominal wage, w_3, and a new AS_3 curve.

REPRISE

The Phillips curve is a relationship between inflation and the unemployment rate that was first observed for England and since has been observed during particular time periods in many other countries. This observed correlation was viewed as a strong confirmation of the Keynesian model, since just such a relationship can be generated by that model with naive expectations. Expectations are naive (or static, as some economists call them), when an individual thinks that what is, will be. The current value of the variable is expected to be the relevant value in the future or, at least, the near future. "Naive" expectations are not always naive. For some things, naive expectations make a lot of sense. If we expect the sun to come up or to go down at the same time tomorrow as it did today, we will not be very wrong.

All of the aggregate demand side policies that worked in the static Keynesian model will work in essentially the same way in the Keynesian model with naive expectations. The main improvement is that we can now connect periods by this expectations function and look at the longer-run effects of government policies.

EXERCISES

1. Consider the problem shown in Figure 9.6. Suppose that the government does not change any of the exogenous variables after the initial changes that generated AD_2. Follow the time path of output, prices, real wages, and unemployment through period four, remembering that the initial AD move occurred in time period one. What does this suggest that the long-run effects of some one-time-only policy might be be?
2. In Chapters 7 and 8 we considered the Reagan version of supply side economics, where a cut in government expenditures and taxes would show up as an equal-sized increase in investment. Suppose that the government does decrease taxes and government expenditures in period one, and that investment increases during that period. The economy is initially in a stationary state equilibrium and the supply side policy moves it out of that equilibrium. Follow the economy through period three, with the stationary state being period zero, and describe the path of output, prices, real wages, and unemployment.
3. Suppose that investment is a function of current income. Let $I = i \times Y$, where $i = .05$. Suppose there is a tax cut in period one (period zero is a stationary state). Follow this economy through period three.

10

Adaptive Expectations

In which the Keynesians are observed attempting to patch up their models by incorporating adaptive expectations as the Phillips curve fails in the 1970s. People, at least in economic models, are getting smarter, and the world changes faster.

INTRODUCTION

It is possible to imagine a large number of economic situations in which naive expectations seem very unreasonable. Germany just after World War I is an especially powerful example, and although it should be viewed as an extreme case it makes our point very forcefully. Table 10.1 shows a quarterly time series for the wholesale price index, in which 1913 is represented by 100, from March, 1921, through December, 1923.

TABLE 10.1

YEAR	MONTH	
1921	March	1,340
	June	1,370
	Sept.	2,070
	Dec.	3,490
1922	March	5,430
	June	7,030
	Sept.	28,700
	Dec.	147,480
1923	March	488,800
	June	1,938,500
	Sept.	2,394,000,000
	Dec.	126,160,000,000,000,000

It would take some very special circumstances for someone living in the economy described above to believe, in the middle of September, 1923, that prices in the middle of October would not be higher than the prices were then. The reason is not, as it is with us, that they knew the December wholesale price index. Rather it was their recent history of rapidly changing prices, right up to the middle of September, that suggested that the prices in the middle of October would be much higher. Germany was in the middle of a hyperinflation, an extreme inflation that Phillip Cagan defines as a situation where the rate of price change exceeds fifty percent a month.[1]

In trying to construct an econometric model—that is, a model that uses economic statistics—of the way money and prices behaved in Germany and other countries during hyperinflations, Phillip Cagan needed to construct an expectations function for prices. He hypothesized that the way in which individuals corrected their expectations of price changes—inflation or deflation—could be described by a function of the error between their expectations from the period

[1] Phillip D. Cagan, "The Monetary Dynamics of Hyperinflation," in *Studies in the Quantity Theory of Money*, ed. Milton Friedman, (Chicago: University of Chicago Press, 1956), pp. 18–21.

before and the actual price change during that earlier period. This is written, in discrete time,[2] as

$$E_t\pi_{t+1} - E_{t-1}\pi_t = \beta \times (\pi_t - E_{t-1}\pi_t) \tag{10.1}$$

where π_t is the inflation rate at date t and $E_t\pi_{t+1}$ is the expectation, at date t, of the inflation that will occur at date $t + 1$. Note that $E_{t-1}\pi_t$ is the inflation rate that was expected, at date $t - 1$, to occur at date t, *and* $\pi_t - E_{t-1}\pi_t$ is the amount by which the expectations were incorrect, the error in the prediction. Equation 10.1 shows that we form our expectations of the inflation at date $t + 1$ by correcting our previous estimate of inflation by a fraction, β, of the error of that earlier prediction.

Cagan manipulated this equation to get an expression for the time, t, expectation of the inflation at time $t + 1$ of

$$E_t\pi_{t+1} = \beta \times \sum_{i=0}^{\infty}(1 - \beta)^i\pi_{t-1} \tag{10.2}$$

where the summation goes from zero (π_{t-0} is today's inflation rate) back into the infinite past. The weights, $(1 - \beta)^i$, get smaller the further into the past we go, giving less weight to older inflation rates. Equation 10.2 can be rewritten both in terms of the price levels at time t and before, and with the unknown variable changed to $E_t p_{t+1}$, the price expected for time $t + 1$. After some algebraic manipulation, equation 10.2 becomes

$$E_t p_{t+1}/p_t = \beta \times \sum_{i=0}^{\infty}(1 - \beta)^i p_{t-i}/p_{t-1-i}$$

The ratio between the expected price level and the current price level is a weighted average of the ratios of past price levels.

Cagan's formation of the expectations function is one of the early cases of an explicit model of **adaptive expectations.** Instead of expecting the price level today to be the same as the price level last period, as naive expectations would, adaptive expectations use all the useful past information on the path of prices to estimate the next period's price. A general, adaptive price expectation function is

$$E_t p_{t+1} = f(p_t, p_{t-1}, p_{t-2}, \ldots) \tag{10.3}$$

where $f(.)$ is some function that might use *all* past prices. The name "adaptive expectations" comes from the fact that individuals change, or adapt, their expectations of future **price levels** based on the entire path of past price levels, and of these price levels alone. When econometricians attempt to estimate the adaptive expectations functions that individuals have, they usually assume that the function is

[2] Cagan's model was written as a continuous time model. We are using a discrete time approximation of his model.

linear. A linear, adaptive expectations function (linear in prices, that is; Cagan's was linear in inflation) is

$$E_t p_{t+1} = \partial + \sum_{i=0}^{\infty} \beta_i p_{t-i} \tag{10.4}$$

where β_i is the coefficient on the price i periods ago, ∂ is some constant, and Σ is the summation operator, summing over i's that range from zero to infinity. Whenever anyone estimates one of these equations, they make all of the β_is equal to zero for all is greater than some number. In other words, they decide that individuals use only ten periods of information, for example, in this equation. In this case i would range from zero today to ten ten periods ago. Note that this equation shrinks to the naive expectations function if β_0 equals 1, ∂ equals zero, and all the β_is equal zero for i greater than zero. Naive expectations can be thought of as adaptive expectations restricted to only current information.

Although Cagan's development of an adaptive expectations function was done in 1956, fairly long ago, and a number of economists used this formulation in the intervening period, it wasn't until the early 1970s that adaptive expectations became very popular in United States macroeconomics. This was in part because the data that came in on unemployment and inflation no longer fit the simple Phillips curve of Figure 9.2. Figure 10.1 shows the data up to 1980 with the "shifted" Phillips curves that some have suggested existed during the later part of the 1970s.

As you might have guessed by now, the assumption of adaptive expectations gives rise to a Phillips curve that can shift out. It permits data points with both high inflation and high unemployment (a situation that was tagged "stagflation" while it

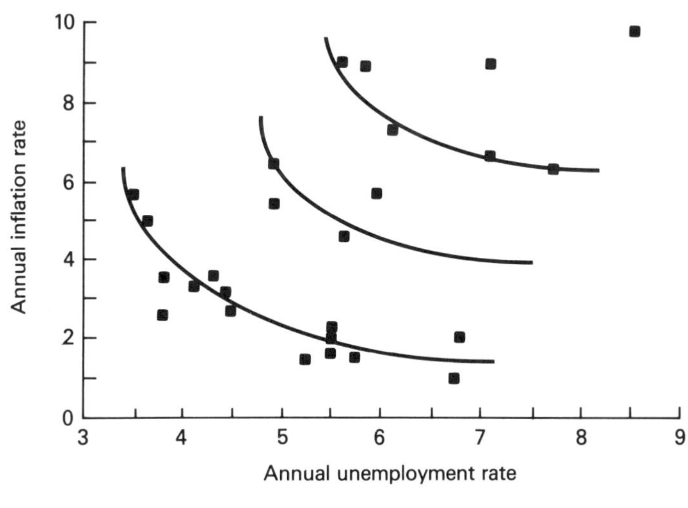

Figure 10.1

was going on), but a Phillips curve type trade-off still exists. It merely requires ever-increasing rates of inflation to make the same kind of unemployment or output gains. This we will show below. Note that if the "ever-increasings" go far enough, the result is hyperinflation.

If past prices have been constant at some p, then it seems reasonable to conclude that the price expectation, $E_t p_{t+1}$, should equal that same p. Naive expectations always give that prediction. If prices have been constant for a long enough time, adaptive expectations yield—and probably should yield—the same prediction as do naive expectations. Notice that this condition imposes some restrictions on the β_is and ∂ of equation 10.4. The β_is must sum to one and ∂ must equal zero if this condition is to hold for any constant price p. One can see this, since with a constant p,

$$E_t p_{t+1} = \partial + \sum_{i=0}^{\infty} \beta_i p = \partial + p \sum_{i=0}^{\infty} \beta_i \tag{10.5}$$

should equal p and that occurs for all p only when ∂ equals 0 and the β_is sum to one.

However, if price levels have been changing recently, naive and adaptive predictions of the price at time $t + 1 (i.e., E_t p_{t+1})$ will be very different. In general, the adaptive expectations function will use information on trends in prices to help predict the future price. If prices have been increasing ten percent the last few years, then many adaptive expectations functions are likely to give a prediction of something like a ten percent increase for next year. This gives us some direction for choosing a particular, simple adaptive expectations function to use in our Keynesian model in this chapter. While the one we use is not the most complete—certainly it is not as complicated as the one used by Cagan—it will exhibit all of the important characteristics of more general adaptive expectations functions.

PUTTING ADAPTIVE EXPECTATIONS IN THE KEYNESIAN MODEL

Assume that firms and unions adapt their expectations to include inflation. Specifically, the expectation is that next period's price will be today's price increased by the inflation rate that occurred between yesterday and today. Written out, this is

$$E_t p_{t+1} = p_t(1 + \pi_t) = p_t + p_t[(p_t - p_{t-1})/p_{t-1}] \tag{10.6}$$

where $\pi_t = (p_t - p_{t-1})/p_{t-1}$. The inflation rate this period is equal to the price change from the last period to this period divided by last period's price. Manipulating equation 10.6, we get that

$$E_t p_{t+1}/p_t = p_t/p_{t-1} \tag{10.7}$$

or that the ratio between price expected for next period and the current price is equal to the ratio between the current price and the price from the period before. Note that equation 10.7 is a simplified version of Cagan's adaptive expectations function written in terms of prices. Graphically, this could be described as a uniform expansion—a stretching—of the price line until the old price, p_{t-1}, lay on top of the current price, p_t. The old p_t is now where the expected price, $E_t p_{t+1}$, will be. The physical *ratios* between 0 and p_{t-1}, and 0 and p_t, are the same as the physical **ratios** between 0 and p_t, and 0 and $E_t p_{t+1}$. Figure 10.2 shows this relationship.

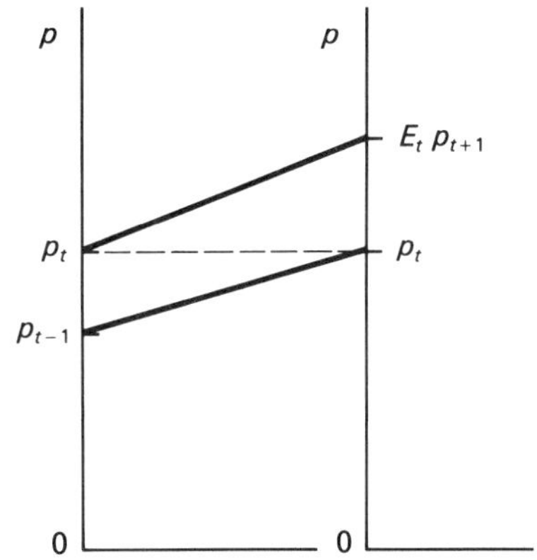

Figure 10.2

We use the ratio effect of Figure 10.2 when we analyze problems in which we are assuming that unions and firms have adaptive expectations. As we did in Chapter 9, we begin in a stationary state equilibrium. The stationary state under adaptive expectations is identical to the one under naive expectations because when the prices are not changing the two expectations functions give the same value for price expectations in the next period. (From equation 10.6, if π_t equals 0, then $E_t p_{t+1}$ equals p_t.) In the stationary state, the continuing result of the negotiations between unions and firms, which result in the same nominal wage each period, is that the unions receive their preferred real wage and the unemployment and output are consistent with this real wage. Given some initial nominal wage, to have a stationary state the AD curve must intersect the AS curve at a price level that generates the preferred real wage and the appropriate output. The (p_1, Y_1) point in Figure 10.3 is such a stationary state equilibrium.

Now suppose that the government decides to follow some type of activist fiscal policy that causes a shift out in the AD curve to AD_2 during period one, just as it did in Figure 9.5 in Chapter 9. (We are continuing to follow the convention that we began in Chapter 9, in which the stationary state is referred to as period zero.) The price level and output equilibrium for period one is now at (p_2, Y_2). There has been inflation equal to $\pi_1 = (p_2 - p_1)/p_1$. The output has increased, real wages have dropped, and unemployment rate has declined. Up to here, the

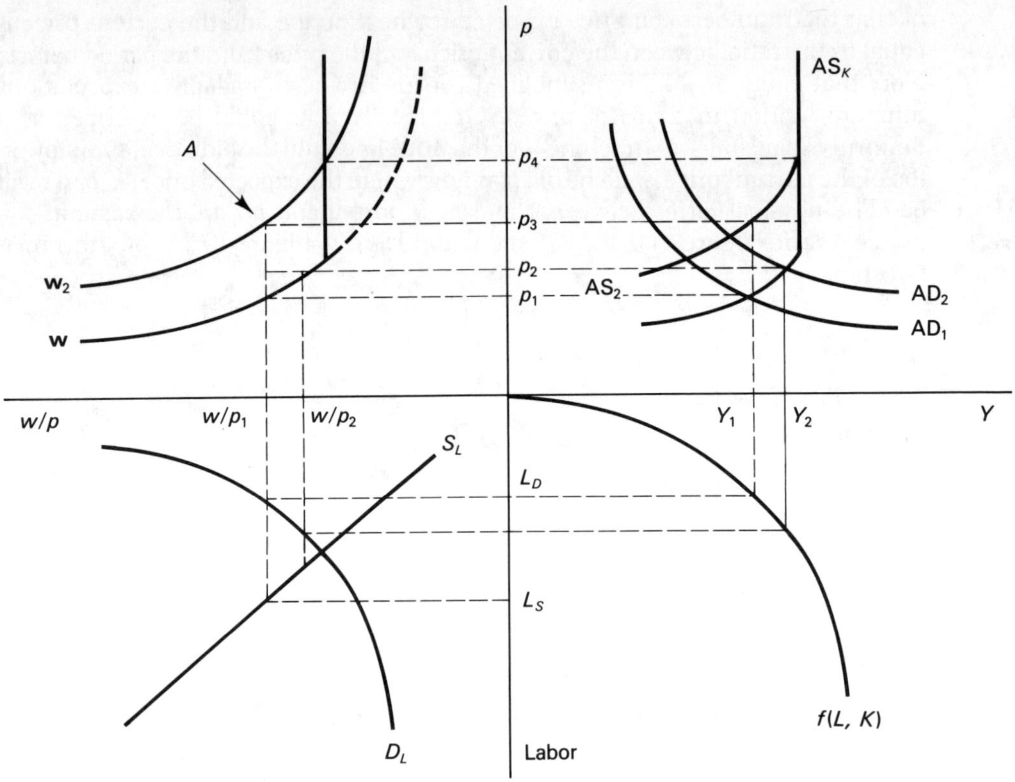

Figure 10.3

example is identical to the one in Chapter 9. Given that this is a world in which agents have adaptive expectations unions and firms expect the inflation rate to continue, and the price level they are expecting for period two is equal to p_3.

As period three begins, the new AS curve is generated (this is the highest of the three AS curves shown) and if no new government policy were followed, p_3 is found by keeping the ratio between p_1 and p_2 the same as the ratio between p_2 and p_3.

The new nominal wage curve, $\mathbf{w}_2$, passes through the point marked A in Figure 10.3. Point A is at the firms' and unions' desired real wage, w/p_1, and the expected price level, p_3. Compare this $\mathbf{w}_2$ curve to the similar, but different, $\mathbf{w}_2$ curve in Figure 9.6. In Figure 9.6, with naive expectations, the price level p_2 was expected, and the $\mathbf{w}_2$ curve passes through the point at w/p_1 and p_2. That $\mathbf{w}_2$ curve in the example with naive expectations is below the one in this example of adaptive expectations. Following points from the new $\mathbf{w}_2$ curve to the labor market, to the production function, and up to the price–output quadrant, we can construct the new aggregate supply curve, AS_2. Note that the kink in the new, "Keynesian" AS gives output level Y_1—the output that corresponds to the desired real wage, w/p_1, and the expected price level, p_3.

The new equilibrium (if the government continues the fiscal policy that it followed in period one into period two) is at the intersection of the AD_2 curve and the new AS_2 curve. In Figure 10.3, one can see that this equilibrium is at a price level (and therefore inflation rate) that is lower than the expected one, p_3, and with output less than the unions' preferred level of output, Y_1. At this equilibrium, the unions are getting real wages higher than expected—higher than the firms are willing to pay in a stationary state. A line traced from the equilibrium over to the nominal wage curve, w_2, will give a real wage that is higher than (that is, to the left of) w/p_1.

We can summarize the events we have just discussed, beginning with the stationary state.

Stationary State. At price p_1 and output Y_1, unions and firms contract for the wage w/p_1.

Period One. The government's policy shifts AD to AD_2. The equilibrium price is p_2, and output increases to Y_2. The real wage declines to w/p_2. The inflation rate, π_2, equals $(p_2 - p_1)/p_1$, and the price expected for the next period is $p_3 = p_2 \times p_2/p_1$. The firms and unions sign a new contract for a nominal wage, w_2, such that $w_2/p_3 = w/p_1$. This wage goes into effect in period two.

Period Two. The new wage, w_2, takes effect. A new AS curve, AS_2, is generated. The equilibrium is at the intersection of AS_2 and AD_2, with a price, p_4, below p_3, and output below Y_1. At the end of the period, a new expected price, p_5, is calculated, and unions and firms agree on a wage for period three of w_3 such that $w_3/p_5 = w/p_1$.

COMPARING NAIVE AND ADAPTIVE EXPECTATIONS ON A LONG TERM POLICY

One useful way to think about the policies that governments follow is to imagine that governments have a political preference function that represents the kind of trade-offs that they are willing to make between important economic variables.[3] These trade-offs usually represent, in some form, the wishes of the constituents of the government, and, if democratically elected, of their party. Of the political

[3] This kind of discussion of government policy is independent of the particular form of government. Democratically elected governments, military governments, dictatorships, and even revolutionary governments can all be thought of in this way. The specific trade-off functions that each of these types of governments have are likely to be very different, but the idea is useful for all types of governments.

parties in the United States, one could imagine that the Democrats have a function that puts a lot of importance on maintaining low levels of unemployment—they see unemployment as very bad for their constituents—and less weight on maintaining low rates of inflation. The Republicans can be characterized as having a function that puts somewhat less weight on acheiving low rates of unemployment—the same percentage of unemployment is not viewed by them as being as bad as it is by the Democrats—and a bigger weight on maintaining low rates of inflation—more Republicans than Democrats own nominally denominated assets. In West Germany, the inflationary experience of 1923 has generated a political trade-off function that finds high rates of inflation to be very bad, much worse than in any major United States political party. Given the set of policies that the political parties have available to them when in power, each attempts to use those policies to find a mix that optimizes their political trade-off function.

In general, the wishes of the political parties, as expressed by this trade-off function, do not aim for single-period goals. Rather, they attempt to generate a set of policies from period to period. Suppose that we have a party—the Demreps—that wishes to achieve, period after period, a level of unemployment lower than the unions' preferred level of unemployment. To do this in one period, the government needs to follow some policy that shifts out the AD curve. This generates some small level of inflation and an increased output as it reduces unemployment. (This occurs in period one in both naive and adaptive models.) Now, in order to simplify things, suppose that the production side of the economy doesn't change. By that, I mean that the production function, the demand curve for labor, and the supply curve for labor remain constant during the entire experiment. The output level associated with the government's preferred unemployment rate will be called the government's preferred output level, Y_p, and with no changes in the production side of the economy this level of output will always occur with the preferred level of unemployment. Let us follow this policy of attempting to maintain the preferred unemployment level, and therefore the preferred output level, in a world with naive expectations. Then we will follow the same policy goal in a world with adaptive expectations.

Figure 10.4 shows the results of the government's attempt to maintain an output level of Y_p and the preferred unemployment rate that goes with it. In period one, the AD curve was shifted out to AD_2. The preferred output was achieved, but prices rose to p_2. At the end of period one, unions contracted with firms for a nominal wage, $\mathbf{w}_2$. Then period two began. The new nominal wage curve generated the new AS curve—the middle of the three AS curves shown—and, if the government did nothing to change the AD curve, the equilibrium between the new AS curve and the AD_2 curve would result in a slightly higher price level, but with a lower-than-preferred output level. To gain its preferred output level, the government must shift out the AD curve again to AD_3. With this AD curve, the new equilibrium is at p_3 and Y_p. To maintain the preferred output level, prices had to be raised from p_2 to p_3. The inflation in period two was $(p_3 - p_2)/p_2$, which is the same rate of inflation that occured in period one. Period two ends with unions and

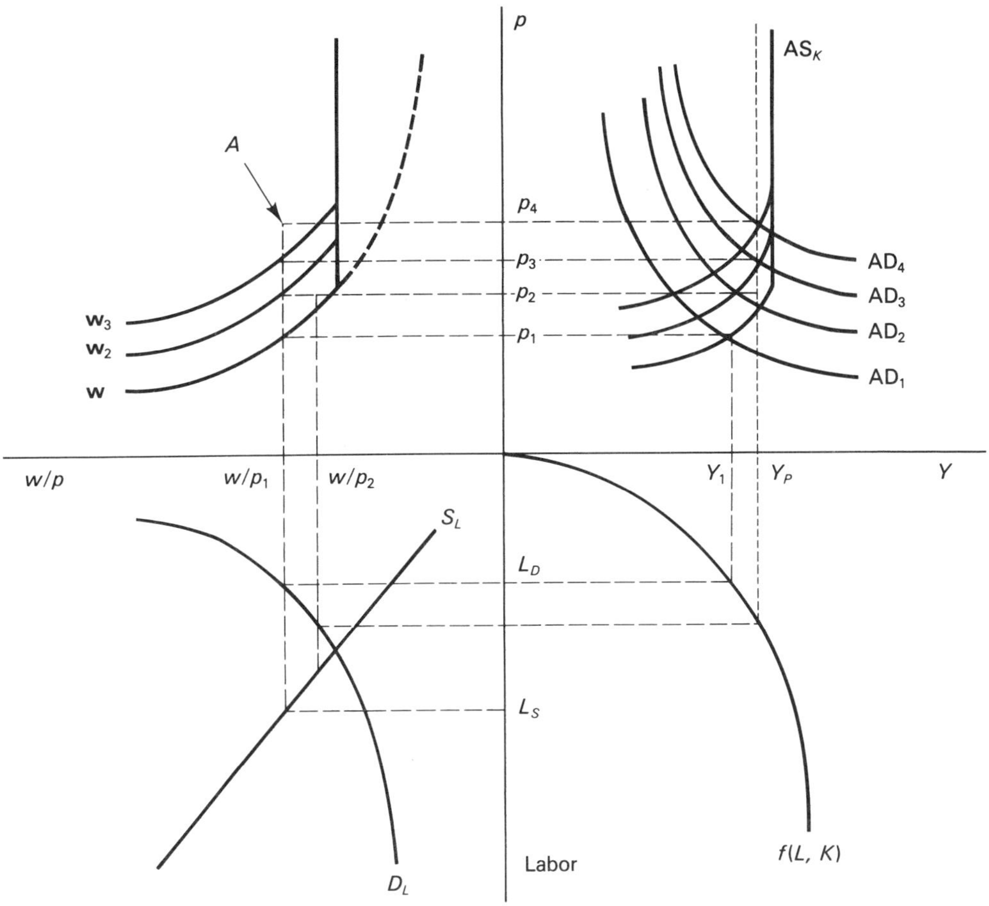

Figure 10.4

firms contracting for the nominal wage, $\mathbf{w}_3$, since the price p_3 is expected to continue into period three.

As period three begins, the new AS curve is generated (this is the highest of the three AS curves shown) and if no new government policy were followed, the output would fall, as it would have in the second period. To maintain Y_p, the government needs to shift the AD curve outward again, this time to AD_4. The new equilibrium between AD_4 and the highest of the AS curves generates price p_4 as the equilibrium price level. The inflation in period three was $(p_4 - p_3)/p_3$. These inflation rates (see Figure 10.4) look very much alike (and, given the shape of the nominal wage curve, *are* alike) and it is fair to say, if we extrapolate from periods two and three, that in an economy with naive expectations, the government can maintain its preferred output and unemployment rates with a constant inflation.

In a world with naive expectations, the results of the Phillips curve holds

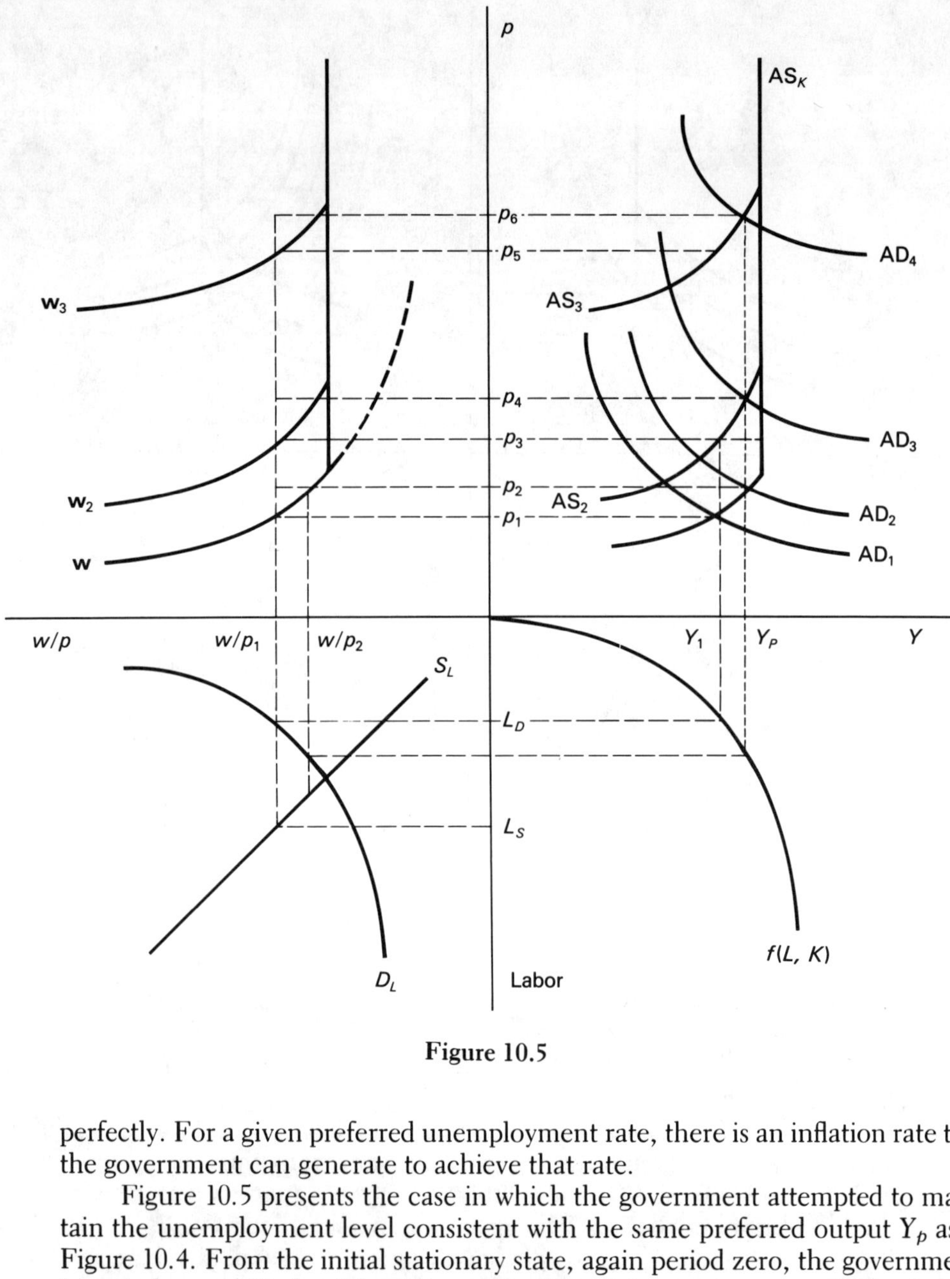

Figure 10.5

perfectly. For a given preferred unemployment rate, there is an inflation rate that the government can generate to achieve that rate.

Figure 10.5 presents the case in which the government attempted to maintain the unemployment level consistent with the same preferred output Y_p as in Figure 10.4. From the initial stationary state, again period zero, the government, in period one, shifted out the AD curve to AD$_2$. Price went up to p_2. With adaptive expectations, the price expected for period two was price p_3, which was higher than the one expected when agents had naive expectations. At the end of period one, the unions and firms contracted for a nominal wage, $\mathbf{w}_2$, that reflected that higher expectation. Period two began with the generation of the new AS curve, AS_2. In order to achieve the desired output and unemployment level, the government shifted out the AD curve to AD_3. The equilibrium price level that occured for period two was price p_4, a price level higher than expected, and which, since the expected inflation rate was equal to the previous period's inflation rate, represented an increased inflation rate. Since the inflation rate in period two was $(p_4 - p_2)/p_2$, the expected price level for period three was price level p_5. At the end of period two, unions and firms contracted for the wage, $\mathbf{w}_3$, that reflected those expectations. When period three began, the AS curve AS_3 appeared, and, to maintain the output level at Y_p, the government needed to shift out the AD curve to AD_4. This achieved a new, higher-than-expected price level, p_6, which represented an inflation rate for period three larger than the inflation rate in period two. The government could reach the desired unemployment rate every period, but, with adaptive expectations, would have to generate *increasing* rates of inflation to do so.

Notice that this set of policies, along with the adaptive expectation function we assumed, results in an ever-increasing inflation rate. When a naive expectation function was used to tell the same story, it would need a constant inflation rate to achieve the same result. Increased employment can be achieved by appropriate government policies, but with ever-increasing inflation. This model is similar to the one that Cagan used to help explain the hyperinflations that occurred in Europe before World War II. Such a model does not give a single Phillips curve. Rather it gives a Phillips curve that shifts whenever a government attempts to exploit it. This is because ever-higher inflation rates are expected, and even higher inflation rates are needed to obtain the same unemployment—output—level.

It is generally believed that the United States government began to attempt to exploit the Phillips curve in about 1965. Figure 10.2 shows the Phillips curve data from 1954 to 1980. The data and the lines drawn on it indicate that the Phillips curves shift until no single Phillips curve can be found at all. The hypothesis is that a Phillips curve exists during times of no activist government policy, but cannot be used except by continually increasing the inflation rate necessary to exploit it.

A comment on the unexploited Phillips curve: An unusually observant student might ask, "If the government follows no activist policies, how do we get a Phillips curve at all? Wouldn't we get a Phillips point, zero inflation and the unemployment determined by the contracted money wage?"

In the world we have been looking at, the answer is yes. Not surprisingly, the real world is slightly more complicated. Various random shocks occur. These shocks are unexplained and possibly unexplainable movements in exogenous economic variables. One can imagine small shocks to 1, the production function, possibly caused by changes in weather which generate changes in output in the farm sector; 2, investment, which we assumed to be exogenous but seems to be to a large extent driven by expectations, so that new information about world events can change investment; and 3, government expenditures and taxes, caused by the government not being able to predict exactly how much it will spend or raise in tax revenues. These shocks, if they are truly random, can have an average value of zero, but much of the time their value is not zero. These shocks cause small changes in the aggregate supply function (in case 1) or in the aggregate demand function (in cases 2 and 3). These changes in the aggregate demand or aggregate supply functions would cause movements in the price level—inflation or deflation—but these movements would be completely unpredictable. These small unpredictable movements in the price level would drive changes in the real wage in a manner that could cause an observable, systematic relationship between changes in the price level and the unemployment rate. Graphing the data generated by these random fluctuations would give a Phillips curve.

REPRISE

The inflation and unemployment rate data that were observed in the United States in the early 1970s were inconsistent with the concept of a single Phillips curve. A change in the assumption of naive expectations to one of adaptive expectations (where all past information on the variable of interest can be used in forming the expectations of future values of that variable) permitted the Keynesian economists to maintain most Keynesian theory and get predictions that matched the data rather well. The addition of adaptive expectations generated the possibility of a shifting Phillips curve. This new Phillips curve is centered around the expected inflation rate, and inflation rates different from the expected one will change the unemployment rate.

Government policies to reduce the unemployment rate, to take one popular policy example, can still be achieved in a Keynesian world with adaptive expectations, but only at a cost of ever-higher inflation rates. The results from the process we observed in going from a naive to an adaptive expectations model would suggest that the more information we let individuals have about the economy, the harder it is for a government to achieve some of the policies it might desire. The next chapter takes this idea to the limit.

EXERCISES

1. Consider the problem shown in Figure 10.3. Suppose that the government does not change any of the exogenous variables after the initial changes that generated AD_2. Follow the time path of output, prices, real wages, and unemployment through period four. (The initial AD move occurred at time period one.) What does this suggest that the long run effects of some one time policy will be?

2. In Chapters 7, 8, and 9, we considered the Reagan version of supply side economics, where a cut in government expenditures and taxes would show up as an equal-sized increase in investment. Suppose that the government does decrease taxes and government expenditures in period one, and that investment does increase during that period. The economy is initially in a stationary state equilibrium and the supply side policy moves it out of that equilibrium. Follow the economy through period three, with the stationary state being period zero, and describe the path of output, prices, real wages, and unemployment.
3. Suppose that the government uses fiscal policy in an attempt to keep the output at some level preferred by the government (and greater than the output level that results when unions and firms get the agreed-upon real wage). Suppose that investment is based upon current income, and the investment function is $I = .05 \times Y$. The government begins its policy in period one. Follow the path of the economy for three periods. Consider the cases where the firms and unions have a) naive expectations and b) adaptive expectations. How are the results different with the two different types of expectations?

11

Rational Expectations

In which we see that, driven by the failure of the predictions of Keynesian models in the 1970s, economists get smarter by letting people get smarter. Naturally, with rational agents in these new classical models, government policy becomes much more difficult to form and, in the limit of rationality, may become impotent.

INTRODUCTION

Suppose that a government wants to change some set of endogenous variables to some other, socially preferred value. For example, suppose that it wants to reduce unemployment. Directly decreeing that unemployment should be less than it is currently is likely to be as successful as the Irish hero Cu'Chulainn was when he decreed that the tides should not come in. Except for direct government employment, as occurred during the WPA projects in the 1930s, a government that is not totalitarian, or does not maintain direct control of the economy, cannot directly change the unemployment rate. The government can only change the variables in its policy set—in our case: T, G, B_g, M—and must attempt to use these policy variables in such a way as to achieve the desired results. To do this rationally, the government needs some model of how the economy works.

This model can be one of two general types: explicit and implicit. The explicit model is similar to the models we have been discussing. Behavioral patterns are carefully written out, and expressed either mathematically or verbally; careful logical deductions relate changes in policy variables to the economy's response. An implicit model is probably more common in government. Policy makers have years of experience in observing the economy and an "intuitive" understanding of economic relationships. Although these implicit models remain intuitive, it would probably be unfair to claim that most of them could not be written out as a consistent set of economic relationships. (However, since they remain intuitive and are *not* written out there is no way to check whether they do indeed form a consistent set of economic relationships.)

Whether the models are implicit or explicit, an important feature they share is that they are systematic. Any time a policy maker faces a specific economic condition or economic environment, that policy maker will respond with the same policy. Other members of the economy—firms and households—soon begin to anticipate the government's policies and include the results of these policies in determining their expectations. When *all* information, including information about how the government forms its policy responses, is used to predict future economic values, the expectations agents are said to display are called **rational expectations.**

Two historical examples might be of some help in seeing how agents' responses to government policy can be important in determining both the path of the economy and the effectiveness of any particular policy. During the 1960s the United States economy experienced a bit of a recession. A law was proposed in Congress to allow firms to take an investment tax credit. This tax credit would, for a limited time, allow the firms to deduct an unusually large portion of any new investment from their corporate income taxes, thereby reducing the cost of those investments by an amount equal to the reduction in taxes. When the law was passed, firms behaved exactly as one would expect them to and spent additional funds on the now-cheaper investment goods. This increased spending in the capital goods sector, increased employment in that sector, and started the economy out of the recession. Once the economy was growing again, Congress could—and did—remove the temporary tax credit. So far, so good.

Time passed. The economy had gone through a boom and was heading into another recession—output was dropping off, and unemployment was rising. In this kind of situation, firms will remember what Congress did the last time there was a recession, and will believe that Congress will institute another investment tax credit when things get bad enough. Because of this belief, firms delayed making the investments they otherwise would have made, so that they could make them after the reenacted investment tax credit made them cheaper. By cutting back on investment as they held off those they were planning to make, they caused the economy to go into a recession faster than it might otherwise have gone, and possibly made it worse than it might have been. Congress did indeed pass the temporary investment tax credit law, firms then made the investments that they were planning to make anyway, and in doing so paid less taxes. A policy—the investment tax credit—that was intended to help get the economy out of a recession had the effect of hurrying the economy into the next one.

Events during the Nixon administration provide a second example. Once again the economy was in a mild recession. Congress began debating the possibility of reducing personal income taxes via an income tax rebate. Bills were introduced in both houses of Congress, and it seemed as if most of the members of Congress would vote for this kind of bill once it reached an acceptable final form. This process took several months. In the interim, people began to go out and spend the income tax rebate that they were expecting to get. The Household Finance loan company even went so far as to offer rebate loans to individuals who brought in their income tax forms so that the firm could calculate the amount of tax rebate they were to get. They could then get the money from the company to use immediately. All of this increased economic activity caused the economy to pull itself out of the mild recession that it had been in. Congress finally decided that it didn't need the income tax rebate after all and did not pass the bill. Imagine what those people who *spent* their income tax rebate will do next time Congress starts talking of such a thing. At the very least, they will wait until the promised rebate is in their hands before spending it.

THE PHILLIPS CURVE–THE DATA

One way of interpreting the data that came in during the late 70s and early 80s is to say that the Phillips curve continued to deteriorate. Figure 11.1 shows the inflation–unemployment points from 1950 to 1986. The line drawn through the graph is an estimate of the straight line that best fits the data. One could continue to interpret this graph as showing a shifting Phillips curve, but that interpretation is becoming increasingly difficult to believe. It might be safe to say that few who look

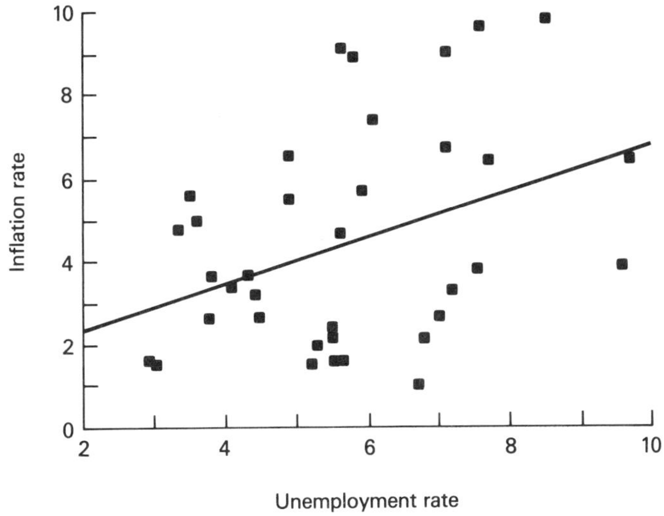

Figure 11.1

at this data without a previous notion of a Phillips curve would find one here. The "Phillips" relationship seems to have disappeared, and it might therefore be best to try to find a new way of looking at the economy that doesn't involve its somewhat questionable inverse relation between unemployment and inflation.

Robert E. Lucas, Jr., did a study on the Phillips curve and government policy in a number of countries.[1] The general result seemed to be that whenever a government attempts to exploit a Phillips curve, as the United States could be viewed as having tried to do in the 70s, the curve disappears. The Phillips curve relationship between inflation and unemployment was strongest in those countries that did not try activist fiscal policies, and the weakest in those that habitually did so. Following these observations, it would be useful to find a model in which a Phillips curve exists, but where it cannot be exploited by government.

MODELING RATIONAL EXPECTATIONS

Let us formalize these notions a bit. Individuals, as consumers, as workers, as members of a union, and as firms, continually observe the government. As time passes they become aware of what economic model the government follows. They become better and better able to predict what the government will do in a given situation. Further, they, as unions and firms, use this information when they sign

[1] Robert E. Lucas, Jr., "Some International Evidence on Output–Inflation Trade-offs." *American Economic Review*, 63 (June 1973): 326–334. Also "Errata" in *American Economic Review*, 66 (December 1976): 895.

contracts with each other for the next period's money wage. The use of all available information, not just past prices, and including expected government actions, in determining next period's money wage is known as rational expectations. In terms of the notation used in Chapter 9, this can be expressed as

$$E_t p_{t+1} = f(p_{t+1} \mid p_t, p_{t-1}, \ldots, \mathbf{Z}_t, \mathbf{Z}_{t-1}) \tag{11.1}$$

where $f(\bullet)$ is the expectations formation function, and $\mathbf{Z}_t$ is a vector of all information from time t that is useful in predicting the time $t + 1$ price level. (A vector is an ordered list of data, so, for each time period s, the information about some particular variable from period s is in the same location in the vector $\mathbf{Z}_s$.) Equation 11.1 merely says that individuals use *all* useful information when they form their expectations.[2]

The use of rational expectations in macroeconomic models has two results, one stronger than the other. The first of these results has to do with the usefulness of government policy in general. As will be shown below, in certain extreme versions of macroeconomic models rational expectations yields ineffectual government policy. This is a very strong result, and more recent work in economics has focused on what kinds of government policies continue to be useful with rational expectations, especially if there is limited or asymmetric information. In less extreme versions of rational expectations models, it is possible to think of the government policy makers as having better knowledge of their own model of the economy than the other agents in that economy could have; and of their own preferences among trade-offs between different economic outcomes. As we will see in Chapter 16, these policy makers might be able to use strategic manipulation of the information that is let out to the public to gain some policy advantage.

The second result has to do with the applicability of estimated macroeconomic models in predicting the outcome of new types of policies. If the macroeconomic model is not—as many are not—based firmly on microeconomic foundations in which expectations are explicitly included, then it is very difficult to have confidence in predictions about policies that have not yet been used and therefore are not included in the data. If a government wants to repeat a policy that it has tried before, the in-sample results (the results of polices that are included in the data sample that was used in estimating the coefficients of the model) may be of some use in prediction. It is quite possible that the values of the coefficients of the model will change as people change their behavior in response to a government policy. If these behavior changes are large enough, then the predictions of an

[2] In a deterministic world, complete information about an event would imply the ability to make perfect predictions about the outcome of that event. The amount of information that is implied by the use of the word "complete" is extremely large, probably larger than the human mind can contain (at least for minimally complex events). All decisions are made based on incomplete information and so interpretations of the sources of uncertainty are based on how well the collected information approximates complete information.

estimated model that used data from a time in which a particular policy was not in effect will misrepresent the behavior of the economy during that policy. These results are developed below.

AN EXTREME VERSION

Consider Figure 11.2. Today, in the stationary state, the money wage has been contracted at **w**. This results in the aggregate supply curve AS_1 (which is not labeled in Figure 11.2, but is the lower of the Keynesian-style AS curves). Suppose the current aggregate demand is AD_1 and resultant price level is p_1, so that the desired real wage $(w/p)^*$ is achieved. This results in employment of L_D and unemployment of $L_S - L_D$. Suppose further that unions and firms have information about the upcoming implementation of government policy. The result of this information is that firms, unions, and the government are making their decisions during the end of period $t - 1$ about the policies they will follow in period t. As an extreme example, assume that the firms and unions know exactly what the government is planning to do the next period, but that the government doesn't know what

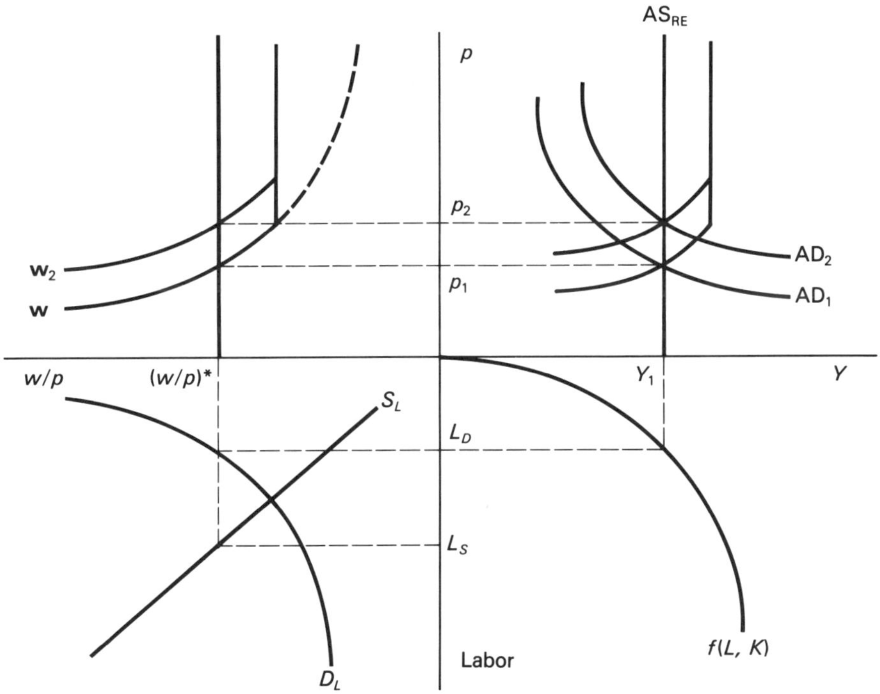

Figure 11.2

the firms and unions will do. This means that the unions and firms can—and do—respond to the government's policies.

In the past, whenever unemployment of $L_S - L_D$ has occurred, the government has responded by increasing government expenditures and causing the aggregate demand curve to shift outward to AD_2, thereby reducing unemployment and increasing the price level. Firms and unions expect this type of behavior to continue. They expect the AD curve for next period, period one, to be AD_2. They will therefore contract for the money wage w_2, a money wage that raises the aggregate supply curve enough so that the final real wage, at period one's equilibrium price, p_2, is $(w/p)^*$. In their negotiations with each other, unions and firms have used their knowledge of the economy and their expectations of the government's policy pattern to maintain their real wage. This defeats the government's policy. Prices increase, but the government's objective, of reducing unemployment, has failed. One can imagine that this pattern of attempted reductions in unemployment caused by shifts in the AD curve will be met by nominal wage hikes that will result in stationary state output and unemployment levels.

If we summarize this behavior, we see that the resultant price–real wage line is vertical, similar to the one in the classical model, but with continual unemployment rate $(L_S - L_1)/L_S$. Some economists refer to this as an example of a "natural" rate of unemployment, a rate inherent in the structure of the system. The resultant AS curve, summarized as AS_{RE}, is also vertical at the output level Y_1. As long as unions and firms can predict the government's actions using rational expectations, the AD curve will cross an AS curve on the summarized AS curve, AS_{RE}. This AS_{RE} curve describes the behavior of the economy under an extreme version of rational expectations. Given this kind of AS curve, which looks much like the one in the classical model but with unemployment, it should not be surprising that models with these types of results are called representations of the new classical economics. If one were to ask these extreme models the kind of policy questions that we have been posing to our models, the results would be very similar to those answers given by the original classical model. The major difference is that in these models there will be unemployment. Unfortunately, if these extreme models are true, there is little that the government can do to reduce this unemployment.

In this world, the government cannot effectively follow a systematic policy. A randomly generated policy would have effects on the economy, but these would be like any other kind of random shock, sometimes good, sometimes bad. It would have effects because people wouldn't be able to forecast the random variable. Government policy attempts of this kind might only increase uncertainty. (We will speak more about this in Chapter 16.) Random shifts in the AD curve that have natural causes are discussed below in the section on the Phillips curve.

There is another consideration worth pondering. Suppose unions and firms included an escalator clause in their contracts. Such a clause would adjust the money wage received by the union upward whenever prices rose, so that the real wage rate, $(w/p)^*$, was kept constant. If this were the case, then the escalator clause would guarantee that firms and unions were always correct in their expectations, since the escalator clause replaces the need for expectations. The results of the extreme rational expectations model would occur. There is one difficulty with escalator clauses in contracts, though; they usually operate with at least a short lag. This happens because people don't normally know the inflation rate at the moment but they might know, for example, the rate for last month. In Argentina in 1985, when the *monthly* inflation rate was over forty percent, the wages were indexed to ninety percent of the inflation of the previous month. This is really a case of institutionalized adaptive expectations, and our models would predict that an ever-increasing inflation rate could be used to generate a lower unemployment rate. If the wage correction were instantaneous, the extreme rational expectations result would hold, and no improvement of the unemployment rate would be possible. Such instantaneous adjustment is probably impossible. A policy that would have the same results would be one that did an after-the-fact adjustment of wages to the inflation that occurred in the previous period. Some economists in Argentina suggested that estimated wages be paid each month and, once the actual inflation rate were known, an adjustment be paid, so that wages after the adjustment were completely corrected for inflation. This is one way of eventually indexing current wages on current inflation.

The second rational expectations result mentioned above deals with the microeconomic foundations of macroeconomics. The consumption function, the investment function (in our case, merely an exogenous variable, but we did discuss other forms) and some of the aggregation characteristics of the production function are, at best, only weakly based on microeconomics. Especially when the economic environment gets more complicated, with lots of taxes and much subtler government policies, the appearance of expectations of future variables and the effects of future government policies can mean that the entire model of the economy is required for the estimation of each of the equations in that model. This was illustrated in the discussion about the life cycle model of consumption, where consumption during early years depends, in part, on the expected income in later years. The model we constructed, but have quietly put aside, of investment behavior based on firms maximizing their discounted value of expected future profits, gives us an investment function with expected future prices and wages as important variables. If we really believe that our consumption and investment functions are descended from these more complicated models, then the coefficients of the equations of our model should depend on these expected future values, just as the more microeconomic models do. The coefficients of our models probably change as government policies change. Because new current government policies imply new future government policies, they will change the expectations of the citizens in a way that changes the coefficients of all the equations. This can happen even if there are no new current policies, if individuals have good reason to believe that there will be new government policies in the near future. (The tax rebate that was never given is an example of this.) If we ask our models (in a form where the coefficients were estimated from the past behavior of the economy) about policies that were not tried before, the coefficients do not include predictions about how people will change their behavior when confronted by these new policies. The predictions of our models, therefore, will likely misrepresent the real outcome of these new policies.

Of course, the way around this problem is to construct macroeconomic models that are really microeconomic models. These models should include functions about how individuals form their expectations and about how changes in these expectations will change their behavior. Predictions generated by these kinds of models would not suffer from the problem of incorrect coefficients. Unfortunately, these types of models are arduously difficult to construct and solve and some important aspects of these models—for instance: How fast do people learn about new policies? How fast do they incorporate this information in their behavior?—have not yet been well studied. Much interesting current work in economics is being done on learning models, and on models where different individuals have different information.

THE PHILLIPS CURVE–THE THEORY

As mentioned above, we want a theory in which a Phillips curve exists but is not exploitable. Not surprisingly (since I bring this topic up) our model of rational expectations gives us just such a result. To get this result, we must slightly weaken the extreme rational expectations version of the model to allow for some naturally-generated, unpredictable movements in the AD curve.

Suppose that we are initially in a stationary state. We are going to use a slightly different notion of a stationary state than the one we used before. In this formation, the location of the AD curve is not perfectly determined. There are either some errors in the government's ability to generate its specific policies, or there are some random shocks in the investment or consumption functions that show up as random shocks in the AD curve. However they are generated, these random shocks cause the AD curve to appear, much of the time, in a slightly different place than expected. Since the "random shock" is random, the slight error in the AD curve cannot be predicted. The "expected" AD curve is the one most likely to occur, but the unpredictable shock causes the one that actually occurs to be somewhat different from the expected one.[3] (It is possible that, once in a while, the unexpected shock has a value of zero, and then the expected AD curve occurs.) Let's consider a more specific representation of this problem.

[3] This is not exactly true, except for random processes that have symmetric distributions, like the normal distribution. The "expected" AD curve is the mean or average of all possible AD curves, with each possible curve weighted by the probability that that curve will occur. The term "the most likely" means that a particular AD curve has the highest probability to actually occur. If the distribution of the probabilities is asymmetric, then it is often the case that the average AD curve is not the one that has the highest probability of occurring.

Figure 11.3a shows the upper right hand quadrant of our main four quadrant graph, the price–output quadrant. The curve labeled AD_e is the AD curve that is expected by the unions and the firms. There is a probability distribution of the error terms, so that it is possible that the AD curve actually occurs somewhere between AD_U (U for upper, in this example) and AD_L (L for lower). Figure 11.3b shows one of the many possible probability distributions for the AD curves between AD_L and AD_U. This probability distribution is approximately a truncated normal distribution. The height of the curve in Figure 11.3b shows how likely it is that each particular AD curve will be the one that occurs. The total probability—the area under the curve—is equal to one, so one of these AD curves will occur. Everyone in the economy expects that AD_e will occur. They know that they will be wrong most of the time, but, since their errors will not be systematic, there is no better choice.

When and if AD_e does occur, output is equal to the expected output, Y_e, and the price level is the expected price level, p_e. Since this is the expected output level, it is also the one where the unions receive their desired real wages from the firms. The unemployment rate at this point is the one associated with that desired real wage. At this point, we need to define a **stochastic stationary state.** A stochastic stationary state is one in which the expected equilibrium for the economy does not change, and *is* the current equilibrium, but the realized equilibrium, the ones that occur, can change, although only as a result of a random variable that has a value different from the expected, or average value.[4] The (Y_e, p_e) pair represents the expected equilibrium for next period in this stochastic stationary state. If an AD curve different from AD_U is the one that actually occurs, and this is very likely,

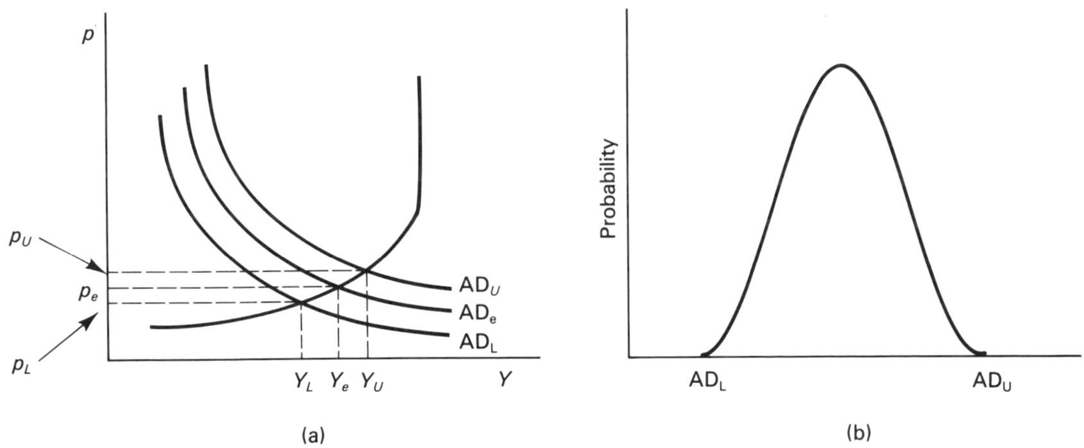

Figure 11.3

[4] The stationary state is called stochastic because it has random, unpredictable elements to it. Tossing a coin is a stochastic—random—process. The side of the coin that comes up is the realization of that toss. A head or a tail are the two events that can be realized in this coin-tossing game.

then the equilibrium values will be different. Since the AD curve can range between AD_L and AD_U, the equilibrium can range, in a random faction, between (Y_L, p_L) and (Y_L, p_U).

Notice that AD_L is associated with the lower-than-expected price level, and therefore a lower-than-expected inflation rate; a lower-than-expected output level; and a higher-than-expected unemployment rate. This higher-than-expected unemployment rate occurs because fewer workers are hired in order to generate the lower-than-expected output. The curve AD_U is associated with a higher-than-expected price level and inflation rate; a higher-than-expected output level; and a lower-than-expected unemployment rate. These variations in the price level and unemployment rates around the expected value, which in a stationary state is a zero inflation rate, gives us a Phillips curve

The thick vertical line over U^* in Figure 11.4a is the Phillips curve that results from a perfectly anticipated government policy that shifts out the AD curve. In the extreme version of the rational expectations model—the perfectly anticipated policies version—changes in the inflation rate have no effect on the unemployment rate. U^* is the unemployment rate that accompanies unions' desired real wage rate, w/p^*. Since the real wage does not change, neither does the unemployment rate.

In a stochastic stationary state, if the government follows a policy that generates an expected inflation rate of zero—that is, if it does not try to exploit the Phillips curve relationship—the random shocks to the AD curve generate changes in the unemployment rate around the rate U^*. The lowest of the angled lines in Figure 11.4a shows the Phillips curve that this stationary state can generate. This line occurs because of the unpredicted movements in the AD curve and the effects

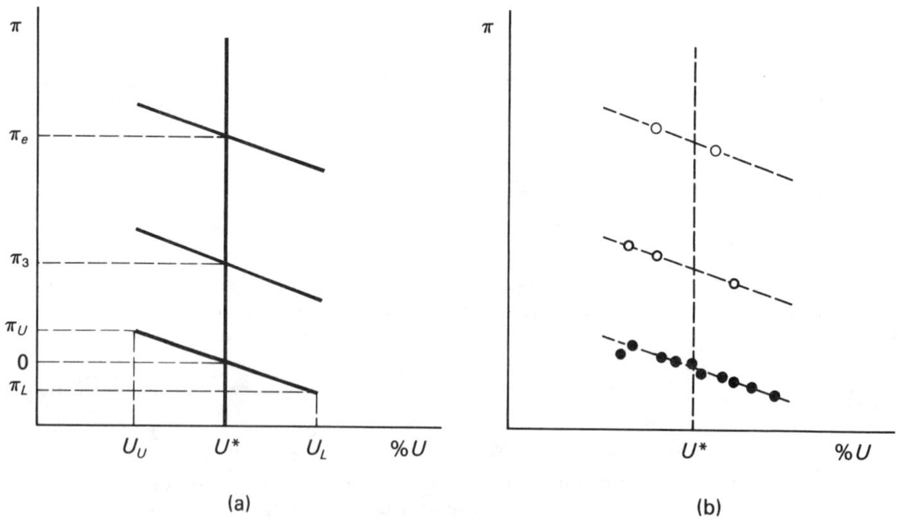

Figure 11.4

of unpredicted inflation on the economy. If the expected rate were always π_e, then the middle of these angled lines would rise, as a kind of shifted-out Phillips curve. Again, the observed inverse relationship between inflation and unemployment comes entirely from the unpredicted component of inflation.

Figure 11.4b shows the kind of data one might get, depending on the kind of policies the government might attempt. The black dots are the inflation–unemployment points that might occur if the government did not try to exploit the Phillips curve. The random shifts in the AD curve generate points along the lower line. If the government started to try to exploit the Phillips curve by shifting out the AD curve to get the inflation π_3 and then shifted it out again to π_e because the initial shift did not generate the desired reduction in unemployment, the points marked by circles might be the observed data. If one looked only at the circles and attempted to see what "curve" best fit the data, something like the vertical line appears. The more the government attempts to exploit the Phillips curve by increasing the expected inflation rate, the more vertical the Phillips curve becomes. Note that the variations in unemployment come from the errors in the prediction of inflation. They come from the nonsystematic (if one can call it that) part of the government's policy.

AN INCOME TAX CUT

It is possible to see how a tax cut can have effects in a rational expectations model if one considers the microeconomic nature of these cuts. Imagine a cut in taxes caused by a cut in the income tax rate. In the world of this model, as in the United States, individuals pay taxes as a percentage of their incomes. A cut in these tax rates reduces tax collections and shifts out the AD curve, just as the cut in the lump sum taxes that we have been assuming up to now did. In a rational expectations world the new equilibrium in the price–output quadrant is at a higher price, but at the same output level. If the analysis is restricted to the aggregate demand curve, this policy does not have an immediate effect on output. Figure 11.2 illustrates this shift.

The change in the percentage of income that an individual must pay as income taxes however, does change the labor market. At each gross real wage (before tax real wage) more individuals will want to work because the net wage (after tax real wage) has increased as a result of the reduction in the income tax rate. If we think in terms of dollars, a gross wage of five hundred dollars a week gives a net wage of three hundred dollars if the tax rate is forty percent ($500 minus .40 times $500 equals $300). If the tax is reduced to twenty percent, the net wages increase to four hundred dollars. This will have an important effect in the labor market if people care about their net wages, not their gross wages.

Let's look at the labor market to see how a cut in the income tax rate changes the equilibrium. Figure 11.5 shows the labor market. The supply curve for labor,

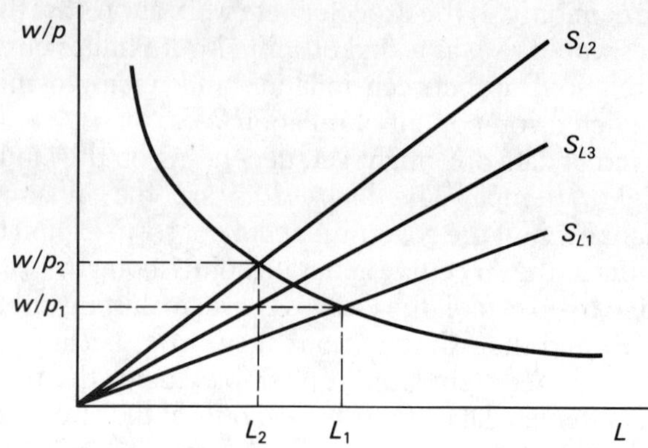

Figure 11.5

S_{L1}, gives the quantity of work that households are willing to offer to the labor market as a function of the wage that they get to keep—the after tax wage. Suppose that there is an income tax of fifty percent. The supply curve for labor, S_{L2}, shows the quantity of labor that the households will provide to the market as a function of the pre-tax wage. Note that this second supply curve for labor offers the same amount of labor to the market as does the S_{L1} curve, at a wage that is twice as high as on the S_{L1} curve. This is because a fifty percent tax on twice the original wage gives the same net wage as no tax on the original wage.

Nothing needs to be done to the demand curve for labor in this example. The demand curve for labor is based on the marginal product of the workers, and firms do not care if the payment that they make to workers goes to the worker for private consumption or to the government as tax payments. The normal demand curve for labor continues to be appropriate.

The equilibrium in the labor market is quite different depending on the rate of taxes. With no percentage income tax, the equilibrium real wage is w/p_1, and the quantity of labor that clears the market is L_1. With the fifty percent income tax rate, the equilibrium real wage is the higher w/p_2, and the quantity of labor that clears the market is the lower L_2. The income tax raises the equilibrium real wage and lowers the equilibrium quantity of labor.

Our assumption about the behavior of unions is that in the long run, in their negotiations with firms, they can gain real wages for their membership that are some fixed percentage greater than the equilibrium real wage. If the equilibrium real wage increases, then unions can get a higher real wage for their members, but the percentage that they can get above the equilibrium is unchanged.[5] So when

[5] This assumption is not exactly correct, but it is a fairly good approximation of union behavior. One of the things that influences the ability of the union to extract increases from firms is the competition that the union faces from nonunion workers. In times of high unemployment, and when many unemployed workers are available, the firm is more likely to let the union strike and to hire some of the unemployed as strikebreakers.

the tax rate change lowers the tax rate, and lowers the supply curve for labor to S_{L3} as it does in Figure 11.5, the real wage that the unions can get must drop as well.

All of this is put together in Figure 11.6. Remember that the labor market quadrant has been flipped in both directions, so read it carefully. The drop in the income tax rate and the tax revenues shifted out the AD curve to AD_2. The cut in the tax rate caused a shift in the supply curve for labor to S_{L2}. The renegotiation of the union's contracts means that it can only get paid the real wage indicated by the thicker of the two lines in the price–real wage quadrant. This lower real wage, or gross wage, for the unions may or may not represent a lower net wage. That depends on the shift in the supply curve for labor and the collective bargaining negotiations. The firms pay lower gross real wages to their workers, and so they are willing to hire more. The demand curve for labor does not move because firms only care about what they have to pay out, not what their workers can keep. So with the lower real wage, the firms hire more people and the output increases. The

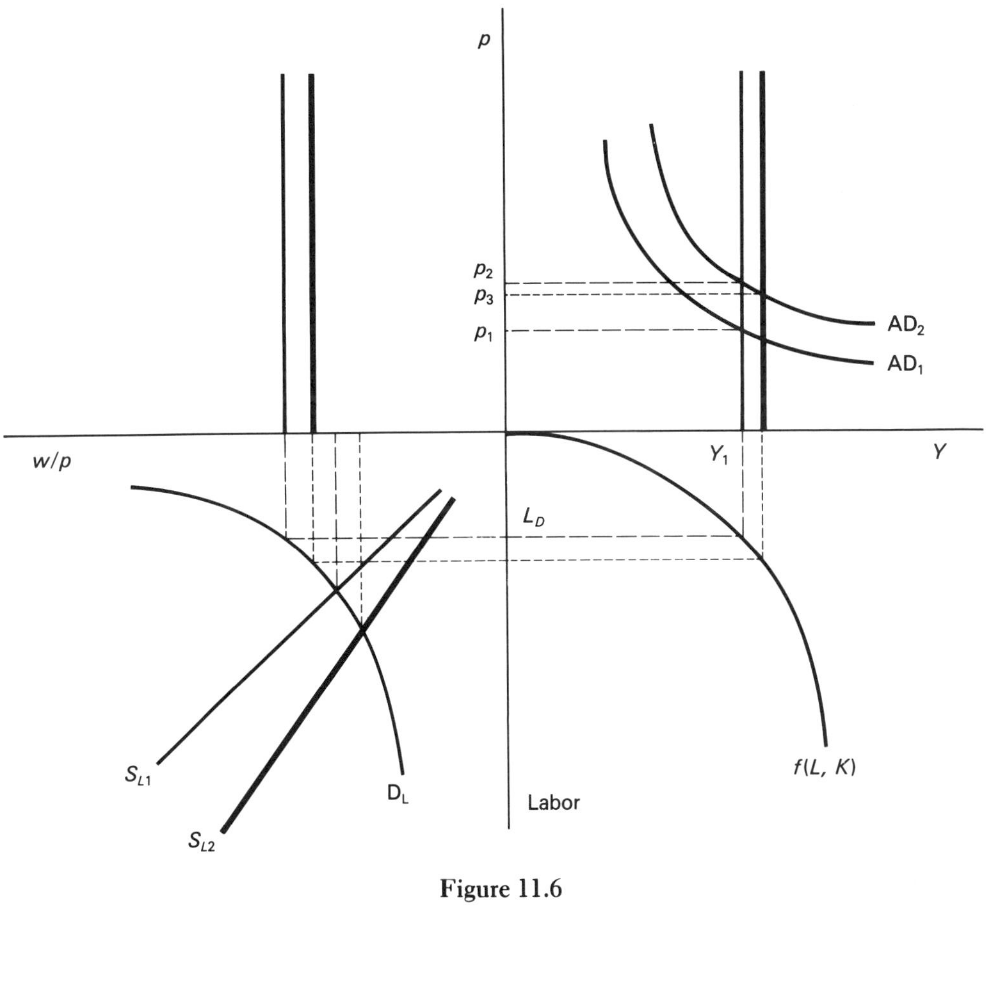

Figure 11.6

new, thicker aggregate supply curve and the price level, p_3, give us a new equilibrium and an increased output.

The result of this policy has been to increase prices and output. If one were to analyze this tax-cutting policy in a standard, naive expectations, Keynesian model, the result would be an increase in prices and output. It is interesting that, during his administration, President Reagan would make references to the tax cut that was put into place by the Kennedy administration as being the source of his own tax cuts. The Reagan administration, however, professed an economic model much more along the lines of a rational expectations or classical formulation than did the Kennedy administration, which was explicitly Keynesian. The two administrations got essentially identical results from their tax cuts, at least in terms of prices and output. The fact that both of these models give the same result from a tax cut means that it is very difficult to use data on prices and output to differentiate between these two models. An attempt to use data from periods in which the government applied tax cuts should give the same results and cannot tell us which is the true model. This kind of "observational equivalence" between economic models is one of the more discouraging aspects of economic science.

NOT EXACTLY A REPRISE

The rational expectations version of our Keynesian model given above is rather extreme. It presumes that firms and unions can determine what the government is going to do, but that the government cannot determine what the firms and unions will do. In this case unions and firms always win. The real world happens to be a bit more complicated in that firms, unions, and government make their decisions at the same time. None of them really know what the others are going to do, even though each of them needs to guess what the others will do when they make their own plans. An analogy from sports might help make this notion clearer.

Consider a football game (American football, not real "futbol"). During each play of the game, the offense attempts to move this piece of pigskin—the ball—in one direction on the field and across a white chalk line. The defense is trying to prevent the offense from moving the ball in that direction and, if possible, to move it in the other direction. The offense will attempt a play based on what it thinks the defense will do. The defense tries to guess what the offense is planning to do and to arrange itself so as to prevent the offense from succeeding. Whoever guesses best makes the gain on that particular play. In this sense, the economy is like a football game. Each of the players in the economy has to determine what the others are likely to do, and each makes these decisions at the same time as the other players, based on limited information about what the others might do.

Let us continue the football example a little further. What each team will do on a particular play is determined to a large extent by the rules of the game. Under the current rules, if the offense has ten yards to go for a first down and this is their fourth try at that first down—they are on the 50 yard line, say—they are likely to punt the ball. The defense knows this and the particular way they set themselves up, with one man back to receive the ball and everyone else on the line, is based on the presumption that the offense will kick. If the rules of the game were changed—you were allowed only three downs, for example; forward laterals were permitted; or no substitutions were allowed—the strategic behavior of each of the teams would be different. Predicting what a team would do under the old rules might often lead to the wrong behavior under a new and different set of rules.

If government policies are viewed as the rules of the economic game that firms and unions play, changes in those rules are likely to cause different outcomes for the economy than could have been predicted under the old rules. In this sense, attempting to use data from a period when the government was following one kind of policy to predict what the economy will be like under a different policy is likely to generate incorrect results. One would like to have the models constructed to explicitly include the decision process of agents as they react to the constraints imposed by the policy rules of the government. Unless this is done, one would be worried about how to interpret the model's predictions in response to changes in those constraints.

These two ideas, the strategic *nature* of agents' decisions and the observation that changes in government policy can change the *way* in which agents make those decisions, are the heart of the rational expectations critique of Keynesian macroeconomics. We will deal with some of the issues of strategic games, and how economies can be modeled as a strategic game between the policy maker and the rest of the economy, in Chapter 16. Chapter 15 will analyze some government policies in a world with perfect foresight. The agents in the models of that chapter will know current and future government policies. There are still some things a govenment can do in that kind of world, but it must operate within narrower-than-Keynesian constraints.

EXERCISES

1. In Chapters 7, 8, 9, and 10, we considered the Reagan version of supply side economics, where a cut in government expenditures and taxes would show up as an equal-sized increase in investment. Suppose that the government does decrease taxes and government expenditures in period one and that investment does increase during that period. The economy is initially in a stationary state equilibrium, and the supply side policy moves it out of that equilibrium. Follow the economy through period three, with the stationary state being period zero, and describe the path of output, prices, real wages, and unemployment when expectations are rational.
2. Suppose that the government uses fiscal policy in an attempt to keep the output at some level preferred by the government (and greater than the output level

that results when unions and firms get the agreed-upon real wage). Suppose that investment is based upon current income and the investment function is $I = .05 \times Y$. The government begins its policy in period one. Follow the path of the economy for three periods. Consider the cases where firms and unions have rational expectations. How are the results here different from the results that you obtained in Exercise 3 at the end of Chapter 10?

3. In a world with rational expectations, suppose that there is a "surprise" tax cut in period one. What does that do to wages and unemployment in period one? What happens to wages and unemployment in periods two and three?

12

Business Cycles

In which economies, like the rest of us, are shown to have their ups and downs. Not only that, they tend to have them sympathetically. Explaining these movements is where modern economics is going.

INTRODUCTION

Economists have observed that certain macroeconomic variables move together through time in a roughly cyclical pattern. These cyclical co-movements in output, prices, wages, investment, and consumption (among others) are known as business cycles. In this chapter we will briefly discuss a number of the earlier models of these cycles and consider in more depth two of the more interesting recent models that economists have developed to explain these movements and co-movements.

Every economic time series, which is a collection of data from sequential periods, can be viewed as being comprised of a **trend component** (sometimes referred to as the deterministic component) and a **cyclical component** (referred to as the random or stochastic component).[1] The trend component can be thought of as a growth or decay component, reflecting the general, long term growth of the economy. The cyclical component is much more difficult to explain. Why should economic variables tend to move in at least vaguely cyclical patterns? What is the nature of these patterns, and, in particular, are they explosive or do they converge, and if they converge do they do so smoothly, or do they oscillate? Why do certain variables tend to move together?

Figure 12.1a illustrates some typical economic variable—in this case the natural log of GNP in the United States from 1947 through 1982. Figure 12.1a also shows an estimate of the trend component, the straight line; Figure 12.1b shows the **residual cyclical component.** The residual cyclical component is what is left over after we remove the trend component. It is the path of the variable around the trend line. We will concentrate on this residual cyclical component and will refer to its movements as a business cycle.

A business cycle in its simplest form has a standard shape. This shape is shown in Figure 12.2. Every business cycle has an expansion, peak, recession, and trough. These characteristics of the business cycle are marked on the oversimplified diagram of Figure 12.2. A complete business cycle is measured from any one of these reference points in a cycle to its next occurrence; for example, from peak to peak. As one can see from Figure 12.1b, the observed business cycles are nowhere

[1] Some economists believe that there is an important distinction to be made between modeling economic variables as composed of 1, a combination of deterministic and stationary stochastic processes, or 2, nonstationary stochastic processes. Stationary stochastic processes are those that have finite limit values—they converge to some finite value—and those where the relationship between different time periods depends only on the time difference and not on the particular time. If we are interested in the stationary process that describes the path of some variable Z_t and we want to know the relationship between the value of that process at time t and time $t + 15$, all we need to know it that these points are 15 periods apart; we do not need to know at which t we are. Certain types of nonstationary stochastic processes may explode. An equation of the form $Y_t = bY_{t-1}+e_t$, where e_t is an error term with a zero average value, will be stationary if b is less than one in absolute value and nonstationary if it is greater than or equal to one.

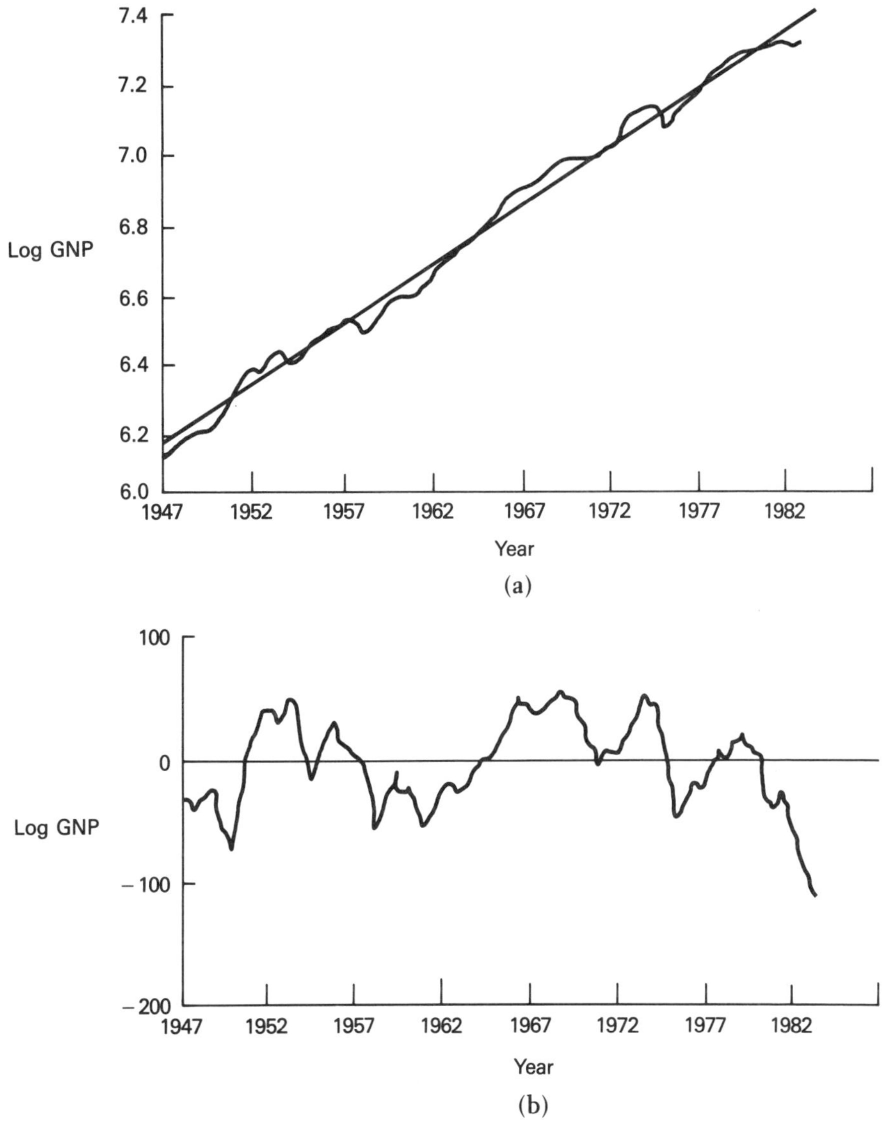

Figure 12.1

near as smooth as the nice sinasoidal curve in Figure 12.2. In order to get models that look like these complicated data series, we can either construct very complicated equations that describe them perfectly but have little predictive power, or we can model them with fairly simple equations that have a random component added. If these simple models capture a lot of the interrelations between the

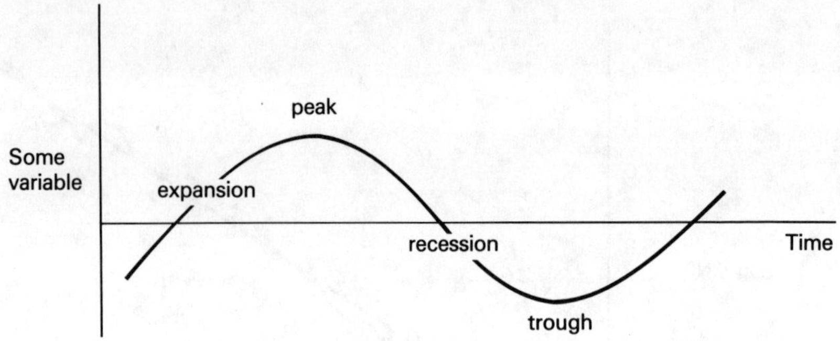

Figure 12.2

variables, then they can have fairly good predictive power within the limit of the random component, which, being random, cannot be predicted at all.

The co-movement of several variables during business cycles is illustrated in Figure 12.3. This figure shows the graphs of the detrended values of the natural logs of GNP, consumption, and investment.[2] Note, first, that there is a similar cyclical pattern in each of the three variables. This similarity in movement is what is meant by the co-movements in variables. In general, these variables move together during business cycles. There are, however, important differences in the way these variables behave during a cycle. The investment graph seems to show the most variation.[3] This suggests that investment is more volatile than the other variables. This volatility is one of the reasons that economists have looked to investment as a source of business cycles. It is also one of the reasons that some economists look to expectations for a theory of investment. They believe that expectations are more volatile than the actual movement of the economy. It is possible that new information shows up in investment decisions much more rapidly than in the other variables because of the effects of this information on expectations and the effects of expectations on investment.

It is clear from the graphs that consumption is the smoothest of the illustrated variables. Larry Christiano has recently argued that the relative smoothness of the consumption cycle is supporting evidence for the life cycle–permanent income hypothesis theory of the consumption function.[4] (This theory of consumption decisions was presented in Chapter 5.) While his model is fairly mathematical, the basic idea is that individuals' predictions of their whole lifetime income pattern change much more slowly than do their current incomes (as measured by GNP, for example). If this lifetime income path is an important determinant of current consumption, aggregate consumption should not show as

[2] In this example, the variables have had the linear and quadratic trends removed.

[3] This is certainly the case if we consider variation as a percentage of the average value. Investment, on average, is much smaller than GNP or consumption, so variations about the trend of equal size imply a much greater percentage of variation in investment.

[4] In Larry Christiano, "Why is Consumption Less Volatile than Income," *Federal Reserve Bank of Minneapolis Quarterly Review*, (Fall 1987), 2–20.

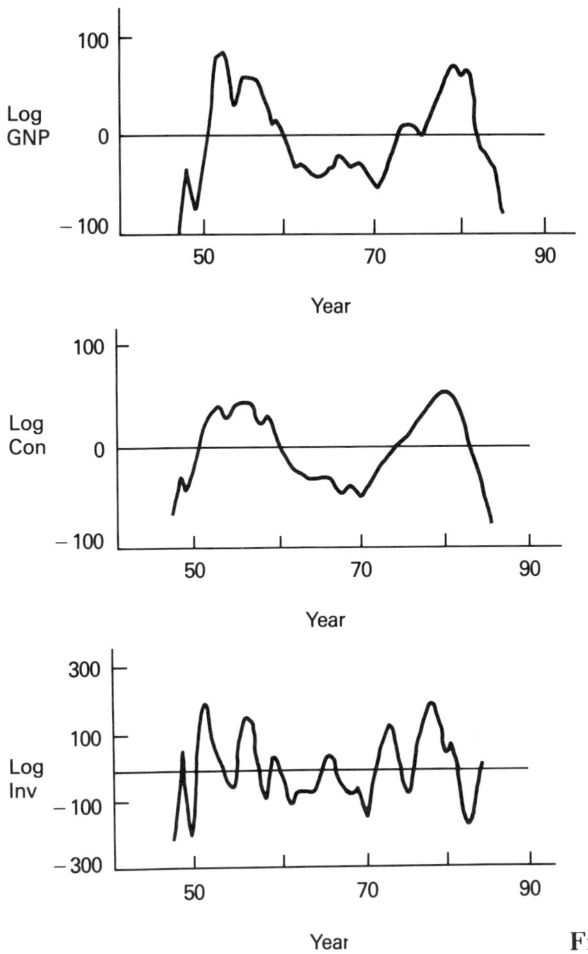

Figure 12.3

much variation as does aggregate income. Consumption does indeed show both less variation around the trend and a smoother path throughout each cycle than do either GNP or investment.

Business cycles are categorized as being of at least three types. These types differ in length. The shortest of the business cycles is the **seasonal business cycle.** Seasonal business cycles are a year or less in length. It is thought that the seasonal business cycle catches those oscillations of the economy that occur within a year but repeat themselves from year to year. For example, every year there is an increase in business activity during December as people make their holiday purchases. Many large retail stores make about fifty percent of their annual sales during December and then there is a decline in business activity in the summer as people take their vacations. This is especially true in France, where most people take their vacation in August; in that month, the country's output falls to some sixty percent of other months. Agencies for government statistics often attempt to remove this seasonal cycle so that the nonseasonal changes can be better examined. This process is called **deseasonalization,** and the resulting series are called **deseasonalized.** Suppose that we want to compare the GNP in December of one year with the GNP of the following January. Normally, the January GNP would be smaller, and if we want to see how we are doing in comparison to other years, we can take out the seasonal drop; computing and removing the average drop from December to January over the last so many years is a rough way of doing this. That way we can see if this particular January represents a boom or bust, relative to other Januaries.

Business cycles of two to six years in length are known as **"the" business cycle.** These business cycles are thought to be caused by the investment decisions of firms and the lag that occurs from the initial investment decision until the investment actually comes on line and begins to be productive. The Hicks-Samuelson Multiplier-Accelerator model we will discuss below attempts to explain this type of business cycle in a fairly simple model.

The third type of business cycle is known as the **long cycle.** This was of major interest to an economist named Simon Kuznets, who also did important work in the development of the United States's national income accounts.[5] In the 1930s, Kuznets became convinced that there existed a business cycle of approximately twenty years in length. He set out to find this cycle in the data. To look for a cycle of this length, especially with the crude annual data that was available at that time, Kuznets needed data gathered over a great many years. The earlier the data, he felt, the less faith he should have in its accuracy. In order to "improve," or "clean up," the accuracy of his data, Kuznets subjected them to a filter. Kuznets first took five-year averages of the data. If the output of the economy at date t is $Y(t)$, he let the five-year average centered around year t be $\mathbf{Y(t)}$ where

$$\mathbf{Y(t)} = 1/5[Y(t-2) + Y(t-1) + Y(t) + Y(t+1) + Y(t+2)]$$

Kuznets intended this filter to help eliminate some of the measurement error that was certain to appear in data this old. If the data are measured badly enough, some goods that were produced in one year would show up in the data as belonging to a different year. Smoothing out the data, as the above filter will do, could make these kinds of mistakes less important. Kuznets then claimed that since he was interested in looking at cycles, he needed to further filter the $\mathbf{Y(t)}$ series by taking five-year moving averages. He used as his final data a series Y(t) where

$$\mathrm{Y(t)} = [\mathbf{Y(t+5)} - \mathbf{Y(t+5)}]$$

In the data that had passed through both of these filters, Kuznets found his twenty-year cycles. Unfortunately for Kuznets, in 1968 a young economist named

[5] Simon Kuznets, *National Product Since 1869* (New York: National Bureau of Economic Research, 1946).

Howrey discovered that the transformations that Kuznets used would *create* a twenty-year cycle.[6] The filters that were intended to clean up the data would, if applied to completely random data, have produced cycles that were twenty years in length. Kuznets did not find his hoped-for long cycles. Because of the error in the technique he used, the question as to whether or not such long cycles do exist is still unanswered.[7]

There is another long cycle that one may read about at times, mostly in the popular press. This is a supposed fifty- to fifty-five-year cycle written about by the Soviet economist N. D. Kondratieff in the 1920s and early 30s.[8] In his theory, major technical innovations, which occur every fifty years or so, set off a cycle of prosperity and depression. A new set of technological innovations then sets off another period of prosperity. There is not much discussion of this Kondratieff cycle in the major economic literature, in part because there is a question about whether we have sufficient data to analyze a cycle this long. Kondratieff paid dearly for his work. The continued periods of prosperity that these models predicted for the capitalist economies did not wear well with the Soviet hierarchy, and Stalin or one of his apparatchiks had him sent to Siberia, where he died.

SOME EARLY BUSINESS CYCLE THEORIES

In his 1927 book on business cycles, Wesley Clair Mitchell surveyed the business cycle theories then current.[9] A selection of these theories is interesting because the theories reappear over and over again in economic literature, especially in the popular press.

As early as 1801, William Hershel suggested that sunspots could be a source of the cyclical movements in the economy. If sunspots changed the weather and the weather changed crop production, then this could lead to cycles in the economy emanating from the agricultural sector. This theory was picked up by W. Stanley Jevons, who noted the (then incorrectly estimated) 10.45 year cycle in sunspots and the (then calculated) 10.46 year cycle in commercial activity. This theory was damaged by the recalculation of the sunspot cycle that found these cycles to last more than eleven years.

Two other theories depended on the weather. Jevons's son, Herbert Stanley Jevons, claimed that a 3.5 year cycle in solar radiation and barometric pressure

[6] E. P. Howrey, "A Spectrum Analysis of the Long-Swing Hypothesis," *International Economic Review* 9(1968):228–60.

[7] There is an important lesson about the value of mathematics in the story of Kuznets's error. What seems simple and/or reasonable can have disastrous results.

[8] Nikolai Kondratieff, *The Long Wave Cycle* (New York: Richardson and Snyder, 1984).

[9] Wesley C. Mitchell, *Business Cycles, The Problem and Its Setting*. New York: National Bureau of Economic Research, Inc. 1927, pp 50–53.

lead to business cycles through its effects on crops. The 7 or 10.5 year business cycles were generated by the accumulated effects of two or three crop cycles. Other United States weather data were used to show both a 33- and 8-year rainfall cycle in the central United States. The eight-year rainfall cycle was also observed in data from France and England. Henry L. Moore concluded that these eight-year cycles were generated by the passage of Venus between the Earth and the Sun, which blocked important solar radiation.

A. C. Pigou blamed business cycles on the optimistic and pessimistic errors of businessmen in their attempts to deal with uncertainty about the future. These errors of optimism spread throughout the business community, and lead to a general overproduction that reflect the "psychological interdependence" of those individuals who make business decisions. A prosperity of this type is founded on errors and must eventually collaspe into a recession. This theory is not too different from the Lucas model presented below in the way errors are propagated through the economy. The source of the errors, however, is quite different. Another, somewhat similar, theory from Maurice Hexter noted that changes in the death rate *precede* changes in wholesale prices, and that these movements in the death rates are what cause the optimism or pessimism that generates the business cycles.[10] Seeing all of your friends die around you makes you pessimistic.

A number of early writers made a distinction between savings and investment and considered this distinction important in generating business cycles. A Russian economist, Michel Tugan-Baranovski, writing in 1894, divided the loan fund—the savings available for investment—into the part provided by the industrial sector and the part provided by the agricultural sector. He claimed that during a recession, the agricultural part of the economy usually does fairly well and accumulates savings. These additional savings eventually lower the interest rate enough so that the industrial sector begins to borrow and starts growing again. Eventually, this pool of funds, along with the savings of the industrial sector, is used up, and interest rates rise. This rise causes a decline in investment and initiates the next recession.

The last of the ideas we will list here comes from Alvin Hansen.[11] It is a bit like the savings–investment discussion, but concentrates on that aspect of the behavior of banking institutions that could lead to business cycles. The banks make loans to the business community when there are considerable profit opportunities available; that is, when interest rates are low and labor is easily obtainable. This causes the upturn of the cycle. The downturn comes about when the loanable funds are used up and the increased demand for labor has raised wages and reduced profitability.

[10] Maurice B. Hexter, *Social Consequences of Business Cycles* (Boston and New York: 1925), pp. 55–57.

[11] Alvin H. Hansen, *Cycles of Prosperity and Depression in the United States, Great Britain and Germany*, University of Wisconsin Studies in the Social Sciences and History No. 5. (Madison, Wisconsin, 1921), 104–108.

Not surprisingly, there have been many other ideas about the causes of business cycles. The above sample is intended to suggest the breath of the ideas that have been suggested. Some of these ideas have returned over and over again in slightly varied disguises, for economic theory has its own cycles. Some of them are sufficiently inexact in their formulation to be impossible to test.

The dynamic Keynesian models that we built in the earlier chapters give rise to business cycles. The naive and adaptive expectations models describe different paths that the economy can take while experiencing different government policies. It can be shown, using those models, that one-time government policies—a change in some government variable that lasts only one period, after which that variable returns to its old value—has a continuing effect on the equilibrium values of the economy.

Two fairly recent examples of business cycle theories follow. The Hicks-Samuelson model is a Keynesian-based business cycle theory that does not have a supply side and for that reason cannot be called an equilibrium model. It is especially interesting in the way in which it considers the different type of cycles that the economy can follow. The Lucas model is more based on microeconomic theory and, with both supply and demand functions for all goods, is an equilibrium model. The Lucas model best describes the co-movements that are experienced in variables like consumption, income, wages, and investment.

HICKS-SAMUELSON MODEL

The **Hicks-Samuelson Multiplier-Accelerator model** illustrates one way in which lags in the investment-decision process and the consumption-decision process can lead to business cycles. The Hicks-Samuelson model is a simple, three-equation macroeconomic model that will look a lot like the aggregate demand part of our earlier models. This three-equation model collapses to a simple second order difference equation system that, depending on the parameters of the first model, will generate the required oscillations. These three equations represent the consumption function, the investment function, and a National Income Accounting Identity; however, there are lags in the consumption and investment functions, since investment level will no longer be exogenous (this cannot be the case if one is attempting to explain an investment drive business cycle), and all of the variables will be time-subscripted. First, we will set up the model; then, we will look at the different kinds of results this model gives us.

Consumption during this period is solely a function of last period's income. (We are dropping the Pigou effect.) This can be viewed as a version of the consumption function we discussed earlier where consumption was based on permanent income. Since individuals do not know the income that they will receive this period, last period's income is used as an approximation for this period's permanent income. The consumption function is

$$C_t = \text{mpc} \times Y_{t-1}$$

Consumption today, C_t, is equal to the marginal propensity to consume, mpc, times yesterday's income, Y_{t-1}. That does it for the consumption function.

Investment is based on the difference between last period's income and the income of the period before that. It is the observed change in the income level that causes firms to increase or decrease their investment. One can imagine that firms use the observed change in income to predict expected future changes in income. This prediction determines the amount that they will invest in order to permit themselves to produce the goods that the public will want to purchase at their new income level. The most recent information that individuals have available to allow them to determine the movement of the output level of the economy is from these two periods. The investment function is

$$I_t = \beta \times (Y_{t-1} - Y_{t-2})$$

This equation says that investment today, I_t, is a constant, β, times the difference between yesterday's income and the income of two periods ago, $Y_{t-1} - Y_{t-2}$.

The model needs a national income accounting identity. We need to keep track of time here, so this is a National Income Accounting Identity with time subscripts. The time subscripted national income accounting identity is

$$Y_t = C_t + I_t + G_t$$

which says that current output goes to current consumption, current investment, or current government expeditures.

Substituting into the National Income Accounting Identity the consumption function and investment function that we just described and including G_t, we get that

$$Y_t = \text{mpc} \times Y_{t-1} + \beta \times (Y_{t-1} - Y_{t-2}) + G_t$$

This simplifies into the Hicks-Samuelson difference equation,

$$Y_t = (\text{mpc} + \beta) \times Y_{t-1} - \beta \times Y_{t-2} + G_t \tag{12.1}$$

which is the second order difference equation mentioned above.

A second order difference equation is one in which the current value of some variable is based on some linear function of the values for that variable for the two previous periods. In the equation above, today's income is a linear function of the income level for the two previous periods and the current level of government spending.

As we did when we discussed the dynamic macro models with various types of expectations, we will begin here with a stationary state. In a stationary state we have that $Y_i = Y_{t-1} = Y_{t-2} = Y$ for all times t. Substituting Y for what it is equal to in the Hicks-Samuelson difference equation above, and setting government expenditures at some constant level, G, we get

$$Y = (\text{mpc} + \beta) \times Y - \beta \times Y + G$$

We can find the stationary state output level of this model by solving the above equation for Y. We get that

$$Y - (\text{mpc} + \beta) \times Y + \beta \times Y = G$$

and, since the βs cancel out this solves to

$$Y = G/(1 - \text{mpc})$$

If an economy is at this stationary state value, some shock, such as a one-time change in the value of government expenditures, will set the economy into motion—that is, will move it from the stationary state.[12] The nature or form of this motion or business cycle depends on the values of the parameters of the Hicks-Samuelson difference equation. There are four possible types of paths that the economy could follow. The economy could follow damped growth, damped oscillations, explosive growth, and explosive oscillations. These four possible paths are illustrated in Figure 12.4. Output is measured in the vertical and time is measured in the horizontal direction in each of the diagrams. In each of the diagrams in Figure 12.4, an economy is initially in a stationary state, with its output constant for some period of time. There is then some small, onetime shock, which causes the value of output to shift up. This is illustrated by the short vertical line in each of the diagrams. Figure 12.4a illustrates the behavior of an economy that displays what we call damped growth. The output level smoothly returns to the stationary state level. (In the figure, the path looks like a straight line, but it should approach the horizontal axis more gradually.) Figure 12.4b diagram illustrates the behavior of an economy that displays damped oscillations. The economy returns to the stationary state, but the output level follows a sine-type wave as it does so. Figures

[12] The way this model is set up, the only possible source of shock is from changes in government expenditures. If we thought about the model a bit casually, we might imagine that output could directly experience such shocks as unexpected weather that damages the crops. This is important because it would be unfair, in many countries, to put all of the blame for shocks on the government.

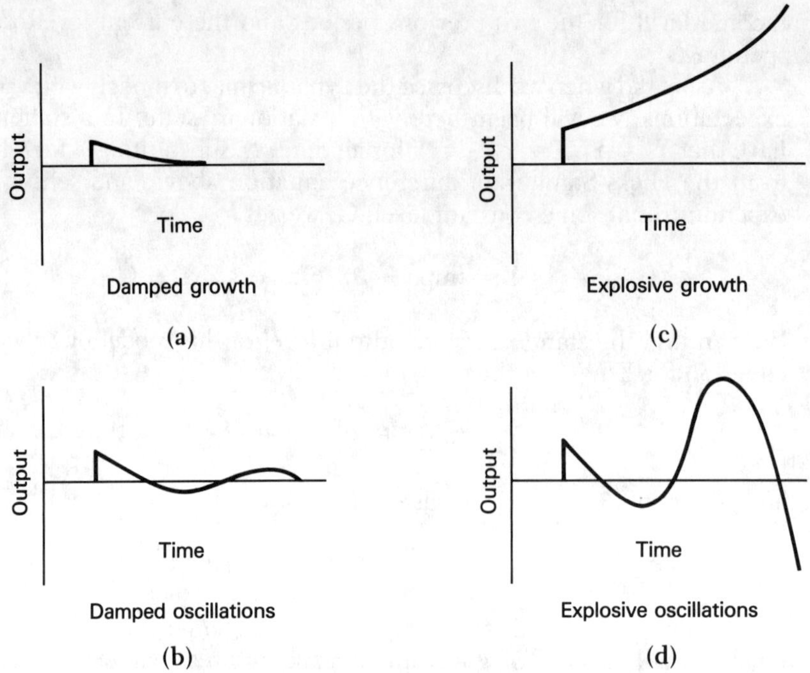

Figure 12.4

12.4 c and d illustrate explosive economies. These economies diverge from the initial stationary state, either oscillating or not.

Which of these paths the economy will actually follow is a function of the values of the mpc and the β. Define **a** = mpc + β, where **a** is the coefficient of the Y_{t-1} variable in the Hicks-Samuelson difference equation. Define **b** = $-\beta$, where **b** is the coefficient of the Y_{t-2} variable of the same equation. (Notice that this is equal to *minus* beta.) The equation 12.1, above, can be written as

$$Y_t = \mathbf{a} \times Y_{t-1} + \mathbf{b} \times Y_{t-2} + G_t \tag{12.2}$$

This **a** and **b** pair can be used directly to determine the type of path the economy will follow. Figure 12.5 (derived from difference equation theory, which we take as given) shows the path of the economy for any **a** and **b** pair. An economy where mpc equals .9 and β equals .1 will give us an **a** = 1.0 and a **b** = −.1. An examination of figure 12.4 shows that these coefficients fall into the region of damped growth. Therefore, this economy will smoothly return to the stationary state after some shock. An economy where the mpc equals .5 and β equals .5 will give an **a** = 1.0 and a **b** = −.5. This economy will exhibit damped oscillations as it returns to the stationary state. Other values for the mpc and β can be found to generate the explosive paths.

A brief comment on Marxian economics is in order here. One of the major tenets of Marx's economics is that the capitalist economic system is unstable. This

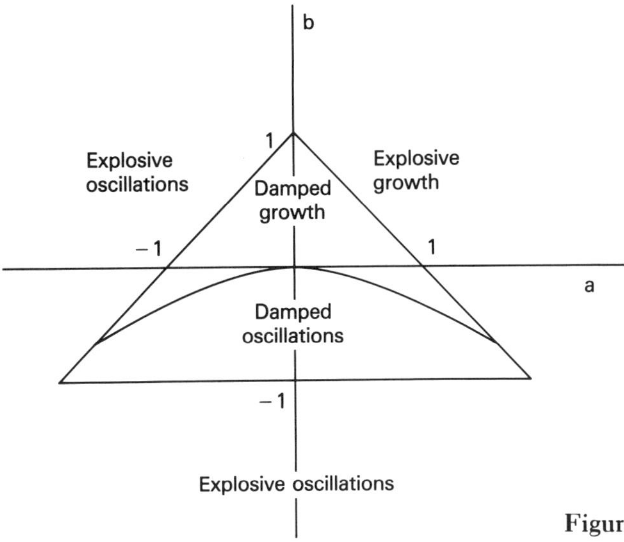

Figure 12.5

would mean that a capitalist economy would follow one of the explosive paths if Marx were correct. Capitalist economists believe that the economy will follow one of the damped paths in response to some shock. Whether Marx or the capitalist economists are correct is an empirical question and one that should be answerable from the data if the Hicks-Samuelson difference equation system were estimated for values of mpc and β. Unfortunately, the world is considerably more complicated than this model and the intertemporal interactions more involved than the simple model we are considering here. At the very least, the issue mentioned at the very beginning of this chapter appears again. If one estimated this system of equations using the basic data, one might find that the system is unstable—that is, that the roots are greater than one. Yet the data can also be viewed as a composite of deterministic and random components, if the deterministic component—the trend—were removed, the resulting system could have stable roots. There is insufficient data or theoretical justification to choose one of these possibilities over the other, so the question of the stability of the capitalist economy is still unanswered.

It is important to keep in mind the fact that the Hicks-Samuelson model is *not* an equilibrium model. Notice that only the aggregate demand side of the model is constructed (this from the National Income Accounting Identity). The model assumes that all of the goods that are demanded in the economy are somehow produced. There is no aggregate supply curve and all of our earlier considerations of the production limitations of an economy, including the problems of the labor market, are ignored. We will next consider a model of business cycles that is an equilibrium model. This will be a model in which both the demand and the supply decisions of the economy are taken into account, and each period's results are generated by completely defined equilibria.

LUCAS'S EQUILIBRIUM BUSINESS CYCLES

Robert E. Lucas Jr., in a paper called *Understanding Business Cycles*, constructed a simple model that generates equilibrium business cycles.[13] This model is one in which all markets clear (prices adjust so that supply equals demand at all times), but where individuals make production and investment decisions in a world with imperfect information. The nature of these information imperfections, and individual's responses to it, give rise to the kind of co-movements in economic variables that we recognize as business cycles.

Lucas identifies business cycles as co-movements in output, prices, short-term interest rates, the money stock, money velocity, consumer and producer durables, and corporate profits (the last two of which display greater than average amplitude in their fluctuations).[14] Since these co-movements are observed in all business cycles, regardless of their size and duration, it is in terms of these co-movements that business cycles are all alike. A good theory of business cycles should then, according to Lucas, explain these co-movements.

In this model the economy is made up of a large number of individual producer–consumers. Each day—or period—these individuals go to their shop (Steve Jobs's garage, for example), observe the price that is being offered that day for the good that they produce, and decide how much of the good to produce that day. Suppose that people get to work and discover that the price for their good is higher than it had been the previous day. Since there is no intermediary between the firm and the worker, any changes in prices are changes in the wage that these individuals receive for producing an additional unit of their good. Therefore, today's wage for these workers has gone up. What will these workers/owners do? Will they produce more, less, or the same as before?

The answer to this question depends on how individuals view the price change. They will behave differently depending on whether they view it as a temporary or a permanent change in the price of their good, possibly caused by a temporary or a permanent change in the demand for their particular product. If they believe that the increase is temporary, it is most likely that they will work more, and so produce and sell on this day more of their good. They will use some of the leisure that they had planned to consume today to produce additional goods; they will plan to consume the leisure that they gave up today in order to get the additional production, at some time in the future, some time when the price of their good is down, and the income loss of their leisure is lower. They are consuming less leisure when it is expensive because the wage is temporarily high and will probably consume more leisure once the wage is lowered, and so price of leisure

[13] Robert E. Lucas Jr., "Understanding Business Cycles," *Carnegie-Rochester Conference on Public Policy*, 5 (1976):7–29.

[14] The percent changes for these variables are greater during each cycle than for most of the other variables.

drops. If individuals view the price increase as permanent, we know from economic research that not only will they *not* increase their production, they might even reduce their hours of work by some small amount. If the wage (price) change is permanent, there will be no future time when leisure will be cheaper, so there is no personal intertemporal trade in leisure to be made. To try to make this discussion a bit more concrete, try to imagine how much workers would want to work in a situation in which they got a regular increase in hourly wages versus how they would react if they were told that the increase in hourly wages would only be in effect for the next two weeks—during the Christmas season, for example.

Consider the investment decision that these consumer–producers make in the face of a price increase. These people are more likely to make an investment—in a machine, say, or in some education that would increase their marginal product—if they thought that the price increase they observed was permanent rather than temporary. If an individual had the "right" amount of capital (right, that is, in the sense that the marginal produce of capital equaled the rent that was paid for using it) the temporary price increase would increase this marginal product. However, if the individual increased the capital stock, because the marginal product of capital (or labor, for that matter) would be decreasing, this additional capital would not produce enough income to cover its rent once the price of the good returned to its regular level from the *temporary* increase. Unless there was some general decline in rents, the profit-maximizing manager of a firm would not make such an investment. Therefore, a price increase that was viewed as temporary would not increase investment.

A price increase that is viewed as permanent will increase investment. This higher price for the good increases the marginal product of the current quantity of capital, and the firm will gain additional profits as it increases the capital stock up to the level where marginal product once more equals the rental. This increase in capital may be in the form of machines or of human capital. However, since human capital normally requires a time input that reduces production, individuals may also acquire additional human capital by getting additional schooling during periods of temporary price decreases. In any case, price increases that are viewed as permanent will increase investment.

On any given day, the price change that our consumer–producers observe for the good that they produce is likely to be made up of a temporary component and a permanent component. At the very least, individuals are likely to *view* any price change that they observe, given imperfect information, as being comprised of both a permanent and a temporary component. This means that their response to that price change will be mixed. In response to a price increase, people will increase the amount of time they work based on how much of the price increase they think is temporary, and they will increase their investment based on how much of the price increase they think is permanent. Since they are unable to separate completely the temporary and permanent components of any price change, both investment and employment will move in the same direction as that price change.[15] This is consistent with the observed co-movements of the business cycle.

If this economy does not exhibit general price movements; if, in other words, neither inflation nor deflation is permitted, every time a good has a price increase, there must be another good for which the price declines. Otherwise, there would be a general price level change. For each of those individuals who observes a price rise and increases both her hours worked and her investment, there is someone else who observes a price decline and decreases both hours worked and investment. The net change for both employment and investment in that economy, given that the responses are symmetric and assuming that they are equal or nearly equal, would be zero. Even though individuals would act in a way that is consistent with business cycles, if no general price level changes could occur, no business cycles would be observed.

However, in an economy in which there can be general price level changes, individuals have an additional problem. If they observe a change in the price of the good that they produce, they need to determine whether this price change is a relative price change or whether it is part of a general price change. We have seen how individuals will respond to a change in the relative price of their specific good. We need to consider how individuals respond to known general price changes, or changes in the prices of all goods relative to money.

From microeconomics we know that both an individual's demand for a particular good and a firm's supply of a good are unchanged in response to an equal increase or decrease in all prices, wages, rents, and, from the last two, incomes. If our consumer–producers observe a general price change and know that it really is a general price change, they will not make any change in the amount of the good that they produce or in the number of hours that they work. A known change in the general price level will have no effect on real output or consumption. All prices and wages, as measured in terms of money, will change exactly the same amount, and no one will work more or less.

Now suppose that the individual consumer–producers observe an increase in the money price of the good that they produce. Suppose that they are unable to tell if this price change is a relative (specific) or a general price change. Their response should be mixed. They are likely, under almost any kind of expectation other than perfect foresight, to assume that part of this observed price change is a relative price change, and another part of the change is accounted for by a general price change. They will respond to the part that they think is relative in the way described above. The portion of the price change they think is a relative price increase will result in an increase in hours worked and in investment. The part that they think is a relative price decrease will result in a decrease in hours worked and in investment. (Note that it is the part of the relative price change that they think is

[15] At different times and with different information, there will be different probabilities that the individual will assign to the permanence of the price change. These different probabilities will be reflected in the amount of the change in work and investment.

temporary that generates the change in the hours worked, while the part that they think is permanent causes the change in investment.) The part of the price change that they think is general will have no effect on either hours worked or investment. Figure 12.6 summarizes these concepts.

Suppose that there is some kind of general price change in this economy. For the sake of exposition, assume that this change is a price increase. All the consumer–producers in the economy observe the price increase. All of them think that some portion of that price increase is a *temporary* relative price increase in their particular good. This causes them to increase their hours worked on that day and therefore the amount of their good available then. All of them think that some portion of the price increase is a *permanent* increase in the relative price of their particular good and invest during more this period. The part of the price increase that individuals think comes from a *general* price increase has no effect on either hours worked or investment. The general price rise has generated the kind of co-movements in prices, wages, output, and investment that is a characteristic of the business cycle. The rest of a cycle follows from this beginning. The increase in investment causes the price of investment goods to go up, and this causes an increase in the production of investment goods. The perceived increased income of the majority of individuals in the economy causes them to increase their demand for most goods (but to decrease their demand for inferior goods). This leads to additional increases in prices for these goods and additional increased production.

The downturn is already built into this model. The expansion was caused by a general price increase that was *perceived* by producers as specific. As producers learn that the price increase for their good was caused by a general price increase and not by an increase in demand for their good, they see that they have overpro-

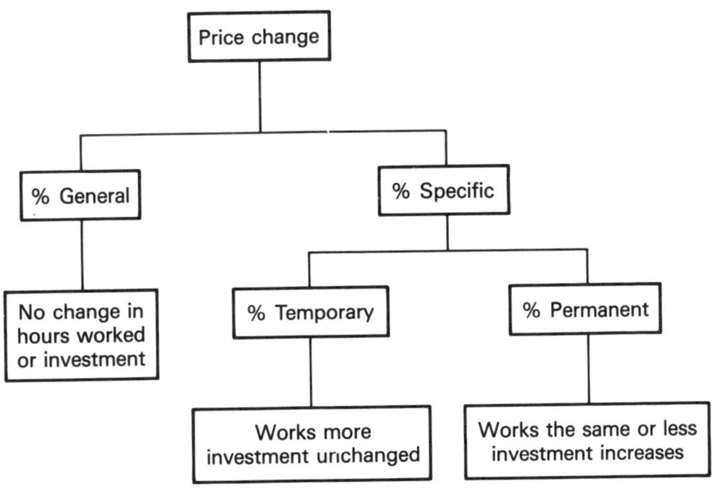

Figure 12.6

duced and overinvested. They then begin to cut back on their production and investment in order to get their capital stock and inventories—that is, the finished goods that they have not yet sold—back to the levels that are appropriate to the specific price changes, if any, that really did take place. This causes output and investment to decline and with declining demand the prices also begin to decline.

Note that a sustained general price increase will *not* generate a business cycle because, on average, the individuals in the economy will come to recognize the price increase as being almost entirely general in nature. Therefore, they will not make the production and investment decisions that they would have made if they thought that the price increase was specific to their particular good.

It is time to see how we get the money stock to move with the business cycle.[16] It is generally accepted in the economics profession that long-term movements in prices and the money stock are correlated. The causal direction for this movement is generally, though not universally, thought to be from increases in the money stock to increases in prices. In other words, in the long run increases in the money stock *cause* increases in prices. The short-run behavior of prices in response to changes in the money stock is much less well understood. This lack of evidence concerning the short-term relationship between prices and money is actually a benefit to this model. Suppose that the money stock is increased. In the short run, price increases that might come from this money-stock increase are difficult to detect. Certainly, in the long run, this increase in the money stock will drive up prices, but it is hard to know the timing of these price increases. A price rise observed today *might* have come from the money stock increase, but it might *also* have come from some increase in the demand for any particular good. This lack of knowledge of the short-run relationship between money and prices actually increases the uncertainty about the source of observed price changes. Increases in the money stock that *do* drive up the price level are not necessarily perceived as such, and this misperception would help generate the business cycles described above. This would then give us the co-movements in the money stock, prices, investment, and output that we observe.

COUNTERCYCLICAL POLICY: A COMMENT

One of the trademarks of Keynesian economics is the belief that the government can operate an effective countercyclical policy. Countercyclical policy is the expressed intent of the government to adjust its policies so as to cause the cycles of the economy around the trend to be smaller than they might otherwise be. If the

[16] This is a little premature since we haven't really introduced money into our economies yet. However, this possible importance of money is an important result of Lucas's model and even though the relation between money and the price level has not yet been made clear from a theoretical point of view, it seems to be sufficiently well known by the general public to be worth including at this point.

economy has entered or is entering a downturn or recession, the government will follow policies that it believes will cause output to increase. If the economy is in an expansion, the government will follow policies that will cause the economy to slow its growth. The caution often heard is that the economy should not get too heated up. The government attempts to cause the economy to follow the trend with as little fluctuation around that trend as possible.

To do this the Keynesians concentrate on short-run policies. Is the unemployment level too high? If so, follow policies that will increase employment: Increase government expenditures, reduce taxes, or the like. If the economy seems to be heating up too fast, follow the opposite policies.

The rise of Keynesian economics in academic circles in the 1950s, and the accompanying interest in short-run countercyclical policies, was achieved at the expense of the traditional study of business cycles. During the first half of the twentieth century, many economists specialized in studying business cycles. The rationale behind this study was that looking for the *causes* of business cycles, and attempting to understand the *institutions* of the economy that give rise to them, would allow policy makers to change the institutions in such a way as to reduce the frequency and severity of the business cycles. This line of analysis was almost completely dropped in favor of the Keynesian, short run, comparative static macroeconomic analysis. For most of the 1950s and 60s, few respected economists wasted their time on studying the complex intertemporal relationships implied by "classical" business cycle theory.

To get some flavor of the difference between these two approaches, one could imagine that the classical business cycle theorists were trying to modify the economic ship so that it would be able to withstand the storms of business cycles without much damage, while the Keynesians were trying to seed the clouds to modify the economic storm. One of the great fears of those who were not of the Keynesian camp (and for a while during the 1960s, this was a very small camp) was that economists were not sufficiently skilled in the operation of this seeding process to weaken the storm. In fact, they feared, it could be strengthening it instead. This was a problem even if the notion that the seeding *could* be effective was granted. The process of government in a democratic society is very slow, and in the United States there was considerable doubt about Congress's ability to enact fiscal policy with appropriate timing.

Suppose the economy behaves like the Hicks-Samuelson model in the damped cycle manifestation described above. Any shock to the economy would set off a series of cycles, including a shock that would be generated by some government policy that was intended to counter cycles. During a downturn, a Keynesian prescribed government expenditure increase would serve to kick up the output level and reduce unemployment of the economy at that moment, but that very same government expenditure increase would be a shock to the economy that sets off its own cycle, a cycle that already has its own upswing and trailing downswing. Analysis of the interaction of an existing cycle and the additional movement of the economy that is generated by the *counter*cyclical policy is extremely difficult.

There is no guarantee that the resulting combined cycle will not have a trough that is lower than that of the cycle that was initially in progress. In the longer run, countercyclical policy could cause a depression even worse than what would have happened if no policy at all were applied.

REPRISE

Business cycles are the movements and co-movements of economic variables around their long-term trends. Some of the interesting facts about business cycles that a good theory should explain are 1, the existence of business cycles; 2, the co-movements of sets of economic variables during the cycle; and 3, the different magnitudes of the oscillations of different variables during each cycle. Business cycles are often divided into three groups based on the length of the cycles. This division into seasonal cycles, The Business Cycle, and long cycles is based on the assumption that different forces are driving each one of them.

The Hicks-Samuelson model of business cycles is capable of generating both the required cycles and some of the co-movements that have been observed. Both the consumption function and the investment function will cause these variables to move with the cycle. The main problem with the Hicks-Samuelson model is that it is really only half a model: It is completely demand side model, and says nothing about how the output of the economy is determined.

Lucas's model takes us towards equilibrium business cycle models. His model generates cycles and co-movements based on information problems faced by the producer–consumers who make up this economy. These individuals are unable to separate the signal, which is the real price movement of their own good, from the noise, the general price trend. This inability to know what is really happening in their own industry is the source of the cycles.

Some recent work in business cycle theory has attempted to build "real" business cycle models. Different sectors are linked together so that real supply or technology shocks, a bad harvest or a new invention, will generate oscillations. In part, this effort is aimed at producing a supply-side business cycle theory to contrast with the Hicks-Samuelson style demand side theory. Cycles in the real world are probably a combination of both real and demand shocks.

EXERCISES

1. Consider a Hicks-Samuelson model with a mpc equal to .9, a β equal to .1, and government expenditures (G_t) from $t = -\infty$ to 0 of 100. At time $t = 1$ government expenditures go up to 110 but drop back to 100 for $t = 2$ to $+\infty$. Calculate the path of this economy for enough periods to enable you to determine which of the four possible Hicks-Samuelson paths it is following.

2. Using the model from Exercise 1, suppose that government expenditures continue at 110 for $t = 1$ to $+\infty$. How does this path differ from the one in Exercise 1?
3. Do Exercises 1 and 2 for a Hicks-Samuelson economy where mpc is equal to .5 and β is equal to .4.
4. In Lucas's business cycle model, why is the possibility of general price movements required to generate business cycles?

13 Money

In which we find that, if money doesn't make the world go round, it at least greases the wheels. The history of money is long and varied. We take an overview of that history, and then look closely at how it has fared in the United States.

INTRODUCTION

Our study of money has three parts. First, we will look at some of the general characteristics of money and at the history of money and banking in the United States from colonial days to the present. We will then consider some of the current institutions in the United States banking system. These institutions will permit monetary policy to have interesting effects in our earlier models. Finally, we will study a theoretical model of money and the question of why people hold money. These models permit us to look at some theoretical aspects of the system of financial institutions. Before we go into any of these more interesting discussions, we need to know what money is and what it does.

Most economists describe money as having three uses. In a real sense, anything that has these three uses should be considered as money. The thing we call money doesn't need to be pieces of paper especially printed by the government, or certain kinds of metal stamped into disks with the head of some purportedly important person on it. Historically, things like salt; tobacco, (both loosed and preformed into cigarettes); large, sometimes immovable stone disks; clam shells; beads; and animal skins, among others, have served as money.

Money serves as a **medium of exchange.** This means that people are willing to accept the stuff as one side of a trade. People will give up goods in order to receive money. They then give up this money to someone else to receive some other good. This use of money makes trades easier and helps to get around the problem that arises in a pure trade or barter economy, that of the possible **non-coincidence of wants.** In a pure barter economy, if trade is to take place each person must have something to trade that the other wants to acquire. Not only that, but both must think that they are better off giving up what they have in order to get what the other has. (This is the reason why trades improve the material well-being of individuals.) Matched wants are not likely to occur very often. It is more likely that one of the individuals will want something the other has but will have nothing that the other individual values to trade for it. Money, or any of those things that function as money, solves this difficulty. If the individuals in an economy know that the other people in that economy will always accept the money object for goods, then they will be willing to give up goods that they have in their possession for an appropriate amount of the money stuff. This characteristic of money makes trades easier, and almost certainly allows a greater number of trades to take place.[1]

[1] Some economists have made much of the notion that when people trade goods for something that they use as money, they perceive the bundle of goods that they have after the trade as less preferred, when considered as goods, than the bundle of goods before the trade. This is because the good that is used as money is worth less to them when thought of as a good than the stuff they traded away. It is the use of the good as money that makes them willing to hold it. This is not, however, a complete model of money, since it doesn't indicate which goods are used in trading, and why those goods become the money good.

Money also serves as a **store of value.** An individual may be interested in trading away some item now, especially if the item doesn't store well, like a strawberry souffle, and make the other side of that trade, in which he gets some item he wants, sometime in the future. People need a way to store the value of the goods given up in the first trade in order to regain that value when they trade in the opposite direction. Money allows them to do this. Money is storable and maintains at least some of its value. Most of the physical items that have been used as money have had physical properties that permit them to be stored without significant deterioration. Some economists think of this use of money as a mere extension of the first use. They say that the noncoincidence of wants that money solves in this case is merely a temporal noncoincidence of wants. People want to consume the two sides of the trade at different times. When one side of the trade occurs today and the other side will occur at some known or unknown time in the future, money as a store of value is operating as a medium of exchange across time.

The third use of money is as a **unit of account.** Even when money is not used in trades, it is possible that the value of the items being traded will be specified in terms of money. Money, or the price in terms of money, is used to compare the various items in trades. Money in this use need not even have a physical manifestation. It can be a kind of bookkeeping money. This money allows us to calculate the value of a large mixed bundle of goods.

We now have the three uses of money—as a medium of exchange, as a store of value, and as a unit of account. Throughout history, many different items have served these uses. We can usefully divide these kinds of money into three *types*. The three types of money are 1, commodity money; 2, backed paper money or backed currency; and 3, fiat money.

Commodity money, just as the name implies, is some good or commodity that provides the services of money. History has seen many different kinds of commodity money, and at various times and places salt, fish, large rocks, cigarettes, and scarce minerals or metals have been used. Some of these monies have had what would seem to be unfortunate properties: rocks were difficult to move, salt disappeared in the rain, and cigarettes had a tendency to go up in smoke. Given the difficulties of these other types of commodity monies it is easy to see how scarce minerals and metals, especially gold and silver, became popular as commodity monies. They were easy to store (they may tarnish, but they do not rust or combine easily with other substances), easily divisible, and fairly easy to protect from, or test for, debasement or forgery. Since the metal was usually fairly difficult to find and refine, the quantity of money could not be changed very quickly. If it were to be possible to use this metallic commodity money, possibly after it had already been stamped into the form of coins—a process that was meant to guarantee the weight and purity of the coin's metal—for long term store of value, it would be important to ensure that the supply of the stuff wouldn't suddenly increase by enough to radically reduce its value in trade.

An interesting example of a commodity money occurred in the Germans' prisoner-of-war camps during World War II. In these camps, cigarettes became an important commodity money. The cigarettes had a value to those who smoked, and they were not produced in the camp. Instead, they arrived at somewhat unpredictable intervals in Red Cross packages. Just after a delivery of Red Cross packages, there was a lot of money about—lots of cigarettes—and it took many cigarettes to buy anything—a haircut, for example. As time passed, many of the cigarettes were used, money went up in smoke, and the quantity of money in the prison "economy" declined. With this decline in quantity, the value of each cigarette rose. The short ends of used cigarettes were combined together to form new, inferior cigarettes, which traded at a value lower than that of manufactured cigarettes. When a new shipment of Red Cross packages came in the price of cigarettes would fall as the "money supply" increased. There are stories of individual prisoners who made "fortunes" by hoarding cigarettes when a shipment came in and selling them off for other goods when the supply got low. When the new shipment came in this prisoner would trade the items he had collected for even more cigarettes and would repeat the whole process. Some held on to their supply of cigarettes too long, being a bit too greedy, and a surprise shipment of Red Cross packages destroyed the value of their accumulated fortune.

A **backed paper money,** or currency, consists of paper notes, specially printed pieces of paper that circulate in the economy as money, with someone, usually a bank or a government, promising to convert this paper money into some real good, usually gold or silver, on demand. The advantage this kind of money has over a commodity money is chiefly one of convenience for its users, in that these paper notes are simpler to carry and hide than commodity money. One possible danger with a backed paper money is that the institution backing the currency may issue pieces of paper for more of the real good than it actually has. In that case, we have a partially-backed currency. In the nineteenth and the first half of the twentieth centuries, most of the major nations of the world had partially-backed paper monies. Partially-backed paper monies are a perfectly workable system, as long as everyone doesn't try to turn in his paper money at the same time.

In the mythology of economics there is what is called "the goldsmith story." Once upon a time, in the 1700s or earlier, people kept their gold for safekeeping in the only vault in town. This vault was owned by the goldsmith, who needed a vault to protect his own gold and was usually willing to rent out space in it to others so that they could safely store their gold.[2] The goldsmith would give receipts to those who deposited gold in his vault so that they could have proof of ownership. If someone needed to make a payment of gold to someone else in the town, he did not have to go to the vault, take out his gold, and deliver it, just to have the recipient then deposit it back into the same vault with the same goldsmith. Instead, it was much easier for him merely to sign over some of his vault receipts. Then, the gold never left the vault and was never at risk of theft, or, at any rate, of street theft.

[2] There is some danger generated by the concentration of the town's gold in one location. Remember that Willie Horton said that he robbed banks because that is where the money is.

The receipts became fully backed bank notes. After a while, the goldsmith realized that he always had some of other people's gold in his vault. If he lent that gold, at interest, to some other people who, he believed, would repay it, he could make additional profits. This might be thought of as a kind of theft or fraud, but it is merely banking. (In a way, this system of goldsmiths could also have generated the precursor to checks. Individuals could write orders to the goldsmith to transfer the ownership of some of their gold to someone else. This is much like a local check, written on the only bank in town.)

Domestically since 1936 and internationally since 1973, the United States has had a **fiat currency money.** (The term "fiat money" comes from the Latin word *fiat*, which means "to make" or "to do." Fiat money is anything the government *makes* money.) To qualify as fiat money, a currency should have three properties. A fiat money is intrinsically worthless, unbacked, and, relative to its trading value, costless to produce. The currency of the United States is intrinsically worthless. It has no value in and of itself. It is not very attractive, cannot be used to produce any other good, and has no use outside its role in trades.[3] If one were placed on a deserted island, an accompanying bag full of paper dollars would serve little use except possibly as a pillow or a fire-starter.

The United States' currency is unbacked. There is no one who will guarantee to exchange it for a specific amount of some other real good. This is indicated on the pieces of paper we use as money. They are labeled as "Federal Reserve Notes," which only indicates that they are official pieces of paper issued by the Federal Reserve System. Older pieces of United States currency were labeled as "silver certificates," and this label indicated that they could be turned in at the Treasury for "money." Federal Reserve Notes are not redeemable for any fixed amount of some real good. Any Federal Reserve Bank will, however, be willing to exchange some old notes for an equal number of new ones, or will be willing to give you ten one-dollar notes for only one ten-dollar note. The currencies of many of the other countries of the world are also unbacked. Some countries back their currency with another country's fiat money. Technically, such a currency is not a fiat currency. Some financial institutions offer paper notes that are better than their country's fiat money. American Express travelers' checks are a kind of backed currency with insurance. The company promises to exchange their checks for currency on demand and will replace, free of charge, any of their money has been stolen or lost.[4]

Compared to their value in trades, dollars are relatively costless to produce. There is some cost to their production and especially to the attempt by the government to prevent other agents from producing money. One of the interest-

[3] The Talking Heads have claimed that the United States has the ugliest money in the world.

[4] The Treasury of the United States will replace badly damaged currency. They will even take the ashes of currency that was inadvertently burned and determine the quantity and denomination of the destroyed bills.

ing theoretical aspects of fiat money is why money trades at a price so much higher than its marginal production cost.

When you read what is written on the one-dollar Federal Reserve Note, you will notice that it says, along with the rather cryptic "In God we trust", that "This note is legal tender for all debts, public and private." The term "legal tender" means that the government has promised to recognize this stuff as being able legally to satisfy debts. If one were to attempt to pay back a debt with whatever it is that the government calls legal tender, then the court system of that government would consider the debt cancelled, or would consider the contract that generated that debt fulfilled. These current legal tender laws are somewhat less severe than some that have existed in the past. Marco Polo, in his *Travels*, reports that in China under the rule of Genghis Khan there was a paper money—an entirely new concept to the Europeans of the time. Moreover, the government issued this money, and made it legally equal to the gold coins that also circulated.[5] Failure to accept this paper money, either in payment of a debt or as payment for the purchase of some good, was punishable by death. A similar punishment for failure to accept the legal tender of the Liga del Norte was threatened by the leaders of that confederation of the northern provinces of Argentina in the 1840s. Normally, however, the punishment is somewhat less severe and only the debt, not the debtor, is cancelled.

The following section presents a brief history of money and banking in the United States. There are several reasons for including this material in an introduction to macroeconomic *theory*. First, since the development of theory has often followed the history of events, we outline some of the main monetary events of the last two hundred years. A second reason is to illustrate the institutional changes the United States has undergone, both by evolution and by legislation. In the fairly short history of the United States, there has been a surprisingly wide variety of monies and financial institutions. Given how much institutions have changed in the past, we should expect the current set of institutions to be revised with time. A third and final reason is to show the process from a commodity money towards a government-controlled fiat money that paralleled the increased government participation in the rest of the economy.

A SHORT HISTORY OF MONEY AND BANKING IN THE UNITED STATES

In colonial North America coins were considered to be the main form of money. Unfortunately, there never seemed to be a enough of them, and other commodities came to serve as money. One of the more interesting commodity monies was wampum (which was then called wampumpeage, meaning "white string of beads"

[5] Marco Polo, *Travels* (New York, Orion Press; distributed by Crown Publishers, 1958).

in Algonquian) among the early colonists in New England. Wampum was made of strings of circular pieces cut from shells. The black pieces, made from quohog, were twice as valuable as the white, which were made from periwinkles. On November 15, 1637, the colony of Massachusetts made wampum legal tender for sums not exceeding 40 shillings and several of the other northern colonies followed this example. The use of wampum as legal tender was rescinded in Massachusetts on May 22, 1661, but it remained legal tender in New York until 1701. (One of the problems associated with wampum was that private production was possible and, for some industrious colonists, very inexpensive. There was a considerable wampum inflation that led to its decline as a currency.) Tobacco was an important commodity currency in the southern colonies and taxes were denominated and paid in tobacco. Because the tax was initially based simply on a particular *quantity* of tobacco, without any reference to its *quality*, people chose to use only the lowest-quality tobacco for payment of their taxes. This led to the debasing of the tobacco currency. Overproduction also drove down the value of the tobacco currency. The receipts for tobacco in the government's warehouse passed as currency.

The colonists's early need to import many goods from England caused a general flight of coins from the colonies. In order to provide some coins to aid local trade, Massachusetts established its own mint on May 26, 1652. This mint produced small silver pieces, the most famous of which is the "pine tree" shilling, which had the image of a pine tree on one side. By royal decree, in 1665 the mint was closed, and the colonies were prohibited from issuing their own money. The right to issue coins was therefore a monopoly of the British government as a royal prerogative. Trade with the colonies, and through that the extraction of wealth from the colonies to Britain, seemed to be the main goal of British economic behavior. Limited trade between the colonies and other international powers, Spain and Portugal, was allowed, but not if it conflicted in a serious way with British colonial rule. Even when it was not allowed, there was a high level of illegal trade between the colonies and the Spanish West Indies. This limited and illegal trade did serve as a source of foreign monies in the colonies. In particular, it provided colonists with the Spanish peso, which was equal to eight reals. This peso was known in the English colonies as a piece of eight or the Spanish Dollar (which is why two bits equal twenty-five cents). The word "dollar" is supposed to have come from a corruption of the German word "thaler," which, minted in Germany beginning in 1517, was about the same size as the Spanish peso. By the way, the sign for the dollar, the $, apparently does not come from a combination of the initials for the United States (a U placed on top of the S) but rather from an early abbreviation for the word "peso." This sign for peso was used until recently in Argentina. Much of this Spanish money found its way back to Britain through the mercantilist practices of the British state and traders.[6] The British government's

[6] Daniel R. Fusfeld, *The Age of the Economist*, (New York: William Morrow, 1986, 8–14).

restrictions on the production of manufactured goods in the colonies were an integral part of this mercantilist perspective.

This drain of coins from the colonies to Britain made money scarce for local trade. Commodity money, in the form of salt, wood, and other products, became common. The individual colonies had difficulty finding money to pay for the local militia, and on February 3, 1690, Massachusetts began issuing low-denomination debt certificates—bonds—to pay for it.[7] The rest of the colonies soon followed Massachusetts' example. These "Bills of Credit," as the debt issue was called, could be used to pay taxes and was therefore a sort of one-sided legal tender. It circulated as one of the first examples of a paper currency in the West. (Notes from the Bank of Stockholm were circulated in 1661, but were discontinued two years later.) Some of the colonies issued rather a lot of these Bills of Credit, and their values varied widely by period and place. Those issued by Rhode Island fell in 1740 to only four percent of their face value. Because of the uncertainty of the value of these bills and because it wanted to reinforce its economic dominance, in 1751 the British Parliament outlawed additional issue of this kind of debt. With few exceptions, the colonies returned to the coin and commodity monies they had used earlier.[8]

During the War for Independence, the Continental Congress, which had no powers to collect taxes, and many of the thirteen states issued bills of credit as a form of money to finance the war effort. The Continental Congress issued so many of these bills of credit (eventually $241 million worth) that the young United States began with a mild hyperinflation. It is interesting that these bills of credit were denominated in dollars—(the Spanish Milled Dollar[9])—and represented one of the early official departures from the British and colonial usage of pounds, shilling, and pence. In 1780, Congress stated that the bills of credit were to be paid off at one fortieth of their par value. As the states removed the legal tender status from these bills, their price fell further and they eventually disappeared, essentially unpaid.

The Articles of Confederation gave few powers involving money to the central government: it had the right to coin money, a right shared with the states;

[7] These bills of Credit had written on them that "This Indented Bill of Five shillings due from the Massachusetts Colony to the Possessor shall be in value equal to money, and shall be accordingly accepted by the Treasurer and Receivers subordinate to him in all public payments and for any Stock at any time in the Treasury. New England, February the Third, 1690. By order of the General Court."

[8] In the 1980s four of the northwesternmost provinces of Argentina issued small denomination bonds that traded as money within the provinces. These "Bonos para la cancelacion de la deuda" were bonds that promised to pay the bearer an unspecified interest rate at a time and place to be later determined by the governour.

[9] Milling is the marking of notches or words around the edge of a coin. These notches make it much more difficult to whittle or cut away some of the metal from the edge of the coin without its being detected. The process of cutting off small chips of gold or silver from coins is called "chipping the coinage." This reference to the Spanish milled dollar meant one of full value, not reduced by chipping.

the right to set the value of the coins struck both by the states and by itself; and the right to issue bills of credit. The Congress under the Articles of Confederation chartered a national bank, but it was not clear that it actually had the authority to do so, and so several states co-chartered this bank to ensure legitimacy. The bank was intended to aid the government in financing its debt issues and to handle other financial transactions of the central government. This Bank of North America actually operated on behalf of the central government for two years (1782–83) and it then became only one more of a large number of state banks, chartered by Pennsylvania, that issued their own notes. It is during the time of the Articles of Confederation that the dollar became the official currency of the United States; by a resolution passed by Congress in 1785, the decimal division of this dollar into cents (a name suggested by Jefferson) and dimes was enacted.

The Constitution, which came into effect on March 4, 1789, says that Congress can "coin money." Initially this phrase was strictly interpreted to mean that the federal government could issue coins, but not paper money. Banks issued "bank notes," and these early commercial banks were controlled by the states. Individuals would deposit gold or silver money at a bank and receive paper money or bearer notes in return. (Bearer notes were so called because "real," or metallic, money would be paid to the person presenting or bearing them to the bank.) Banks would also make loans with their bank notes. This paper money would then be used in general commerce, usually relatively near the issuing bank.

Most of these commercial banks issued more notes than they had gold or silver to back. They would loan out notes that individuals would use to buy some real asset, or real property. The liabilities and assets of the bank would balance, since the borrowers owed the bank the value of the notes loaned. They could do this because under normal conditions only a small fraction of the outstanding notes would be surrendered in exchange for gold. The bank had to make sure it had enough gold or silver **reserves** to cover the redemptions that were likely to occur on any given day. Sometimes, especially when people were afraid that the bank had too few reserves, many people would try to convert their notes to metal coins. These **runs** on banks caused some banks to fail or go bankrupt, because they couldn't call in enough loans to repay all the depositors who wanted their money back.

Although the amounts of metallic—coin—reserves varied across banks, relatively few commercial banks failed in the late 1700s and early 1800s. There were two major reasons for this. First, these early commercial banks tended to be fairly conservative in their loan policies. Second, on February 14, 1791, Congress created the first Bank of the United States. The policies of this first "national" bank helped keep the state banks from overextending themselves.

The Bank of the United States was a publicly held corporation—the government initially owned twenty percent, but sold off its shares after a few years—that was chartered with three major purposes. It issued a national currency, served as banker for the federal government, and was intended to serve as a safe funnel for foreign investors who would invest in the young United States and increase its capital stock. Even though foreign investors owned a fairly large percentage of the bank's capital, no foreign citizens were permitted to be on the board of directors. So while there was a fairly significant foreign ownership of the bank, there was very little in the way of foreign control.

The national bank notes that this bank issued provided the first nonmetallic money that kept its value across the entire country—small as the country was at the time. This was important because the notes issued by the different state banks were discounted (converted at less than face value) as one moved further away from the issuing bank; the farther the distance, the greater the discount. The bank notes from some banks in Kentucky were exchanged with a discount that reached seventy-five percent. A lack of good information on distant banks, their trustworthiness, the possibility that the genuine-seeming notes of distant banks were really counterfeit, and the likelihood of those notes being redeemed caused this discount. A national bank, with offices in each state, or at least in each major city, provided a security not available before and this made long-distance transactions much easier. Further, the Bank of the United States received state bank notes as payment on loans it had made. Since it was a large bank, could collect many of these notes, and had the right to turn them in at any state bank for coins, the threat of this happening caused the state banks to maintain larger gold and silver reserves than they might otherwise have gotten away with. This provided the second reason for the relatively small number of bank failures.

The formation of the Bank of the United States was the work of Alexander Hamilton, who was Secretary of the Treasury under George Washington. His second important long-term contribution during his term as secretary was the establishment of a mint and the subsequent determination of the coins of the United States. This Coinage Act of April 2, 1792, set the dollar as the unit of money for the country and specified a decimal division. The coins to be minted were to be of both silver and gold; this bimetallic system proved to be so difficult to operate that the country would eventually shift to a pure gold standard. (However, the issue, if not the reality, of a bimetallic standard would return in the late nineteenth century.) The specified gold and silver content of the dollar was 24.75 grains of gold and 371.25 grains of silver. This made the dollar a distinct monetary unit, since these quantities of metal were different from all existing currencies. The dollar was no longer the Spanish dollar, but something of our own.

The charter for the Bank of the United States came up for renewal in 1811. Thomas Jefferson, who had strongly opposed the bank when it was originally chartered, was president. The state banks were unhappy with the constraints the Bank of the United States imposed on them. In addition, much of the stock of the bank was owned by British citizens (foreign citizens owned seventy-two percent of the bank's stock) and this foreign ownership made some of those not bothered by the other issues uneasy. There were also continuing concerns about the constitutionality of the bank. The charter was not renewed.

From 1811 to 1815 the number of state banks in the country increased from 88 to 246. The removal of the regulation provided by the Bank of the United States and the need of the federal government to fund the War of 1812 caused the money supply to increase rapidly, and in 1814 most of the state banks suspended convertibility to gold. In 1816 there were over 200 different bank notes circulating, most of them at some fraction of their face value. Reference books were issued to provide information on the relative security of one note versus another.

On April 10, 1816, Congress chartered the Second Bank of the United States with a charter very similar to that of the original bank. The major differences between the banks were that the capitalization was raised from ten million to thirty-five million dollars, and that the President of the United States was to appoint twenty percent of the board of directors. This attempt to correct the monetary difficulties caused by multiple currencies did not fare well. Initially, the bank was not well managed. It was correctly viewed as a threat to the state banks. During the presidency of the populist Andrew Jackson, the charter came up for renewal. The charter was renewed by Congress but vetoed by President Jackson. Even before its charter expired, the bank had ceased to have a significant effect on monetary policy because the Treasury had withdrawn most of the federal funds and transferred them to "depository" state banks.

One of the more noteworthy outcomes of the Second Bank was a Supreme Court ruling that the states did not have the power to impose taxes on the federal government. One of the states, Maryland, attempted to impose a surcharge only on transactions that took place using notes issued by the Bank of the United States, while not taxing transactions that used state bank notes. A cashier in a Maryland branch of the bank, one James McCulloch, was brought to trial for putting untaxed bank notes into circulation. When the case was before the Supreme Court, Daniel Webster, in his defense of McCulloch, argued for the supremacy of the federal government with the famous admonition that "the unlimited power to tax is the power to destroy."

The demise of the Second Bank of the United States allowed tremendous growth in the number of state banks. By the beginning of the Civil War there were over sixteen hundred state banks in the country, and most of them issued their own bank notes. Again, most of these bank notes circulated at a discount from **specie** (gold and silver) and long-distance transactions remained difficult.

Monetary policy in the country became the province of the Treasury. Federal government receipts were generally greater than expenditures until the advent of the Mexican War in 1846. The revenues were mostly from tariffs and the sale of government-owned land in the new territories, and the federal government was able to retire much of its debt and to disperse some of the funds from land sales to the states in an early revenue-sharing scheme. The federal government held deposits in designated depository state banks and these banks, which were usually large were supposed to redeem federal drafts in coin. This forced them to maintain larger reserves and provided for more stability in the banking system.

During the late 1830s and early 1840s the federal government issued two kinds of notes. These notes were short-term government bonds and were used to cover federal expenses. One type was a note that was issued in exchange for coin and gave an interest rate of five to six percent. The other was a note that circulated much like currency and gave a return of .01 percent. Both of these notes possessed a slightly limited form of legal tender; they could be used for payment of taxes and had to be accepted as payment for government purchases.

The Civil War forced the United States government (that is, Lincoln's government in Washington) to find new and more effective ways of raising revenue. Three methods were employed. First the federal government increased its borrowing by issuing long-term government bonds. Second, it increased taxes and imposed the first federal income tax in the country. This tax was difficult to set up, met considerable popular resistance, and in the end raised only a small amount of revenue. Third, it issued the United States notes called greenbacks, which were a general legal tender money but could not be used for the payment of tariff revenues on imports. This restriction was aimed at providing the Federal government with at least one source of gold coin, which it needed for purchases of war material from other countries. These were notes that had to be accepted as payment of both private debt, and debt owed to the government.

In order to increase the acceptance and purchase of government bonds, the National Banking Act was passed in 1863. This was designed as a war measure that allowed individuals to form banks, which would be chartered by the federal government, by purchasing a fixed amount of federal bonds, depositing them with the Treasury for security, and receiving federal bank notes (a paper money different from greenbacks) worth ninety percent of the value of the bonds. If this caught on, the central government could improve the market for its bonds. These bank notes could be lent out at interest, as at any bank, and the government thought that the double interest on the capital—the money used to purchase bonds—would make this type of charter very attractive. Reserve requirements were specified for all national banks, as such federally-chartered banks were called, with the city or commercial center banks required to hold twenty-five percent of their deposits as reserves, and country banks fifteen percent. All national banks had to accept national bank notes at par in coin, and thus was established the first effective national currency.

In 1865, Congress made national banks more attractive by imposing a ten percent tax on all bank issues of state bank notes. At the time this was called a "death tax" on state banks. This law was intended to cause more state banks to apply for federal charters and thereby to increase the sale of federal bonds. It was wildly successful, since the number of national banks increased from 638 at the end of 1864 to 1582 at the end of 1865. The law had the additional effect of tightening the national banking system and making it more difficult for states to separate from the union. (The Confederacy had the state banking system in operation before splitting off, and it was thought that a single federal system would have made such independence more difficult.)

The Confederacy, meanwhile, had financed a great portion of the war by printing Confederate notes. When the southern states went to war with the Union, the flow of Confederate notes from the north (mainly from Massachusetts, where they were being printed because of a lack of printing facilities in the south) stopped. The Confederate government couldn't get enough paper currency printed to meet its expenditures.

> As early as November, 1861, Secretary Memminger reported that "daily requisitions exceeded the supply of money by nearly 50 per cent." He expanded the Treasury note-signing bureau from seventy-two employees in July, 1862, to two hundred and sixty-two in July, 1863. Even so, an insufficient amount of currency was issued. As the war continued, paper, suitable engravings, and printers became harder to find. In desperation, Secretary Memminger recommended that the South resort to honoring counterfeits. Any person holding a bogus note should be able to exchange it for a 6 per cent call certificate. The counterfeits could then be stamped 'valid' by the Treasury and reissued.[10]

As the Union's blockade drastically reduced imports, the issue of money became the only possible source of revenues for the Confederacy. Prices rose rapidly and near the end of the war one journalist reported that coffee was selling for forty dollars a pound, the daily paper cost a dollar, and "wretched tallow candles" were selling at ten dollars a pound. By the very end of the war, the value of Confederate currency, especially after the North indicated that it would not honor the currency, fell to zero. The victorious North forced the South to honor the debts they incurred during the war, with the payments, made in northern dollars, indexed by the value of southern currency with respect to the northern dollar at the time of issue of the debt.

During the war in the North, banks ceased to convert bank notes, either federal or private, into gold at par. At one low point of the war, thirty-eight dollars of gold coin could purchase one hundred dollars of bank notes. When the war ended, the federal government, through the Treasury, slowly reduced the money supply, and by 1879 the dollar returned to convertibility with gold at the pre-war rate. The United States had been on a bimetallic (gold and silver) standard until 1873, even though convertibility had been suspended. In 1873, silver was demonetarized although minting was continued at a substandard rate in subsidiary coinage (small change) and the United States was officially on a gold standard.

An interesting legal note: In 1870, the United States Supreme Court ruled that the greenbacks issued as a legal tender before the Civil War were unconstitutional. The Chief Justice, Salmon Chase, wrote the court's decision finding that the activities of the Secretary of the Treasury, in issuing these greenbacks, were unconstitutional. The Secretary of the Treasury who initiated the greenbacks was the same Salmon Chase. Since this ruling found contracts written *before* the war as not covered by the Legal Tender Act, there was considerable concern that contracts signed *after* the war would also not be bound the ruling. This was viewed as

[10] E. M. Lerner, "Inflation in the Confederacy, 1861–1865," in *Studies in the Quantity Theory of Money*, ed. Milton Friedman (Chicago: University of Chicago Press, 1956, 168).

very undesirable, and in 1871, the court, with two new members, reversed itself and found the greenbacks constitutional legal tender. This later ruling was confirmed by another case in 1884. Salmon Chase, as Secretary of the Treasury, had his own portrait put on one denomination of the greenbacks. He was the only living person to have his portrait on these notes and, in 1866, Congress passed a law prohibiting the image of any living person on a note of the United States.

The contraction of the money supply that led to the resumption of the convertibility of bank notes with gold at the old par also caused a considerable decline in the price level. In 1873, there was a banking panic, followed by a serious recession that didn't end until 1879. Much of the blame for this recession, especially among the debtor classes, was placed on the gold standard and the "insufficient" money supply. The declining prices meant that debtors had to pay back their debts in money that was worth more than the money they had borrowed. The solution suggested by the debtors, which was to be repeated for years to come, was to remonetarize silver.

The price decline that came along with the reestablishment of the gold standard was to continue until 1897 at a rate of about one percent a year. It is believed that the root cause of this price decline, which was pretty much worldwide, was the increased economic activity in the face of a relatively steady gold—read "money"—supply, since there were few major discoveries of gold made during this period. It was this continued decline of prices and the outcry of the debtor class (which included the farming community) that this generated, along with the interests of the silver-mining establishment, that led to the free silver movement of the late nineteenth century. The debtor groups complained, quite rightly, that the money that they paid back on their loans was worth more than the money that they borrowed. They argued that if silver was allowed to be freely coined (in that any silver that was brought to the mint would be converted into coins and returned with no charge to the person who brought it in) that would have an inflationary (or at least counter-to-deflationary) effect on the economy and would lessen the burden of their debts. The gold–silver exchange rate, fixed at sixteen to 1, was favorable to the silver mining interests, and this won their support for "free silver." The free silver movement was defeated in 1896 by the election of William McKinley, who is said to have represented the banking interests. The discovery of gold in South Africa and other countries at the turn of the century ended the price decline, anyway, and with that the enthusiasm for free silver disappeared. The history of the problems with the bimetallic system before the Civil War does not make it clear that the addition of silver would have increased the money supply as the free silver people had hoped that it would. If the exchange rate between silver and gold were not exactly equal to the free market rate, one of the monies would disappear as a money, and would probably have been exported.

The late nineteenth century also witnessed the rise of the check, or demand deposit. Most of the state and national chartered banks in the country were required to maintain a percentage of their deposits as reserves. They were, however, allowed to maintain these reserves as deposits in other banks. For most of the rural banks, the most reasonable place was in a bank in one or more of the major cities. These depositories became "correspondent" banks. When someone sent a check, drawn on a local bank, to someone in another part of the country, as payment for some service or good, the check's recipient would want to turn it into cash. He could not take it to just any bank and get money for it there. Rather, he had to take it to a bank that had some of the reserves of the issuing bank—that is the bank of the person who wrote the check. If there was not such a bank in town, he had to take it to a bank that had reserves in a bank that also had reserves of the issuing bank. This tiering of banks could become quite complex and checks could take a long time to clear if someone in some small, rural district sent a check to someone in some other far off, small, rural district. There was also the banks' annoying habit of charging a small fee, called an exchange charge, for every check that moved through them. This fee was paid by the person who cashed the check.

A possibly more important problem with the correspondent banking system was the rate at which funds could flow *out* of the major city banks. If a number of the rural banks thought that the bank in which they had their reserves in was not especially sound, that it had made a number of loans that might not get paid back, they could all try to take out their reserves at the same time. During the "panic," the city bank could have difficulty in meeting the demands of the rural banks and might be forced to declare bankruptcy. The rural banks' attempts to protect themselves could put the entire banking system into jeopardy. If the correspondent bank was unable to pay back the deposits of the rural banks, the rural banks then would not have sufficient reserves, and they too might be forced into bankruptcy. The specter of this complete collapse of the banking system was one of the things that led to the institution of the **Federal Reserve System** (called the Fed) on December 23, 1913.

The Federal Reserve System provided two major services to both the national banks, and those state banks that chose to become members. First, the member banks were required to maintain their reserves at the regional Federal Reserve Bank. (There are twelve of them, scattered about the country.) These reserves were used to clear checks for all of the member banks, so there were only twelve central points through which checks could clear. Second, the Federal Reserve could exchange reserve account balances—money—for commercial debt instruments, in a maneuver called discounting, and could therefore provide the banks with additional cash if they needed it. This was intended to help prevent failures in banks that were in short-term difficulties.

Milton Friedman and Anna Jacobson Schwartz argue that the Federal Reserve did not fulfill its duty with respect to the exchange of money for debt instruments during the beginning of the Great Depression.[11] When the Bank of United States (not at all related to the earlier Banks of the United States, but a small New York immigrant bank) got into difficulties in late 1930, the Federal

[11] Milton Friedman and Anna Jacobson Schwartz, A *Monetary History of the United States, 1867–1960* (Princeton: Princeton University Press, 1971).

Reserve did little or nothing to help it, and it failed in December of that year. The unfortunate name of this bank, linking it in peoples' minds to the government, initiated a banking panic and runs on many of the country's banks. The later liquidation of the bank showed that it had sufficient assets to cover its debts and that with proper help from the Federal Reserve it need not have gone under.

The United States was on a full gold standard until January 17, 1934, early in the Franklin Roosevelt administration, when citizens were required to surrender all of their gold except for art and jewelry and gold certificates to the government in exchange for paper currency. Congress passed a joint resolution in 1933 voiding provisions in contracts that specified repayment in gold coin. Two weeks after all gold was turned in, Roosevelt reduced the dollar for international transactions from $20.67 per ounce of gold to $35 per ounce, thereby collecting a tax, or making a profit, of $14.33 on each ounce of gold that was turned in. While citizens of the United States were not allowed to hold gold as an asset (they could hold it as art or jewelry), the country was still on a gold standard as far as the rest of the world was concerned. Faced in 1968 with increasing difficulty in providing gold to private users—and to the French government, which being difficult, was exchanging its dollars for gold—a two-tiered price system was set up. The official price was kept at $35 an ounce and that was the price at which governments exchanged gold. A private market was allowed to develop in which private individuals who were not United States citizens could make their personal purchases, and that market would determine whatever price it wanted for gold. Governments were prohibited from buying or selling in that private market, since they could buy gold at the lower official price and sell at the usually higher free price.

In August, 1971, the Nixon administration imposed the first wage and price controls on the United States since World War II, and, in December of that year, it devalued the dollar, which it was not exchanging for gold, anyway, to $38 an ounce. (At that time the free market price was over $100.) This new international dollar price of gold was short-lived and on February 12, 1973, the dollar devalued to $42.22 per ounce. Within two weeks, most of the United States's major trading partners had allowed their currencies to float against the dollar so that the dollar went on a de facto float. (Currencies float when the government doesn't choose and then defend some officially determined rate for exchanging it with other currencies. Some sort of market forces determine what the exchange rate will be.) The United States dollar became a fiat money both domestically and internationally.

In 1975, United States citizens were once again allowed to hold gold as an investment. Driven by some fears in the Middle East, the price of an ounce of gold went up to over $800 by early 1980. In early 1985 it dropped to around $300 an ounce and in 1988 it was in the $400 to $450 range.

In the 1980s there were no countries on the gold standard. Most of the major currencies of the world floated against one another. The European countries had what was called "the snake in the tunnel." All of the major European currencies were to be maintained at a fairly fixed exchange rate with respect to one another—

the snake—but the entire set was allowed to move more widely—the tunnel—against other currencies, particularly the United States dollar and the Japanese yen.

Innovations in banking during the 1970s and 80s were mainly innovations in the electronic transfer of funds. One of the main innovations is called Fedwire, an electronic transfer network run by the Federal Reserve System that permits depository institutions, such as banks and savings and loan associations, to transfer funds nationwide with great speed. Another innovation is the automated clearinghouse services (ACH) that allow firms and other institutions to make recurring transfers via magnetic tape. These are used primarily for payroll deposits. These changes were more in the *speed* at which the banking system could move money than in the basic *way* in which it moved money.

Two major laws involving the United States banking system were passed by Congress, one in 1978 and the other in 1980. The more recent of these was the **Depository Institutions Deregulation and Monetary Control Act** of 1980. This act did several things. The high inflation rates of the late 1970s, which were above 10 percent, made the fixed-rate savings accounts of commercial banks unattractive, especially with respect to the then newly-formed money market mutual funds, which provided much higher interest rates with very little risk. The DIDMCA, as it is called within the government, allowed banks to offer the same kind of interest rates as the money market mutual funds by removing the interest rate upper limit previously set by the Fed's Regulation Q. Possibly the most important effect of the Monetary Control Act of 1980 was to require all depository institutions in the United States (national and state chartered commercial banks, savings and loan associations, credit unions, and United States agencies and branches of foreign banks) to maintain reserves either as cash in their vaults or in their local Federal Reserve Bank. The ability to clear checks through the Fed was extended to this same set of institutions, but the service was no longer free. These institutions were also given the right to use the Fed's discounting facility. The reserve requirements were also changed fairly dramatically and were defined over broad classes of types of deposits and not so narrowly as before. Table 13.1 shows the classifications and reserve requirements for each class as it was defined before and after the Monetary Control Act of 1980. Notice the significant decrease in the number of categories and the more general definitions of those categories. The more general definitions were required by the new types of institutions that now had to maintain reserves in the Fed.

The **Full Employment and Balanced Growth Act** (the **Humphrey-Hawkins Act**) of 1978 amended the original mandate of the Federal Reserve Board. The new mandate reads

> The Board of Governors of the Federal Reserve System and the Federal Open Market Committee shall maintain long-run growth of the monetary and credit aggregates commensurate with the economy's long-run potential to increase

TABLE 13.1

BEFORE MONETARY CONTROL ACT		AFTER MONETARY CONTROL ACT	
TYPE OF DEPOSIT	RESERVE REQUIREMENT	TYPE OF DEPOSIT	RESERVE REQUIREMENT
Demand Deposits, in dollars		*Transaction Accounts, in dollars*	
0 to 2 million	7%	0 to 31.7 million	3%
2 to 10 million	9.5%	Over 31.7 million	12%
10 to 100 million	11.75%		
100 to 400 million	12.75%		
over 400 million	16.25%		
Savings Accounts	3%	*Time Deposits*	
		Less than 1.5 years	3%
		1.5 years or more	0%
Time Deposits		*Eurocurrency Deposits*	3%
0 to 5 million			
30–179 days	3%		
1/2–4 years	2.5%		
over 4 years	1%		
over 5 million			
30–179 days	6%		
1/2–4 years	2.5%		
over 4 years	1%		

> production, so as to promote effectively the goals of maximum employment, stable prices, and moderate long-term interest rates.[12]

The Chairman of the Federal Reserve Board was mandated to go before the Senate Banking Committee after the January and July meeting of the Open Market Committee to report on the long term policies of that committee. The novel part of the Humphrey-Hawkins Act, as it relates to the Fed, is the insistence on long-run goals and, in particular, on the long-run goals of maximum employment. It is not clear how this act has generated real changes in the behavior of the Fed, but it does point to increased intervention by Congress in the independence of the Fed and a shift in responsibilities from the banking and commercial sectors to a more general responsibility for aggregate economic performance.

[12] "Full Employment and Balanced Growth Act," *Federal Reserve Bulletin* (December 1977):1076–1078.

14

Banks and Financial Institutions

In which we study many institutional details. The Federal Reserve system, bonds and how they work, banks, and inside money are all here. We bring back our earlier model to look at monetary policy.

INTRODUCTION

Monetary policy in the United States is operated by the **Federal Open Market Committee (FOMC)** of the Federal Reserve Board, through the effects its policies have on the banks and financial markets. In other countries, the country's central bank controls monetary policy in much the same way as the Fed does in the United States. In order to understand the way the Federal Reserve or central banks control the money supply, you will need to understand how banks help "create" money and what a bond is. The discussion of bonds cannot go very far without a discussion of interest rates. First, we need to consider how the government measures money.

Monetary policy aims at controlling the money supply in order to produce some set of optimal properties, yet to be defined, for the general economy. There is not complete agreement as to what comprises the money supply. Some years ago, the Federal Reserve System had over thirty definitions for money or things that act like money. The definitions were numbered. The simplest definition was called M_0, followed by M_1, M_2, and so on. These definitions were inclusive in the sense that M_1 included the things in M_0, M_2 included the things in M_1 . . . Only the first few of these definitions are in general use today. The definitions were revised in 1980 and again in 1982. Now there are only four definitions of money; M_1, M_2, M_3, and L. $\boldsymbol{M_1}$ contains 1, currency outside of bank vaults; 2, demand deposits at commercial banks; 3, other checkable deposits, mainly interest-earning deposits on which checks can be written; and 4, traveler's checks from nonbanking firms. $\boldsymbol{M_2}$ contains M_1 and 1, overnight repurchase agreements and Eurodollar deposits in Caribbean branches of United States banks; 2, shares in money market mutual funds; 3, other savings accounts; and 4, small time deposits, with small meaning less than $100,000. $\boldsymbol{M_3}$ contains M_2 and 1, large time deposits; 2, large and longer-term repurchase agreements; and 3, money market mutual funds held by other financial institutions. $\boldsymbol{L}$ contains even less liquid assets, assets that are harder to convert to cash. It contains M_3 and 1, United States savings bonds; 2, short term United States government securities; 3, some short-term commercial assets and Eurodollar assets held by U.S. citizens. (Eurodollars are dollars that are deposited in banks in countries other than the United States.)

To give some idea of the difficulties encountered in calculating these numbers, consider just one item, currency. The Federal Reserve System counts as part of the money supply of the United States *all* of the currency issued by the Fed minus the currency in the vaults. Yet this number is not the amount of dollars in the United States. Many individuals in foreign countries, especially in countries such as Israel and Argentina, with their very high inflation rates, use and hoard dollars as much as possible. There are probably more one hundred dollar bills circulating in Argentina than in the United States. These dollars circulate in these foreign countries and are not an active part of the United States money supply, yet they are counted in M_1. They are included by default because there are no good estimates about how much currency is outside the country.

THE FEDERAL RESERVE

The Federal Reserve System is comprised of the Federal Reserve Board in Washington, D.C., and the twelve regional reserve banks. The reserve banks are in Boston, New York, Philadelphia, Richmond, Atlanta, Cleveland, Chicago, St. Louis, Minneapolis, Kansas City, Dallas, and San Francisco. These regional banks are semipublic corporations. They are owned by the local member banks (members are all national banks and any state bank that chooses to join) and are run by a board of directors, some of whom are appointed locally and some of whom are appointed by the Federal Reserve Board.[1] Notice that there are two reserve banks, in St. Louis and in Kansas City, that are in the state of Missouri. It may just be coincidence that when the legislation to enact the Federal Reserve System was working its way through Congress in 1913, the chairman of the Senate Banking Committee was from Missouri.

It seems that the primary business of the regional Federal Reserve banks is to clear checks. This is accomplished by the use of the reserve accounts that all member banks and all other depository institutions maintain in their local reserve bank. When someone deposits a check in a bank, that bank **credits,** or adds that value to, the depositor's account for the amount of the check. The bank then sends the check to the local reserve bank, where the amount of the check is *credited* to the reserve account of that bank. The check then gets sent to the local reserve bank of the bank on which the check was drawn—the bank of the person who wrote the check—and that reserve bank **debits,** or subtracts that value from, the reserve account of the appropriate bank. The check then gets sent to the bank on which it is drawn and the account of the person who wrote the check gets **debited.** This way the check-clearing process operates through only twelve hubs as opposed to the earlier correspondent system where there could be hundreds of hubs. The Federal Reserve banks in the larger regions have branches that aid in the clearing of checks. For example, the Minneapolis Federal Reserve bank has a branch office in Helena, Montana.

In many countries the central bank is not involved in clearing checks. In these countries (and in the United States before the Federal Reserve System was established) checks are cleared by private or publicly owned clearinghouses, which charge banks for the service they provide. In these cases, the connection between check cashing and reserves is not so direct. Some countries have very high reserve requirements on their banks. These very high reserves pay interest from the

[1] A bank can be chartered (legally formed) by either the Federal government (national banks) or by a state government (state banks). All national banks join the Federal Reserve System, but state chartered banks may choose not to.

central government to the banks, because these reserves are really an indirect method of government borrowing.

The Federal Reserve Board has seven members who each serve fourteen-year terms. The chairman is appointed by the president of the United States and holds office for four years, although most chairmen have served for more than one term. It is the Federal Reserve Board that sets monetary policy in the United States. There are three principle methods for directing monetary policy: 1, changes in the reserve requirement; 2, changes in the discount rate; and 3, open market operations. Open market operations is the method most frequently used for control of the money supply and is managed by the Federal Open Market Committee. How each of these can change the money supply will require a bit of explanation, and for the first two will require a description of the process by which banks "create" money. To explain open market operations will require a careful description of bonds. While the exact details might be different in different countries, most central banks use the same three tools for monetary policy.

HOW BANKS "CREATE" MONEY

Individuals deposit money, either as cash or as a check from some other agent, into their bank account. (Assume a demand deposit or checking account.) The bank credits them with this deposit, which these individuals then view as money that they can use whenever they need. The bank does not store this money in the vault for them, but lends all of it, except for the portion that it maintains as reserves, to some other agent under an agreement in which the borrower promises to give the money back at some specific time in the future and in the interim to pay the bank something, called interest, for the use of the money. Either the agent who received the loan or some other agent, who received it from the first one, eventually deposits it into an account in a bank. These new agents view their bank deposits as money, and the bank can lend them out, minus reserves, to someone else. Consider an example.

Imagine that there is only one bank in some closed economy. This one bank really is standing in as a proxy for the country's banking system. The Fed introduces $1000 in new money into the economy by giving it to someone whom we will call Alvin.[2] Alvin deposits this money into his checking account in the bank. The bank sends the reserve requirement, fifteen percent, for this example, to the Fed and lends out the rest—$850—to Bertha. Bertha uses this money to buy a new stereo at Cain's Amazing Sound House. Cain deposits the $850 into his account in the bank. The bank sends fifteen percent of this deposit to the Fed as a reserve and loans out the $722.50 left over to Deborah. Deborah uses this to buy a car at Ishmael's Whale of a Deal Used Autos. The owner, Elmo, deposits this money in

[2] Of course, the Fed seldom gives people money. Alvin might have traded a government bond he owned with the Fed for money.

his bank account. The bank sends fifteen percent to the Fed and loans \$614.12 to Fritz. This cycle continues, as shown in Table 14.1.

From an addition of one thousand dollars of new money into an economy with a reserve requirement of fifteen percent, the banking system adds an additional \$5666.67 to the money stock. Notice that the entire one thousand dollars of new money eventually ends up as reserves. The total addition to the money supply that results from adding one additional dollar into the economy is a function of the reserve requirement. To see this, look at Table 14.1 as if the one thousand dollar initial amount were one dollar. Remember that in the case above, the reserve requirement (RR) was fifteen percent (or .15).

In cycle 1, the initial dollar enters the money supply. In the second round the dollar minus RR reenters the system (this is $1 - RR$). In the third round, of this $1 - RR$, a fraction equal to $1 - RR$ of it reenters the money supply, while the rest goes to reserves. So the total amount entering in the third round is $(1 - RR)\times(1 - RR)$ or $(1 - RR)^2$. In the fourth round, a fraction equal to $1 - RR$ of the $(1 - RR)^2$ reenters the money supply. This is equal to $(1 - RR)^3$. If you recall that for any finite number x, $x^0 = 1$, the sequence of increases in the money supply that result from the addition of one dollar into the economy can be written as,

$$(1 - RR)^0 + (1 - RR)^1 + (1 - RR)^2 + (1 - RR)^3 + \ldots$$

Writing this out in summation notation and recalling a bit of mathematics, we find that from one new dollar we get

$$\sum_{i=0}^{\infty} (1 - RR)^i = 1/RR$$

TABLE 14.1

CYCLE	DEPOSIT	RESERVES	LOANS
1	\$1000.00	\$ 150.00	\$ 850.00
2	850.00	127.50	722.50
3	722.50	108.38	614.12
4	614.12	92.12	522.00
.	.	.	.
.	.	.	.
∞	00.00	00.00	00.00
Total	\$6666.67	\$1000.00	\$5666.67

dollars in the economy.[3] The number 1/RR is called the **money multiplier.** For a reserve requirement of fifteen percent, the money multiplier is 6.66667, if we round off at the fifth decimal place.

The money multiplier represents the **upper bound** of the increase in the money supply—also called the money stock—that results from an addition of one dollar into the economy. It is an upper bound because not every dollar gets put back into the banking system. Some of it gets held in pockets, pocketbooks, or pillowcases; flows out of the country; or gets lost; so that the actual increase in the money supply is something less.

RETURNING TO THE FEDERAL RESERVE SYSTEM

Now, how does all of the above relate to the way the Federal Reserve System can control the money supply? It was said above that seeing how banks "create" money was necessary in order to understand how changing the reserve requirement and changing the discount rate can change the money supply. Let's begin with the reserve requirement.

The **reserve requirement** (**RR**) is that portion of the deposits in a bank that *must* be kept in the local Federal Reserve Bank. This requirement is different for different kinds of accounts in any given bank and is different for different types of banks. For smaller banks, those with less than 31.7 million in transaction deposits, the reserve requirement on those deposits is three percent and can be varied by the Federal Reserve Board between zero and nine percent. For larger banks, the reserve requirement is twelve percent and can be varied between eight and fourteen percent. Other kinds of deposits tend to have lower reserve requirements.

For simplicity, suppose all banks have a reserve requirement of twelve percent. For each new dollar that *had* entered the economy, the banking system expanded the reserve by an amount up to the money multiplier. (These new dollars are called **high powered money** or the **monetary base** because it is the amount of money that serves as a base for the multiplicative effect of the banking system.) In this case, the high powered money is multiplied by 1/(.12) or 8.33 to get the money supply. If the reserve requirement were lowered to ten percent, then the money multiplier would be 1/10 or ten. So the money supply could expand to be ten times the high powered money rather than the 8.33 times that it could be when the reserve requirement was twelve percent. Consider an example. If the money supply (we are using M_1 here) were $756.5 billion, as it was in December 1987, and the reserve requirement were twelve percent, then the monetary base would be $90.82 billion ($756.5 divided by 8.33). If the reserve requirement were

[3] As an example for those readers who have not seen this math before, let RR = 20% = .2. Then 1 − RR equals .8. We sum up the infinite sequence. For the first ten elements of the sequence we have 1 + .8 + .64 + .512 + .401 + .328 + .262 + .21 + .168 + .134 = 4.463. Adding the next ten elements of the sequence gives a total of 4.942. Adding ten more (now we have 30 elements of the sequence) gives a total of 4.995. The sequence is approaching 5 or 1/.2.

lowered to ten percent, then this monetary base would be multiplied by ten and the money supply could be $908.2 billion. The change in the reserve requirement from twelve to ten percent permitted the money supply to increase by $151.7 billion. Note that reducing the reserve requirement *allows* banks to increase their loans and thereby increase the money supply. Banks are not forced to make new loans. During the Great Depression, banks accumulated a large amount of voluntary reserves, in part because they were afraid of runs. In this situation, reductions in the required reserves might not cause them to make more loans. (As it happened, for some reason the Federal Reserve Board increased the required reserves and reduced the protective cushion of voluntary reserves that the banks had built up. This caused them to make even fewer loans than they might have and, some argue, increased the severity of the depression.) Increasing the reserve requirement *forces* the banks to reduce their loans and reduce the money supply. There is asymmetry in the effects of applications of this type of policy. Changes in the reserve requirement can have very strong effects on the money supply and, in part for this reason, these changes are relatively infrequent.

The **discount rate** is the interest rate that banks pay when they need to borrow money from the Federal Reserve System. They need to borrow when their reserves are insufficient to meet their reserve requirement. The discount rate is set every two weeks by the Fed Board, but it will often remain at the same rate for months on end. Banks that borrow reserves for two weeks in a row or for more than four weeks a year pay a four percentage point surcharge on the discount rate. Note that banks sometimes borrow reserves from other banks that have excess reserves. In this way they do not face the penalties they would if they were forced to borrow from the Federal Reserve System. The interest rate that they pay to the other banks is called the **Federal Funds rate** and has been as much as five percentage points higher than the discount rate.

Raising or lowering the discount rate affects the money supply in two ways. With lower discount rates, banks are more likely to lend very close to the limit of their reserves because the cost of overlending is smaller. At higher rates they are likely to maintain more of a cushion and not to loan so close to their limit. The second effect of changes in the discount rate is that it is interpreted as signaling what the Fed will be doing with its major (in the sense of "most frequently used") money control instrument, open market operations.

BONDS

Because open market operations involve the buying and selling of government bonds, we must first discuss the interrelation between bonds, money, and interest rates.

A **bond** is a contract. It is a promise to pay a certain amount of money at fixed intervals and then to pay an additional amount of money at the end of some fixed period of time. Individuals purchase these promises by giving some money *now* to the agent who promises this *stream* of payments. Bonds are differentiated by the size of the individual payments, the amount given back at the end of the time period, and the length of that time period. The first and second items determine the **interest rate** or yield on a bond, the second determines the **denomination** of the bond, and the third determines the time till **maturity.** A twenty year, ten thousand dollar, eight percent bond will offer yearly payments of eight hundred dollars (eight per cent of ten thousand dollars) for twenty years and will give an additional ten thousand dollars at the end of the twentieth year.

An artificial distinction, which we will use to help explain open market operations, can be made between old and new bonds. Old bonds are those whose denomination, interest rate, and date of maturity are already determined. New bonds have their denomination and date of maturity determined and will sell in the market at their denomination price. Their interest rate will adjust until their denomination and sale price are equal. Old bonds need not sell at their denomination. This distinction between old and new bonds is useful for seeing how the price of bonds changes with changes in the market interest rate and the related notion of yield.

Imagine that you own an old bond of the type described above; a twenty year, ten thousand dollar, eight percent United States government bond. You will be receiving the eight hundred dollars each year for twenty years, and will receive ten thousand dollars in the last year. You paid ten thousand dollars for this bond. You have held this bond for ten years and now need cash and want to sell the bond. How much will you get for it? At this point the bond is a contract that promises to pay eight hundred dollars a year for *ten* years and then pay ten thousand dollars.

Suppose that new, *ten* year, ten thousand dollar United States government bonds are now giving ten percent interest; that is, paying a stream of one thousand dollars a year in interest. Since your bond has only ten years left, this is the relevant bond for comparisons. This new bond is offering one thousand dollars a year for ten years and pays ten thousand dollars in the tenth year. If this bond is currently selling at par (my *definition* of a new bond, that the sale price equals the denomination), then you will not be able to receive ten thousand dollars for your bond, since it gives a smaller payment than the new one every period. If you sell your bond, its price will be *less* than the price of new bonds. The price of your bond must fall until its stream of payments and final payment are as attractive as the stream and final payment of the new bonds.[4] If interest rates had gone down to six

[4] Note that the price will *not* drop so that the interest stream payment divided by the sale price is equal to the interest rate of the new bonds. In the example above, that would mean that the price of your bond would have to fall to eight thousand dollars. If it did this, then the eight hundred dollars each period divided by the eight thousand dollars would equal ten percent. But the final payment is equal to ten thousand dollars, and in the last period of the bond the person who bought it would get that period's interest payment and ten thousand dollars, or two thousand dollars more than she paid for it. This additional two thousand dollars must be counted. The price will fall less than two thousand dollars and the interest rate calculated by dividing the payment stream by the sale price is less than ten percent. The difference between the sale price and the ten thousand dollars will "make up" for the lower payment each period.

percent, say, instead of up, then new bonds would be offering six hundred dollars a year and the ten thousand dollars the tenth year. In this case the stream of payments from your bond is greater than those from a new bond and you will be able to get a greater than par (greater than ten thousand dollar) price for your bond.

To summarize the main points of the above paragraphs: If the interest rates go up, the price of old bonds goes down. If the interest rates go down, the price of old bonds goes up.

Some comments on interest rates: There is not *one* interest rate for an economy. There are many interest rates. One reason for this multiplicity of rates is because there are many bonds with different times till maturity, and there tends to be a difference in short- and long-term interest rates. This is true for a number of reasons, the most important of which is that long-term bonds are somewhat riskier than short-term bonds. One of the important sources of risk in longer-term bonds is inflation. Because the payments that make up a bond are denominated in money, changes in the inflation rate will change the real value of the interest and the principle that a bond pays. If individuals are concerned with the real value of the payment stream, then it is necessary to take this inflation into account.

Consider a bond that lasts only one period. It is purchased today and pays back the principle and some interest in the next period. Suppose, as an example, that it is a twenty percent, one thousand dollar bond that is purchased for one thousand dollars today. Next period, the total payment will be twelve hundred dollars. If, between this period and the next, there would be an inflation—a rise in the general price level—of ten percent (again, as an example) then one would need eleven hundred dollars to maintain the purchasing power of the one thousand dollars that was used to purchase the bond. If one maintains the purchasing power of the initial payment, then the interest paid, after the inflation correction is made, is only one hundred dollars. This approximately represents an interest rate of ten percent.[5] In this case, the **real interest rate,** ten percent, the rate paid after corrections have been made for the effects of inflation on the principle, is the **nominal interest rate,** twenty percent, minus the **inflation rate,** ten percent. The historical average real interest rate in the United States over the past two hundred years is around two percent.

The different nominal interest rates on long- and short-term bonds is generated, in part, by expectations about inflation in future periods. If these expectations of inflation translate into different expectations about the expected short-

[5] The reason that one must use the term "approximately" is that the purchasing power of the $100 of "real" interest has also declined. If one were to correct for that, the $100 has the purchasing power of only $90.9 of the initial period's money. This is found by dividing the $100 by 1 plus the inflation rate as a decimal and 90.9 equals 100/1.10. The correct calculation of the real interest rate is 9.09%. This correction for inflation in the value of the nominal interest payment is most important when the inflation rate is large. For low levels of inflation, simply subtracting the inflation rate from the nominal interest rate is close enough for any practical purpose.

term nominal interest rate in some future period, then current short-term nominal rates will be different from current long-term nominal rates. From this we can develop a theory of the **term structure of interest rates.**

In the market there exists a two period bond. This is a bond that will become due (that is, pay the principle and the accumulated interest) two periods into the future. There is an interest rate for a bond of this type that is sold in period t. We will label the interest on a bond of this type $i_{2,t}$. Since this bond only pays two periods into the future, it must pay interest on the interest earned the first period.[6] The total payment on a bond that costs, or is denominated as, one dollar is $(1 + i_{2,t})(1 + i_{2,t})$. One has earned $1 + i_{2,t}$ by the end of the first period, and this total amount of money then earns a rate of $i_{2,t}$ to the end of the second period. In the market there exists a one period bond. This bond will pay the principle and interest in the next period. The interest rate on this bond in period t is $i_{1,t}$. One can imagine that there will exist a one period bond that, purchased in the next period, will yield the principle and interest two periods in the future. The interest rate on this bond is not known now, but there is an expectation as to what the interest on that bond will be. We will call that interest $E_t i_{1,t+1}$ and it is the expectation at time t of the interest rate on a one period bond sold in period $t + 1$. If one were to purchase a one dollar, one period bond today and buy another one period bond tomorrow with all of the earnings from the first bond, the total expected return would be $(1 + i_{1,t})(1 + E_t i_{1,t+1})$.

Since it is possible to purchase either a two period bond or a sequence of two one period bonds, the total return on either of these routes should be the same. Therefore,

$$(1 + i_{2,t})(1 + i_{2,t}) = (1 + i_{1,t})(1 + E_t i_{1,t+1})$$

In the above equation, $i_{1,t}$, the interest rate on a one period bond purchased today, and $i_{2,t}$, the interest rate on a two period bond purchased today, are known. They can be observed in the market. $E_t i_{1,t+1}$, the expected interest rate on a one period bond purchased tomorrow, is not known, but can be calculated since it is the only unknown in the above equation. We find that the expected interest rate on a one period bond purchased in the next period is

$$E_t i_{1,t+1} = [(1 + i_{2,t})^2/(1 + i_{1,t})] - 1$$

The expected interest rate on a one period bond purchased two periods in the

[6] This is a somewhat different bond than we have been using up to now. Normally, bonds paid out the interest each period and gave the final interest payment and the principal in the last period. The bonds we are using to discuss the term structure of interest rates will make only one payment at the final maturity date. If it is a two year bond, the interest that the bond earned during the first period is not paid to the holder of the bond, and therefore this interest earns interest. This is a slight modification in the form of payouts of the bonds that make the mathematics of the analysis much simpler. It is possible to carry on the discussion in terms of bonds that pay out each period, but the math is quite messy.

future can be calculated in a similar manner. If the interest rate on a three period bond purchased today is $i_{3,t}$, then the expected interest rate on a one period bond purchase two periods in the future is

$$E_t i_{1,t+2} = \{(1 + i_{3,t})^3/[(1 + E_t i_{1,t+1})(1 + i_{1,t})]\} - 1$$

where $E_t i_{1,t+1}$ was calculated as above. In this way, all of the expected future one period interest rates can be calculated from current market rates. From the above analysis one can see that the long-term interest rates will be different from the short-term rates if the expected future short-term rates are different from the current short-term rates.

Another reason for many different interest rates is that there are many different agents in an economy, firms and governments, who offer bonds; there are different probabilities that these agents will be able to pay off those bonds. The United States federal government offers the most secure bonds in terms of United States dollars. This is because the government controls the printing presses for currency and will almost certainly be able to pay off the bonds. States and very large corporations are the next most secure. Local governments and smaller firms are less secure. Each of these agents offers a different interest rate. If there is a higher risk that some small firm will not be able to pay off its bond, then it has to offer a higher interest rate in order to get people to be willing to accept that risk. This risk premium increases as the likelihood that the bond will be paid off decreases. (The risk premium of a firm changes as people get new information about that firm. If you hold an old bond from some firm that is getting into difficulties, the interest rate on new bonds from that firm will go up because of the increased risk, and the selling price of your old bonds will go down.) There are firms, such as Moody's Investors Service and Dunn and Bradstreet, that specialize in rating different firms and governments as to the likelihood that they will meet their obligations. The interest rate that these firms and governments have to pay on their debt issues reflects the ratings they get from the investors' service companies.

OPEN MARKET OPERATIONS

The Federal Open Market Committee, often called the FOMC, buys and sells government bonds in the bond market through the New York Federal Reserve Bank. This is called **open market operations.** The New York Federal Reserve Bank handled more than one trillion dollars worth of purchases and sales of bonds in open market operations in 1988. When it sells government bonds, it receives money for them. This takes money out of the economy, since money in the vaults of the Federal Reserve System does not count as money. When it buys bonds, it gives money for them and this adds money to the economy. When money is added to the economy, it enters into the banking system and goes through the money multiplier process. If one billion dollars of bonds are bought by the Fed, then one billion dollars is added to the system; this may multiply, depending on the reserve requirement, to a much larger amount—one billion times one over the reserve requirement is the upper limit. When bonds are sold by the Fed, the money—part of the monetary base—leaves the economy and the money stock shrinks by that amount times the money multiplier. Note that this is how open market operations can shift the aggregate demand curve in our earlier model.

In order to sell additional bonds—some old federal government bonds that it owns—the Fed must offer to sell them at a price lower than the price currently being offered by the market. As seen above, this decline in the price of bonds causes the interest rate to rise. When it buys bonds, the Fed offers a price higher than that prevailing in the market, and this lowers interest rates. Therefore, open market operations change not only the money supply, but the interest rates as well. These changes in the interest rates are likely to have effects on investment.

There is a concept in economics called the **crowding-out effect.** The idea is that when the Fed or the U.S. Treasury sells additional bonds, these sales replace the sales of bonds by firms. The firms had been selling the bonds in order to finance new projects. The government bonds, which are usually sold in order to finance current consumption, crowd or drive corporation bonds out of the market by driving up the interest rate that the firms would have to pay in order to get people to hold their bonds. This makes fewer of the projects that firms might want to invest in profitable. It is unclear from the data how important this crowding-out effect is. Some economists suggest that the increased interest rates generate enough additional savings in the form of delayed consumption so that there is little or no loss in investment. Most, however, believe that the crowding-out effect can be substantial. The investment function mentioned in Chapter 5, where investment is a function of the interest rate, is in keeping with the notion of a crowding-out effect, since that function says that higher interest rates will result in reduced investment.

MONEY IN OUR MACRO MODELS

Here we will use the models developed in Chapters 5 though 11 to see how monetary policy can have effects on the rest of the economy. Suppose that the Fed decides to increase the money supply. It can do this by reducing the reserve requirement, which works through the banking system to change only the money supply; by reducing the discount rate, which operates the same way, but with a much smaller change; or by buying bonds in open market operations. We will look more carefully at open market operations.

To increase the money supply, the Fed buys bonds and gives money in exchange for them. In order to buy these bonds, it must offer higher prices for these bonds than others are willing to offer. This increases the price of the bonds and, as a result, lowers the interest rate. If we no longer think of investment as exogenous, but assume that it is determined by the interest rate, we see that this reduction in the interest rate increases the amount of investment that firms are willing to make, and will, over time, cause the capital stock to increase. In all of our models, the increase in the money stock and investment cause the AD curve to shift out. This can be seen from the AD function that at some fixed price level p_1, initial output is

$$Y_1 = [1/(1 - \text{mpc})] \times [\mu \times (M_1 + B_p + B_{g1})/p_1 + I_1 + G - \text{mpc} \times T]$$

and the final output is

$$Y_2 = [1/(1 - \text{mpc})] \times [\mu \times (M_2 + B_p + B_{g2})/p_1 + I_2 + G - \text{mpc} \times T]$$

Since $M_2 - M_1$ is equal to the purchases of bonds (the absolute value of $B_{g2} - B_{g1}$) times the money multiplier, $(M_2 - M_1 + B_{g2} - B_{g1})$ is positive and equal to the money multiplier minus one times the change in bonds. The decline in the interest rate causes I_2 to be larger than I_1. Combining these two effects, we get that Y_2 is greater than Y_1. At price p_1, the demand for output increases, so the AD curve shifts out.

In a static classical model and the extreme rational expectations version of the Keynesian model, this shift in the AD curve drives up prices in period one, but does not effect output. Consumption is down because, with unchanged output and government expenditures and increased investment, there is less left for consumption. (The increase in prices must be more than the increase in the nominal wealth generated by the increase in the money supply minus the decline in bonds. This must be so in order to have consumption decline, because neither income nor taxes change.) In period two, the production function and demand curve for labor shift out because of the increased capital stock. This causes equilibrium output to increase. Things then get a bit difficult to follow for consumption, (but not for output, which increases) since the decrease in consumption caused by the increased investment is being offset by the increase in available output.

In the other Keynesian models, the shift in the AD curve will result in an increase in output. In these models, open market operations not only have long-run effects through the changes in investment, but have short-run effects as well. It is suggested that the reader follow the above open market operations in the naive and adaptive expectations models for a few periods to be comfortable with these results.

THE RETURN OF THE SUPPLY SIDE

Let us consider the Reagan "supply side economics" example that we have used earlier once again, but now let us keep the discussion about money and interest rates in mind. Remember that for the following discussion we will be working in a closed economy—one without international trade.

If taxes are cut and government expenditures are not reduced, the government budget constraint says that ΔM, ΔB_g, or both will increase to make up for the reduction in taxes. In a Republican administration, which is predisposed against inflation, the inclination is to use a flow of new bonds rather than a flow of new money to cover this increased deficit, since the bonds do not have the money multiplier effect. That means that ΔB_g will increase and ΔM will remain constant. Now, just as the Fed had to raise the interest rate on its bonds thus lowering the price, in order to sell more of them, the Federal government will have to do the same thing in order to sell the bonds that make up ΔB_g (especially if ΔB_g is large, say as large as two hundred billion dollars). Therefore, the increased sale of government bonds generates pressures for the interest rate to raise, and, if it does this will *reduce* investment.[7]

The government is selling bonds equal to the cut in taxes. This cut in taxes is in the form of an income tax cut biased towards the wealthy, who are, according to this theory, going to save it all to provide the additional savings necessary for the **increases** in investment that this theory predicts. However, even if they do save it all, this would only makes up for the lost taxes that are financed by the government bonds, and so there would be no increase in real investment. If all the reduction in taxes would be saved, there would also be no increase in the interest rate. (If savings equaled investment before the policy, the new higher savings will equal the same investment plus the ΔB_g. Therefore, investment and the interest rate are unchanged.) However, we should remember the consumption function. The consumption function says that

$$C = \text{mpc} \times (Y - T) + \mu \times (M + B_g + B_p)/p$$

or that consumption is determined by disposable income and real wealth. A cut in taxes that does not increase output results, at some constant price, in an increase in desired consumption equal to mpc × (the decrease in taxes) and a desired savings increase by (1 − mpc) × (the decrease in taxes). In the interpretation of the mpc that is most favorable to Reagan's supply side economics, according to the cross-sectional data (which might be applicable because the tax cut was not equal for all income classes) the mpc has a value between .5 and .7. Therefore, desired savings increase by between thirty and fifty percent of the cut in taxes, and the rest goes to increased desired consumption. The second half of the consumption function shows the result of changes in the price level on real wealth and therefore on consumption. If the price level rises, then real wealth falls and individuals will

[7] This problem is a little more complicated than is being suggested here. In order to have a complete model, in which investment is a function of the interest rate, we need to have at the least an additional equation that lets the *system* solve for this interest rate. Simply adding an additional variable in the investment results in a system that is underdetermined. Such a system does not have sufficient restrictions to give solutions for all of the variables. We are implicitly adding another restriction with savings equal to investment plus the sale of government bonds.

increase their savings—reduce their consumption—in an effort to regain some of the lost wealth. So savings may increase by more than thirty to fifty percent of the cut in taxes if that cut results in an increase in prices.

One of the things that would help generate an increase in the price level would be a shift out in the AD curve. Since the Aggregate Demand curve is determined by the function

$$Y = [1/(1 - \text{mpc})] \times [\mu \times (M + B_p + B_g)/p + I + G - \text{mpc} \times T]$$

this function might help to tell us if prices rise or not. The cut in taxes is reflected by a decline in T, $\Delta B_g/p$ rises to pay for that decline in taxes, and that increase works its way into an increase in B_g/p. We have been suggesting that I falls. So the three variables that can change are T, I, and B_g/p. Together in the AD function, their relationship is

$$\mu \times B_g/p + I - \text{mpc} \times T$$

The effects on B_g and T are to increase the value of the above expression, while the effect on I is to decrease it. How the AD curve shifts is determined by the balance of the three effects. The drop in investment might just exactly balance the effects of the other two, but this is not likely.

Is there an increase in output? In a classical model, output is determined by the aggregate supply behavior. A cut in taxes could change the supply curve for labor. If there is a reduction in income taxes (that is, those taxes that are determined as a percentage of income) at each wage paid by the firms, workers will get to keep a larger portion of that wage. In Figure 14.1, at real wage w/p_1 a reduction in

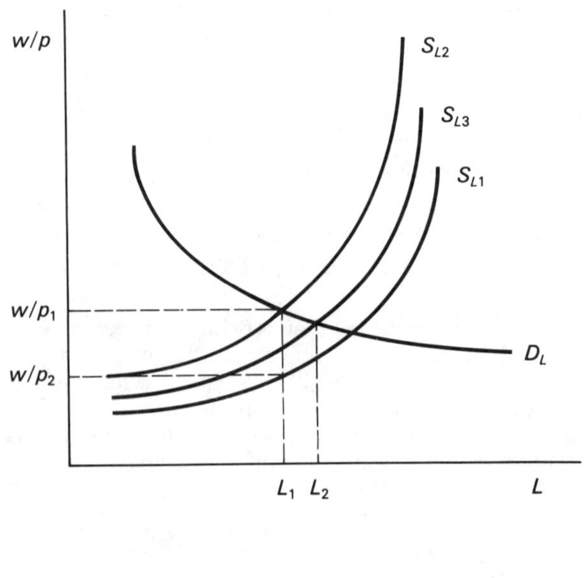

Figure 14.1

taxes will increase take-home pay and thus increase the number of people willing to work at that wage. If S_{L1} represents the amount of labor that will be provided based upon take-home pay, S_{L2} can be thought of as the supply curve for labor when a percentage income tax of $(w/p_1 - w/p_2)/w/p_1$ is imposed. If the percentage tax rate is reduced, this will give a labor supply curve similar to S_{L3}. Notice that in response to this reduction in the income tax rate, the equilibrium quantity of labor increases from L_1 to L_2. With this decline in the tax rate, the real wage paid by the firms is reduced but the real wage that the workers keep has gone up. The increased quantity of labor will increase output in the classical model.

What happens if there is already unemployment, such as in the Keynesian model? Suppose that there was a contract for the nominal wage from the period before. Because the demand curve for labor determines the quantity of workers who are hired, the only change in the aggregate supply curve is a shift of the vertical portion. If the intersection of the AD and AS curve is not in this portion of the AS curve, then the change in the equilibrium real wage has no effect on the equilibrium between the AS and AD curves. If the unions are using the equilibrium real wage as a major factor for determining the unions desired real wage (say, for example, that the desired real wage is always thirty percent higher than the equilibrium real wage) then the change in the supply curve for labor will change the equilibrium real wage and that will, in this period or the next, depending on how much information the unions have, change the desired real wage.

REPRISE

The Central Bank of a nation operates the monetary policy. This policy includes changes in the discount rate; changes in the reserve requirements; and, in countries with well-functioning bond markets, open market operations. All of these methods rely on the observation that banks create money in the sense that they can keep recycling deposits into loans that show up as additional deposits. The reserve requirement determines the upper bound of the multiplicative effect that is generated by the recycling.

Open market operations involve the exchange by the public of government bonds for money or money for government bonds. Bonds are different than money in that they do not enter as deposits into the banking system and do not have a multiplier effect. It is this multiplier effect that lets open market operations shift the AD curve. Any sale by the Fed or Central Bank of bonds for money will reduce the money supply more than the bonds are increased. Open market operations also have important effects on the market interest rate. These interest rate changes feed into the investment function and generate additional changes in the AD curve and, over time, in the capital stock and through the production curve on the AS curve.

EXERCISES

1. Consider the Keynesian model with 1) naive and 2) rational expectations. Describe the changes in prices, output, and unemployment that results from a drop in the reserve requirement from ten to eight percent.
2. The current interest rate on one year government bonds is 7.3%, the current interest rate on two year government bonds is 6.8%, and the current interest rate on three year government bonds is 8.1%. What are the expected interest rates on one year bonds to be offered one and two years from now? If the real interest rate is always two percent, what is the inflation rate that is expected for this year and the next two years?
3. Suppose that investment is a function of the interest rate and that higher interest rates mean lower investment. Suppose that an economy is initially in a stationary state. What are the results in a Keynesian model with adaptive expectations over four periods of an open market policy that is intended to reduce unemployment in period one and remains unchanged for the rest of the time period?
4. What is the result of the policy in Exercise 3 in a rational expectations world?

15

Money and Policy under Perfect Foresight

In which we introduce a new model, full of the drama of life and death; we see the future; and we discover what the government can do when all its policies are known beforehand. As a bonus, we get reasons to use money.

INTRODUCTION

In Chapter 11 we developed an extreme version of the rational expectations model. This extreme version implied that there were no policies that the government could use to improve the welfare of the members of the economy. Since in those models we were only concerned with the level of output and the price level, the inability of the government to increase output meant that it could not improve welfare. This idea is very distressing to government policy makers and to those who, for political reasons, favor government intervention in the economy; it is heartwarming to those who favor minimal or no government intervention. In this chapter will we consider a world in which agents have perfect knowledge of government polices, and we will ask what policies the government can follow that might improve the welfare of the citizens.

One can think of a world with perfect foresight—one in which the actual behavior of the government and therefore the economy is known—as the limit of rational expectations. If rational expectations represents situations in which forecasters use all of the available information to predict the future, in the limit it is possible to have *all* information (as occurs in some theories of god) and, therefore, to *know* the future.[1] We can look at models where we are exactly correct in our expectations, and can wonder, in those models, what kinds of government policies still are useful. The example of a perfect foresight model that we will build is called the **overlapping generations** (**OLG**) model of money. This model follows one developed by Paul Samuelson in 1958, which he called a "**consumption–loan**" model. For us the model has two important features: how the stuff we call "money" gains value and how some policies can work even when they are completely known.

We want to build a model in which people hold fiat money and trade it for real goods. One standard way of doing this has been to assume that individuals have demand curves for money, as a function of the interest rate perhaps; that the government supplies the money; and that an equilibrium is found by using these demand and supply curves. There are some difficulties with beginning with demand curves; before constructing a more complicated model, we should consider them.

The "begin with a demand curve for money" approach begs the serious question of why people hold money. Money is not like real goods. One does not

[1] There is a question as to whether the universe is deterministic or if it really has random components. If it is deterministic, then full information of the current state of the universe would imply perfect prediction. If the universe really is random, then full information of the current state of the universe would still not permit perfect predictions. The random nature of the universe would mean that the future is never completely knowable.

gain utility or happiness directly by having money.[2] No one would choose to take money with her if she were going to a deserted island where she would be alone for the rest of her life. Rather, it is the fact that *other* people will exchange real goods, the things that *do* provide utility, for money that gives money its value. This implies that there must be something in the structure of an economy, some kind of friction in the normal, optimal flow of goods, that money helps to smooth. If this is so, it should be instructive to consider the exact nature of this friction and observe how an individual's behavior in using money to circumvent the friction changes as the government's policy concerning money changes.

The OLG model hypothesizes a special kind of friction. An economy is set up with young and old people, but with only the young owning goods. The problem of interest is to ensure that the old get some goods to consume. Normal, quid pro quo contracts between young and old are not possible because, once the young become old and have no goods, the previously old people are no longer around (that is, they are dead). Anthropologists have provided some examples of how primitive societies solve this problem by the use of rituals and the veneration of the old. Economists provide other answers, and the institution of money is one of them.

Before we consider monetary and nonmonetary equilibria for this problem (for it is these equilibria that will interest us) we must carefully describe the physical world—the economy—and the particular frictions that occur there.

THE ECONOMY

Time is discrete. It is comprised of distinct periods. If you wish, you can think of these periods as years or as generations (thirty-year periods). The periods are demarked by the integers, so one can speak of period 1, 2, . . . , period 5026, and so on. It is as if they were years and we are referencing them from some arbitrarily chosen initial year. In each period N individuals are born (N is a positive integer). The way this is stated assumes that the same number of individuals is born each period. (This assumption can be relaxed, and the model can include population growth or decline without any serious changes in the basic results. The zero population growth assumption is, therefore, made for simplicity's sake.) Each of these individuals lives for two periods: They are *young* during period in which they are born, and *old* in the next period. Each group of individuals born during the same period is called a generation and is demarked by the date of its birth. So,

[2] One might say that the pathological case of the miser is an example of someone desiring money for its own sake. Literature, including children's literature, is replete with stories of people who hoard money for its own sake. These stories are meant to illustrate the error of holding unproductive assets. While in literature the miser holds "money," he (and the miser of literature is always a he) might just as well hold minerals other than gold, stockpile wheat, or collect machinery that is left unused.

generation thirty-eight is the group of individuals who were born and were young in period thirty-eight and who are old and will die in period thirty-nine. Figure 15.1 shows the relation between time and generation and indicates when each generation lives. An O signifies that the individual is old, and a Y signifies that the individual is young. Two blocks connected from left to right is a life. Two blocks connected top to bottom shows which generations are alive in the same period.

In this model, all individuals are identical. (This assumption will be relaxed later.) What this means in economic terms is that they have the same lifetime pattern in their endowment of goods and the same preferences—likes and dislikes—about their consumption. This is independent of their date of birth. There is only one commodity (one good). Each individual is endowed with g units of the good when young and none of the good when old. The good is nonstorable, so that it can't be saved and eaten when old. If a young person tried to store any of this good while he was young, he would find that all of it would have rotted before he could consume it in his old age. As with many of the other assumptions, it is possible to weaken this one and to have the good only partially deteriorate during storage.

The assumption that the young are endowed with the good may seem a bit strange. If you have difficulty accepting that idea, think of the young as being endowed with the vigor or energy that allows them to produce goods; the old have lost this vigor or energy. The reason that we are not operating under this assumption is that we don't want to worry about the problem of production—this is a theory of exchange—so it is easier just to assume an endowment of goods.

Individuals all have the same preferences. Since there is only one good, these preferences must be about the quantities of the good that is consumed in both periods of a person's life. We will assume first that in each period more is preferred

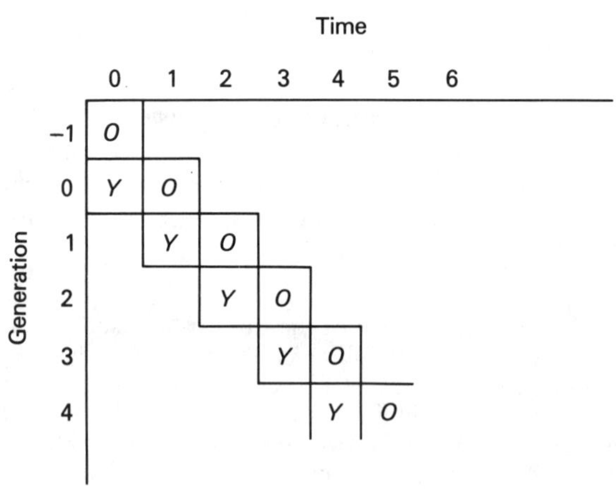

Figure 15.1

less preferred ← | most preferred ↓ | → less preferred

Young	0	1	2	3	4	5	6	7	8	9	10
Old	10	9	8	7	6	5	4	3	2	1	0

Figure 15.2

to less. There is no satiation; one never has enough. Second, we assume that individuals prefer to consume the good in equal quantities in both periods of their lives.[3] Figure 15.2 shows how individuals might partially order their choices of ways to consume a total of ten units of the good. The "five when young, five when old" pattern is the most preferred, with deviations from equal consumption each period becoming less preferred the further the deviation. Given the chance, individuals would want the 5/5 consumption instead of any other combination that totals to ten. If this same person had the chance to divide twenty units of the good between the two periods of life, the division of ten when young and ten when old would be the most preferred.

The decision on the allocation of goods across the two periods of life can only be made when the person is young. Once he is old, his youthful consumption is history and cannot be changed. Once he is old, only the consumption during the current period matters, since there are no future periods of life and the past cannot be changed. Figure 15.2 lists eleven ways in which ten units of the good might be divided between the two periods of life. The three over seven pair represents the case where the individual consumes three units of the good when young and seven units of the good when old. In the figure, we are only considering the integer possibilities for dividing up ten units of the good between two periods of an individual's life. Given that the choice is limited to something that totals ten units, we are saying that the individual's preferences will make the five over five choice the most preferred; allocations of ten units into more unequal consumptions that sum to ten are strictly less preferred.

[3] Preferences are usually expressed in terms of utility functions or indifference curves. In the case of indifference curves, one axis would represent the consumption when young and the other axis would represent the consumption when old. There would be indifference curves indicating the appropriate trade-offs between these two consumptions (as is shown in a normal introductory microeconomics course). The method of representing preferences given in the text is inferior from a technical standpoint, but captures much of the flavor of the decisions that individuals have to make and is somewhat more intuitive for those without a microeconomics background. (See the appendix to this chapter.)

LAISSEZ FAIRE EQUILIBRIUM

In a free market situation, there is no way for the young and the old to make trades. The young own everything, all of the goods; the old own nothing.[4] The old have nothing to give up in order to gain some goods for consumption. This generates an equilibrium in which all individuals consume all of their endowment (which we are denoting as g) when young and consume nothing when old. Suppose that some old person tried to form a contract with a young person in which the young person gave the old person something to eat in this period and the old person promised to give the young person something to eat in the next period. Since the old person will be dead in the next period, and it is exceedingly difficult to get dead people to honor their contracts, any young person who might sign this type of contract would know that this old person will be dead the next period, and so no young person would ever sign such a contract. Therefore, there is no type of private contract that, while allowing transfers of goods from the young to the old, will allow the young to receive something when they are old. Figure 15.3 shows the consumption sequences for this type of equilibrium. The figure is the same as Figure 15.1 but with consumption amounts listed in the boxes instead of age. We will refer to this equilibrium as a nonmonetary equilibrium.

EQUILIBRIUM WITH A LONG-LIVED GOVERNMENT—A TRANSFER SCHEME

Suppose that in some period—let's call it period 1—the young and the old get together and form a government. This government takes goods from the young by taxation if necessary, and gives them to the old. It can do this because, in the next period, the government will take some of the good from *that* period's young and give it to the old, who were young the first period. These taxes and transfers continue forever and allow everybody to be better off than they were in the nonmonetary equilibrium. If the individuals have the preferences indicated in Figure 15.2, the government will take $1/2g$ from each young person and give that much to each old person. The consumption pattern is as in Figure 15.4. Looking down the columns of Figure 15.4, one can see that consumption adds up to g for each pair of old and young at each time period. The individuals who are old when the government begins doing this make out very well; they get to consume all of their own endowment when they are young, yet they get to consume an additional $1/2g$ when they are old. (This is generation 0 in the figure.) All generations after

[4] Since there is neither storage nor capital goods, there is no way the young can save some of their real commodities for when they are old. This seems a bit strange, especially when it is the old in the "real" world who own most of the assets. You should think of the model in its own terms and not worry about this seeming confusion. We will add assets soon.

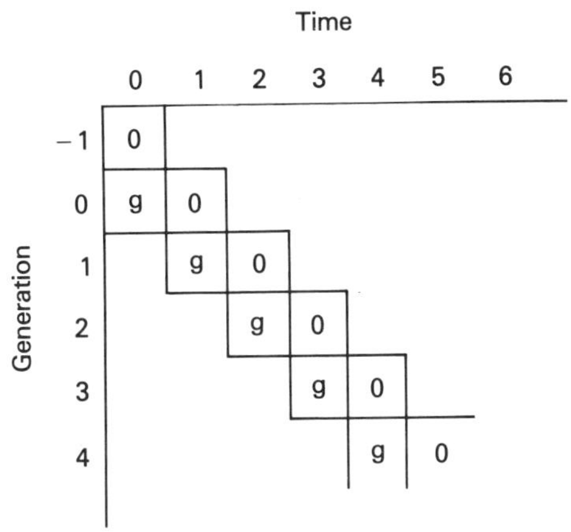

Figure 15.3

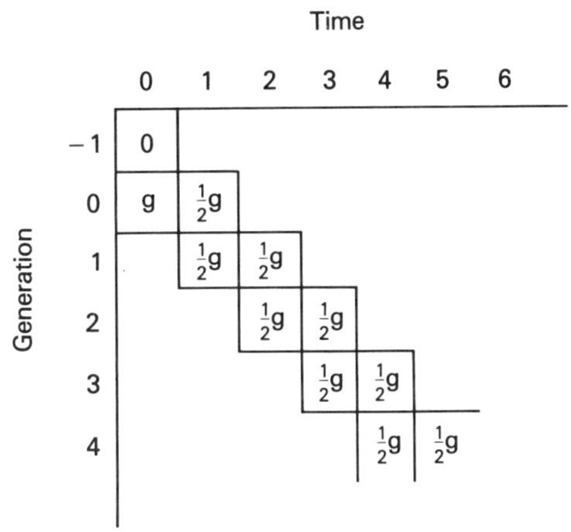

Figure 15.4

that consume 1/2g when young and 1/2g when old. This is the preferred way of consuming their endowment of g goods.

This equilibrium should seem quite familiar to you. It should remind you of a Social Security system similar to that of the United States. Generation 0 was the Franklin Roosevelt New Deal generation. One of the interesting lessons of this model is that it is not necessary to have an endowment fund for a Social Security system. Such a system can be merely a transfer system. Remember that the model we are using here has a constant population for each period. Some of the difficulties that are occurring with the current system may come from demographic changes. In this model, if the population is shrinking each young person will have to give up more than she will get when old.

Summing this up, a social security style transfer system in which a long-lived government is invented and given the right to take from the young and give to the old is a policy that has the effect of increasing the well-being of all of the citizens, now and forevermore.

MONETARY EQUILIBRIUM

Suppose a government issues something it calls money—fiat money—to the old people in some period.[5] This money is storable, so it can be carried over from period to period. Assume further that individuals have perfect foresight. For us,

[5] It doesn't matter what this money stuff is. It only matters that the government is able to have a monopoly on the production of this stuff and that this stuff is storable from one period to the next. It could be pieces of green paper, as it is in the United States, but it doesn't have to be.

this means that they know, when young, what the price of money in terms of the good will be when they are old. By the way, this money stuff doesn't have to come from the government, although now it generally does. It might just be that there is a particular good around that people start using exactly as they might use this money stuff. The stuff that they start using for this must have the ability to be stored. Even if it had no other use, something like gold could gain value from a private, as opposed to government-mandated, decision to use it as the money stuff.

The perfect foresight assumption may seem a bit strange. We are familiar with individuals having expectations about the future, and we normally make provisions for these expectations to be wrong to some extent. Assuming perfect foresight assumes that these expectations are always correct. We are therefore avoiding models where the interesting equilibria arise because people guess incorrectly, or where policies work because people are fooled.

The old sell the money to the young, who give up some of the good for it. The young store the money until they are old and then sell it to that period's young. The young know the price they will receive when old (because of perfect foresight) and can plan exactly how much money they want to buy. The old will sell all of their money because, in this model, you can't take it with you.

There are at least two types of equilibrium that are possible. One of these is a **nonmonetary equilibrium.** This is a case where the price of money, in terms of the good, is zero. The stuff that the government issues as money is not accepted by the citizens as having any value and so no one ever trades any goods for it. Suppose that you printed up some green pieces of paper, put your picture on them, and then attempted to exchange them for some real goods.[6] This "money" may well have a zero price in terms of goods. This equilibrium is identical to the one in Figure 15.3.

Monetary equilibria, those where the price of the money stuff is greater than zero, also exist. It is possible that more than one of these equilibria exist, but we would only observe one of them. In this model a stationary state monetary equilibrium exists where the good allocation perfectly matches the equilibrium in Figure 15.4 (the Social Security system). In this equilibrium the young sell half of their goods to the old and purchase all of the old's money. When these folks get old, they then sell the money for one half of that period's young's goods. The price of money in terms of goods stays constant. If each old person has m units of money, the price of the money is $g/2m$ units of good per unit of money. Since the population is constant, each young person gives up one half of his endowment of g good for all of the money (m units) that some matching old person has. That is how we get a price of $1/2g$ units of the good for m units of the money, or $g/2m$ units of the good per unit of money.

[6] There really is an artist who does this. He draws "money" with, among other things, his own picture on it, and offers it in place of "normal money" in shops and restaurants in payment for goods. Sometimes his offer is taken and sometimes not. He often buys back the "money"sometime later and presents it, along with the object bought—or a description of it if it were a meal—as art pieces that he sells in art galleries.

A rather interesting aspect of this model is that if money ever, even very far in the future, takes on a price of zero and people know that, it will always (for example, now) have a price of zero. Suppose that people know that the price of money will be zero in 1020 periods. In 1019 periods, the young will know that the price of money will be zero when they are old; they will not be willing to pay anything for it. Money thus has a price of zero in 1019 periods. The young in 1018 periods know that the price of money will be zero when they are old and they will not pay anything for it. Money then has a price of zero in 1018 periods. Keep doing this, and today's price of money is zero.

This last point was well illustrated in the classic 1950s science fiction film *When Worlds Collide*. In this saga of mankind's fight against very large rocks, a rogue planet has been sighted out in space, and it is on a path so as to directly intersect with the path of the earth. When it hits the earth, the earth will be destroyed—and this will end the film. Now the really interesting part of the film is that as soon as people find out the earth will end (and therefore they discover when the price of money will be zero) the price of money goes to zero. This is only one of many fine examples of prescience in cinema.

INFLATION AND MONEY

We have been discussing a number of cases where inflation is generated by government or some other agent or event shifting out the AD curve or shifting in the AS curve. (Chapters 7 through 11 contain examples.) The inflation comes about from the adjustment process that equates aggregate demand and aggregate supply. In many countries, large persistent inflations (the German hyperinflation detailed at the beginning of Chapter 10 is one extreme example) are generated by the continual issuing of new money that the government is using to purchase goods for its own use. During the peak of the German hyperinflation, October, 1923, only .9% (less than one percent) of government expenditures were paid for from normal tax sources. The rest was paid for with government bonds, most of which the government sent to the Central Bank where they were exchanged for paper money.

All of the more recent big inflations have the same basic source as the 1923 German inflation. In Argentina, Bolivia, Brazil, Israel, and Peru, all of whom have had inflation rates above 500% a year at some point in the 1980s, issuing new money was an important way to cover government expenditures not paid for by taxes. In each of these countries, during the peak of their inflations new money issue was used to pay for a government deficit in excess of five percent of GNP. The overlapping generations model is very useful for analyzing inflationary financing of government deficits because its simplicity shows us quite clearly what the cost of this type of inflation is and who is bearing those costs.

All inflations are not equal; not just in the different rates of inflation that occur, but also in their effects on households and firms in the economy. It is possible to have inflations that are perfectly neutral with respect to welfare. These neutral inflations are not observed very often, but they could exist. All of our inflations come about by the government's issue of new money. In these examples, the link between money and inflation is very strong. However, one should remember that it is possible in these models to have nonstationary equilibria with fixed money supply but inflating prices.

The monetary equilibria we have been considering so far are stationary states, where allocations of goods and the price of money in terms of goods remain constant through time. It is possible to add policies to the model that generate equilibria with inflation. The inflationary equilibria we will consider are stationary states in the sense that the allocations of goods remain constant, or stationary.[7] They are not stationary in the sense that the price of money changes as time passes. The reason we can view them as stationary states is that the rates of change of prices will be constant. Prices can change, but the rate of change of those prices will be kept constant. It is the rates of change that are stationary.

We will consider three different ways in which the government can generate inflation in these models. In the first, in each period the government gives each old person an amount of money equal to some percentage of the amount of money they hold. We will use ten percent as our example. In the second, the government will give to each old person the same amount of money, regardless of the amount they already hold, so as to increase the total money stock by the same ten percent. In the third case, the government will issue an amount of money equal to some percentage of the outstanding stock—still ten percent, as above—but will sell it to the young in exchange for goods and will thus be competing with the old in the market to sell money. Each of these models will generate the same inflation rate, but since they will have different real effects on the citizens in the sense that consumption patterns will be different, they should demonstrate that the way the government generates inflation is important, possibly even more important than the amount of inflation. Each of the models can result in a different allocation of goods. The real welfare of individuals—how well off the individuals actually are—is different in each of these models.

In the first case, where government issues new money to the old as a proportion of the old money they already hold, there exists an equilibrium where the allocation of goods for each individual across time is identical to the allocation in the no-inflation monetary equilibrium. In such an equilibrium, the young know—because of perfect foresight—that the price of money will drop 9.0909 . . . percent (10%/110%) from this period to the next. Normally, this drop in the price of money would make money seem less valuable to them and make them willing to pay less

[7] There is the very real possibility of non-stationary states that generate inflation. Some of these are called bubbles in the economic literature because prices seem to float upwards without any support. The mathematics for these equilibria is very difficult and we will not deal with them here.

for it today. (If money loses value, one would be more inclined to consume one's endowment today and save less because the more one saves, the smaller the portion of the initial endowment would be total consumption.)[8] However, in this model the government's gift of money to the old, based on the amount of money each one owns, exactly compensates for the drop in the price of money; the nominal ten percent return on money, because of the government gift, compensates for the price drop and results in exactly the same consumption pattern as in the no-inflation monetary equilibrium.[9] Inflation in this case is perfectly neutral—in the sense that nothing changes—in terms of the welfare of individuals.

The second method for generating inflation would result in an equilibrium identical to the first if all individuals were the same in their tastes and endowments. An issue of x units of money to each old person would result in the same percentage increase in their money holdings if they are all alike (if they all already hold the same amount of money). However, if there are some rich and some poor people (individuals with a large or a small endowment of goods when your relative to the community average), the issue of the same **quantity** of money to each of them changes the *relative* money holdings. The rich will end up with a smaller portion of all outstanding money after the transfer and the poor with a larger portion. These different rates of return on holding money will result in the rich and poor desiring to sell different portions of their endowments for money and will therefore cause real welfare changes (changes, that is, in the allocation of goods). This policy is likely to make the poor better and the rich worse off. How the rich will respond is a little difficult to tell, exactly. The lower rate of return on money holdings means that they will consume less when they are old than in the initial case. They may consume less or more when they are young. Depending on how important consumption when they are old is to them, they might use more of their goods when

[8] Let g equal a young person's endowment, C_y equal consumption when young, S equal savings (the goods used to purchase money), and C_o equal consumption when old. As a simple identity, $g = C_y + S$; endowment is either consumed or spent on money. In the no-inflation monetary equilibrium above, $S = C_o$; consumption when old equals savings. Suppose that young people know that, because there is inflation, the price they get for their money when old will be less than what they paid for it. In that case, $S > C_o$, or if the inflation rate is π,

$$(1/(1 + \pi)S = C_o$$

This loss of goods (since $C_y + C_o < g$) will cause young people to save less and therefore to shift consumption from old age to youth. (For students who have had a microeconomics course, whether they save more or less depends on the elasticity of demand for consumption when old.)

[9] If the price of money at time t is one unit of money for one unit of good, then the savings, S_t, is both the real and money value of savings. If inflation is π, then the price of each unit of money at time $t + 1$ is $1/(1 + \pi)$. If the government has increased the amount of money held by the old at time $t + 1$ by π percent of holdings, the money holdings equal $(1 + \pi)S$. Then $C_o = [1/(1 + \pi)](1 + \pi)S$ or $C_o = S$. All savings become consumption when old.

young than they would have before, in order to buy money that gives them less than before when they reach old age. If consumption when they are old is not too important, then they will use less of their goods when they are young to buy money and will consume more, when they are young, than they would have in the earlier case.

In the third way of generating inflation, the government purchases goods from the young for money. This new government-issued money reduces the purchasing power of the money held by the old. This is likely to have two effects. First, if the demand for consumption in the second period of life is elastic the reduced rate of return, caused by the lack of compensation for inflation, is likely to cause young people to want to allocate less of their income to consumption when they are old, and so they would sell less of their endowment for money. (If the demand is inelastic, then they will allocate more of their income to consumption in old age.) Second, since the government is purchasing some of this savings of goods from the young by issuing additional money, the old get a reduced amount of this reduced savings. Consumption when old and when young add up to less than the total endowment and provides a reduced amount of welfare to individuals. (One might argue that if the goods that the government purchases are used to compensate individuals for some of the lost consumption or to provide goods and services that might not otherwise be provided, individuals might be better off. While this is possible, the distortion in consumption patterns caused by the inflation makes this method not as efficient as others for raising the same revenues. However, under certain political [although normally not economic] constraints, some government financing by inflation might be optimal.)

Figure 15.5 should help show how this form of taxing by inflation works. Both the government and the old are sending money into the market in which money is sold for the good. The old send the old money that they bought the period before and the government sends the new money that they are issuing. The old have no choice except to send all of their money to the market (the "you can't take it with you" theorem). The young decide how much of their good to send to market based on the rate of money issue that they know (that they expect, in a less-than-perfect foresight world) the government will issue the next period. They exchange this amount of money for goods. If the government always issues the same percentage of the outstanding money stock, then the percentage loss from purchasing money will be constant and the relative price of goods when old in terms of goods when young will be constant. This generates a stationary state equilibrium with inflation.

This last equilibrium is a case where the government can extract revenues via seigniorage, and there is nothing that the citizens can do to prevent it.[10] They must use money to gain consumption when they are old, and this provides a perfect

[10] Seigniorage originally referred to all of the rights of a king or prince. Today it is used only for the inflation tax that the issue of money generates for the government.

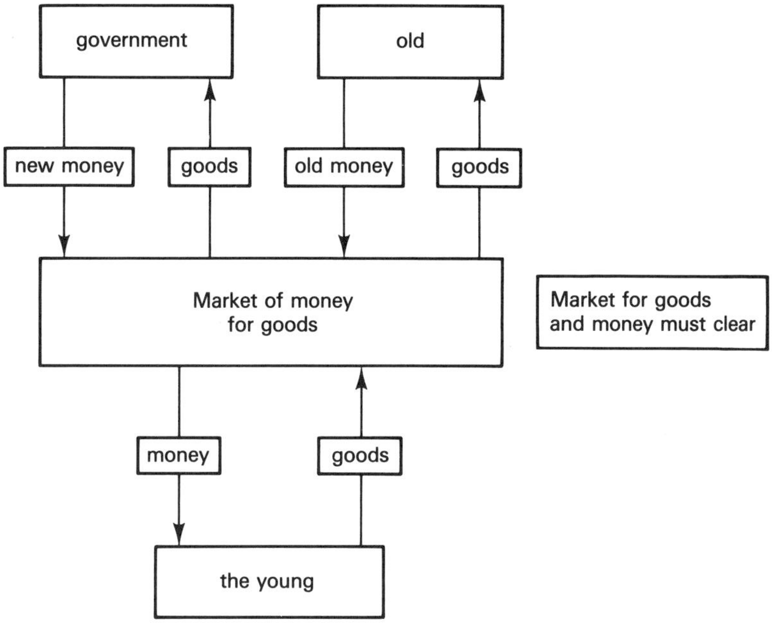

Figure 15.5

place for the government to extract taxes. Note, however, that this tax is like most, and if the government attempts to increase the tax rate the attempt will, at some point, reduce tax revenues. As the inflation rate goes up, people will—depending on the elasticity of the demand for consumption when old—reduce the portion of their endowment that they allocate for consumption when they grow old. This reduces the base from which the inflation can extract taxes. This deterioration of the tax base is more serious when there are alternative assets.

Figure 15.6 shows a hypothetical graph of the government revenues as a percentage of the endowment of the young that can be extracted by different stationary state inflation rates. This graph is generated by calculating the revenues from inflation in stationary states for a large number of different rates of money issue. When the inflation rate is zero, no revenues are generated. As the inflation rate increases—as the rate of money issue increases—the revenues increase up to the point where the increases in the inflation rate are dominated by decreases in the amount of the good that the young allocate for consumption when old. As stated above, this allocation decreases in the face of declining returns on the holding of money. If the inflation rate gets high enough, there might be a point at which people do not hold any more money. If some consumption when old is important enough, then the revenues might not go to zero, but might approach some asymptote.

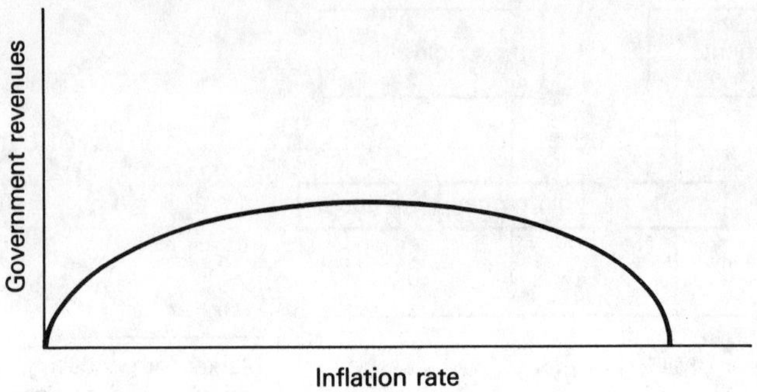

Figure 15.6

OTHER ASSETS

In the models we have looked at up to now, money has been the only asset available to allow consumption when old. In the stationary-state, no-inflation monetary equilibrium, the rate of return on this asset—money—is zero.[11] If one gives up one unit of the good to purchase money when young, one gets one unit of the good back when old. In this case, one neither gains additional goods (gets a positive rate of return) nor loses any goods (gets a negative rate of return). In the third example of inflation, the rate of return on money was negative, since you got fewer goods back than the quantity you used to purchase the money.

Suppose some other asset is available and that this asset offers a positive sure (certain or guaranteed) rate of return. Land might serve as an example. The old own all the land. They sell this land, for some of the endowment of the young, to the young, who keep ownership of it until they are old. This land produces some of the good (which grows on it) between periods. The old get this good as a return for owning land. (Suppose that the return is the same per acre. Then, the more land you own, the more of the good you get.) They also get to consume the amount of the good that the young give them when they sell their land.

In a world with this kind of land as an available asset, no one will want to hold money. The land, with its positive rate of return, *dominates* money. All of the land will be sold each period and all young people will buy land equal to their portion of total savings. Since no one will buy it, the price of money—fiat money—will be zero. One can always do better owning land than owning money.

If the land did *not* generate a positive rate of return, but was just something that was traded from the old to the young, just as large stone disks could be, then we would get an indeterminate price between land and money. It is possible that both the land and the money have value. The total value of land and money is

[11] "The rate of return" will be used to refer to the implicit interest rate that is earned on some asset. So if you invest one unit of the good when young, and end up with one unit of the good when old, the interest rate, in real terms, is zero.

equal to the total amount of the good that the young give up to acquire them. There are an infinite number of possible equilibria in this case. There are stationary states, in which money might account for ten percent of the goods sold by the young, and land for ninety percent. This is as good an equilibrium as one in which money accounts for fifty percent of the value, and the goods sold by the young and land the other fifty. In the first case, the price between land and money is such that it takes all of the money to buy 11.111 . . . percent (11.11 . . . percent of ninety percent equals ten percent) of the land. In the second case, 11.1 . . . percent of the money will buy 11.1 . . . percent of the land.

When land doesn't generate a positive rate of return, there are two possible equilibria when the government issues new money to collect an inflation tax. In one of these equilibria, money and land maintain the ratio between them (that is, the price of money in terms of land does not change) and the new currency issued by the government reduces the price of both of these in terms of the good. In the other equilibrium, the price of money is zero and only land is used as an asset. This is the case if the new money were to change the rate of return on money but not on land. Since there is perfect foresight, people know this, and no one wants to own money. The price of money in terms of the good goes to zero.

The dominance of land—an asset with a guaranteed positive return—over money does not mean that we cannot have models with other assets yielding positive (expected) returns. This can be demonstrated by considering a world in which the other asset is risky. (By risky we mean that there is some positive probability in this case of a negative return or loss.)

Consider a world where the two assets available to the young are money and shares in a ship that sails to another economy and will provide a large profit if it returns. Its return is scheduled for the next period, when the investors will have become old. The sea is fraught with danger; the ship might be sunk in a storm, be devoured by a sea monster, or, possibly, fall off the edge of the earth. (Remember, many economic models are linear.) In any case, there is a known probability that the ship won't return.[12] Since the young want to ensure that they will have some consumption even if the ship doesn't return, they will diversify their portfolios and put some of their savings into the ship and some of it into money. Therefore, there exist equilibria in which money will have a positive price every period; but, with the

[12] To calculate the expected rate of return of a project, one multiplies the probability of a state of the world occurring times the return in that state and sums up over states. Consider a world where there is a forty percent chance the ship will sink (a state of the world) and a sixty percent chance the ship will return (another state of the world); since their probability sums to one, these are all of the possible states of the world in this model. An investor gets nothing if the ship sinks and four units of good back for each unit invested if the ship returns. The expected rate of return is

$$.40 \times 0 + .60 \times 4 - 1 = 1.40$$

or a 140 percent expected rate of return on each unit of investment. The one is subtracted because that was the initial investment.

same amount of money in this model as in the model with only money as an asset, the price in terms of goods will be lower than in the model with only money.

There is another way in which individuals can diversify their portfolios. It is possible to send out more than one ship, and, if the probability of each one returning is independent of whether other ships return, then individuals stand a much better chance of having something when they are old if they put their savings into shares of many ships. Even if some of the ships sink, the probability is higher that one of them will return. However, if there is some independent probability that each of the ships could sink, there is some nonzero probability that *all* of the ships would sink. If the probability that any one of the ships could sink is .4 (forty percent) and seven ships go out, the probability that all of them sink is

$$(.4)^7 = .4 \times .4 \times .4 \times .4 \times .4 \times .4 \times .4 = .0016384.$$

This probability is quite small, but the prospect of having nothing in old age could easily be frightening enough to get people to hold some (but a small amount) of money even with all of these ships going out.

Both of the examples above are of attempts to diversify a portfolio of assets. In the first case, the diversification is between money, which offers a low but sure rate of return, and the ship, which offers a high but quite uncertain rate. Therefore, it is best to hold some of both. In the second case, the diversification is among many ships. The probability that all of the ships will come in is small (.6 to the seventh power, or .028), so the investor is less likely to hit it as big as she might if she invested in only one ship, where the probability of hitting it big is sixty percent. Diversification of this type is common for normal asset portfolios. Individuals invest in a large number of things; in stocks, in bonds, in land, and so on. While the wide range of investments reduces the possibility of making a huge rate of return, it promises that the probabilities of a total loss are also very small.

Suppose that the government attempts to use the issuing of new currency to generate tax revenues. If the only other assets are risky ones, then individuals will still want to hold at least some money. Remember that with other, risky, assets, the portion of the endowment of the young that is used to purchase money is smaller than when money is the only asset. Therefore, the amount of taxes that can be raised by issuing new money is smaller to begin with. As the cost of holding money increases as the government attempts to collect more of the endowment from the inflation tax, people rely more on the risky assets and less on money. The government can still collect some seigniorage, but less than before; with higher inflation rates—reductions in the rate of return on money—this should result in a faster reduction in the revenues. Figure 15.7 illustrates the differences that might exist between the seigniorage that is possible when there is no other asset available (the thinner line) and the seigniorage that is possible when there are other, risky, assets (the thicker line).

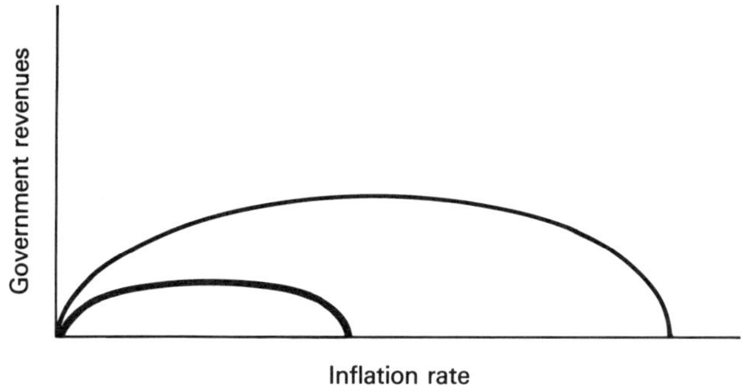

Figure 15.7

REPRISE

In this chapter we constructed a model in which individuals were willing, under some circumstances, to hold money. The friction that money—and a social security system before it—solved was the inability of the young and old to make contracts that would provide the old with some of the good to consume.

The model was used to generate inflation in three ways, and each way had a different effect on the well-being of the members of the economy. Inflation can be neutral, have distributional effects, or, most frequently, can be used by the government to collect revenues. While it may seem silly to go to all the trouble of generating a model with inflation that doesn't do anything, and it may seem unlikely that a government would follow that type of policy, it does serve to highlight the observation that inflation need not be detrimental to an economy. It depends on the type of policy that generates the inflation and what it does to the real allocation of goods in the economy. The issue of the neutrality of money and inflation is one that has been in economics for a long time, and I believe that these examples illustrate how likely it is that inflation will, indeed, be neutral.

The addition of other assets makes the model seem more real. These other assets can dominate money when they offer a positive real rate of return. They can exist alongside money, as individuals diversify their portfolios by holding some money to cover some of the risk that the other assets present. If the other asset generates a rate of return that is the same as money (another paper money is a possible example) then the price of one of these assets in terms of the other is undetermined. Any price is as good as any other. This indeterminacy is interesting as an observation about exchange rates—the price of one country's money in terms of another country's—in a world where many countries have fiat monies. The overlapping generations model does not provide assistance in determining the price of one of these monies in terms of others. That a given real economy might have an infinite number of possible exchange rates, none of them more likely than any other, might be worrisome to some.

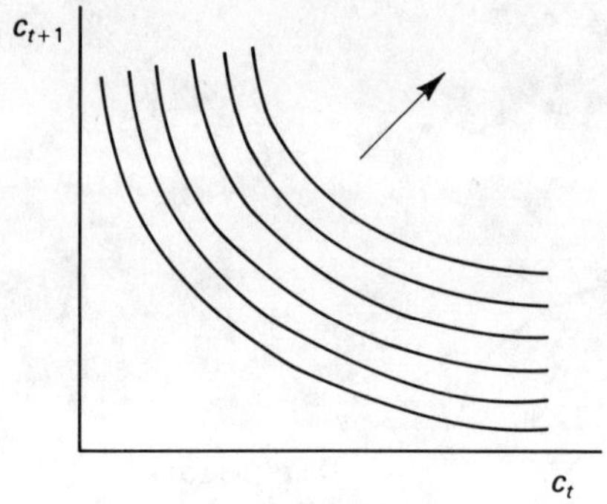

Figure 15.A.1

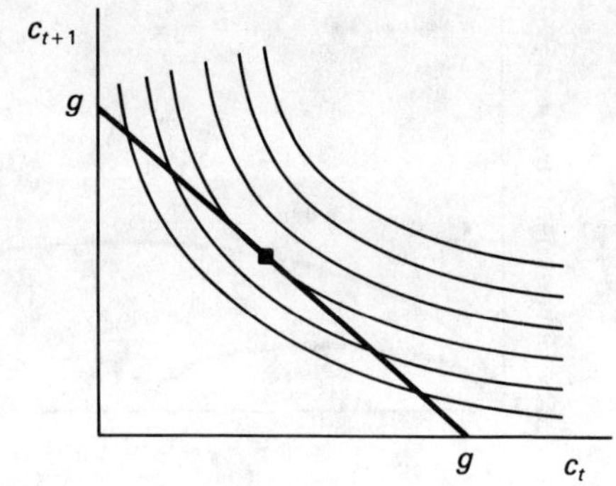

Figure 15.A.2

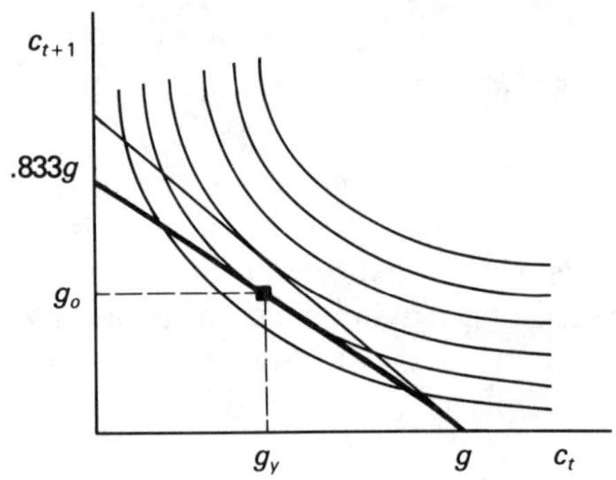

Figure 15.A.3

Appendix

It is better to think about these overlapping generations economies in models where the preferences are expressed as utility curves and indifference curves. If we use the same technology we developed in the appendix at the end of Chapter 3, we can do exactly that. The main difference between the use of indifference curves in this model and the ones used at the end of Chapter 3 is the way in which we define goods. Instead of having different types of goods, we have goods at different times. So, we can speak of a member of generation t as having preferences between time t good and time $t + 1$ good, or between consumption when young and consumption when old, because they are the same thing. Figure 15.A.1 shows one such indifference curve set.

The choices that young people face can be shown by a budget line in the same commodity space that is used to show the preferences. If we have an economy where there is money and no inflation, then it is possible to exchange goods one for one between the two periods of life. The budget line that represents this set of possibilities is a 45° line with the starting point at the endowment g as a possible time t consumption. The line from g to g in Figure 15.A.2 shows this kind of budget line. An individual chooses to consume at the point on this budget line that gives the highest utility, and that is the point on the budget line tangent to the highest indifference curve. This point is marked in Figure 15.A.2. The two coordinates of that point give the preferred consumptions of the good when old and young.

If the government is generating inflation (say, of twenty percent), the g goods when young can be exchanged for only $g/1.2$ (or $.8333g$) units of good when old. This change in the ability of the young to exchange consumption when young for consumption when old is illustrated by a rotation of the budget line. The thick line in Figure 15.A.3 is a budget line with inflation. Notice that $g_y + g_o$ is less than g. The difference, $g - g_y - g_o$, is the inflation tax revenues of the government.

16

Strategic Government Policies

In which the government and the rest of the economy face off against each other in a game of policy. Winners gain a temporary bonus. Reputations are on the line in this game.

INTRODUCTION

We want to consider government policies to which the government knows individuals in the economy will respond. The individuals know that the government knows that they will do so. A world in which the welfare of each individual or agent depends on the reactions of the other agents to the decisions of every other agent is the realm of **game theory.** Game theory is the study of situations, much like those in sports, where there are a set of rules, all players try to achieve optimal results for themselves, and the outcome for each player of the game depends on the actions of all players.[1] Many nonsport situations fit into the game theory definition. Political positioning, almost any type of negotiating, pricing of goods in markets where there are few manufacturers, buying a house, submitting sealed bids, and developing a reputation; all are examples where game theory is applicable for analyzing the possible outcomes.

Before we can use game theory as a way to think about these problems, we must develop a few of the simple single game analytical tools. These single game tools will then be extended to generate repeated games. A repeated game is one in which the agents meet in a single game situation over and over again and their behavior during each of these games is important to the outcome of future games. In a game of American football, each play can be thought of as a single game whose specific outcome depends on the actions of the players on both sides. The whole game of football is a series of repeated single plays and the strategic interconnection of the plays is very important in the outcome of the entire game. Games comprised of a series of repeated games are called **supergames.** The invention of the analytical tool of supergames has caused a resurgence of interest in game theory. Earlier work using only single play games gave a lot of predicted results that did not fit observed behavior. Supergames give many more results that fit casual empiricism.

Single games are either cooperative or noncooperative. Cooperative games are those in which the participants, possibly after initial negotiations, can form binding contracts. Noncooperative games do not allow binding contracts. We will concentrate on noncooperative games because it seems that this better fits the relationship between the government and the rest of society. Although the government usually operates under some set of rules—a constitution, for example—it can and often does make policy promises that it does not live up to and that it cannot be forced to live up to by the other agents in the economy.

In certain types of supergames, especially those in which future or expected government policies are important in the determination of this moment's equilibrium, a **time inconsistency** problem can arise. If one thinks of a government policy as a promise to follow a certain series of actions, which might be quite

[1] This definition comes from James W. Friedman, *Game Theory with Applications to Economics*, (New York: Oxford University Press, 1986).

complicated, now and into the future, then choosing an optimal government policy involves choosing and promising to follow a path of actions that generates currently desired results. The time inconsistency problem arises if, at some time in the future, the government recalculates the optimal policy path, and the optimal policy action at that future time is different from the policy action that the government had promised to follow initially. Suppose, for example, that the optimal monetary policy at this moment is to increase the money supply this period by ten percent but not to increase it for any other future period. This might be because the (believed) promise not to increase it in the future will make people want to hold more money than if they believed that the inflation in the future would be ten percent and therefore the government would be able to collect a larger seigniorage. In the next period, however, the optimal thing for the government to do is to generate ten percent inflation and promise never to inflate the currency in the future. The government would not follow the promised policy because, when the future became now, that was not the best policy to follow. In a policy where this is the case, this time inconsistency between promised behavior and the behavior that would be optimal at that future date, ignoring the promise, means that no one will believe the initial policy promises and the desired results will not occur.

SINGLE GAME MODELS

Individuals are interested in their own welfare. They wish to make themselves as well off as possible given the constraints that they face. Part of the constraints that they face are the possible actions of the other agents in the economy. They need to take these possible actions into account when deciding what is best for themselves. Consider an example.

In a model much like our static Keynesian model in Chapter 8, both the unions and the government need to make their decisions about what to do in the next period at the same time (at the end of some period).[2] We will limit ourselves to a case in which each of them has only two options. The unions can ask for a zero increase in the nominal wage (we will call this NC_U for no change) or a five percent increase in their nominal wage (called $5\%_U$). The government can either not shift out the aggregate demand curve (called NC_G) or increase government expenditures so that the AD curve shifts out five percent (called $5\%_G$). There are four possible outcomes from this game and they can be illustrated by the matrix (box) in Figure 16.1.

Each of the boxes in Figure 16.1 is a possible outcome. The box labeled A

[2] Remember that we are using the unions here to represent the joint decisions of the unions and the firms. The text will refer to the results of these negotiations as the strategic plays of the unions, but they really represent the combined play of both the unions and the firms.

		Government	
		NC	5%
Unions	NC	A	B
	5%	C	D

Figure 16.1

represents a resolution where neither the government nor the unions make any changes. The box labeled B represents a resolution where the unions make no change but the government shifts out the AD curve by five percent. Boxes C and D represent similar situations but where the unions ask for and get a five percent increase in their nominal wage.

Using the model, both the unions and the government can calculate the results of each of these four combinations of policies. They each assign a number to each result that represents their relative happiness with that particular result. Suppose that the unions see the result that is generated by the $[NC_U, NC_G]$ pair, which is the no change equilibrium, as having a value of zero. The government also assigns a value of zero to this result.[3] The **payoff** for this pair of choices is written as (0,0), where the number in the first position represents the payoff to the unions and the second number represents the payoff to the government. Suppose the unions assign a value of −5 (because their real wages drop) to the $[NC_U, 5\%_G]$ pair, where the government shifts out the AD curve but the unions did not change their nominal wages while, because the unemployment drops a lot and there is only a little inflation, the government assigns a value of 4 to this result. This payoff pair is written as (−5,4). The equilibrium that results when the unions increase their nominal wages by five percent but the government makes no change, the $[5\%U, NC_G]$ pair, is assigned a value of 1 by the unions, because there are higher real wages, even though fewer of the unions' members are working, and −3 by the government, since the increased unemployment is bad for the government. This payoff pair is (1, −3). The final case is $[5\%_U, 5\%_G]$, where both the unions and the government generate five percent increases. Assume that this equilibrium leaves the real wages unchanged but generates some inflation.[4] The value the unions assign is zero, since real wages didn't change; the value the government assigns is −1, because, although the unemployment is unchanged, it doesn't like the in-

[3] It doesn't matter very much what we use for a reference point. In this case we are giving the initial situation a value of zero for both participants.

[4] We can simply assume that the shift out in the AS curve generated by the five percent increase in the nominal wage just compensates for the five percent shift out in the AD curve. "Just compensates" means that the output level is unchanged, real wages are unchanged, but inflation occurs.

flation and this equilibrium is a little worse than the $[NC_U, NC_G]$ case. This payoff is written as (0, −1). Putting all of this together in Figure 16.1 we get Figure 16.2.

Figure 16.2 now represents the payoff matrix of this game. We can use this payoff matrix to help us find a solution to the game. Consider the payoffs that the players assign to each of their actions. For the government, a policy of NC offers payoffs of 0 and −3, depending on what the unions do. A policy of five percent offers payoffs of 4 and −1, again, depending on what the unions do. Note that the government is better off—gets a higher payoff—if it follows the five percent policy in each of the possible policies for the unions. The five percent policy *dominates* the NC policy and will always be chosen by the government. This choice of this policy offers a better payoff regardless of the choice of the other player.

For unions, the NC policy offers payoffs of 0 and −5, depending on what the government does. The five percent policy offers payoffs of 1 and 0. For the union, the five percent policy dominates the NC policy. So if, as seems reasonable, each player chooses a policy that dominates the other policy choices, then both the unions and the government will choose to follow the five percent policy and the solution is Box D of Figure 16.2. Given the setup—the set of possible choices—that we described, that solution is the equilibrium. Interestingly enough, this implies that in an economy of this type one should expect inflation, even though both players would be better off, or at least as well off, without it. (If the value of the solution in the [5%,5%] box were (−1, −1), it would still be the equilibrium. In this case both players would be worse off than in the no inflation equilibrium, but inflation would occur. Reflecting on this example, it should not be surprising to observe that we get inflation fairly regularly in our economy.)

Note that this is *not* the best of the possible solutions for both players of this game. The Box A payoff is one in which the unions are as well off as they are in the chosen outcome and the government is better off, at 0 rather than −1. The surprising thing about this game is that the best outcome is not chosen. If either one of the players knew that the other player was choosing NC, then this player would be better off by choosing five percent. The player who chose NC would be much worse off. Because each of the players could individually do better than the [NC,NC] solution, that "best" solution is unattainable. Games of this type, where individual maximizing behavior does not yield a collective maximizing behavior,

		Government	
		NC	5%
Unions	NC	A (0,0)	B (−5,4)
	5%	C (1, −3)	D (0, −1)

Figure 16.2

are sometimes called a "prisoners' dilemma." The prisoners' dilemma gets its name from the problem faced by a pair of crooks who have been caught (but not in the act) and have been separated by the police. The police separately promise each of them a light sentence if he confesses and testifies against the other. If neither confesses, then both go free. Individual welfare maximization—choosing the dominant strategy—will have both of them confess and each receive a moderate sentence. The "social" optimum (for the den of thieves, at any rate,) is when neither of them confesses, but in the simple form of the prisoners' dilemma game, that doesn't happen.

NASH EQUILIBRIUM

There are some situations in which there is no dominant choice for a player. Figure 16.3 shows an example of a game similar to the one above, but without dominant policy choices for either of the players. Notice how the payoff matrix in Figure 16.3 is different from that in Figure 16.2. The main difference is the increased payoffs of the [NC,NC) choice (Box A). One can imagine a world in which an end result of no inflation but some unemployment might be viewed as a high payoff by all the players. The players might perceive that the [NC,NC] actions offer higher payoffs if, for example, there is already some inflation in the economy; both the unions and the government would believe that getting rid of this inflation is a great success (but from the unions' point of view, only as long as they get their preferred real wage). The [NC,NC] choice (Box A) could stop the inflation and give unions their preferred real wages; therefore it is the box with the highest payoff for each of the players. However, the lowest payoff for either one of the players occurs when that player chooses NC and the other player chooses five percent. In this case, neither the NC choice nor the five percent choice dominates. Our problem is finding a solution for this game.

A **Nash equilibrium point** is a combination of plays—one for each player—where each player chooses her particular play to make herself as well off as possible given that the other player is choosing a play that is part of the equilibrium. There are two Nash equilibrium points in the game in Figure 16.3. Payoffs (3,5) and (0,0)

		Government	
		NC	5%
Unions	NC	A (3,5)	B (−5,3)
	5%	C (1,−3)	D (0,0)

Figure 16.3

are both Nash equilibrium points. This is so because when the unions choose NC, the best choice for the government is NC. When the government chooses NC, the best choice for the unions is NC. So if both choose NC, no one wants to change. If the government chooses five percent, then the best choice for the unions is five percent. If the unions choose five percent, then the best choice for the government is also five percent. If both choose five percent, no one wants to change. Neither of the Nash equilibrium points dominates the other, even though the [NC,NC] choice (Box A) generates a higher payoff for both individuals. There are no dynamics that would cause the players to move from the [5%,5%] solution (Box D) to the [NC,NC] solution (Box A) if they began at [5%,5%]. (Note that in Figure 16.2, with the different payoffs, only the [5%,5%] result is a Nash equilibrium point.) A sports example from Thomas Schelling illustrates these equilibria.[5] A number of years ago, none of the players in the National Hockey League wore helmets. This put them at a real risk of injury or death from falling. All of the players were aware of this and realized that wearing helmets would be safer. However, wearing a helmet cut into your peripheral vision and made you appear to be a wimp, so no player was willing to wear one unless all of the other players did. The Nash equilibrium point that existed—no helmets—was one in which all the players were worse off than another Nash equilibrium, where all wore helmets. There was no way for the players to get from one equilibrium to the other. It eventually required a rule change in the league to get all of the players to wear the helmets.

MIXED STRATEGIES

Sometimes there are games with payoffs for which there does not exist a Nash equilibrium. There are, however, equilibria for these games, although the equilibria are a bit more complicated. In these games individuals follow mixed strategies. A mixed strategy is one in which each player does not choose one of the available plays to follow, but rather chooses a combination of plays and assigns a set of probabilities to each of them. Some random number-generating mechanism, weighed by the probabilities chosen, is then used to choose which of the plays to actually follow. Thomas Schelling has presented a rather dramatic example of this type of play.[6]

Suppose you are in a house and there is an assassin outside who wishes to kill you. (This is an imaginary example—please don't take it personally.) There are two doors to the house, one on either side, and the assassin can only cover one of them. Unfortunately, you cannot tell *which* door before you decide to leave the

[5] T. C. Schelling, "Hockey helmets, concealed weapons, and daylight saving," *Journal of Conflict Resolution*, 1973, 17:381–428.

[6] T. C. Schelling, "Zero-sum Games," *Teaching and Research Materials*, Kennedy School of Government, Number 15T, August 1973.

house. On one side the woods are near, and if the assassin is also on that side when you exit, you have a ninety percent objective probability of reaching the woods safely. (One time in ten, ten percent of the time, you will get killed.) On the other side of the house the woods are further away, and you have only a fifty percent chance of reaching them safely. (Half of the time you will get killed.) If the assassin is on the other side of the house when you exit, you have a hundred percent chance of reaching the woods safely. Your problem is to decide which door to leave by.

It is not clear that it is best to leave by the door which offers you the highest probability of reaching the woods. The assassin is most likely to be waiting for you on that side and so, if you left by the other door, you might not encounter him at all. But the assassin is thinking this too, so maybe he is on the side where the probability is the worst. How can you maximize the probability of escaping without getting killed? (After all, escaping by getting killed is viewed as having little value.)

The way to achieve the best probabilistic result is to randomize the selection of the escape door so that the probability of a successful escape by each door is the same. In this way, the assassin cannot follow the same line of logic that we use in choosing a door, and *he* must randomize his selection of which side to be on. The door on the side closer to the woods is five times better, in terms of getting to the woods if the assassin is there, than the door on the far side. So, while we want to choose our escape route by a random process, we would want the "near" door to show up five times as often as the "far" door. If we use a die (as in the game of dice, a cube with one through six dots on a side and a different number of dots on each side) then we might assign "near" to the sides with one through five dots and the "far" to the side with six dots. A role of the die will tell us which door to leave by. By doing this we get a probability of the assassin's being able to kill us of one in twelve no matter which side he is on—this is the lowest probability we can generate.[7] Since the assassin's chances of killing us are the same no matter which side of the house he is on, he will be indifferent between the two sides. Remember, he is interested in the probability of his killing us, not of getting a shot at us. He then randomly chooses—by a flip of a coin, perhaps—which side to be on; the probability of our being killed is one in twenty-four (one in twelve times one in two).

This method of randomly choosing one policy to follow from a set of policies that has been determined, possibly in advance, and with each of the policies having a probability weight assigned to it, would also work in many other aspects of life. One can picture a football coach throwing the die—or, in this modern age, having a computer randomly choose one play—before each play to see which of the plays on his list appropriate to the current situation will be chosen. That would

[7] We get the one in twelve result because there is a five in six chance that we will get the 10% side and a one in six chance of the 50% side, and 5/6 times 10% or 1/6 times 50% gives us 1/12. Therefore, we have the same probability of staying alive no matter which door we leave by.

certainly make it more difficult for the defense to predict what the coach will have his team do, and that is the whole idea.

Let's get back to examples in economics. Suppose that the government believes that a shift out in the AD curve will help the economy, given the government's political preference function, but only if unions and firms don't respond to it. Is there some way that the government can gain this advantage? We are going to let the unions and firms choose any response to the policies that the government uses, and they will know what the government strategies are.[8] A government's **mixed strategy** is a choice of a set of possible policies and a probability weight for each of them. These probability weights add up to one, so that one of the policies from this set will be chosen. Each period the government randomly chooses—weighted by its subjective probabilities—one of the policies to follow.[9] Before the period starts, the unions and firms know the set of probabilities and the set of policies, but neither they nor the government know which of the policies will actually be chosen when the next period begins. In this rational expectations world, the unions and firms have all the information possible about the outcomes for the next period, but the choice of which policy the government will really follow is random and cannot be perfectly predicted. Does a mixed strategy of this type make sense for the government? The answer is often "yes."

Suppose that the set of policies available to the government is 1, to generate no change (NC) in the AD curve; or 2, to increase government expenditures in a way that shifts it out five percent (5%). The government can choose the probabilities that it will assign to each of these possible policies. It chooses these probabilities in such a way as to maximize the expected value of its political preference function. The government knows how the unions and firms will act in response to the announcement of any particular strategy, and so it chooses the probability weights on the policies [NC,5%] so as to maximize its political preference function. Suppose that in period zero it chooses a probability of .1 for the likelihood that the five percent policy will occur. The unions and firms know that ten percent of the time the AD curve will shift out the five percent, and ninety percent of the time it will not be shifted at all. The shift in the AD curve expected with rational expectations is one half of one percent (.05 times .1 plus 0 times .9, which equals .005). If the unions and firms use the expected value of the shift on which to base their nominal wage contracting, then they will get an increase in their nominal wage of one half of one percent.

[8] Unions and firms will be able to respond continuously in the sense that they willl not be limited to choosing either a NC or a five percent nominal wage policy. Unions and firms will be allowed to make any change in their nominal wage that they can get the firms to agree to. So it is similar to the much earlier model in which unions and firms choose a wage based on their expectations. Here they have rational expectations in the sense that they know exactly what the government's strategy is.

[9] The term "randomly chooses" is not an oxymoron. The government uses some random process to decide which option of the policy set will actually be put into effect. The role of the die in choosing the policy option is important.

When period one begins, the government goes to its random number generator and finds out what the draw is for that period. (In this case, the machine can generate numbers from one to ten and the government has decided that it will shift out the AD curve if a "one," for example, occurs.) If the draw is a "one," then the AD curve is shifted out 5%. Otherwise, the AD curve is not moved.

If the "one" occurred and the AD curve was shifted out the 5%, then that action, combined with the roughly one half of one percent shift in the AS would result in a very large drop in unemployment mixed with some inflation. If a "two" through "ten" occurred, then the AD curve would not move and the one half of one percent shift in the AS curve would generate a very small inflation and a very small increase in unemployment. If the very small inflation and the very small increase in unemployment would not be viewed by the government's political preference function as being very different from doing nothing, and the bigger inflation combined with the large reduction in unemployment that occurs ten percent of the time would be viewed as being very good, then the expected value of this mixed strategy could be very high.[10] The expected value could well be much higher than when the government follows the five percent policy and people know that it will.

Because this strategy is mixed, unions and firms cannot completely respond to it. The government gains a lot every once in a while (in the case above, ten percent of the time) and loses a little the rest of the time. If the gains sufficiently outweigh the losses, then a mixed strategy makes sense.

REPEATED GAMES (SUPERGAMES)

One could take the view that life is not just one period, but rather is comprised of a sequence of periods; people are interested in their welfare over the whole sequence of those periods; and what people have learned from earlier periods can be useful in determining their behavior in later periods. All of these characteristics show up in the theory of repeated games.

Consider the prisoners' dilemma story given above. Much of the time, especially when organized crime is involved, the [confess, confess] solution does not occur. Instead, the [not confess, not confess] solution is the one that we see. How is it possible to reconcile the theory and the evidence?

For many of those who choose a life of crime, being brought into the police station and being forced to submit to an interrogation is not a one-time event. This is more likely to be true of those who are members of a band of criminals. These individuals do not view the interrogation as a one-time event or game, but merely

[10] The expected value is the probabilities of each outcome multiplied by the value of that outcome from the point of view of the government's political preference function. It is a weighed average of the values of the outcomes.

as a part of a sequence of repeated games played between themselves and the police. The band can encourage the behavior that it prefers during interrogations by emphasizing the repeated nature of the game and by instituting a penalty for responses that it does not desire.

Individuals are interested not merely in the value of the current payoff, but in the discounted value of their future stream of payoffs. If the payoff from a certain policy in period t is denoted P_t and the discount parameter is ∂, then value of the future stream of payoffs (call that V_s) at time s can be written as

$$V_s = \sum_{i=0}^{\infty} \partial^i p_{s+i} \tag{16.1}$$

Now suppose that the action of one player in each period is remembered by the other players and is used, in part, to determine their actions. It is possible for a group to get together and to impose a penalty on members of the group who choose undesired actions. This penalty is a promise on the part of the other members to follow an action in response to some individual player's action which, while it will in all likelihood reduce their own payoff, definitely reduces the payoff to the offending player. In the prisoners' dilemma game, if a confession by one player in period one generates sufficiently severe actions by the other players in following periods, then a confession, while it raises the payoff of the period in which the person confesses, will lower the discounted stream of payoffs and generate the "no confession" solution. These kinds of penalties exist in the real crime world and are one of the reasons why witnesses for the government need to take on new identities once they have completed their testimony, and why members of the crime world try so hard to discover these new identities.

Now let us consider an example in macroeconomics. The supergame that is being played is between the unions and the government. Suppose that the unions are the reactors rather than the actors in this game. They observe a shift out in the AD curve, generated by some government policy, that reduces unemployment and generates some inflation. The unions respond by demanding higher rates of increase in their nominal wages for the next five periods. In a sense, the unions lose during the period in which the government generated the lower unemployment rate and are driven by a sense of fear that the government will follow the same policy in the following periods. By attempting to make up for the lost wages, they keep demanding nominal wage increases for five periods. After that they feel as if they have made up for their loss and have gotten over their fears; so, if there are no additional shifts out in the AD curve they will not ask for additional nominal wage increases. In this case, the penalty of reduced payoffs that the government faces from the periods of high wage demands, which generate increased inflation and questionable results on the unemployment side, makes the gains from the one-time policy seem sufficiently unattractive so that it is likely that the policy will not be pursued. The government will be persuaded not to follow this policy because the multiperiod reaction of the unions is bad enough to scare them away from it. However, if the "good" results can be generated during an election year and the penalty years are the first few years of the following term, leaving enough time to recover from the penalties, then the government political preference function might find the gains sufficient to outweigh the continued postelection losses. One additional complication is worth mentioning. If this were the case, then the unions would believe that inflation would be more likely in the year before or of an election and ask for higher nominal wages that year. This could be a complicated rational expectations response to previous government policies.

Figure 16.4 is a possible numerical example for the game played in the above paragraph. Each player sees that the [NC,NC] solution is preferred over the two Nash equilibria, but it is not a Nash equilibrium. If the single-play game were at the [NC,NC], neither player would want to stay there. If the government plays NC, then it is better for the unions to play five percent and have a payoff of five, which is greater than the zero payoff at the [NC,NC] solution. If the unions played NC, then the government would play five percent. Once one of the players played the five percent strategy, then the other would too, in order to get a higher payoff. These moves converge to the [−1,−1] payoff. If for some reason in a single-play game the unions played ten percent, then the government would also play ten percent, and the [−8,−8] payoff would be an equilibrium. These are the two Nash equilibria.

If played as a repeated game, the [0,0] equilibrium can be obtained. If each player wants to maximize her discounted payoff over time, then a credible threat to follow the ten percent policy in the next period whenever the other player plays a five percent move will be sufficient discouragement if each player's discount parameter (the ∂ in equation 16.1) is large enough. In this example, if the ∂ is greater than 5/8, then the penalty period need be only one period in order to prevent either of the players from choosing five percent. Suppose the initial situation is the [0,0] payoff. If no one does anything different, the value of the game for each player in each period is

$$0 = \sum_{i=0}^{\infty} \partial^i 0$$

		Government		
		NC	5%	10%
Unions	NC	A (0,0)	B (−5,5)	C (−10,0)
	5%	D (5,−5)	E (−1,−1)	F (−10,−5)
	10%	G (0,−10)	H (−5,−10)	I (−8,−8)

Figure 16.4

Now suppose that the government chooses five percent some period (Box B). It gains a payoff of five for that period, and the unions get a payoff of minus five. The unions respond by increasing their nominal wages by ten percent—the threat—and the government knows this and shifts out the AD curve by ten percent (Box I). The payoff is minus eight for each of them. After that penalty period, the union returns to the NC behavior (and so should the government). Because of the threat response of the unions, the payoff for the government from this policy was $5 + \partial \times -8$ ($5 - \partial 8$ must be less than zero), which is negative if ∂ is larger than 5/8. The government gains in the first period but loses so much in the next as to make the gains not worth it. (The unions take a beating, but this threat keeps the government from following this policy and *is* worth it to the unions.) If the discount parameter were between .435 and 5/8 then the unions would have to follow the threat for two periods in order to make the penalty greater than the gain. This can be seen because then $5 - \partial 8 - \partial^2 8$ is less than zero if ∂ is greater than .435. The lower the discount parameter, the longer the unions need to keep up the threat in order to counter the gains made in the first period. There is no threat period long enough to counter the government's gains in this example if the discount parameter is below .3846 (which equals 5/13). To show this, we need to consider what discount parameter would demand an infinite penalty period to just compensate the gain of five that the government gets from following the five percent policy. If the discount parameter is below this number, the losses in the following periods are not considered important enough to prevent the policy. In the limit we want $\partial 8 + \partial^2 8 + \partial^3 8 + \partial^4 8 + \ldots$, on to infinity, to be larger than five. That sum is equal to $\partial 8(1 + \partial + \partial^2 + \partial^3 + \partial^4 \ldots)$, which is equal to $\partial 8[1/(1 - \partial)]$.[11] So for ∂ less than 5/13, the summation, $\partial 8[1/(1 - \partial)]$, is below five, and the loss from an infinite penalty period is insufficient to wipe out the gain of five from following the five percent policy. The government would ignore the threat of retaliation to its policy because, in the period during which the government follows the five percent, the gains from the policy outweigh the future discounted losses. The government may, in the future, regret its policy decision, but at the moment of choice that is irrelevant.

REPUTATIONS

The role of reputation and its development is one of the more interesting applications of repeated game theory to economic policy. This is especially true in the context of monetary policy, because monetary policy is usually handled by the Central Bank (the Federal Reserve Board in the United States) and there are normally only a few individuals responsible for decisions involving monetary

[11] This is from mathematics. $\Sigma\, \partial^i = 1/(1 - \partial)$, when the summation is from zero to infinity and the absolute value of ∂ is less than one.

policy. The reputations of these few individuals will have an unusually large effect on the success or failure of a given policy. Reputation is important because of the distinction between public and private knowledge. For example, suppose that each individual knows what type of person she is, but this information is not perfectly available to the general public. The actions of an individual in repeated games generate information that others can use to determine the kind of person she is. This information can then be used to help predict what type of actions the individual is likely to take. First, a simple example from normal life; then, a more economic example.

Suppose that you are considering going on a date with someone new. You haven't played the "dating game" with this person yet, so you have no direct information on how he or she might act on the date. You do know other people who know this person, possibly even some who have gone on dates with this person, and you can ask them about him/her. In any case, information about how this person has behaved on other dates can be collected or is public knowledge. This "reputation" that the other person has developed through past actions will help serve as a guide for your actions and expected responses on this date. You might also choose to go on a date with a different person, who has a different reputation, in order to enjoy other aspects of the dating game payoff vector.[12] You are sure to realize that in this game individuals can manipulate their reputations by behaving in a fashion that does not maximize the immediate, short-run payoff of the dating game but helps them generate a reputation that will allow them to collect a possibly much larger long-run dating game payoff. The desire of each individual to engage in reputation manipulation, since the long-run payoff may be delayed for quite some time, depends on that individual's discount rate (the ∂ in the last section). The lower the discount rate, the more likely that the individual will go for the short-run payoffs of the dating game.

For the economic example, imagine that there are two possible types of individuals who could become the President of the Central Bank (or the Chairman of the Federal Reserve Board).[13] One of these is a tight money person, who hates inflation and hates to increase the money supply; the other is a loose money person who doesn't hate inflation and will accept some of it when some other social good is achieved. In particular, the loose money person will try to use inflation to counter

[12] A more formal way of expressing the ideas of this paragraph follows. In the dating game, individuals (we will call these the seekers) gather information about other individuals (the sought) in whom they are interested. This information is generated by observations on the behavior of the sought in earlier rounds of the dating game (played with either this particular seeker or with other seekers). This public information about past behavior generates the reputation of the sought. Information about this reputation of the sought will be used by the seeker to predict likely behavior of the sought in future plays of the dating game. Individuals trying to maximize their payoffs from the dating game are likely to choose different members of the "sought" set for maximizing different aspects of the payout vector of the dating game.

[13] M. B. Canzoneri, Monetary Policy Games and the Role of Private Information," *The American Economic Review* 75 (December 1985), 1056–1070.

unemployment. That is the *definition* of the loose money person. We can refer to these as the Tight President (we will call this type "Tight") or the Loose President (simply called "Loose"). Unfortunately for the rest of the community, only the presidents can know which type they really are. The other members of the economy can have a prior guess at what type of president the current one is (or a prospective one will be). Then, they use their observations of the president's actions while in office to update their prior guesses.[14]

Within the constraints of the above example, a Tight type will never increase the money supply to attempt to influence aggregate economic variables. If at any time an increase in the money supply occurs, everyone knows for certain that the current president is of the Loose variety. If the money supply is not expanded, then there are two possibilities. The president could actually be of the Tight variety, or the president could be Loose, pretending to be Tight. It should be clear why a Tight president will not increase the money supply, since that would lead to inflation, but we need to consider what a president who is Loose could gain by pretending to be Tight.

Suppose, as in the mixed strategy example above, an increase of the money supply, say by open market operations, has a salutary effect on the economy only if it is unexpected. (Unexpected, here, means that the unions have not responded as they would to an expected increase in the money supply in such a way as to shift out the AS curve to counter the the effects on output and unemployment that the shift out in the AD curve generated.[15]) The unions don't know if or when the Central Bank will increase the money supply. The unions use their prior guess about which type of president the Central Bank has, and its observations of the behavior of that president, to form these expectations. If the Central Bank president does not increase the money supply during times when doing so might seem a useful policy for a Loose president to follow, then the unions begin to give greater and greater probability to the event that the president really is Tight. In this case, the unions will give lower and lower probability to an increase in the money supply, which shift out the AD curve and generate inflation, and will contract for smaller and smaller nominal wage increases.

Given this use of information by the unions, what is the best policy for a president of the Central Bank to follow? If the president really is of the Tight variety, there is no choice. The Tight president will not increase the money supply under any conditions and therefore has no decision to make. All of the interesting options belong to the Loose president. Yet even the Loose president must be careful. One has the option to use loose monetary policy only once. After that the other agents in the economy—mainly unions and firms—will know that the president is Loose, and the unions will request (and receive) large nominal wage

[14] This can be done explicitly with Bayesian statistics.

[15] Remember that open market operations can cause an increase in the money supply, M, and a decrease in government bonds, B_g, with a net effect of a shift out in the AD curve. See Chapter 14.

increases to protect themselves from the loose monetary policies. A president of the Loose variety must decide when it is the most appropriate moment to use Loose monetary policy, use that policy, and then must resign. If this president is not replaced by someone who might or might not be Tight, and so ensures that the other agents once again face uncertainty, then the economy will be forced to endure an inflation generated by the necessary government responses to the unions' nominal wage increases.

Because the other agents in the economy *know* that the old president is Loose, their expectations of inflation are high. This drives up the nominal wage that results from their contract negotiations compared to the nominal wage that results from a Tight president, and shifts up the AS curve. If high unemployment is to be prevented, the Loose president must generate the expected inflation, for this president really will accept inflation rather than unemployment, and the expectations-generated inflation occurs. Since the other agents know that this president is Loose, a period with high unemployment and no inflation promises an even larger inflation to come and increases their wage demands. This can make unemployment worse. If the Loose president does not eventually increase M to shift out the AD curve as unemployment gets worse, then this president is not, by definition, Loose.

In the real world, it is never known, in the sense used above, whether a new president is Loose or Tight, so the wage demands will always be less than if it were known with certainty that the president is Loose. It is possible, in the real world where there is uncertainty and the definitions of Loose and Tight are not perfect descriptions of real individuals, that a Loose president may serve a whole term in office and never have to generate inflation. That might occur because the act of pretending to be a Tight president is successful.

When a new president is chosen for the Central Bank, he has a reputation that was generated by behavior before he was elevated to president. New presidents who know that they are Loose can pretend to be Tight, up to the point where the one-shot use of Loose monetary policy is worth it. Each period that the president pretends to be Tight, the unions and firms reevaluate their estimate of the probability that he actually is Loose. Following the mixed strategy we discussed above, the unions will ask for a lower nominal wage increase. Each period the contracted nominal wage increase will be smaller and smaller, and the potential gains from a Loose monetary policy will be larger and larger. If the Loose president springs the Loose monetary policy, which the Tight will never do, after several years of pretending to be Tight, the payoff in terms of unemployment decreases could be large.

The nomination of a new president of the Central Bank, when the old one had been faithful to the claim of being Tight, will result in large nominal wage increases in the demands of the unions. This is because the old president, by actions, had developed a strong reputation of being Tight and so, almost no matter who the new president is, he will be viewed as having a greater probability of being Loose. Therefore, one would expect that in 1987, when Paul Volker, who had resisted presidential pressure to increase the money supply for many years, retired as Chairman of the Federal Reserve Board and was replaced by Alan Greenspan, who was much more of an unknown, that the agents (unions, consumers, firms, and investors) in the economy would behave as if they expected a greater inflation in the future (and, as an example of the responses, the unions would probably ask for higher nominal wages). It was probably impossible to find someone who had the same reputation as Volker, and certainly Greenspan was known as more of a team player, a dangerous reputation for the Chairman of the Federal Reserve. Whoever the new Chairman was, agents in the economy would have had to respond to the uncertainty the nomination generated with defensive policies; defensive, that is, against additional inflation.

REPRISE

Game theory offers a rich source of techniques for interpreting economic phenomena. The strategic nature of games seems to create a very "real" world, in which each agent responds to the action of every other agent and attempts to collect information about the actions of other agents.

Simple, single-game models can be used in macroeconomics to analyze policy outcomes that are nonoptimal (in the sense that everyone would be happier at some other equilibrium) but occur anyway. Our example of a solution that generates inflation when everyone would prefer the no-inflation solution seems to mirror some actual government policy problems. The theory of mixed strategies shows us why governmental agencies like to keep their policy options open and maintain secrecy about what they will do once and if they decided. In an environment in which a number of individuals are responsible for arriving at any particular policy decision, there is innate uncertainty about which of the possible policies will eventually be chosen. One could almost view committee decision-making as a way of making somewhat random choices; it could also be merely random decision-making with different probabilities on the different possible outcomes.

Supergames recognize the importance of time. If individuals meet often to repeat transactions, then the game they play becomes much more complicated, and the payoff they are interested in is not necessarily the immediate one, but is likely to be a stream of payoffs generated by the repeated exchanges. Principal–agent problems, such as manager–employee relationships; cartel maintenance, such as keeping the producers honest in restricting output to what they agreed to in OPEC; and oligopolistic behavior, such as pricing in a four-manufacturer market are all examples of economic behavior where supergames have been successfully used for modeling. We used supergames to consider two aspects of macroeconomic policies. In one case, we saw that the reactions of one set of players, the unions, increased the cost over time of government policies and could, if the costs were big enough, make these policies unattractive. In the second case, we saw how information about the nature of one of the players, reputation, was important, and how players might behave in a manner so as to hide their real natures, in order to take advantage of it later. The example used was the reputation of the Chairman of the Federal Reserve Board. Reputations are important in many other aspects of life and during an election year one can observe the various candidates spending large sums of money to achieve the desired reputation. But that leads us to the problem of how public policies are chosen from the set of all possible policies, which is our next chapter.

17

Choosing Government Policies

In which we examine how the public decides which policies to foist upon itself. This is an almost impossible task, but government committees take it on; we might gain from the confusion.

INTRODUCTION

In some of the earlier chapters, we considered examples where the government has an objective function, which expresses the desires of the policy makers in terms of their relative trade-offs among some group of important economic variables. We have discussed these objective functions as if they represented the preferences, or trade-offs, of the government among such important variables as government revenues, the rate of inflation and/or unemployment, and the general level of production in the economy. Left untouched was the question of what might be the possible sources of these objective functions. How does the government get an objective function (because it seems strange, except under dictators, to think of a government as an individual with a particular utility function) and how might this objective function represent, in some fashion, the preferences of the population? Work done in the subfield of economics known as **public choice** has attempted to answer, from models based on microeconomic theory, these and other questions about the functioning of government.

One theory of government states that the actions of governments somehow represent some "consensus" (which needs to be defined) of the members of the society. This consensus may arise because the creation of a government allows for private well-being or private utility that is greater than that which would exist without the government because the other, private, agents in the economy are unable or unwilling to provide appropriate amounts of certain goods. Examples of this type of good that have already been used in this book include the creation of the social security system or money in the overlapping generations model (Chapter 15) and, in a Keynesian world, activist macroeconomic policy. Other examples, at a microeconomic level, might include education, if other people benefit from your knowing how to read, for example; weather forecasting services, although this could be private, but the information might then be kept secret; and, in a negative sense, air pollution. Goods that have this character usually generate **externalities** in the marketplace. Externalities occur when one individual can enjoy the use of a good or service without having to pay an appropriate price for it. Goods that have shared use, such as roads, national defence, and police and fire protection, are goods from which, possibly, some individuals can benefit while their neighbors pay the cost of the service. Because their use is open to the public at large, goods of this type are called **public goods.** One worry about these types of goods is that all individuals will want to understate the value they receive from a certain amount of this good and will attempt to pay less for it than the value they receive from its production. In that case, the quantity of the good that can actually be produced is less than that which individuals actually want to consume. There are goods (such as air pollution, mentioned above) where there are negative externalities. In this case an individual pays a cost even though she doesn't receive the services or gains. A firm that can freely generate air pollution and worsen the quality and possibly shorten the length of life of those who live near it is gaining benefits—profits in excess of what it would gain if it did not pollute—by shifting some of the costs to its neighbors. If the firm could produce the good more cheaply, without generating pollution, it would do so (as we know because of our assumption about profit maximization of firms); so, if it is polluting the air, it is doing so because that is a cheaper method of production.

One partial solution for this problem is to have the good produced by or for the government, which collects taxes to pay for its production. There are individuals, usually of the current "conservative" persuasion, who claim that this is the only appropriate role of government, aside from setting and enforcing the "rules" of the economy, and that the number of goods that fall in this category is quite small. Others, today's "liberals," believe that a much larger set of goods falls into this category, and in some countries the set of goods that the government actually places in this category is very large. In some countries the government buys up bankrupt firms in order to prevent the employees from losing their jobs, since it believes that the loss of employment that would result from shutting down the firm is an externality for the rest of the community.

A second area of public choice that is of interest to macroeconomists is the problem of how to arrive at collective decisions. One might hope for decisions that would improve the welfare of everyone, or at least not diminish the well-being of anyone; so that while some individuals might not be better off, they would not be worse off either. It is quite reasonable to think of starting with some definition of the preferences of individuals. These preferences might be defined by actions, so that when a person is willing to choose one combination of goods over other combinations, the chosen one is defined as preferred. Economists believe that an individual can make such choices over a large collection of combinations of goods and that these individual preferences can have such nice properties as transitivity and completeness.[1] One would like to be able to speak of social preferences, in the sense that the society (economy) can somehow also make choices between various bundles of goods. A theory that allows one to move from individual preferences to social preferences would be wonderful in helping to determine government decisions. The main (initial) research in this area was done by Kenneth Arrow in 1951.[2] Arrow's worrisome results showed that if one required five seemingly reasonable characteristics of the relationship between social and individual preferences, then a social preference ordering could not be found for many very reasonable forms of individual preferences. The behavior of governments in which decisions are made by committee can have important macroeconomic repercussions. The ability of citizens to predict future government actions is reduced by the very nature of the committee decision process and the uncertainty that this process generates. Some

[1] Transitivity of preferences means that if A is preferred to B and B is preferred to C, then A will be preferred to C. Completeness means that the preferences order all of the potential choices.

[2] Kenneth J. Arrow, *Social Choice and Individual Values* (New York: Wiley, 1951).

of this uncertainty may not disappear even with full information about the preferences of each of the members of the committee.

Another area of public choice that has macroeconomic importance is the formation of coalitions that shape the choices made by governments that rely on majority voting rules. These coalitions help define the forms of a government's or political party's objective function and can result in the imposition of minority interests in cases where the majority interest is very diffuse. The problem of information and reputation (as we saw in Chapter 16) shows up again in situations where political candidates attempt to present themselves as having opinions likely to gain them a majority coalition of voters. This topic will not be discussed in any detail here.

By the way, don't expect any dramatic answers about how political decisions *should* be made in this chapter. Expect, instead, a different perspective from which to think about political decisions and some hints at the reasons why different economies (countries, for example) make different types of political and economic decisons while operating under different sets of rules.

Before going on to some macroeconomic aspects of public choice (mainly issues about how private preferences can be aggregated and about some of the problems that can result from majority-based decision rules) it is worth the effort to consider how much of a public good a government should provide and how much it should charge each citizen for its use.

PUBLIC GOODS

If an individual considers purchasing a hamburger for personal consumption, the economic decision is fairly simple. She must measure the personal gains from the consumption of the hamburger against the personal cost of its purchase. (Remember from Chapter 3 that the private cost is the opportunity cost, or foregone benefits, of not consuming the best alternative good.) Generally, we do not worry about the gains or losses of welfare to other people because someone has purchased a hamburger. The costs and gains fall on only that one individual.

Suppose that someone builds a public good; for example, a section of road on her own property that connects two other roads. The individual who has built the road now has improved access to the rest of the world and makes some gains in well-being from the road construction. But other individuals can also gain from the construction of the road. They may now have a shorter route to some desired location (to the drive-in, perhaps) and can gain from reduced travel time. If this road shortens the distance from a populated area to a commercial area, the merchants in the commercial area gain by the increased sales that result from the expanded access to their stores. So while the person who builds the road makes private gains from the construction of the road, she is not the only one to gain; the public in general gains. If the other users cannot be obliged to pay for the gains that they make from the construction of the road (by a toll booth, for example), then the gain to society, the social gain, is much greater than the private gain. One apparent solution is to make each road a toll road. This, unfortunately, defeats the usefulness of the new road (unless it is quite long) in that the many stops that would be required to pay the tolls on the many short roads might eliminate the gains from the new road. When we look at goods where potential social gains are much greater than private gains and there is no good way to collect the gains that go to other individuals, we see that too few of them are produced in a private economy. The nonexclusion characteristic of public goods—others can't be kept from using it without paying—is very important in generating the difference between the public and private gains from its production.

Government in one of its manifestations, national, state, provincial, or local, has the ability to produce these public goods and demand payment in the form of taxes—forced contributions—from all members of the community. Governments traditionally provide roads, police and fire protection, defense from other economies, primary education, and more recently, a wide variety of services that include information on aggregate economic behavior (that might be useful in an economy like the Lucas model of business cycles), agricultural price supports, wildlife conservation, and social services such as income support, food and health programs, and job training. It can be argued that all of these items contain some amount of the characteristic of a public good, but there is bitter public debate over which of these contain a sufficiently large difference between public and private gains to justify their inclusion in the basket of government services.

While the public is making decisions about what public goods to produce, and how much of each of them is required, it is also solving the problem of how much each member of the economy should be charged for these public goods. This problem is not so difficult if we could get individuals to reveal (that is, to be truthful about) their demands for these goods. If there is a lot of demand and only one supplier for some public good we can use supply and demand curves to decide how much to produce and how much to charge each individual. The supply curve side is easy, the demand side slightly more tricky.

One of the main features of a public good is that individuals can use it without reducing its use by others. Let's use defense as an example. If the government has an army protecting me, in the northern United States, from an attack by the Canadians, this same army simultaneously protects my neighbor. Each of us has a demand curve that tells how much we will be willing to pay (truthfully) for a given amount of protection, which in this case means a certain size army.

Since each of us can use the protection while the other is also being protected, the total demand for an army is found by summing the demand curves vertically. If I'm willing to pay twenty dollars a year to have an army of ten thousand soldiers at the northern United States border, and my neighbor is willing to pay fifteen dollars to have that same army there, then it is worth thirty-five dollars to us combined to have that army. Notice that prices were added at a fixed quantity. This is the same as adding the demand curves vertically. Where the demand curve for the community (found by summing up vertically all of the individual demands of the members of the community) crosses the military supply curve (marked **S** in Figure 17.1) we find the equilibrium quantity of the public good that would be produced. Notice that the price that I pay for this quantity of defense is different from the price that my neighbor pays, but there is nothing wrong with that. In each case, we are paying what an army of that size is worth to us.

This way of deciding how much to charge individuals for the use of public goods only works if people honestly reveal their demand curves for the good. Unfortunately, it is usually a better private decision *not* to reveal one's preference. If my neighbor lies and claims that his demand curve for military is much lower than it really is, he might be able to pay less than he would otherwise have to and still receive just about the same quantity of defense. If my neighbor can get away with this, he has become a **free rider,** someone who benefits from a public good without paying his appropriate share of the costs. Being a free rider is easier in situations where there is a large number of people who are contributing to the public good than it is in cases where there are only a few. Large cities have a harder time preventing free riders than do small villages, where everyone knows and can monitor everyone else.

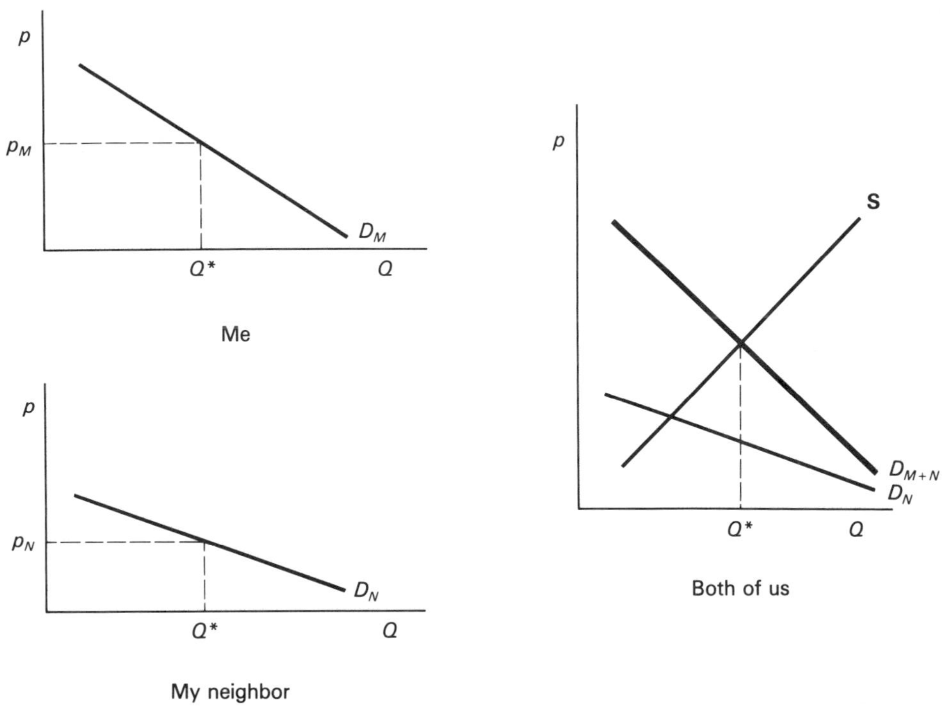

Figure 17.1

Government macroeconomic policy might be considered a public good. For example, there is one small school of thought that views fiat money and monetary policy as public goods. Private production of fiat money is a theoretical possibility, but it may permit or even encourage excessive production of competing fiat monies. Control by the government of the production of fiat money can give credibility to a rule that provides for a limited rate of growth of the money supply. Since the government also controls the legal system, it can make rules to help prevent an equilibrium with a price of money equal to zero. Potential rules include legal tender laws such as those mentioned in Chapter 13, the right to pay taxes in the fiat money, and (as happens with the provincial fiat money in northern Argentina) a lottery based on the serial numbers of the currency. Appropriate control of the quantity of fiat money permits an equilibrium that improves private welfare.

Other aggregate government policies, such as stabilization policies—if they work—might also be public goods since they cannot be provided by private agents. If such policies do improve welfare (whether or not they do is controversial,) then it is appropriate for the government to produce such policies as public goods.

THE UNANIMITY RULE

One method that has been suggested for making decisions about how much of a public good to produce and how much to charge each person is the **unanimity rule.** This rule, suggested in 1896 by the economist Knut Wicksell, requires all members of the community to agree on the quantity of the public good being produced and the tax to be paid by each of them. This rule is not completely hypothetical, for this method of deciding village action has been the traditional decision process in rural Japan and, many claim, is also the decision process used currently in the Japanese business sector.

Traditionally, in Japanese villages, when a repair or construction project that would benefit more than one person had to be done, the village leader would call a community-wide meeting. The meeting would last until all were in agreement about the project and about the contribution required from each. So if an irrigation ditch had to be cleaned to allow proper water flow to a number of rice paddies, the whole village would clean it, but only after a meeting in which there was unanimous agreement on the amount of time each member of the village had to devote to the job.

The reasoning behind this type of decision rule can be demonstrated in a two-person example. Suppose that two neighbors want to build a swimming pool for their mutual use. Each of them has a private value, or gain, she believes she will receive from having the pool put in. This gain represents how much better off each of them will be having a pool instead of not having a pool. The gain will be larger for a larger pool and less for a smaller pool. Suppose that an arbitrator names a pool size and the contribution that each will be required to make in order to have that pool. If the individual believes that having the pool is worth more than the contribution she is being required to contribute, she will vote for that plan. If the gains are less than the contribution, she will vote against the plan. Agreement by both of them means that the contribution that each is making is less than the gains that each will get from having the pool. Everyone gains by this plan. The arbitrator can offer different plans, entailing different sized pools and different contributions, but the neighbors will only vote for one of these new plans if it is better than the one that was last agreed to. This process can go on for a while until no one can find a pool size and contribution plan preferred to the last one agreed upon.

The same strategy can be used for larger projects that involve more people. There are two main drawbacks to the unanimity rule. The first is that it may take a very long time to get everyone to agree to a plan, especially if the group is large. Imagine what kind of plan will be required to get everyone in the country (any country—even the island of Fiji has a large enough population so this can be a problem) to agree on it. Many may not want to contribute that much time to the making of public decisions. (Look at the number of people who don't even spend the time to vote.)

The second possible problem is that some people may misrepresent their positions and vote against plans where they gain more than they contribute because they believe that they can push the others to a different contribution plan where they would have to contribute even less. This strategic behavior makes the decision process last even longer than it otherwise would, and makes even fewer individuals willing to spend the time required to achieve unanimous group decisions.

In spite of the difficulty of reaching unanimous decisions, the unanimity rule is the only known decision process in which all members of the society are certain to gain from public projects. Each member of the group will agree to a project only once the member is certain that the private gains will be bigger than the private costs. This is the appeal of the unanimity rule. The cost in time of achieving such a decision is the main flaw. It is this cost that leads organizations to choose less-than-unanimous decision rules for making their group decisions.

MAJORITY RULES

A large number of organizations, including countries, use some form of **majority rule** to make their group decisions. One of the main concerns of those who draw up these majority rule decision processes is the protection of the rights—the well-being—of those who are not members of the majority coalition. But other questions are also important. In what way can majority rules be thought of as optimal? When will majority rule decision processes fail to achieve any decision? In what way do majority rule decisions reflect individual preferences? How do majority rule decision systems operate in practice? These are some of the issues we will consider.

Once a group decides not to use the unanimity rule, it must decide just how small a subgroup will be required to be in agreement in order to make a public decision. The larger the proportion required, the longer the decision process will take. (That was the main fault with the unanimous decision rule.) One might want to reserve the requirement that subgroups be composed of large majorities for those decisions that are especially important (changes in constitutions, for example). The rest of the time one can probably make do with the assent of smaller subgroups to allow a decision to pass. There *is* something special about the "one more than half the group" (the "normal" majority) voting rule, but it is probably not what you think.

Suppose we had a rule that required *less* than half of the group to be in agreement on a public decision. Group decisions can probably be made very quickly under this kind of a rule. That's good. It is possible to get two distinct and possibly contradictory decisions out of a single group. That's very bad. Suppose that the Board of Aldermen of Chicago has a rule requiring that at least forty-nine percent of the group must agree in order to make a public decision. There are one hundred aldermen on the board. Suppose that the decision that they are contemplating is whether to build a new football stadium in the city. A vote is taken on a bill proposing that the stadium be built and forty-nine board members of the board vote for it. Another alderman offers a law that proposes that the stadium should not be build. A different group of forty-nine aldermen vote in favor of that law. Now the city of Chicago has simultaneously decided to build and not to build a football stadium. Neither decision overrides the other. The mayor has to determine how simultaneously to build and not build the stadium. Such an action is clearly impossible (well, it might be possible in Chicago). A majority rule that requires less than or exactly one half to make a decision allows for the possibility of two simultaneous, conflicting decisions to be made. Such a rule can lead to unworkable "decisions."

Note that voting rules where less than half can determine a winner exist in the world. When there are more than two candidates for public offices in France, Canada, and many other countries, the candidate with the *most* votes wins the election. This is known as **plurality** voting. It is possible, although unlikely with large electorates, that two or more candidates receive the highest number of votes and therefore that election would end in a tie. This tie does not determine a winner, and another election would be held to find the candidate with the most votes. Voting with more than two candidates or policy options is complicated, and we will return to it presently.

The smallest-sized group that prohibits an organization from making simultaneous, conflicting decisions is "**one more than half.**" With this size for a majority, only one of the two conflicting decisions can pass. This is the strong, positive feature of the "one more than half" majority rule: It is the smallest-sized winning coalition with which immediately conflicting decisions are impossible. The "one more than half" rule puts a premium on making decisions as quickly as possible while still prohibiting conflicting decisions. In organizations where the members do a lot of things other than attend meetings to make decisions (such as a country, where many people actually need to produce goods), the simple, "one more than half" majority rule is likely to prevail.

Other, larger majorities are possible and do occur. Consider the trade-off that individuals must make when thinking about the majority size that is optimal for making particular types of public decisions. The bigger the majority needed for agreement, the longer the time needed, on average, to reach any decision, and the more costly the process in terms of time not used for other, preferred activities. However, different classes of decisions have different potential costs to an individual. Changing the tax rate that an individual must pay can be costly, and individuals will spend some time helping decide what that tax rate must be. A change in a basic "law of the land," such as the one that determines when and how the government may kill any particular individual, might be viewed as much more important than a tax change, and individuals will be willing to spend much more time in making this kind of decision. An individual is willing to spend more time at these kinds of decisions, because the potential losses from a decision that puts him in the "killable group" are much higher than the potential losses of being put in a high tax group. The optimal majority for a given *type* of decision is the one where the potential gains in well-being from being able to prevent unfavorable decisions just matches the losses in well-being from the time needed to arrive at a group decision (and the bigger the majority, on average the more time needed). That is why the Constitution of the United States of America is so difficult to change and why making decisions within that Constitution is relatively easy, although more difficult than simple majority.[3]

THE MEDIAN VOTER

Now we will begin discussing the problem of more than two options. The example given here offers a one-dimensional continuum of options. Any value over a range of values may be chosen. That means that there are infinitely many possible choices. Under certain conditions, we can use voting mechanisms to make social decisions with these many choices.

Suppose that a government is trying to decide how much it will spend on some public good such as the expenditure on defense or aid to the poor (which might be a public good). It will need to tax the citizens of that society to get the

[3] This kind of rule is true for the majorities needed to change the constitutions of many other countries as well. Smaller groups (clubs, for example) also normally require larger majorities to change the group constitution than to make decisions within that constitution.

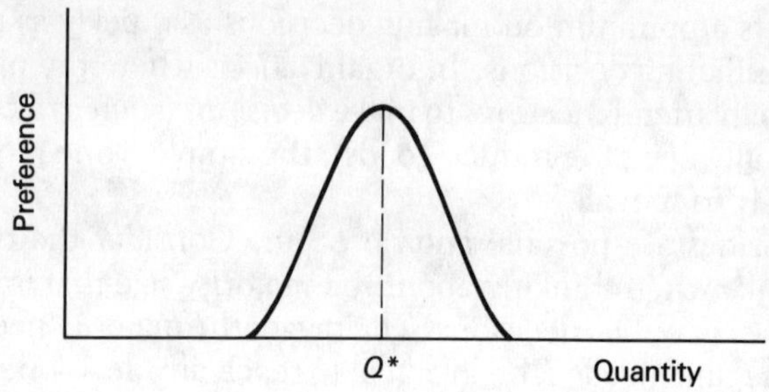

Figure 17.2

funds to pay for that public good. Suppose, also, that the citizens have different ideas about the optimal quantity of this good that should be produced. Each citizen can rank the quantity that she thinks the government should produce. Figure 17.2 shows how Annabel B. ranks the amount she believes that the government should spend on defense.

The height of the curve at each quantity indicates how much Annabel likes that much expenditure on defense. The quantity Q^* is the quantity that she prefers most, and the quantity that she would choose if the decision were up to her. Other members of the society have similar curves representing their preferences, but they have different optimal values (different Q^*s) and the curves may be shaped somewhat differently. To keep it simple, assume that there are four other members of this society and that they have preference curves shaped just like Annabel's, but that the optimal point, Q^*, is at a different level for each of them. Figure 17.3 shows the set of these curves for the entire group.

The quantity of defense that this group chooses is Q^*, the quantity desired by the **median voter.** The median voter is the one whose preference places him or her exactly as the middle or swing person in the group. It is not necessary that this person's preferred quantity be the average of the preferred quantities. In the example above, the quantity Q^* is not the average of the most preferred quantities of the members of the group. If this group is asked to vote for the quantity of Q^* or more, Annabel and the two with preferences to the right of hers will vote for that quantity, which is preferred to anything less, and the other two will vote against it.

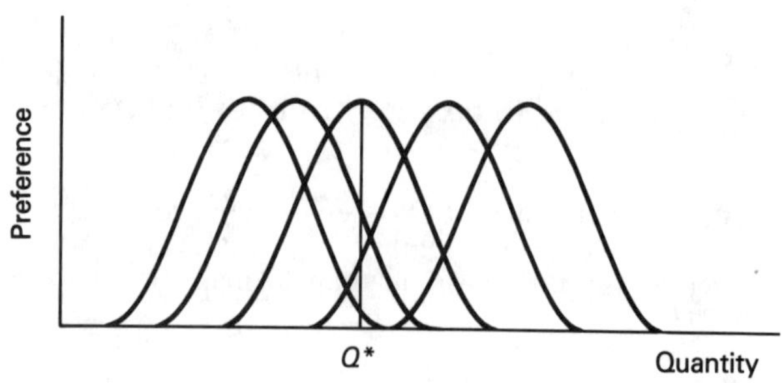

Figure 17.3

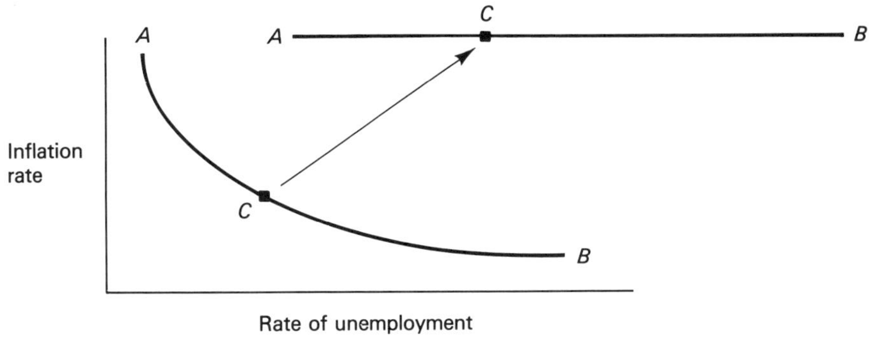

Figure 17.4

If the vote is for the quantity of Q^* or less, Annabel and the two to her left will vote for it, and the other two will vote against it. Around this median voter can be built a winning coalition. Note something about this median voter. She is the one whose preferences determine the outcome of the election (that is, of the decision process). In societies where two parties dominate, each candidate attempts to capture this median voter. This is why both candidates in presidential elections in the United States generally move toward the political center after they are nominated by their parties.[4]

Certain macroeconomic policies might be decided on by a median voting rule, even though the policies might have more than one dimension. Consider the often mentioned (but, as we know from earlier chapters, questionable) Phillips curve trade-off between inflation and unemployment. If there really is a Phillips curve, and that curve doesn't shift, the only policies available are those *on* the curve. So while the curve is in a two-dimensional space (unemployment and inflation) restricting oneself to the curve reduces the choice to a one-dimensional set of alternatives.

A standard Phillips curve is shown in Figure 17.4. The curved line AB is that Phillips curve. Mathematically, it is possible to straighten out the curved AB. We can do this so that every point on the straight line AB has a matching point on the curved line AB. Each point such as C on the straight AB represents a particular combination of inflation and unemployment. If individuals have single peaked preferences on the straight line AB, such as the preferences shown in Figure 17.3, then the median voter will decide the inflation rate–unemployment rate that is chosen by the society.

[4] The process is actually slightly more complicated than that. The candidates are attempting to capture the median voter of enough states to win the election there in order to win the electoral college. The shift toward the center is the same, but the center can be different in different states, and finding that center can be more difficult.

CYCLING

Annabel's preferences, as shown above, have a particular shape. This shape is called **single peakedness.** Over the set of possible choices, as the possible quantity moves away from her most preferred point Annabel likes it less and less. This occurs in both directions. Finding a majority vote solution to public decisions is not always possible if the preferences are not single peaked. (The cycling problem occurs with three or more outcomes, and is not a problem when only two outcomes are possible. One or the other is chosen.)

Consider a group of three people (Robert, Sam, and Thomas) who are to choose to buy one of three possible outcomes (Apples, Bananas, or Cantaloupe). The group must choose only one of these to buy. Suppose that Robert has preferences such that A>B>C (apples are preferred to bananas, which are preferred to cantaloupe). Sam has preferences such that B>C>A (Sam prefers bananas to cantaloupe, and apples are the least preferred) and Thomas has preferences such that C>A>B (cantaloupe is his favorite followed by apples and then bananas). We can display these preferences in a table if we use the convention that for items in a list, the earlier an item occurs, the more preferred it is. The three sets of preferences above can be written as

person	*preferences*
Robert	ABC
Sam	BCA
Thomas	CAB

One way to try to find a "social decision" when there are multiple possibilities is to let the voting take place in pairs (choose one of Apples or Bananas, choose one of Bananas or Cantaloupe, choose one of Apples or Cantaloupe). If one of the possibilities wins in all of the pairwise elections in which it occurs, it is called the **Condorcet winner.**

We can check to see if there is a Condorcet winner in the problem given above. In choosing between A and B, Robert and Thomas vote for A and Sam votes for B. In an A against B contest, A wins. In choosing between B and C, Robert and Sam choose B and Thomas chooses C. In a B against C contest, B wins. Note that this says that A is socially preferred to B and that B is socially preferred to C. One would normally think that this would mean that A is preferred to C. But in choosing directly between A and C, Sam and Thomas vote for C and Robert votes for A. In an A against C contest, C wins. The social ordering (the outcome of the voting) says that

A is preferred to B (R and T vote for A)

B is preferred to C (R and S vote for B)

C is preferred to A (S and T vote for C)

In this example there is no Condorcet winner. The social order (let me use >> to mean "is socially preferred to" or "wins in a pairwise vote against") says that

A>>B>>C>>A>>B>>C>>A . . .

In pairwise voting, the choice cycles forever and no decision is made. Robert, Sam, and Thomas can't decide which of the three fruits to buy.

A graph of the preferences used in this example will help illustrate the problem. Remember the median voter examples, in which we could find a social optimum when there were single-peaked preferences. Graphing the preferences of the three individuals illustrates that single peakedness does not occur.[5] Figure 17.5a shows that Robert's and Sam's preferences have a single peak (at A for Robert and at B for Sam) but that Thomas's preferences have two peaks (at A and C). In a situation where cycling takes place, this failure of single peakedness will be maintained even if the order of the choices is changed on the horizontal axis of the

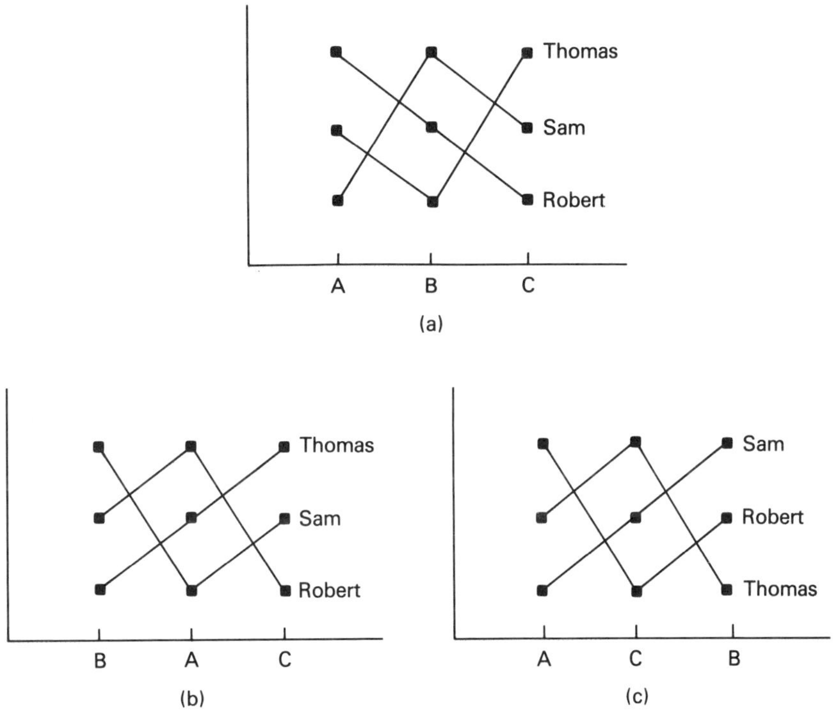

Figure 17.5

[5] The vertical dimension in these graphs measure preference. The higher up a point is, the more preferred it is. The exact height doesn't matter. Something twice as high up is **not** twice as preferred. The connecting lines are only there to keep track of whom we are talking about. The points above A, B, or C are *indicators* of preference.

graph. Figures 17.5b and 17.5c show two other orderings and the continuing failure of single peakedness.

In Figure 17.5b, the two peaks in the preferences occurs for Sam (at Bananas and Cantaloupes) while both Thomas and Robert have single-peaked preferences. In Figure 17.5a, it was Thomas' preferences that had the double peak. Robert is the one whose preferences display two peaks in Figure 17.5c. The order of the choices can change on the horizontal axis, but if the problem really has a cycle, every ordering will have two peaks for at least one of the participants.

This example shows that some sets of preferences can have two peaks when the graph is drawn with one ordering, but is single peaked in another ordering. This kind of problem has a Condorcet winner. Suppose that Robert, Sam, and Thomas have a slightly different preference ordering among Apples, Bananas, and Cantaloupe. This ordering is

person	*preferences*
Robert	ACB
Sam	BCA
Thomas	CBA

In this example, Robert has changed his ordering of Bananas and Cantaloupe, and Thomas has changed his ordering of Apples and Bananas. Notice that Cantaloupe is the Condorcet winner. In a vote between A and B, Bananas win (Sam and Thomas vote for Bananas). In a vote between A and C, Cantaloupe wins (Sam and Thomas vote for Cantaloupe). In the vote between B and C, Cantaloupe wins since Robert and Thomas vote for Cantaloupe. Cantaloupe wins in each of the elections in which it appears. If one were using the Condorcet winner as the decision rule, then Cantaloupe would be chosen. Figure 17.6a shows the graph for this decision problem.

In Figure 17.6a, Robert's preferences show double peaks, one at Apples and one at Cantaloupe. This double peakedness might make one think that the Condorcet pairwise voting would fail to get a winner. However, when the ordering of the choices on the horizontal axis is changed, as in Figure 17.6b, then the double peakedness disappears. Note that the preferences of the three individuals have not changed between Figures 17.6a and 17.6b. Merely the way in which they are displayed is different. The set of preferences is single peaked when looked at correctly, and we get a winner. The group goes out and buys a cantaloupe or two.

A similar but somewhat different result can occur with a voting scheme in which, first, amendments can be added and voted on individually; then, the whole bill is voted on. This can result in socially nonoptimal results. The classic United States example happened in the 1960s, and involved a bill for federal payments to local schools.[6] Congress can be thought of as having been then composed of three

[6] For readers from outside the United States: primary and secondary education in the United States is the responsibility of local (state, city, and town) governments and is not federally controlled. It is funded mostly by local taxes.

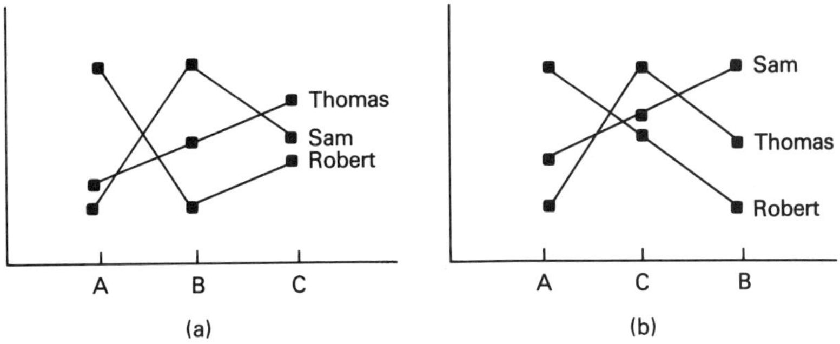

Figure 17.6

groups: northern Democrats, southern Democrats, and Republicans. The Democrats were a majority in Congress and for many years had proposed a bill to have federal assistance to local education. If the bill had been voted on directly, the northern and southern Democrats would have voted for it and the Republicans would have voted against it, since they were against the federal aid. Each year, the Republicans would propose an amendment to the bill that required schools that received the federal funds to be racially integrated. This amendment would be approved, with the Republicans and the northern Democrats voting for it and the southern Democrats against. The amended bill, which said that the federal government would help local schools but that they must be racially integrated, would fail every year, with the Republicans and the southern Democrats voting against it and only the northern Democrats supporting it. In this way, the Republicans were able to prevent the federal government from funding local schools.

ARROW'S IMPOSSIBILITY THEOREM

In earlier sections of this chapter we demonstrated that majority voting rules work for making social decisions if there are only two options to choose between, or if the options are one dimensional and preferences of individuals are single peaked. Limiting ourselves to public choices, of which choices among available macroeconomic policies are a subset, and imposing the further limit that they all have three or more options or more than one dimension of available policy choices, we can ask a very general question: Do there exist decision rules, majority voting or otherwise, that will generate public choices that fulfill a few seemingly reasonable restrictions?

In one of the most influential economic Ph.D. dissertations of all time, Kenneth Arrow demonstrated that, given only a few fairly reasonable sounding requirements on the relationships between the preferences of individuals and social preferences, no social preference function can be found that fulfills these requirements. This is where the "impossibility" in the section title comes from. It is impossible to find a consistent way of going from the preferences of individuals to a social preference ordering that fulfills these requirements. Arrow's result is fairly old and was not quite correct in its original version, and recent work has shown that similar impossibility results hold for other sets of requirements. We will discuss but not prove Arrow's theorem in the corrected version, and then we will discuss some of the implications of this impossibility result. First we will list these requirements and then define them and attempt to show that they are, indeed, reasonable characteristics to desire from a decision process.

Arrow's theorem says that there *does not exist* a social choice rule that satisfies the following five criteria:

1. a minimally complex world,
2. the strong Pareto condition,
3. independence of irrelevant alternatives,
4. transitivity,
5. no dictator.

Note that the theorem does not merely say that it is difficult to find a social choice rule that satisfies these criteria. It says that it is *impossible!* Majority voting or any other possible rule will fail at least one of these criteria. Criterion number 5 implies something rather frightening to those of us who feel strongly in favor of democratic styles of public choice processes. It might well be possible to find a public choice rule that fulfills the other four criteria, but where there is a dictator.

Criterion 1, that we have a **minimally complex world,** eliminates some of the unreasonably simple results we discussed earlier. To begin with, we assume that there are at least three available possibilities to choose among. This makes the world interesting and more complex and realistic than a two-alternative world would be. Even in cases where we seem to have only two creditable alternatives, as in the United States presidential elections, there is really a much more complex process that determines what those two choices will be. When there are only two alternatives, majority voting will select a social choice that fulfills the rest of the criteria in the list above.

We assume, as part of criterion 1, that there are at least three individuals in the society. We do not want to impose advance restrictions on the preferences that these individuals may have, and so will ask that the social choice function (as we will call the process for making a social choice) work for all logically possible preferences. If we impose enough restrictions on the kinds of preferences we allow, we can guarantee that there exists a social choice rule. For example, if we required that all of the individuals have exactly the same preferences then they would all want the same thing, and social decisions would be very easy to make.[7] In contrast, we permit diversity.

The last assumption of criterion 1 is that we do not restrict the agendas we might ask the social choice function to confront. By agenda, we mean the portion of the set of alternatives that we are deciding among and the order in which we choose to act on those alternatives. (This use of agenda should be familiar. An agenda or order of business of a meeting lists the topics to be decided on in that meeting and the order in which they will be discussed.) We are not going to limit the permissible agendas in advance.

Criterion 2, the **strong Pareto condition,** states that if there are choices A and B as part of the available alternatives, everyone thinks that A is at least as good as B,[8] and at least one person prefers A to B, then B will not be chosen. This condition does not say that A will be chosen, only that B will not be. Consider an example in which choice A is a macroeconomic policy that results in a ten percent unemployment rate, a five percent inflation rate, and an average real wage of five dollars per hour, and choice B is a policy that results in a five percent unemployment rate, a fifteen percent inflation rate, and an average real wage of ten dollars per hour. If everyone is willing to accept five points of additional unemployment in exchange for a ten point reduction in inflation, and one person—a banker who has loaned out money at fixed interest rates—thinks that the lower inflation is definitely better than the lower unemployment, then the strong Pareto condition says that policy B will never be followed. It is possible that policy A will not be the one that eventually will be chosen. All we know from the strong Pareto condition is that policy B will *not* be chosen. This criterion says that if a choice is available that makes at least one person better off and no one worse off compared to some initial choice, then our social choice rule should not select that first choice.

Independence of irrelevant alternatives, criterion 3, has been quite controversial, mainly because it has been misinterpreted. Suppose that we want to choose between the three alternative policies, A, B, and C. Suppose a lot of other

[7] An unproven conjecture this example suggests is that it should be easier to achieve social choices in societies where the preferences of individuals are more alike than in societies where they are very different. The more homogeneous the population of a country (or smaller social unit) the easier it should be for that unit to govern itself. It has been argued that the relative social tranquility of certain countries (the Scandinavian countries are often used as examples) occurs because of the similarity of the preferences of the citizens of those countries.

[8] This does not mean that *everyone* prefers A to B. "At least as preferred as" means that they could be liked equally well.

policy possibilities exist—say ten other possibilities—but that we wish to choose among only these three. Individuals have preference rankings over all thirteen of the possibilities, the relevant three and the irrelevant ten. We want our social choice to depend only on the rankings among themselves of the three relevant choices and not to change if some people change their rankings of the other ten. In the example we are illustrating here, there are thirteen possibilities. The list below (from choice A to choice M) is one ordering of thirteen possibilities. Choices to the left are preferred.

F **B** D **A** M K H E I **C** J G L (ranking #1)

A second possible ranking among the thirteen choices that preserves the ordering of the three relevant alternatives is

J M E **B** F H L I **A** D K G **C** (ranking #2)

Notice that the order of A, B, and C (in bold) when the other ten are discarded is the same in ranking #1 and ranking #2. In both cases the ordering is BAC.

There are two main reasons that this criterion is desirable. One is that it limits the social choice function to feasible alternatives. It does not matter how we rank the current presidential candidates when compared to Franklin Pierce, the fourteenth president of the United States, or to Bernardo O'Higgins, a hero of the Chilean war for independence; only how we rank the current candidates when compared to each other. This limits the amount of information that is needed; it is probably impossible to collect information of individuals' rankings of all infeasible alternatives. Speaking of restricting ourselves to relevant infeasible alternatives merely generates an oxymoron. All known electoral systems restrict themselves to feasible alternatives.

The second reason that this criterion is desirable is that it prevents individuals from misrepresenting their preferences. If one could change the outcome of a social choice process by lying about one's preferences over infeasible alternatives, there would be considerable incentive to do so, especially since the infeasible alternative by definition never can occur. Restricting the process to only the feasible alternatives provides incentives for truthful revelation of preferences—for telling the truth. (Note: Several years ago at a major university, a rock won the election for student body president. This strategy, which represented dissatisfaction with the available candidates, did not work except to point out the dissatisfaction, since the rock was not a registered student and therefore was not eligible. The presidency went to the student with the highest number of votes.)

The criterion of **transitivity** is fairly noncontroversial. If a social choice rule chooses A over B and B over C, then if we had to choose between A and C we would hope that the rule would choose A over C. If it does, it fulfills the criterion of transitivity. The idea of transitivity is deeply ingrained in normal thought processes. If John is taller than Sam and Sam is taller than Arnold, then John had better be taller than Arnold. However, there are situations where we don't really expect transitivity to hold. Sports is one of the most frequently observed of these examples. Suppose that during one season of an imaginary baseball league the Lions beat the Cubs, and the Cubs beat the Celtics. While one might expect that the Lions will beat the Celtics, most sports fans would not be too surprised if the Celtics beat the Lions. This is because teams have a range of characteristics, and while one set of characteristics might dominate another set (the Lions beat the Cubs and the Cubs beat the Celtics), in the final matchup between the Celtics and the Lions some of the strong characteristics of the Celtics might dominate some of the Lions' weaknesses, and allow the Celtics to win. If individuals are asked to rank complicated bundles of goods that provide many different kinds of characteristics, it is sometimes observed that these rankings are not transitive. Bundle A is preferred to bundle B and bundle B is preferred to bundle C, but the person chooses bundle C over bundle A. However, transitivity is normally observed and is viewed as a desirable property for a social choice rule.

In the context of a social choice rule, a **dictator** is an individual whose ranking of the alternatives is decisive regardless of the rankings of the other members of the society. The alternative preferred by the dictator is the one chosen by the social choice rule unless he ranks two or more choices as equal and as the preferred choice. In this case, the rankings of other individuals can be used to determine which of these alternatives, equally preferred by the dictator, is finally chosen. Criterion 5 expresses the desire that no one person shall have such power.

Arrow proved that a social choice rule does not exist that fulfills all the five criteria listed above. This means that any rule fails at least one of these criteria. This failure occurs in small committees with at least three members as well as in the society as a whole. What interpretations relevant to macroeconomics can be made of this theorem?

One of the important themes of this text has been the use of information. In Chapters 9 and 10, the government's information about the unions' wage behavior gave power to government policy.[9] This power disappears once the order of information is switched and the unions have rational expectations—perfect information—about the government's policies (see Chapter 11). How well the public can predict the government's policies determines how well it can protect itself from the unpleasant private effects of those policies. This predictability was one of the main themes of the strategic policy chapter (Chapter 16). An individual's reputation is useful to help predict behavior. What happens to the theories of rational expectations and strategic policy formation if the decisions are not made by single individuals, but are made by committees?

It is reasonable to assume that most public macroeconomic policy choices are made by committees. In the United States one such committee might include

[9] Remember that we are using unions as a proxy for the results of negotiations between unions and firms. It is more accurate to say that the government knows about conditions in contracts signed by the private sector. Note that the government is expected to enforce these contractual conditions in its courts.

the president, several members of his cabinet, and at least a few of the significant members of Congress. In some other countries it will only include members of the ruling party. It is very unlikely that the preferences of these individuals will match perfectly, so some rule will be needed to decide the actions to be taken. Arrow's theorem says that no rule exits that fulfills the five criteria. If we assume that the president is not a dictator, at least one of the other criteria will sometimes fail to hold.[10] The majority of economic policy problems are complex, so let's assume that criterion 1 holds. So at some time, at least one of criteria 2, 3, or 4 fails to hold. The most interesting of these criteria are the independence of irrelevant alternatives and transitivity.

The failure of either of these two criteria to hold affects the predictability, for economic agents who are not members of the committee, of the results of committee deliberations. Remember from the discussion above that the inclusion of the criterion of independence of irrelevant alternatives prevented strategic misrepresentation of preferences. Once this misrepresentation is allowed, the committee process becomes a complicated strategic game, a game that is a mix of cooperative and competitive behavior. The information set needed to accurately predict the likely government policy becomes very large and includes the preferences of the committee members over irrelevant as well as relevant alternative policies. Determining a "reputation" for a committee based on the reputations of the members of that committee becomes a formidable task.

The failure of transitivity in the committee's policy choice ranking presents a problem for the private sector similar to the one that results from the failure of independence of irrelevant alternatives. Cycling is the result of the failure of transitivity. The social choice rule for the committee can determine that macroeconomic policy A is preferred to policy B, which is preferred to C, which is preferred to A. In this case, even perfect knowledge (by the public) of the entire preference orderings of the members of the committee and of the committee's social choice rule will not allow the public to determine which policy the committee will choose. The selection of one policy from the available set might well be entirely fortuitous. This committee can have no reputation, and information about the reputations of the members has a greatly reduced value. Rational expectations of the committee's policies, made with full information about the preferences of the members of the committee, provide little help in forecasting. In the example of cycling given above, each of policies A, B, and C is equally likely.

Governmental committees like to keep their decisions secret. The Fed's Open Market Committee, which determines the week-by-week open market operations of the Fed, is particularly careful about secrecy. Members of the Fed staff have been sent to jail for revealing the decisions of the committee before the official announcement. That the prices of stocks and bonds in the Wall Street

[10] An impossibility theorem says that there is no rule that will hold all of the time. It is very possible that there are rules that will result in outcomes that fulfill the five criteria much of the time, especially if the preferences of the members of the committee are very similar for the set of options being considered.

markets change after these announcements indicates that they do, indeed, contain new, unexpected information. If the decisions of the committee were accurately predictable, then there would be no effects of the announcement: The prices of stocks and bonds would already reflect that information. (At certain times, the Chairman of the Federal Reserve System has had a particularly forceful character and the FOMC has almost had a dictator. In those times, the decisions of the committee were more predictable, since only the preferences of the chairman mattered.)

Arrow's impossibility theorem says something important about the existence of some unpredictability in government policies. This unpredictable behavior is not generated from attempts by the government to fool people or to hide its real nature. Unpredictability is an inherent part of complex, nondictatorial committee processes. This unpredictability may contribute to the effectiveness of the government policies eventually chosen (as in Chapters 9 and 10), to the existence of business cycles (as in Lucas' model in Chapter 12), and to the potency of strategic behavior (as in Chapter 16). It also increases the uncertainty that individuals face in their private lives and makes their economic planning more difficult.

REPRISE

Goods with externalities that cannot be resolved by existing private institutions are often handled by the government and are classified as public goods. The main externality that these goods have is the difficulty of preventing those who have not paid for them from gaining from their production by some other member of the society. Roads, national defense, and public education are some examples of goods that are often included in lists of public goods. Taxes are a forced payment for the use of these public goods and are imposed as a second best solution since the first best is not possible. Macroeconomic policy might be thought of as a public good.

Decisions about what types of public goods should be produced or what kind of macroeconomic policy should be followed by the government must be made. We considered the benefits and difficulties of using unanimity and different sized majority or plurality rules. Majority rules can be used when there are only two alternatives to chose between, or when the choice is over a one-dimensional space and preferences are single peaked. In more complicated cases cycling is possible, and majority rules do not yield a solution.

Arrow's impossibility theorem gives some not very optimistic results for the outcomes of attempts to use some rule, majority voting or otherwise, to make collective social decisions based on individual preferences. Given the requirement that any rule obey his five postulates, no such general rule can be found. In specific cases, it is possible to make social decisions using majority rules or other processes, but in even slightly complicated worlds, no general process exists.

18

Open Economy Macroeconomics

In which we finally let in the rest of the world. We discuss international finance, exchange rates, and the flow of goods and assets; then we return to our original model to observe the effects.

INTRODUCTION

Up to this point, we have pretty much limited ourselves to closed economies—those economies that do not trade goods or assets with others. Some economies—for example, the United States, China, India, the Soviet Union, and Brazil—are so large that studying their macroeconomic policies as if they were closed might not damage reality too much.[1] For most of the other countries of the world, trade in goods and financial assets is crucial to a high level of economic welfare. We have already shown some cases where interactions with other economies are important. In Chapter 2, we showed that countries can gain from trade, and in Chapter 7 we illustrated the changes in output and price levels in Venezuela that resulted from a decline in the price of its main export, oil.

International trade in commodities was partially responsible for leading Europe out of the really great depression that lasted from the fall of the Roman empire to the Renaissance. Even during the darkest portions of the Dark Ages, trade between the East (the Islamic countries, at least) and southern Europe was maintained. In fact, at the level of grand commerce (trade between kings) the medieval period was fairly active. The climb out of the poverty of that period was lead by the great merchant bankers in the city-states of Italy, who traded along the Mediterranean; it was later dominated by Portuguese and Dutch sailing fleets. The European discovery of the Americas resulted from the financing by a desperate Spain of an ill-conceived search for a short international trade route that would let them compete with the Portuguese, who then had the route to China around Africa.[2]

In 1985, of an estimated nonsocialist world output of eleven trillion dollars worth of goods, some two trillion dollars of these were traded between nations. On the asset (financial) side, by 1987 cumulative lending by private banks to citizens and governments of other countries was at four thousand seven hundred billion

[1] We haven't discussed the economic structure of socialist or centrally planned economies such as China and the Soviet Union. They are included in this list because they are large enough so that a closed economy might be a good approximation and not because the macroeconomic theories we have been studying are particularly relevant to their economic systems.

[2] Columbus was wrong in all but one major aspect of his proposal for his voyage of discovery. All reasonably educated people of that time knew that the world was round, and there existed quite good estimates of the westward distance from Europe to China. Those who rejected Columbus's proposal did so because his estimate of the diameter of the earth was much too small and his estimate of the distance from Portugal to China (the eastern route, over land) was much too large. His wildly optimistic calculation of the westward distance to China was less than half of the actual distance. The real distance was well beyond the reach of any of the ships of that period. If Columbus had not accidentally run into the Americas, all of his crew would have starved to death before he reached China. Columbus was a very good sailor and he was right about the route of the trade winds. His path west is still the best route for sailing ships.

dollars worldwide. Nonbank foreign assets are much, much more. The less developed countries owe the banks of the developed countries some 1.3 trillion dollars.

There is great divergence in the importance of trade for different countries. At one end of the scale, countries such as Albania and Burma have chosen to have almost no international trade. (We say that countries that are not trading are in **autarky**.) At the other extreme, exports for Luxembourg were over ninety-nine percent of its GNP and almost twice the level of private consumption. Table 18.1 lists thirty countries, with their exports and imports given as a percentage of the countries' GDP.[3]

This table illustrates some interesting points. Notice that trade for the United States, Brazil, and India are relatively small percentages of their GDPs. For all the talk of its dominance of world trade, the trade for Japan (whose exports are only thirteen percent of its GDP) is surprisingly small. Korea has a much higher percentage of its GDP in trade than does Japan. Notice that the European Economic Community countries have fairly high levels of international trade. Most of this trade is with other members of the EEC with whom they have special arrangements. Notice that for the majority of the Latin American countries exports are more than imports. This is because in those years much of their exports was used to pay service (interest and principle payments) on their debt and could not be used to purchase imports. Trade for the centrally planned economies is fairly high. The international trade ministries of these countries are known for their aggressive negotiations of trade agreements and their deep knowledge of international commodity markets. (This is especially true of the Soviet Union, which is not on this table.) Several of the poorest countries (Bangladesh, Burkina Faso, and Egypt) have levels of imports much higher than their exports. This represents gifts or borrowing from the rest of the world. In 1986, oil prices were low, and so Saudi Arabia was importing more than it exported, using assets it had purchased in previous years to pay for the imports.

Some words of warning about this chapter: We are going to suggest more than we can demonstrate. The models from Chapters 5 through 10 are the basis for the open economy macroeconomic theory we will discuss. It is assumed that you have a good understanding of these earlier, closed economy models and that you will work through the graphs that are not done in this chapter.

EXCHANGE RATES

An **exchange rate** is the price at which one currency sells for another. Some commonly used exchange rates are the yen/dollar rate, the franc/mark rate, and the pound/rupee rate. An exchange rate is a ratio between two currencies, so it

[3] These numbers were calculated based on IMF International Financial Statistics from April, 1988. The numbers in parentheses are the year the data was collected.

TABLE 18.1

COUNTRY	IMPORTS/GDP	EXPORTS/GDP
Algeria (86)	20.57%	23.93%
·Argentina (83)	9.80%	14.68%
Bangladesh (86)	15.36%	5.56%
*Belgium (86)	61.95%	65.29%
·Brazil (86)	6.98%	12.04%
Burkina Faso (86)	48.40%	17.17%
Canada (86)	26.02%	27.33%
·Chile (86)	26.70%	30.51%
Congo (84)	33.04%	57.28%
Egypt (87)	24.79%	14.14%
*France (86)	20.49%	21.52%
*Germany (87)	26.30%	31.75%
†Hungary (86)	41.08%	39.61%
India (84)	9.11%	7.44%
*Ireland (86)	53.22%	56.66%
Israel (86)	57.16%	41.56%
*Italy (86)	18.13%	18.65%
Japan (86)	8.76%	13.16%
Korea (86)	35.09%	35.13%
*Luxembourg (85)	86.06%	100.87%
·Mexico (84)	9.65%	17.75%
·Peru (85)	18.82%	25.67%
†Poland (86)	16.78%	18.20%
Saudi Arabia (86)	44.90%	35.79%
Switzerland (86)	35.51%	36.58%
*U.K. (86)	27.00%	26.22%
U.S.A. (86)	10.23%	6.92%
·Uruguay (86)	18.59%	24.03%
·Venezuela (86)	25.16%	24.22%

* European Economic Community countries
· Latin American countries
† Centrally planned economies

doesn't matter which is compared to which. It is equally correct to speak of the yen/dollar or the dollar/yen rate. Normally, United States newspapers give the rates as numbers greater than one, so if it takes 150 yen to purchase one United States dollar, the rate is given as 150 yen/dollar; if it takes .8 British pounds to purchase one United States dollar, the rate is given as 1.25 dollars/pound. This is only convention, and this convention is not always observed in print. One can hear of exchange rates improving or worsening (value-laden phrases that tend to confuse the issues); by "improving" it is usually meant that one's own currency can now purchase more foreign currency and "worsening" means it can purchase less.

From the 1830s until the early 1970s, the vast majority of countries attempted to maintain a fixed exchange rate between their currencies and either gold; the United States dollar, which had a fixed price in terms of gold; the British pound; or, for some francophone African countries, the French franc. With a system of **fixed exchange rates,** the government of each country promises to intervene in the market to keep the price of its currency at some preannounced rate. The country sets a floor and ceiling price for its currency (recall floors and ceilings from Chapter 3). The most common type of intervention is buying gold or other currencies, or selling gold or other currencies, from stockpiles that the country had previously accrued. These stockpiles are called **international reserves.** Many countries, especially the less developed ones, still attempt to maintain fixed exchange rates. Gold is no longer used much as a reference point. Most countries that fix exchange rates fix them against the United States dollar, the french franc, the **Special Drawing Right,** (SDR),[4] or an index based on a basket of other currencies. The majority of the developed countries no longer promise to intervene in the market to maintain a specific price for their currency. They allow the prices of their currencies to move to wherever the market mandates. They do, however, intervene to change the rate at which their currencies move—mostly to slow up the rate of change. Governments call this kind of intervention "maintaining an orderly market." In the case where the government does not intervene to maintain a particular exchange rate, but may intervene to slow up the rate of change of the exchange rate, we say that the currency has a **floating** or **flexible exchange rate.**

In the major financial centers of the world (London, New York, Chicago, Paris, Zurich, Tokyo, Hong Kong, Singapore, and Bahrain) are foreign exchange **brokers** who are willing to exchange any one of the major currencies of the world for any other major currency. Some of these brokers are independent firms and some are divisions of major banks. In any case, these brokers adjust the price they offer as they attempt to balance off the supplies and demands for different currencies. These brokers are in the business of exchanging currencies (the broker makes a profit on the difference between the buying and selling price of currencies) and do not wish to end up holding too much of any one currency. They have a portfolio of currencies that is their working capital and they try to keep this portfolio balanced. This business is very highly pressured, since millions of dollars can move through these brokers in a few seconds. If some United States bank wants to exchange, say, dollars for yen, the agent handling this transaction for the bank calls up a broker and indicates what two currencies they wish to exchange (but not which they are buying or selling). The broker then announces the buying and selling price, mentioning only the third or fourth decimal place (since everyone is supposed to know the rest of the price). The agent from the bank then has

[4] The Special Drawing Right is an index of a basket of currencies calculated by the International Monetary Fund. The U.S. dollar was the initial currency of reference for the IMF, but once the dollar was no longer fixed to gold and was experiencing inflation, many countries wanted a different reference point.

thirty seconds to decide to accept this price or not. Only if the agent decides to make the transaction at that price does the agent tell the broker how much to exchange. Since each broker adjusts the exchange rate to attempt to keep equal the value of the flows of currency going in both directions, this process adjusts the exchange rate so that total flows into and out of each currency is balanced.

One way to understand how policies might effect the exchange rate is to analyze the sources of the flow of funds into and out of the economy. Consider first the flow of goods: the exports and imports of goods and services. An export is a flow of goods out of the country and is paid for by a flow of funds (money) into the country to pay for the goods. If the only allowable international transactions are trades in merchandise and services, then the corresponding flows of funds are illustrated in Figure 18.1.

In a floating exchange rate world, the exchange rate changes to equalize the dollars in and the dollars out of the foreign exchange market. It also equalizes the foreign money in and the foreign money out of the same market. The changes in the exchange rates change the cost of imports and the domestic currency received for exports and eventually change the flow of exports and imports. The word "eventually" is used because a large portion of international trade is done on short-term contracts, and these contracts are met even if the exchange rates change. For that reason, it may take a year or so for significant changes in exchange rates to show up in the flow of goods. The trade flows of the United States following the decline in the yen/dollar and mark/dollar exchange rates in 1986–88 changed with this kind of lag. As long as the ratio of the flow of dollars and the flow of foreign money into the exchange rate market stays the same, so does the exchange rate. If the ratio of these flows changes, in a floating exchange rate world, so does the exchange rate.

If we have a fixed exchange rate world, one of the governments must intervene to keep the exchange rate unchanged. To illustrate this, suppose that the rest

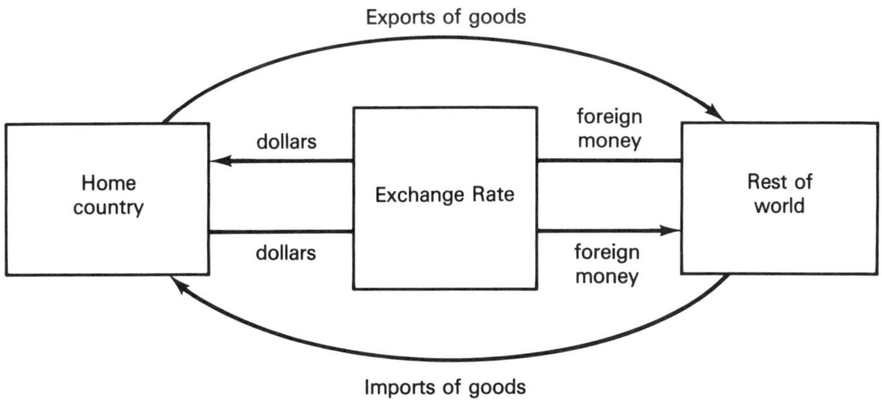

Figure 18.1

of the world now purchases less from the home country than in Figure 18.1, but the home country continues its purchases abroad. Figure 18.2 shows an example.

To keep the ratio of the flows of currencies the same as before—to keep the same exchange rate—the government uses some of its international reserves and sends either foreign currency or gold to the foreign exchange market to buy up the extra dollars, those that are not matched by a flow of currency from the rest of the world. If this change in the flows continues for a long enough time, the home country begins to run out of reserves, for it has only a finite stockpile. It must then allow the exchange rate to change so that at the new rate, the flows in both directions are equal.

Suppose we allow citizens of other countries to invest in the home country. This means that they can purchase factors (that is, they can own land and machines) or financial assets (such as government or private bonds, or stocks. They can also have deposits in the local banking system). Suppose that, initially, the trade flows were in balance (at the original exchange rate, the value of exports equaled the value of imports for both the home country and the rest of the world). What happens to the exchange rate if the citizens of the rest of the world decide to invest, or place their savings, in the home country?

The sequence of events goes as follows: The increase in the flow of foreign money into the market drives up the exchange rate of the home currency, so that it now takes more units of the foreign money to purchase one unit of the home currency. This makes foreign goods cheaper and home country citizens purchase more of them. This increase in the exchange rate also makes the home country's goods more expensive to the rest of the world, so they buy fewer goods. The flows of money eventually balance (this is why the dollar flows in both directions are equal) but exports from the home country are less than imports to the home

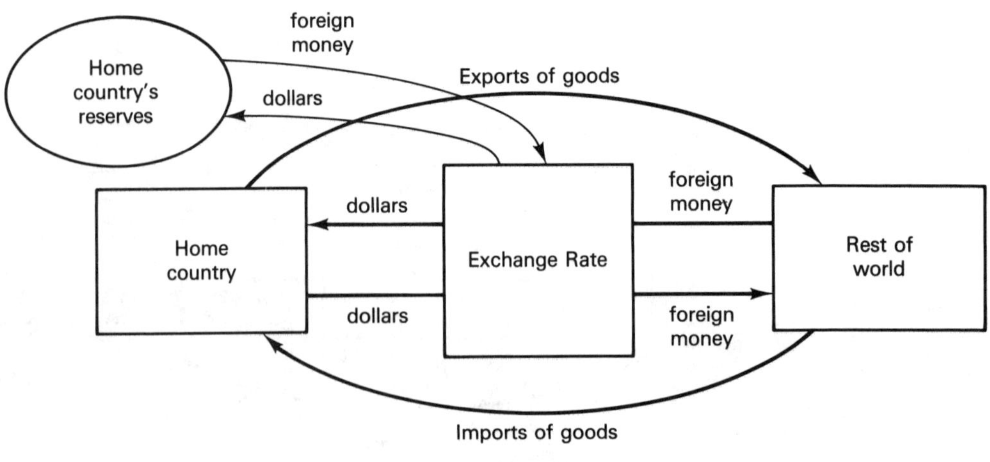

Figure 18.2

country. The difference in the value of the goods flows is the value of the asset flows. Figure 18.3 illustrates this discussion.

Another way to think about the exchange rate is to use a supply and demand analysis. Suppose that there are only two countries: France and Germany. Consider the market for French francs. The price (the exchange rate) is in German marks per French franc, *M/f*. The Germans demand francs either to purchase French goods, which become imports into Germany, or to put their savings into French assets—for example, Volkswagen purchases a factory in France. The supply of francs comes from the demand by the French to purchase German goods—imports into France—or German assets. Figure 18.4 shows where S_1 and D_1 cross to be an initial equilibrium for this franc/mark market. We have defined both supply and demand curves as being generated by the demand in each of the countries for the other country's currency. This demand for the other country's currency is a derived demand. It is derived from the demand for the other country's goods and assets. We will simply assume that these demands exist, although we know from Chapter 15 that it is not easy to characterize demand curves for assets.

Changes in the French desire to purchase German goods or assets will cause a shift in the supply curve for francs. Changes in the German desire to purchase French goods or assets will cause a shift in the demand curve for francs. Without government intervention, either one of these changes will cause a change in the equilibrium price in this market; or, as is more commonly said, will change the exchange rate.

In Figure 18.4, the free market or floating mark/franc exchange rate goes up to M/f_2 when a shift out in the demand for French goods and/or assets by the Germans shifts out the demand curve for French francs to D_2. On the other hand, the exchange rate goes down to M/f_3 when there is an outward shift in the demand

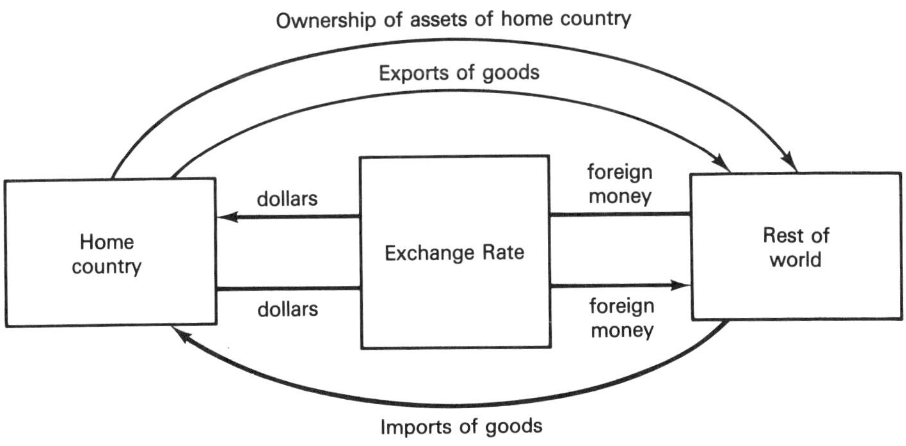

Figure 18.3

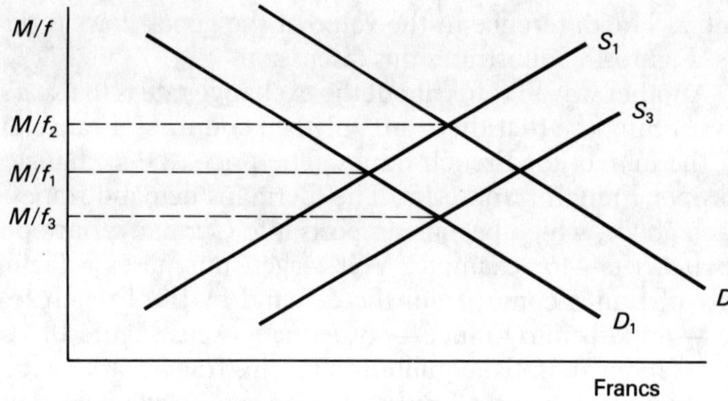

Figure 18.4

by the French for German goods and/or assets. This shift in the French demand curve for German goods causes a shift outward in the supply curve for francs to S_3. The French are offering more francs to purchase German goods and the new equilibrium is one in which it now requires more francs to purchase each mark, or fewer marks per franc. In a floating exchange rate regime, an exchange rate movement can occur when there is a change in the desires of either the local or foreign citizens in their purchases of the other country's goods or assets.

In a fixed exchange rate regime, the shifts in the demand and supply curves for one currency are not allowed to cause changes in the exchange rate. The French government promises to keep the exchange rate within a small band of some preannounced rate. Figure 18.5 illustrates one such band around the exchange rate M/f_1. Suppose that the Germans no longer desire French goods and assets as they once did. Their demand curve shifts back to D_2. The free exchange rate would be M/f_2, if the governments allowed the market to adjust to this drop in demand.

However, the French government has promised to "defend" the floor of the bank around M/f_1. With the new demand for francs, only Q_{D2} are demanded by

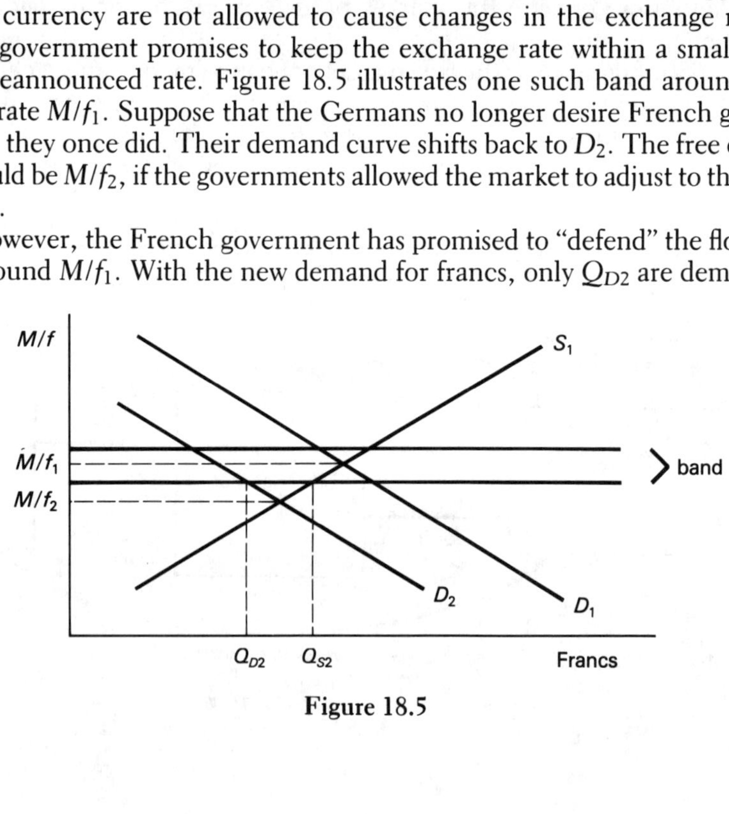

Figure 18.5

the Germans but Q_{S2} are being offered by the French people. To maintain this floor, the French government must buy up the $Q_{S2}–Q_{D2}$ francs with some of its foreign reserves or gold. If the decline in the German demand for French assets and goods is only temporary, then the demand curve will shift back up above the floor and the French government can leave the foreign exchange market. If, instead, the change continues for a long time, the French government may begin to run out of reserves and will be forced to lower the official announced exchange rate to something like M/f_2, where it will no longer need to intervene.

In Figure 18.6 are graphs of the yen/dollar and the mark/dollar exchange rates and the current account, measured in billions of dollars (the current accounts is net exports of goods, services, and transfers) for the United States from 1975 to 1987. Notice how both of the exchange rates rose in the 1980 to 1984 period (the shaded region) and how the trade deficit grew at the same time. There was a very large flow of foreign savings into the United States at this time and this flow of savings increased the demand for the United States dollar and drove up the exchange rates. The flow of savings into the United States equaled the difference in the trade in goods and services. The United States current account deficit and the net inflow of savings had to occur together because the United States is on a floating exchange rate regime.

The 1985 through 1987 data shown in Figure 18.6 is interesting and a bit unexpected. The United States current account deficit continued to grow during this period but the mark/dollar and yen/dollar rates declined. Since this is contradictory to the simple theory we discussed above, something else must have been going on during that period. Part of the something else that was going on was intervention in the foreign exchange market by the seven largest western countries. This intervention, which was agreed upon in a meeting in Canada of the leaders of these seven countries, was aimed at lowering the exchange rate for the United States dollar by increasing the interest rates in these other countries and by direct intervention in the exchange market. The increased interest rates in the other countries made it more attractive to save in the domestic economy, reducing to some degree the demand for dollars, and the intervention supplied additional dollars into the market to reduce the price. As Figure 18.6 illustrates, these efforts were successful in reducing the exchange rate for the dollar.

Between any two countries there is only one exchange rate, although this rate can be expressed two different ways.[5] Between the mark and the franc, the one exchange rate can be expressed as either marks per franc or francs per mark. These are merely two different ways of saying the same relative exchange rate. Among

[5] Some countries have several fixed exchange rates or some fixed exchange and one floating rate. It is fairly common to observe countries with a pair of rates, one for commercial transactions and the other for financial transactions. Some countries have one exchange rate for approved imports (often including many government purchases) and a second, higher rate for other imports. Venezuela at one time in the mid 1980s had four different exchange rates. Three of these rates were for three different categories of imports and the one floating rate was for anything else.

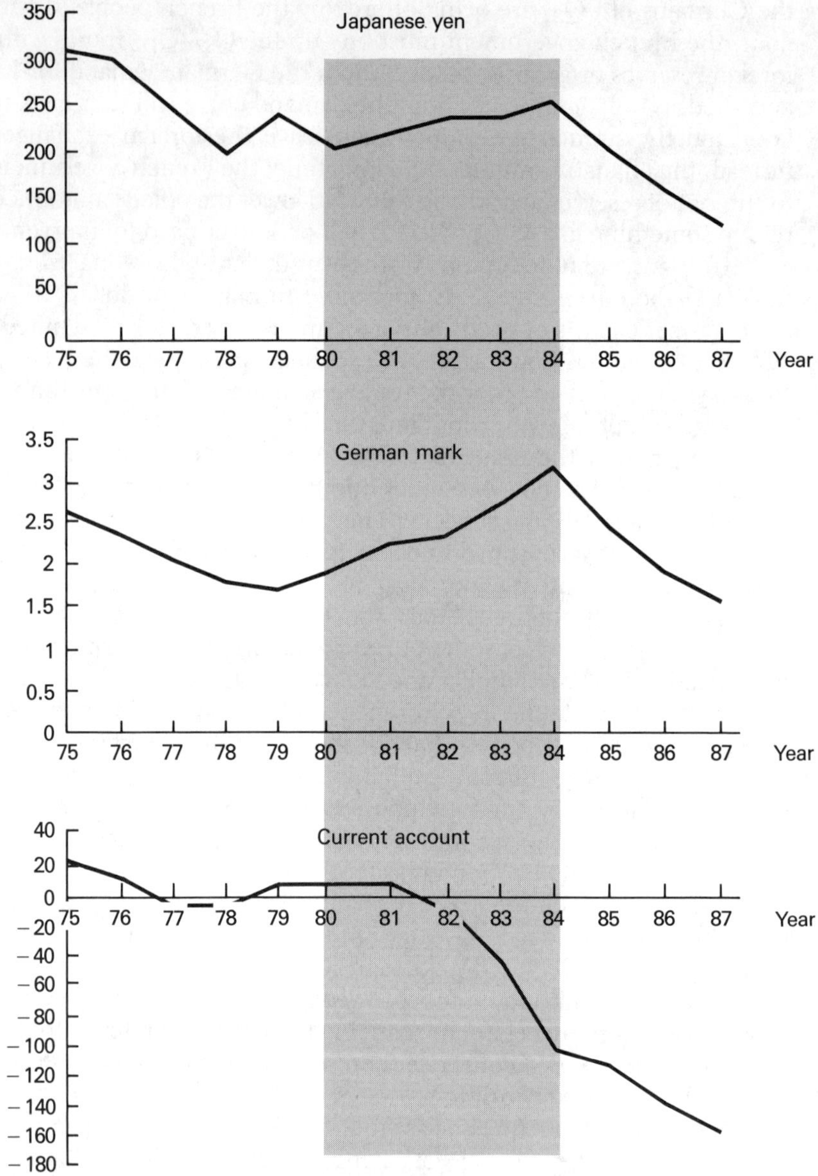

Figure 18.6

three countries (and therefore, three currencies) there are only two exchange rates, even though one can name six different relative rates. Among the dollar, mark, and franc, there are, nominally, the dollar/franc, franc/dollar, dollar/mark, mark/dollar, franc/mark, and the mark/franc rates. Since we already showed that the mark/dollar rate and the dollar/mark rate are merely two different ways of saying the same thing, one might think that among these three currencies there should be three exchange rates. There are, but these three rates are linked in a particular way so that any two of them determine what the third will be. Permit me a minor digression before I illustrate this concept.

Consider the exchange rate between the United States dollar and the British pound. There is a market for these two currencies in London and there is a market in Zurich (as well as all of the other major trading centers listed above). The interesting characteristic of London and Zurich is that both of these markets are open at the same time for much of each day. At any moment, the exchange rate between these two currencies in London should be almost exactly the same as the exchange rate being offered in Zurich. If not, there are opportunities for profits to be made by people called arbitrageurs. What these people do is called **arbitrage.** They watch the two markets all of the time and when there is a large enough difference in the exchange rates in two markets (in London and Zurich in this case), they simultaneously buy and sell the currencies. If the dollar/pound exchange rate is, for example, one tenth of a cent higher in Zurich than in London, then an arbitrageur will sell, say, a million, pounds for dollars in Zurich and buy a million pounds for dollars in London. The number of dollars that the arbitrageur receives in Zurich is greater than the numbers of dollars that the arbitrageur spent for the same number of pounds in London. The difference is the profit from this transaction.

Arbitrage is not the same as speculation. In speculation, an individual purchases a foreign currency in expectation of a *future* favorable price change. In arbitrage, there are two simultaneous transactions. If the arbitrageur begins with dollars, the fact that there are two transactions means that the arbitrageur ends up with more dollars or with the same number of dollars and more of a foreign currency (as in the example above). For the arbitrageur, trades in both directions occur at the same time and at known prices. There is no risk in arbitrage. There is risk in speculation because the exchange rate might move in an unexpected and unprofitable direction.

Now let's get back to multiple currencies. A slightly more complicated type of arbitrage can occur with three (or more) currencies. We will continue with the dollar, mark, and franc example begun above. Suppose that we already know the first two of these three exchange rates: the mark/franc rate is .3 marks per franc and the franc/dollar rate is six francs per dollar. Then the mark/dollar rate had better be 1.8 marks per dollar or there is opportunity for huge profits. Suppose that the mark/dollar rate is 1.9 marks per dollar.[6] Then an arbitrageur would make the

[6] One would never observe a divergence this large from the zero profit exchange rate of 1.8. Once the divergence from the zero profit rate is big enough to cover the costs of transactions (the commissions for handling the exchange) and only a little more, the arbitrageurs who are constantly monitoring these prices would make the appropriate set of trades and the profit opportunities would disappear. These windows of profits only last for seconds. This is a very high-pressure job and the individuals who do this are often burned out by the time they are thirty-five years old.

exchanges illustrated in Figure 18.7, beginning and ending with dollars. One million dollars get exchanged for 1.9 million marks, which get exchanged for 6.33333 million francs, which get exchanged for 1.055555 million dollars. A profit of $55,555 was made in these three exchanges.

Note again that since this is arbitrage, no risk is involved. All of these transactions are made at the same time and at known rates. Note also that this transaction increases the demand for marks with respect to dollars, for francs with respect to marks, and for dollars with respect to francs. If we think of foreign exchange as trading in markets with demand and supply curves, then these transactions shift the demand curves of the currencies and change the equilibrium prices so that the profit opportunities will disappear. If the mark/dollar exchange rate were 1.7 marks per dollar, then the same circle of exchanges would occur, but in the other direction. One million dollars would be exchanged for six million francs, which would be exchanged for 1.8 million marks, which would be exchanged for 1,058,823 dollars. Profit from these three transactions is $58,823. The market forces (the shifting demand curves) should close up this profit window very quickly. So, except for very short periods, knowledge of any two of these three exchange rates will tell you what the other must be. There are only two independent exchange rates among these three currencies. In a world with a hundred currencies there are ninety-nine independent exchange rates.

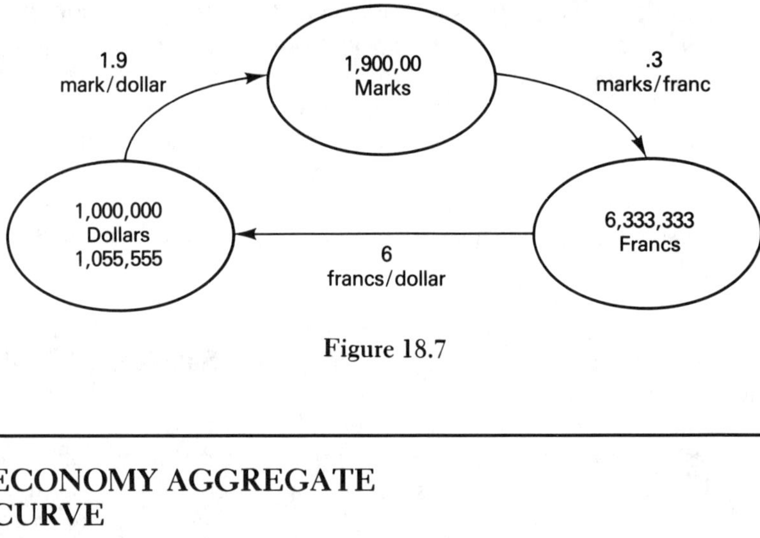

Figure 18.7

AN OPEN ECONOMY AGGREGATE DEMAND CURVE

Let us go back to the material from Chapter 5, the aggregate demand curve, and expand it to an open economy. Our initial National Income Accounting Identity was

$$Y = C + I + G + (X - IM)$$

where $X - IM$ is exports minus imports or **net exports.** We are going to treat both exports and imports as exogenous to our macroeconomic model and see what happens when net exports is either positive or negative. If we include net exports in the National Income Accounting Identity and use the functions we initially used for consumption, investment, and government expenditures, we end up with an open economy *AD* function of

$$Y = [1/(1 - \text{mpc})] \times \{\mu \times [(M + B_g + B_p)/p] + I + G - \text{mpc} \times T + (\boldsymbol{X} - \mathbf{IM})\}$$

where the $\boldsymbol{X} - \boldsymbol{IM}$ is shown in bold to highlight it. The only change in this *AD* curve is the inclusion of $(X - IM)$. Notice that $(X - IM)$ is multiplied by $1/(1 - \text{mpc})$. Since we have assumed that exports are exogenous they show up in the National Income Accounting Identity just the same way the other exogenous variables show up. Since investment, that other exogenous variable, ends up being multiplied by $1/(1 - \text{mpc})$ one should expect net exports to be multiplied by it as well.

If, in Figure 18.8, the curve AD_1 were the aggregate demand curve when net exports was zero, then an exogenous increase in net exports would cause a shift in the AD curve to AD_2. In a similar fashion, an exogenous decline in net exports results in a shift in the AD curve to AD_3. At any price, the AD curve shifts by $1/(1 - \text{mpc})$ times the net exports. Since we have been using a value of .9 for the mpc, $1/(1 - \text{mpc})$ is equal to ten and the shift is ten times the net exports.

Back in the period between World War I and World War II, a number of European countries used exchange rate devaluations, making their currency cheaper relative to other currencies, as a tool for inducing growth in their economies. The story goes as follows: The reduction in the cost of the French franc (for France was one of the countries to attempt this) at least temporarily lowered the cost of French goods to other countries and increased the cost of other countries' goods to the French. Assuming that this has the desired effect of decreasing the

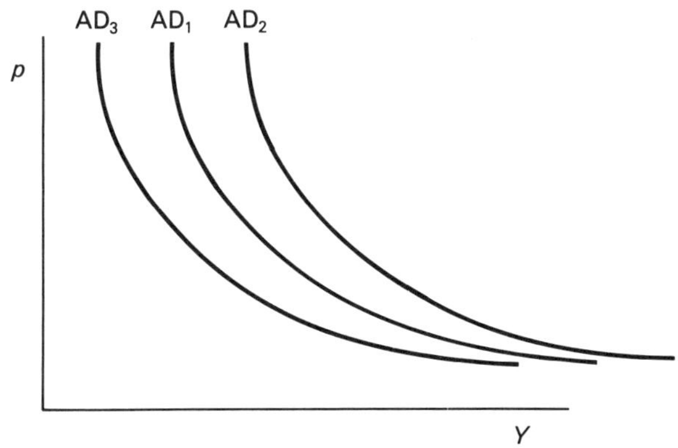

Figure 18.8

amount of imports into France and increasing the exports, this devaluation causes an increase in net exports. Assume that the AS curve is of the Keynesian type, for this is the kind of world in which this policy works best. Figure 18.9 illustrates the results of this policy for France.

The shifting outward of the AD curve results in an increase in output from Y_1 to Y_2 and some inflation, represented by the increase in price levels from p_1 to p_2. This kind of policy at least in the Keynesian model is able to generate the increase in output that the governments were looking for. The reader should be able to show that in either a classical model or the extreme model with rational expectations the increase in output would not occur. But let's stay with the Keynesian model for a while longer.

If the imports for France declined and its exports increased, what happened to the rest of the world? Since total world exports must equal total world imports (ignoring possible exports to outer space or imports from extraterrestrials) if one country is to have positive net exports at least one other country must have negative net exports. For the country that did have negative net exports (and this might include all of France's major trading partners), the shift in the AD curve would be exactly opposite that of France. So for France's trading partners the French devaluation, if it worked as the French hoped it would, caused their imports to go up and their exports to decline. The resulting shift back in their AD curves caused their output levels to drop and deflation to occur. Figure 18.10 illustrates this shift back in the AD curve. Since the trading partners were hurt by one country's attempt to use devaluation to improve its own internal economic situation, such policies became known as Beggar Thy Neighbor policies.

In the interwar period a large number of countries had difficulties with their economies. Remember that this was the period of the Great Depression, and the governments of several countries attempted to use devaluations to help get their economies out of the depression. Once they did devalue, their neighbors calculated that a devaluation of their own would be an appropriate response to the initial devaluation. Retaliatory devaluations took place. Since exchange rates are rela-

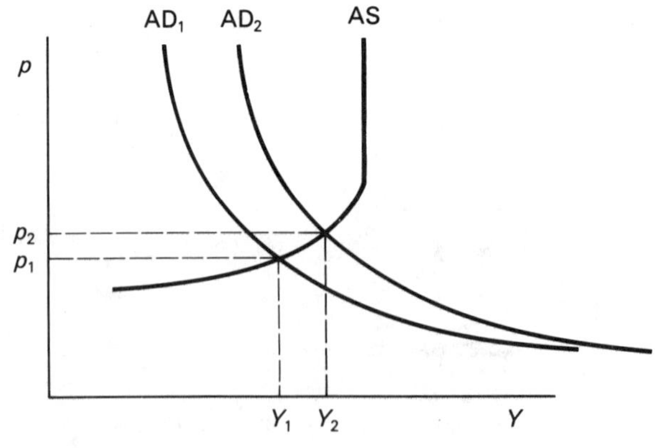

Figure 18.9

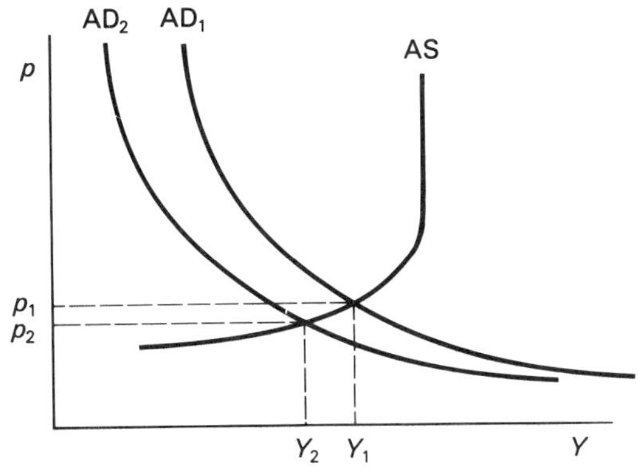

Figure 18.10

tive, it is impossible for all countries to have a devaluation against all other countries. A fifty percent devaluation by all countries leaves the relative exchange rates unchanged. Part of the efforts of the founders of the Bretton Woods agreement (the agreement that set up the post-World War II monetary system) was to design a system that would not permit the cycle of devaluation that they viewed as a very damaging characteristic of the interwar period.

AN OPEN ECONOMY WITH A CLASSICAL AND NEW-CLASSICAL *AS* CURVE

In both classical and the extreme rational expectations (new-classical) models, the AS curve is vertical, although in the new-classical model there is a natural rate of unemployment and in the classical model there is no unemployment. These vertical AS curves mean that the shifts of the AD curves only result in increases in the price level without any effects on the level of output. Figure 18.11 illustrates

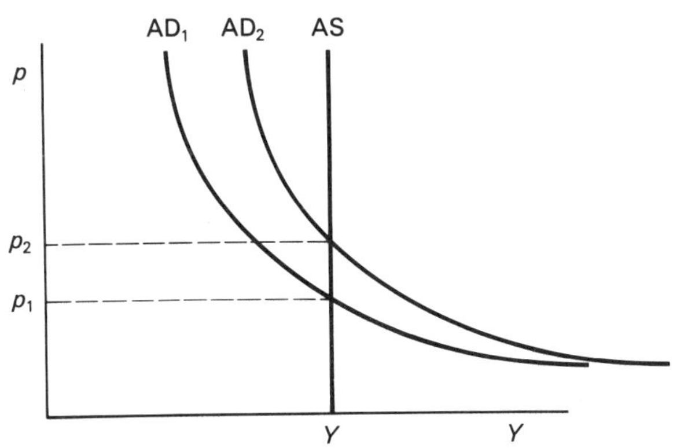

Figure 18.11

these models. The AS curve shown in this graph can be at an output with either no unemployment (the classical model) or with the natural rate of unemployment (the new-classical model). The basic results of a change in the AD curve are the same, but the level of output and of unemployment depend on which model is being used. The shift from AD_1 to AD_2 causes the price level to rise from p_1 to p_2. In one period, a shift in the AD curve due to changes in exports or imports does not change output or employment. In a classical or new-classical world, if trade has effects on employment, output, or rates of growth (which we haven't really talked about much), they must come from some other source than the shifting demand curve.

There are sources for this growth of output or employment from the aggregate supply side of the model. However, we need to think in microeconomic terms to find them.

Increased exports usually mean increased production of goods that the country is already fairly good at producing. If the production functions for these goods display increasing returns to scale—the bigger the factory producing the good, the more output per worker and per machine—then increasing exports means that these goods can be produced even more cheaply and might, if the demand curves for these goods are elastic, increase the quantity sold and the total value of exports. This increased value of exports would allow increased imports of the goods which are relatively more difficult to make in this country. Available output, Y, increases because of the increased quantity of the export good and the increased imports. These increases do not come about by an increased *gap* between exports and imports, but by an increase in *both* exports and imports.

In Chapter 7, the decline in output and the rise in prices in Venezuela came about because of the decline in oil revenues and the concomitant decline in imports of intermediate inputs. Since we claimed that a large portion of the manufacturing production in Venezuela was assembly of imported parts, declines in the ability to get these parts reduced both the quantity of goods and the amount of work to be done. (This was illustrated by a shift back in the production function and a shift in the demand curve for labor.) The long-run effect of the decline in export revenues for a country like Venezuela is a reduction in investment. A large portion of the investment goods that are used in developing counties, or in countries that are simply too small to have a domestic market for investment goods large enough to allow the production of these goods at an efficient scale, are not produced in those countries but are imported from the developed countries—for example, machine tools from Japan and chemical factories from Germany. A decline in export revenues reduces the quantity of these investment goods that the country can purchase. This decline in investment can lead to a decline in the rate of growth or, in the worst case, to actual reductions in output if depreciation is greater than the investment, which is restricted by exports.

The problems of reduced growth rates that the Latin American and African debtor nations face stem from the decline in their ability to import. Since these countries have agreed to devote some portion of their exports to the payment of their debts, their imports are less than their exports. Table 18.1 shows that the difference between the exports and imports for Argentina, Brazil, Chile, Mexico, Peru, and Uruguay for the year given average 30.4% of their exports. This difference comes out to average 5.7 percent of their GDPs. Although Brazil is a large country with a well developed heavy industry (they export airplanes) and Argentina has been a fairly closed economy for years, all of these economies depend on the rest of the world to supply them with some of their intermediate inputs and investment goods. Argentina and Uruguay lack mineral resources and import most of what they use. Neither Chile nor Peru have much in the way of heavy industry. They import most of their machinery and the completely knocked down (CKD) kits of the consumer durables (automobiles, washing machines, refrigerators, and stoves) that are assembled and sold there. The diversion of a large portion of export earnings of these countries to the banks of the developed world is having severe effects on their levels of output.

An increase in export revenues allows a country to purchase more of the intermediate inputs and investment goods that provide the opportunities for its industries' need to expand. In the 1970s and 80s, Korea, Taiwan, Hong Kong, and Singapore have been following the example of Japan, which went through this process in the 1960s and 70s, and expanding their industries through export-led growth. All of these countries have become aggressive exporters, and the increased revenues from these exports and their high domestic levels of savings have generated rapid growth. The growth of export industries was promoted by an undervalued exchange rate. The governments of these countries intervened in the exchange rate market to keep their currencies trading at a price in other currencies that was lower than it might have been with free markets. These countries also "protected" other domestic goods, especially agricultural goods, by preventing their importation with high import taxes or restrictions on the quantity that could be imported. This set of policies made manufactured goods relatively inexpensive in these countries and promoted their export. They also borrowed heavily in international markets, as did the Latin American debtor countries. However, while much of the borrowing in Latin America ended up subsidizing consumption, these NICs (newly industrialized countries) used the borrowed monies to finance the purchase of investment goods for exportable products. Exports have been growing fast enough to pay for these loans, so much so that in early 1989 Korea became a net creditor country. For most of the 1960s and 70s, Japan and Korea had low levels of domestic consumption, which was heavily taxed by their governments, and high levels of savings.[7] These savings were used to finance investment.

[7] A tax on consumption will increase savings only if there is an expectation on the part of the citizens that this tax will be lowered in the future. If that is the case, consumption will be shifted (with savings) from the high tax time (now) to the low tax period (the future). If the expectations are that the consumption tax will not be reduced in the future, then it will not encourage savings.

To sum up the policies used in the Asian NICs, they

1. maintained an undervalued exchange rate,
2. limited or taxed imports,
3. taxed consumption,
4. borrowed internationally for investment.

Some have argued that an undervalued exchange rate might discourage exports of manufactured goods because it increases the cost of imported intermediate inputs in terms of the local currency. The Korean steel industry must import iron ore, for example. This argument misses one very important point. Korea, for example, can purchase iron ore in dollars at the world price and then convert it to steel. When this steel is exported, the iron content has the same cost as any other steel made with world price inputs. The undervalued exchange rate reduces the cost in dollars of the Korean factors that converted the iron ore to steel. The Korean steel ends up being cheaper in international markets than the steel from countries that do not follow this policy of undervaluing their exchange rate.

The above discussion on how certain countries have used undervalued exchange rates as a way to promote exports and growth is a possibly strange combination of macro and microeconomics. This mix is unavoidable when discussing international trade because the relative prices of goods (a micro concept) are crucial in determining the quantity and content of a country's exports and imports. Government policies that change the relative, international prices of a country's goods can have macroeconomic effects. In terms of goods, devaluations or undervalued exchange rates have effects because they change the relative prices of one country's goods in another country.

FOREIGN ASSETS

Why might citizens of one country wish to place some of their savings in another country? That is what happens when foreign citizens choose to purchase stocks, government or private bonds, or real assets such as apartment buildings, office buildings, factories, and agricultural land from another country.

At least in terms of the trade flows, purchases of any of these kinds of assets, particularly real assets, can be thought of as the purchase of imports that cannot change their locations. In this context, if we correctly measured the trade flows of a country the imports and exports are always equal in value. It is merely that some of the imports cannot be moved from their foreign location and are therefore called something other than imports; instead, they are called foreign investment.

Motivations that drive decisions to acquire foreign assets are different from motivations to acquire foreign goods. Let's consider some of these motivations.

What is different about a citizen of Germany purchasing stocks from the New York Stock Exchange or from the Frankfurt Exchange? Living in Germany, this citizen has already collected a lot of information about the important German economic variables. Given this information, the calculation of the real rate of return on assets purchased in the Frankfurt Exchange is fairly simple. The expected rate of return minus the expected German inflation rate gives the expected real rate of return. Let r_G be the nominal interest rate (or rate of return) in Germany. Let $E\pi_G$ be the expected inflation rate in Germany. Then the expected real rate is $r_G - E\pi_G$. This return is available in German marks, which is often assumed to be the relevant currency for the German citizen.

If this German citizen considers placing some savings in the United States, calculations of the expected return are more complicated. First, sufficient information on the United States economy is required to make good estimates of the expected rate of return on United States assets. (Call this r_{US}.) If the German citizen is interested in the final returns in German marks, then additional expectations need to be made. The current exchange rate between the dollar and the mark [$X_{\$M}$(today)] is easy to find. This can be read directly from the newspaper. However, the exchange rate that will or might prevail on the date the German wishes to repatriate the asset is unknown. After the collection of additional information, one can form expectations of the future exchange rate between the dollar and the mark [$X_{\$M}$(future)]. One thousand German marks can get converted today to 1,000 × $X_{\$M}$(today) dollars today. These dollars earn a nominal return of r_{US}, so at the end of the investment period, the individual has $(1 + r_{US})$ [1,000 × $X_{\$M}$(today)] dollars. The exchange rate that is expected to prevail at that date is $X_{\$M}$(future), so that the expected number of marks the saver expects to receive from the initial savings of 1,000 marks is

$$(1 + r_{US})[1{,}000 \times X_{\$M}(\text{today})]/[X_{\$M}(\text{future})] \qquad (18.1)$$

Suppose the current exchange rate were 1.8 marks/dollar, the interest rate in the United States were eight percent, and the expected exchange rate (in one year, say) were 1.7. Then the one thousand marks would convert to $555.55. At the end of one year with an interest rate of eight percent, this would become six hundred dollars. Those six hundred dollars are expected to convert (at the expected exchange rate) to 1,020 marks. The entire process earned an expected nominal interest rate of two percent in marks. If the exchange rate in one year were expected to be 1.9 marks per dollar, then the six hundred dollars would be expected to convert to 1140 marks. In this case the process generated an expected return of fourteen percent. To find the expected real rate of return in marks, the expected inflation rate in Germany must be subtracted from the expected return from the investment. Notice that the expected inflation rate in the United States did not appear directly in these calculations.

Figure 18.12 shows the alternatives that a citizen from Germany has for saving marks. It is possible to go directly from marks today to marks in the future

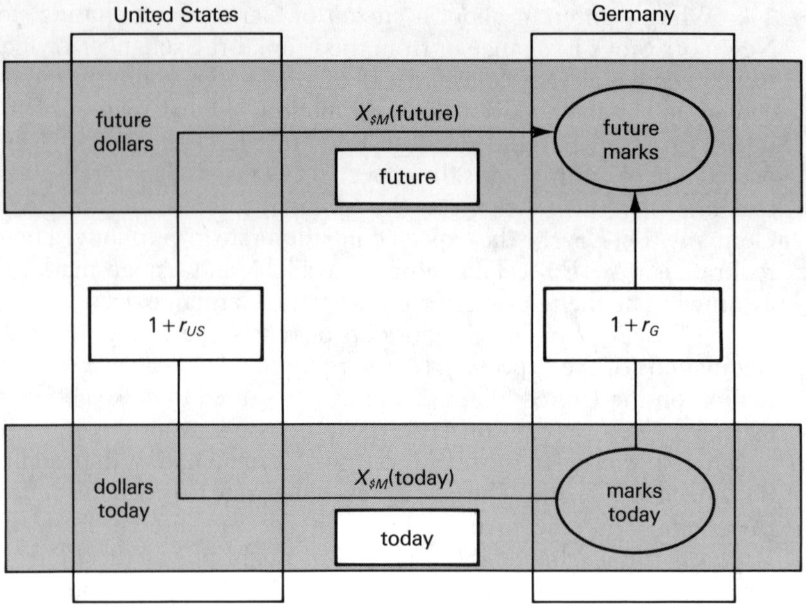

Figure 18.12

through buying assets in Germany. It is possible to go through the asset market in the United States by converting marks today into dollars and using these dollars to purchase assets in the United States. At some future date, these assets in the United States can be converted back to dollars, which can be exchanged for marks at the future exchange rate. At the time that the purchase of assets in the United States is made, the German citizen does not know what the exchange rate will be in the future. Rather, the German citizen has *expectations* about what this exchange rate will be. Because the future expected exchange rate is not known with certainty, there is extra risk in the asset in the United States compared to the asset in Germany. Because of this additional risk, the path through the United States must offer a higher expected return to be equal to the less risky German asset. Figure 18.12 should also make clear where the equation 18.1 above comes from.

There is a way that the expected inflation rate in the United States does enter into the above calculations. One theory of exchange rate movement is called **Purchasing Power Parity.** This name comes from the idea that exchange rates convert the purchasing power of any currency into the same purchasing power in any other currency. The theory states that in the long run exchange rates will adjust, so that if a particular bundle of goods can be purchased with a given quantity of local currency, exchanging that currency for another will allow the purchase of exactly the same bundle of goods in the other country. The bundle of goods that can be bought with ten thousand Peruvian inti can be bought in Brazil with the cruzados that would be received from exchanging those inti for cruzados. Even the most ardent fans of this theory admit it might not hold in the short run.

Now suppose that at the purchasing power parity exchange rate ten thousand inti exchange for two hundred cruzados, at the rate of fifty inti to one cruzado. Suppose that in one year there is an inflation of five hundred percent in Peru and two hundred percent in Brazil. What could be purchased in Peru with ten thousand inti a year ago now costs sixty thousand. What could be purchased in Brazil with two hundred cruzados a year ago now costs six hundred. If purchasing power parity were maintained, the sixty thousand inti should now exchange for six hundred cruzados; that is, there should be an exchange rate of one hundred inti to one cruzado. If purchasing power parity holds, only the expected rates of inflation in the two countries are needed to calculate the expected changes in the exchange rate.

Figure 18.13 below gives the real exchange rate between the United States dollar and the French franc, German mark, Italian lira, and Japanese yen from 1961 to 1987. The real exchange rate is calculated by taking the price index in the United States, P_{US}, dividing that by the price index in the other country, P_F, P_I, P_G, or P_J, and multiplying that by the nominal exchange rate between the other currency and the dollar. If the purchasing power parity theory holds, the exchange rate should change to compensate for changes in the price levels in the two countries and the value of the real exchange rate should be constant. If the

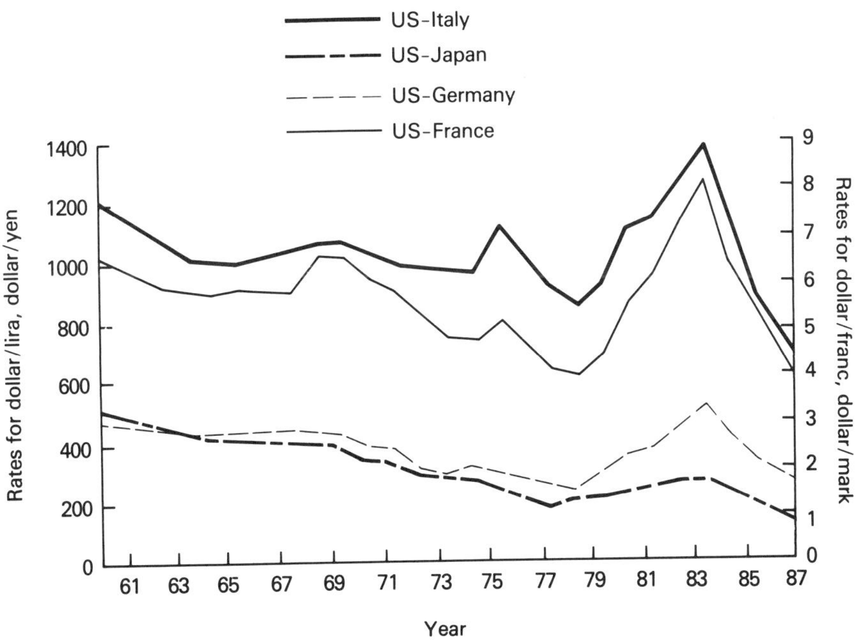

Figure 18.13

inflation in the United States is ten percent and the inflation in Germany is five percent, then each mark should buy five percent more dollars, thus enabling the buyer to purchase the same bundle of goods in each country. If that happened, the real exchange rate would not change. Figure 18.13, with big swings in the real exchange rate, shows that purchasing power parity does not hold for each year. However, even though these countries have all been changing their purchasing power against the United States dollar, the three European ones have been keeping fairly constant against each other. This is caused, in part, by the rules of the European Economic Community, which tries to maintain a partially fixed exchange rate among its members. Notice the difference in the smoothness of these curves during the fixed exchange rate period, 1961–1973 and the period after, especially with the peak in the real exchange rate for the dollar against all of these currencies in 1984.

In spite of what is suggested by Figure 18.13, assume that the purchasing power parity theory of exchange rate movements is true, at least in the long run. Then, if individuals compare the expected real interest rates in different countries (expected real interest rates are the nominal interest rate minus the expected inflation rate) there will be a propensity for them to put their savings in the country that offers the highest expected real interest rate. Correcting this theory for possible occurrence of errors in predicting the future exchange rate, individuals will put their savings in another country when the real interest rate in that country is sufficiently higher than in other countries to cover the added risk of unpredicted future exchange rate movements. The United States in the mid 1980s offered expected real interest rates of over six percent. This may not sound very high, but the historical average real interest rate is about two percent. In 1872, Walter Bagehot, in his book, *Lombard Street* (which was the address of the Bank of England), claimed that movements in the interest rate offered by the Bank of England would bring in funds from France or the rest of Europe.[8] The Bank of England used changes in the interest over one hundred times during the gold standard period—from 1830 to 1914 for England—to balance out gold flows at the fixed exchange rate. It therefore should not come as a surprise, given the current globalized financial markets, that the six percent real interest rate in the United States attracted upwards of one hundred fifty billion dollars a year from the rest of the world.

Higher-than-domestic rates of returns are the most important, but not the only, motive for holding foreign assets. Wealthy individuals in less developed countries with political systems that may change radically often protect themselves from the complete loss of their wealth by placing some of it in the more politically stable developed countries. When domestic insurgent activity in a country increases, so does the flow of wealth out of that country. When the activity subsides without a revolution much of the expatriated wealth will return. Governments that are in constant need of cash for one reason or another and appear likely to tax

[8] Walter Bagehot, *Lombard Street* (New York: Scribner, Armstrong & Co., 1873).

the wealth of the rich will observe cash flows out of the country. There have been innumerable, generally unsuccessful attempts by governments of less developed countries, especially in Latin America, to restrict these outward flows. Such flows will be caused merely if the citizens expect that the government will attempt, some time in the future, to restrict such flows. This is because these restrictions are usually followed by some increased taxing of these assets. Events such as the nationalization of private banks, freezing of accounts, or general economic decline will increase the likelihood that wealthy individuals will export some of their wealth and put it into assets in developed countries.

Sometimes foreign governments wish to own assets in foreign countries. Governments such as the socialist block countries, whose currencies are not freely exchanged for other currencies, often hold dollar-denominated assets to aid in their foreign trade transactions. Countries also use the accumulation of foreign assets to help them smooth out imports when the prices for their exports undergo large and rapid fluctuations. Oil, coffee, tin, sugar, and wheat are merely a few of the commodities that have experienced violent price swings. Oil has exhibited fluctuations in its real price (the quantity of other goods it can buy) that include an eightfold increase in price and drops, slower than the price increases, to less than one fourth of the peak real price. The peaks occurred because of successful market intervention by cartels (organizations of producer countries who agree to work together to gain some monopoly control over the price of their common export good) and the price declines because of the inherent instability of these same cartels as some of the members cheat on the cartel agreement. A country that can get away with cheating on the agreement can make gains even larger than its membership in the cartel allows. Saudi Arabia was one of the countries in the oil cartel, OPEC, that has purchased large quantities of assets in developed countries. During the periods when the real price of oil was very high, Saudi Arabia acquired a large and diversified portfolio of assets in the developed countries. These assets included real estate, both land and buildings; stocks and bonds in major corporations; other governments' bonds; deposits in foreign banks; gold; and reserves of foreign currencies.[9] The reason that Saudi Arabia accumulated these assets was that it could not efficiently increase its imports at the same rate as that of the increase in the value of its exports. The accumulation of assets was designed to allow the government of Saudi Arabia to smooth out the time path of its imports, and therefore its consumption, in the face of a violently fluctuating export time path. From 1984 to 1986, it sold off some of these assets to maintain imports in the face of lower oil prices. Figure 18.14 shows a graph of the imports and exports for Saudi Arabia. Notice that exports are greater than imports for a long period, while recently imports have become greater than exports. These additional imports were

[9] Some have argued that the lending boom of the late 1970s and early 1980s was merely the recirculating of the profits of the OPEC cartel. This is the same period when the middle-income developing countries took on much of their current debt burden.

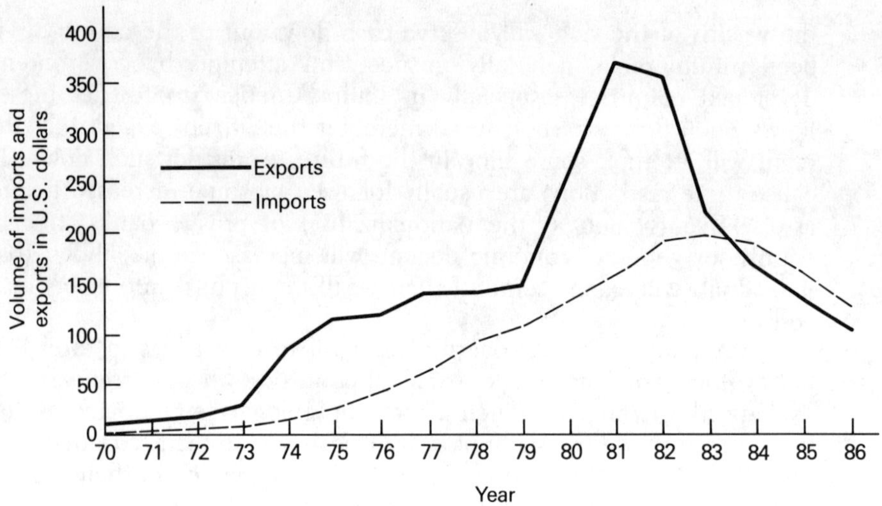

Figure 18.14

paid for with the earlier exports, converted into foreign assets. This graph also shows how much smoother the time path of imports is compared to that of exports.

There are other reasons why citizens of one country might want to purchase assets in a foreign country. Many of these are political. The political reasons might have to do with tax policies of the foreign country. Manufacturers, for example, might wish to build a factory in a foreign country because producing some of their good there permits increased entry of their exports. This is why many Japanese automobile companies have built assembly plants in LDCs and the United States.

It is sufficient to say that international transfers of assets have important effects, both on the exchange rates between currencies and on the short-run movements of goods. These asset transfers can be damaging to the welfare of a country, as they were to the LDC debtor nations, or they can be apparently useful, as with Saudi Arabia and the Asian NICs. In all of these cases it is important to note that that it is easier to transfer savings than goods, so that asset movements can have very large short-run effects on the exchange rate that cannot be compensated for by goods flows.

It is sometimes said that the United States is in great danger of having foreign asset holders decide to withdraw all of their funds at the same time and cause havoc in financial markets in the United States. By now you should see that this danger is not very great. If a large portion of foreign asset holders suddenly wished to convert their dollar assets into assets in their own currencies, this would cause a greatly increased demand for their own currencies. This would drive down the price of the dollar in terms of the other currencies and seriously reduce the returns, based on their initial savings in their own currency, that they would get from those dollar assets. The only way that they can be certain of getting a reasonable return is if they slowly withdraw the assets from the United States. This potential huge loss from a rapid transfer should be enough to prevent its ever happening.

REPRISE

Opening up the macroeconomic models discussed in Chapters 5 to 10 is done by replacing the exports and imports that were originally taken out of the National Income Accounting Identity. Net exports becomes a component of the aggregate demand function, and exogenous changes in net exports will cause the same kind of shifts in the AD curve as would changes in the other exogenous variables. In a Keynesian model, increases in net exports will increase employment and output. In a classical or new-classical model, the demand side effects of increases in exports do not result in increases in either output or employment. If exports are to have any effects on the economy in the classical or new-classical model, these effects must come from increased efficiency or increased access to capital goods (or to the knowledge necessary to increase the human capital of the country, although this point was not emphasized in the text).

Changes in the exchange rate between currencies have effects on the flows of goods (the net exports) and the flow of assets. Foreign assets are held for a wide variety of reasons: funds driven from a country by political unrest, responses to interest rate differentials, or long run diversification of portfolios for risk reduction, to name a few. In floating exchange rate regimes, changes in these asset flows result in exchange rate changes and can produce a trade surplus or deficit. Domestic policies, especially as they influence the interest rate, can cause asset movements that result in exchange rate behavior that is detrimental to the original goals of the domestic policy. The United States trade deficit of the Reagan period is a prime example of this. The borrowing done by the federal government in order to cover its deficit drove up the real interest rates and, for a while at least, caused foreign assets to flow into the United States. The trade deficit, and its resulting effects on industry—as some industries that had been internationally competitive could no longer compete effectively at the new exchange rate—were one of the major sources of political problems for that administration.

Index

D

E

F

G

H

I

K

L

M

N

O

P

R

S

T

U

W